Religion and Canadian Party Politics

Religion and Canadian Party Politics

David Rayside
Jerald Sabin
Paul E.J. Thomas

*To Judi
with love,

David R.

June 2017*

UBCPress · Vancouver · Toronto

26 25 24 23 22 21 20 19 18 17   5 4 3 2 1

Printed in Canada on FSC-certified ancient-forest-free paper
(100% post-consumer recycled) that is processed chlorine- and acid-free.

Library and Archives Canada Cataloguing in Publication

Rayside, David M. (David Morton), author
   Religion and Canadian party politics / David Rayside, Jerald Sabin, and Paul E.J. Thomas.

Includes bibliographical references and index.
Issued in print and electronic formats.
ISBN 978-0-7748-3558-9 (hardcover). – ISBN 978-0-7748-3559-6 (pbk.).
ISBN 978-0-7748-3560-2 (PDF). – ISBN 978-0-7748-3561-9 (EPUB).
ISBN 978-0-7748-3562-6 (Kindle)

   1. Religion and politics – Canada – Provinces – Case studies. 2. Political parties – Canada – Provinces – Case studies. I. Sabin, Jerald, author II. Thomas, Paul E.J., author III. Title.

BL65.P7R34 2017   322'.10971   C2017-901735-7
                                             C2017-901736-5

Canadä

UBC Press gratefully acknowledges the financial support for our publishing program of the Government of Canada (through the Canada Book Fund), the Canada Council for the Arts, and the British Columbia Arts Council.

Printed and bound in Canada by Friesens
Set in Myriad and Sabon by Artegraphica Design Co. Ltd.
Copy editor: Joanne Richardson

UBC Press
The University of British Columbia
2029 West Mall
Vancouver, BC V6T 1Z2
www.ubcpress.ca

Dedicated with gratitude to
  Graham White
who brought us together in this project
and who teaches all of us so much about Canadian politics

Contents

Part 3: Religious Conservatism and the Partisan Right

Part 4: Canada's Most Distinctive Regions

Figures and Tables

Preface

The book you see before you was born of a concern that the role of faith in Canadian politics was insufficiently understood. Episodic attention is paid to moments in which religiously based political mobilization surfaces in particular issue debates, such as Catholic school funding, abortion, the recognition of non-Christian minority faith practices, or same-sex marriage, although this occurs more in the media than in longer-term analytical work. Those who do comment frequently have wildly different approaches, many characterizing Canadian society as secularized to the point at which faith no longer has any sustained impact on this country's political life, and others seeing the religious right as exercising significant influence, even if not at the level of its American counterpart. Still others see religion as a factor shaping political choices only for ethno-religious minorities and declining segments of the Christian majority.

Our decision to focus on how religion affects party politics arose from our own interest in parties. It was also influenced by the fact that we were developing the project during a period in which the Conservative Party of Canada held the reins of government in Ottawa, eliciting considerable public commentary about the influence of religious conservatives in political debate and public policy. Moreover, we were struck by important instances of provincial parties across the country wrestling with pressures from moral traditionalists on a range of policy fronts or, in our increasingly secular society, from others opposed to the official recognition of at least some minority faith practices. We knew, then, that there were stories to tell, to interpret, and to place within a historical context.

David Rayside initiated the project, bringing to it an interest in the role of religion in party politics that extends over five decades. This eventually led him to develop an undergraduate comparative course on religion and politics, which he taught or co-taught for several years. In the last three decades, he has also been interested in the various ways in which religious communities in North America, including non-Christian minorities, have responded to sexual minority advocacy. In that work, he came to realize how little subtlety has been applied to analyses of religious traditionalism in the literature on sexual diversity politics. He feels this despite his advocacy for sexual minority rights, his own experience as a gay man, and his lack of personal attachment to religious belief.

Jerald Sabin joined this project at the moment that major funding was secured. He was keenly interested in mapping the policy outcomes of conservative religious activism and in the increasing secularism of Canadians. As a scholar whose work focuses on northern Canada, he was also interested in broadening the scope of this current project to include the two territorial legislatures without political parties.

Paul E.J. Thomas is associated with a study of Christian activism in Canada conducted by Jonathan Malloy, who introduced him to David while the funding for this project was under review. With his own research examining the interaction between parliamentarians and external stakeholders, Paul's interests in this book project lay in mapping the various organizations (both faith-based and secular) that sought to mobilize religious conservatives and in studying how politicians from different faith communities attempted to act out their beliefs in the political arena. As a Christian who at different times has attended a variety of mainline and evangelical denominations (Anglican, Associated Gospel, Baptist, Mennonite Brethren, Presbyterian Church in America, Wesleyan), he was also interested in exploring how parties targeted their appeals to faith communities.

We began our shared intellectual voyage with a clear question in front of us but without a rigid analytical framework. We were going to examine federal parties and a number of provinces with party systems that spoke to themes that we considered important. We felt that different chapters warranted distinct approaches, sometimes shaped by particular incidents or crises. One such example is the increasingly vocal pro-life advocacy by backbench MPs in the federal Conservative Party. Another is the controversy over sexual health education in Ontario. The recurrent partisan sparring over "reasonable accommodation" of minority religious practices in Quebec also heavily shapes a chapter in this volume. So while there are commonalities across all the provincial cases, there are very distinct stories to tell and patterns to explain.

A couple of themes acquired more prominence in this volume than we imagined at the outset. Schooling is the most obvious example. Any treatment of religious influence on politics would have to include education, of course, but we regularly found that there were contemporary developments and controversies with schools at their centre – more than we expected. The politics of lesbian/gay/bisexual/transgender rights is another example. This would inevitably be part of our analysis, but here too we found more controversies over these issues erupting while our project was under way than we had expected, and this called out for analytical attention.

Even accepting this approach, some readers may wonder about some of the choices we made. In a number of chapters, we provide extensive historical accounts drawn from other sources. While perhaps appearing as unnecessarily repetitive, we believe that there is value in gathering such histories together in one place and in applying to them our specific interest in religious contention.

Others may feel that we pay too little attention to some religious voices or communities. We say very little, for example, about reformist or Anabaptist faith communities devoted to social justice and equity but a great deal about religious conservatives. We do this not because we are unmindful of those reformist voices. We are personally either a member of such a community or highly respectful of friends who are, and we recognize that no single interpretive voice speaks for all Christians, Muslims, Jews, Hindus, or Sikhs. On the other hand, we give religious conservatives the attention we do because it is they who have been most successful at political mobilization in recent decades, and it is they who have most influenced policy debates between or within Canadian parties.

We also spend more time dealing with the Muslim minority than we do other ethno-religious minorities, particularly in the discussion about Quebec (Chapter 8). We do this, too, because, in recent years, there has been more political contention attached to the Muslim community than to others. It has also become the largest religious minority in this country, by some margin.

We do not cover all provinces, and some may wonder why we neglect Manitoba, Saskatchewan, Nova Scotia, and Prince Edward Island. One reason is simply that the project was already an extremely ambitious one, and the addition of more cases was simply impractical. We also believe that, even if the cases we do not address might have had important lessons for us, the provinces and territories that we do include raised the full range of analytical questions that we consider essential.

In exploring the response of political parties to faith-based mobilization, we do not take account of as broad a range of indicators of party positioning as some might wish. We focus a good deal of attention on party leaders and, in some cases, on legislators and voters. We devote little time to party activists and members, especially in presenting hard data. We made this decision not only because of the relative weakness or datedness of systematic data, but also because we share the almost universally accepted view that Canadian parties are leader-dominated. This does not mean that we are inattentive to the possibility of revolts against incumbent leaders – indeed, an entire chapter is largely preoccupied by this issue (Chapter 2), but we also recognize that an examination of the policy priorities of Canadian parties must spend a good deal of time reflecting on the policy priorities of their leaders.

There are real challenges in engaging in the analysis that we have undertaken. The questions that guided our work elicited highly contrasting and passionately held beliefs. In piecing together the stories we chronicle, we confronted very different memories and very distinct views about what is important. In trying to make sense of particular elections or the campaigns of individual parties, we faced claims that religion had no role whatsoever as well as claims that it mattered a lot. We find similar variations in understandings of particular policy developments – for example, in the funding of private schools. We take the measure of all such views and use our own research backgrounds and intuitions to sort out what we believe makes sense and to flag those areas where no clear-cut conclusion is possible.

Among the strongly held views that such a project encounters are those that reflect prejudice against particular religious groups – Roman Catholics, Evangelicals, Muslims – and against those who adhere to any religious belief. In person or in print, for example, we inevitably confronted analyses of religious conservatives that suggested a uniformity or an unchangingness in perspective that does not match the more complex reality that we encountered. At the same time, we found academic supporters of religious rights who do not always acknowledge that these rights can collide with rights claims by women and sexual minorities.

Our challenge has been to remain fair to a variety of voices without denying that we have a point of view on a number of the policy disputes that we discuss. We are each, in our distinct ways, "engaged" scholars who match our serious writing with social and political advocacy. But we strive at least to be analytically careful, to listen to as wide a range of perspectives as possible, and to do so with openness and empathy.

Acknowledgments

Any work of this scale incurs incalculable debts. The first of these is to Graham White, who so strongly recommended to David that he ask Paul and Jerry to associate themselves with this project. The partnership on which this book is based would simply not have existed without him.

From the outset, we knew this book's ambitious scope would call for our little troop to travel across Canada, meeting with religious activists, politicians, journalists, and academics. These trips were a highlight of Jerry's and Paul's time at the University of Toronto, and of course they helped all three of us immeasurably in deepening our analysis of religious contention and politics. We would like to thank the many friends, family members, and strangers who welcomed us in British Columbia, Alberta, Ontario, and Quebec. Our interviews were almost all confidential, thus we cannot name the many people who were so wonderfully available to us and helped us with their own analyses.

For providing access to data before they were publicly available, or assistance in interpreting them, we are grateful to Chris Cochrane, Joanna Everitt, Andrea Perrella, Brian Tanguay, and Fred Cutler. Clifton Van der Linden and Yannick Dufresne also provided a helpful look at Vote Compass data for Alberta. Christopher Dunn gave us an advance look at the third edition of his collection on provincial politics, published by the University of Toronto Press.

For comments provided in response to conference presentations, we thank Agnès Alexander-Collier, Clark Banack, Jim Farney, Trevor Harrison, and David Stewart. For willingness to read draft material and provide helpful commentary, we are extremely grateful to Joanna Everitt, Mark Graesser, Alex Marland, Luc Turgeon, Graham White, and Linda White. For general advice and interpretations of events we sought to understand, we profitably talked to Tom Flanagan, Rachael Johnstone, Jonathan Malloy, Achsah Turnbull, and Lisa Young. For assistance in preparing the manuscript for publication, and in developing visual materials, we have Abouzar Nasirzadeh, Michael Pelz, and especially Erica Petkov to thank.

This book has benefited enormously from the peer review process, and we are grateful for the encouragement that it provided as well as for the detailed commentary provided by one reviewer in particular, who pointed the way towards a much stronger manuscript.

We could not have embarked on this great journey without funding provided by the Social Sciences and Humanities Research Council. Paul also benefited from financial support from the (British) Political Studies Association, enabling him to attend the PSA's 2015 Annual International Conference in Sheffield. All of us are grateful for support provided in the final stages of publication by the University of Toronto's Political Science Department and the Bonham Centre for Sexual Diversity Studies.

At UBC Press, we owe much to the inimitable Emily Andrews, who guided this manuscript through much of the adjudicative process. Randy Schmidt has also been a wonderful successor in that role, with Holly Keller helpfully steering the book through production. We have genuinely appreciated Joanne Richardson's attentive copy-editing and Sigrid Albert's art work for the book cover.

We have dedicated this volume to Graham White, who suggested to David that Jerald and Paul would be talented partners in this project, and who saw them through their doctoral programs at the University of Toronto.

And then there are the people in our personal lives who have lived with the long process through which this manuscript was born. David's twin brother Ron helped, perhaps more than he realizes, simply by being interested in the project and being willing to talk through some of the complicated issues discussed in the Quebec case that he knows so well. David also knows that his partner Gerald Hunt was wary of taking on another large project but he provided indispensable support during the emotional roller coaster ride that such a book inevitably entails.

Jerald thanks his partner Kyle Kirkup for his good humour and support as he balanced both his dissertation research and the completion of this book. Kyle, a sharp observer of gender, sexuality, and the law, also honed some of the analysis presented here

Paul owes a great debt to his wife Heather Limburg for unfailing support, patience, and adaptability as he pursued this project in tandem with his dissertation and a growing family. His daughter Claire must be praised for (grudgingly) accepting the many times when she had to hear, one more time, "Daddy's working." There were also many friends from Grace Toronto Church and Sunnyside Wesleyan Church who provided helpful insights into the evangelical community and religious organizing.

We have to add the usual note that no one else is responsible for any of the errors that appear in this volume. We really mean that – we alone are responsible for those.

Religion and Canadian Party Politics

Introduction:
Faith and Party Politics in Canada

What sense do we make of these stories?

- Conservative parties in Ontario and Alberta select socially conservative leaders who then repeatedly deny that such beliefs will have any role in party policy.
- Alberta's government resisted lesbian and gay rights for years, but in 2011 the Wildrose Party lost an election in part because of an evangelical candidate's anti-gay extremism.
- Quebec's sovereigntist party has increasingly touted assertively secular policies, but it insists on retaining a crucifix over the legislative speaker's chair and remains silent on generous government funding for faith-based private schools.
- The federal Conservative government excluded abortion from maternal health development aid, but it forcefully spurned pressure from its own religious conservatives to make abortion a domestic political issue.
- Yukon is Canada's most secularized region, but in Nunavut evangelical churches and other forms of conservative Christianity are widespread.

- In British Columbia, the Liberal premier openly professed her faith in a 2013 provincial election almost universally perceived as devoid of religious influence.
- Ontario's Catholic bishops actively campaigned against provincial legislation requiring all schools to recognize Gay Straight Alliances, but then muted their advocacy for fear that it was fueling opposition to full funding of those schools.

In Canadian politics, faith matters. Despite secularization, social liberalization, and a steady decline in denominational distinctions in party choice, faith communities shape our politics in important and enduring ways. The issue of religious diversity, which has influenced public policy in Canada for generations, has taken on new dimensions that shape the internal dynamics of political parties and the conflicts between them. Religious beliefs are not as powerful a force as they once were, but in this book we consider the many ways in which they still influence contemporary Canadian political life

The Core Arguments

We make three core arguments about faith in federal and provincial politics in Canada. The first is that religious faith, and particularly its conservative variants, retains an influence over voter affiliation and party policy differentiation even in a society that has become increasingly secularized over the past half-century. The second is that the lines of faith-based political contention have shifted from a period when Protestant-Catholic divisions mattered politically to one in which disagreement over moral issues is more influential in distinguishing parties and their electorates. The third is that religious and cultural diversification has created a new "axis" of contention centred on the place of minority faiths in the Canadian social fabric. Although this new axis has been prominent in Quebec since the mid-2000s, major party leaders at the federal level largely avoided it in their policies and campaigning until it became a major issue in the 2015 election.

The overarching point is that any understanding of Canadian party politics requires attention to the influence of religious beliefs on party leaders and voters, and of particular faith communities on cementing old partisan distinctions or creating new ones. At one point this would have prioritized an exploration of Catholic-Protestant differences. In recent decades, it has meant focusing on conflict between moral traditionalists and social progressives across the range of faith allegiances. In the last few years we have had to pay more attention to the growing visibility of ethno-cultural minorities within Christian religious communities and to the partisan reverberations of growth in the size of non-Christian religious minorities. In addressing these questions, then, we need to be mindful of major changes in the religious make-up of Canada over recent decades and in the political relevance of such changes. We are also conscious of the significant differences in the way that faith shapes party politics in the provinces and territories. This suggests to us that not only should we attend to some themes that are applicable across the country but also that we should use detailed case studies of particular provinces or regions to illustrate their distinctive histories and party dynamics.

Declining Religiosity and Changing Family Values

The dramatic decline in religiosity throughout Canada since the 1950s has meant that religious currents in party conflicts often seem to be historical artefacts. Parties differ on the role of government, economic management, environmental policy, free trade, health care reform, education spending, and (in Quebec) the national question. But faith? Even party leaders who are personally religious frequently avoid the subject, delivering at best minor policy concessions to religious conservatives wanting to revive debates over abortion and sexual minority rights. This seems a very different story from that which still echoes through party politics in the United States, where debating such issues remains prominent and expressions of conservative faith are so visible. It is also at odds with a number of European party systems whose major centre-right parties are rooted in a Catholic tradition, however ill-defined that relationship may be. Such contrasts easily translate into a view that religion was never all that powerful a force in Canadian party politics, with the exception of broad denominational affiliations that long ago lost their linkage to serious policy differences, and that now border on the inconsequential.

Secularization, in All Its Meanings

In 1947, a Gallup survey showed that 67 percent of Canadians attended religious services weekly – a figure that rose to 83 percent among Catholics.[1] As Mark Noll points out, this country was "more observant in religious practice and more orthodox in religious opinion than the United States."[2] Richard Johnston extends the comparison further by saying that, at mid-century, "Canadians were among the world's most church-going peoples."[3] As we see in Figure I.1, things then changed drastically, with large-scale abandonment of church attendance especially evident from the mid-1950s to the mid-1970s. Weekly service attendance is now substantially below 20 percent, with one 2015 survey indicating that 14 percent of Canadians attended weekly services.[4] A 2006 Statistics Canada report shows that fully 40 percent of the country's population scored "low" on an index of religiosity, with only 26 percent of Canadians born in this country scoring "high."[5]

When we argue that Canada has secularized, however, we are referring to more than a decline in faith and religious practice. We are also referring to the institutional separation of faith and politics, or what some would call "institutional differentiation."[6] At its limits, this change is

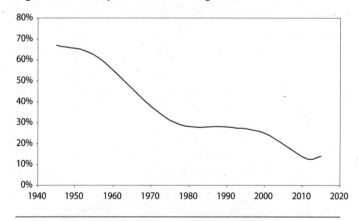

Figure I.1   Weekly attendance at religious services, 1945–2015

Sources: Gallup Surveys; General Social Surveys; Bibby, *Fragmented Gods*, 17; Bowen, *Christians in a Secular World*, 13, 28, 32; Lindsay, "Canadians Attend Religious Services Less than They Did 20 Years Ago"; "Canada's Changing Religious Landscape"; and Ipsos Reid, Canadian Online Omni, August 29–September 6, 2011.

characterized by the removal of faith-based practices from the governmental sphere and from publicly funded organizations as well as the elimination of public support for faith-based institutions. There are divergent views about how far Canadian society has shifted in this direction, but there can be no doubt that state authorities have taken on much of the delivery of social and educational services that were once the province of religious institutions.[7] The role of faith is also diminished in most of those service providers that remain religiously aligned, particularly those whose operations are subsidized by public funds. Such change reflects a shift of public sentiment towards the view that faith is a largely private matter and that church and state should be separate, at least in principle.[8]

Secularization is also manifest in the widespread acknowledgment of the plurality of beliefs in Canada, including greater public (and private) recognition of non-Christian faiths and more acknowledgment of non-belief. Institutional and theological pluralism has, of course, always been a feature of Canadian Christianity, with multiple strands of Protestantism co-existing (often not peaceably) with Roman Catholicism. Over the last few decades, that diversity has been cross-cut with growing populations of ethno-cultural minority adherents to the various Christian denominations, the long-standing visibility of a Jewish minority, a resurgence of First Nations spiritual beliefs, and the more recent growth in numbers of Muslims, Sikhs, Hindus, Buddhists, and so on. Without ignoring the persistence of discomfort with such diversity among adherents to the full range of faiths, it is fair to say that most Canadians have come to accept religious pluralism as a permanent, and routine, feature of Canadian society. They also broadly accept the principle that the interpretation of faith can vary across groups and individuals, and are comfortable with the absence of faith and faith practice within their communities and among their neighbours. As Kurt Bowen puts it in surveying the state of religion in Canada, "religious adherents today manufacture their own eclectic version of their religious beliefs and duties that their faith entails."[9] The powerful force of North American individualism contributes to this process, moulding the interpretation and practice of faith, or its absence, in even the most traditional of communities.

Are there significant regional variations in this pattern of decline in religiosity? In the late 1990s, Kurt Bowen compiled an index of religious commitment, and, as we see in Table I.1, the differences were not radical, with BC and Quebec having somewhat fewer of the very committed, and the Prairies and Atlantic Canada somewhat more. The 2011 census replicates this to some extent, showing that BC in particular stands out for the high numbers who report no religious affiliation. Quebeckers are much less likely to declare no affiliation, although this is unquestionably a result of the many Catholics who have no religious commitment whatsoever but who identify with their religion as an element of their ethnic or national attachment. The 2011 Ipsos Reid poll of attendance at religious services shows just how much less likely Quebeckers are to regularly practise their faith as compared to the inhabitants of any other region. This is congruent with responses to a 2015 Canadian Election Study question on the importance of religion in one's life. On a few questions, British Columbians are noticeably less religious than inhabitants of other English-majority provinces, but Quebec still stands out as the most distinctive region.

Attitude Shifts on Family Values

Secularization, individualization, and a growing acknowledgment of the legitimacy of human rights claims have all contributed to a shift in public beliefs away from what might be called family traditionalism. Of all the issues that have generated public mobilization by faith groups over the last half century, those related to reproduction and sexual diversity have produced the most sustained and politicized contention. For much of this time, analyzing the place of faith in Canadian party politics has required close attention to the policy debates over precisely these questions. Changes in public attitudes on these dimensions speak to the declining hold of traditional religious strictures on public belief systems and suggest that parties seeking to represent family traditionalism have less room to manoeuvre than they once did.

Figure I.2 illustrates changes in family traditionalism by displaying the proportion of Canadians in favour of the view that a woman who wants to have an abortion should be able to have one – a minority view

Table I.1 Religiosity by province and region (%)

	Canada	*ATL*	*QC*	*ON*	*MB*	*SK*	*AB*	*BC*
Bowen, 1997								
Very committed	19	26	17	22	23		13	18
Less committed	13	16	12	14	14		8	12
Conservative Protestants as % of committed	21	19	6	17	27		31	38
Canadian Election Study, 2015								
Very important	26	25	15	29	29	29	34	27
Somewhat important	36	35	35	37	35	38	31	38
Not very important	23	22	32	21	23	20	18	21
Not important	15	18	18	12	13	13	16	15
Statistics Canada, 2011								
Christian (including Catholic)	67	84	82	65	68	72	60	45
Roman Catholic	39	41	75	31	25	29	24	15
Non-Christian religions	8	1	6	12	6	4	8	11
Religiously unaffiliated	24	15	12	23	26	24	32	44
Ipsos Reid, 2011								
Weekly attendance	13	18	6	16	14		14	11
Religion defines me as person*	35	35	37	33	36		32	33

* Combines "strongly agree" and "somewhat agree."

Note: Comparable data are not available for the northern territories, though selected data do appear in Chapter 9.

Sources: Bowen, *Christians in a Secular World*, 54–55; Patrick Fournier, Fred Cutler, Stuart Soroka, and Dietlind Stolle, the 2015 Canadian Election Study (dataset), http://ces-eec. arts.ubc.ca/english-section/surveys/; Statistics Canada, 2011 National Household Survey, http://www12.statcan.gc.ca/nhs-enm/2011/dp-pd/prof/index.cfm?Lang=E; and Ipsos Reid, Canadian Online Omni, August 29–September 6, 2011.

Figure I.2   Attitudes on abortion, 1970–2012

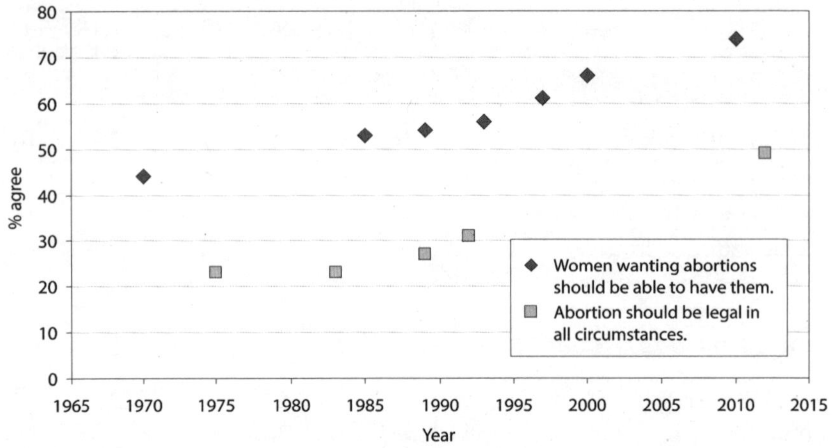

Sources: Gallup polls, Pew Global Attitudes Project; Ipsos Reid; Environics Institute, Focus Canada 2010, 39; Boyd and Gillieson, "Canadian Attitudes on Abortion: Results of the Gallup Polls."

in the 1970s but, by 2000, one held by two-thirds or more of Canadians.[10] When faced with questions that include an intermediate response saying that abortion should be permitted only in certain circumstances, the results are less positive, but by 2012 half of Canadians held to this unequivocally pro-choice position, up significantly from about one-quarter during the 1980s.[11] At the other end of the spectrum, support for a complete prohibition on abortion, covering all circumstances, was never held by as much as one-fifth of the population, and by 2012 it was supported by only 6 percent. A few surveys have asked Canadians if they considered abortion to be morally wrong, and that view is also now a minority sentiment – 40 percent in one 2002 poll, 26 percent in another from 2014.[12] It is worth adding that Catholics are only slightly less likely than others to support abortion access, in contrast to evangelical Protestants, who are more distinctively on the pro-life side of that debate.[13]

Opinion shifts are even more substantial on questions related to sexual diversity. As Figure I.3 shows, a strong majority of Canadians still disapproved of homosexuality through the 1980s, and, as recently as

Figure I.3 Attitudes on sexual diversity, 1975–2014

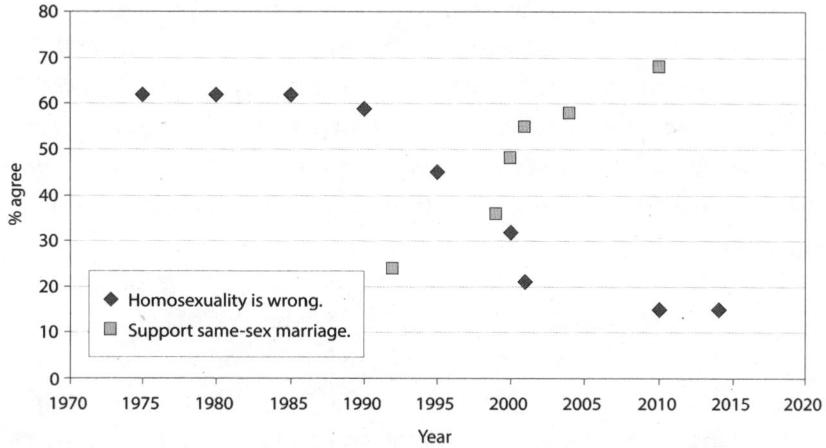

Sources: Gallup, World Values Survey, Pew Global Attitudes; Langstaff, "A Twenty-Year Survey"; Bibby, "The Bibby Report"; Zwelling, "Canada's Pulse; Rayside and Bowler, "Public Opinion and Gay Rights."

1987, only 10 percent of respondents "approved" of it.[14] By the early 2000s, however, a significant majority of Canadians agreed that "society should accept homosexuality," and in 2014 this view was held by 80 percent of respondents. Support for same-sex marriage in the 1990s was low but then moved steadily through the early 2000s towards acceptance.[15] An Ipsos Reid survey in 2012 shows that 62 percent of respondents agreed with the statement that "same-sex marriage should be fully recognized and equal to conventional heterosexual marriage," even when faced with the alternative of same-sex marriage being recognized in civil law but without the same legal weight.[16] Only 18 percent said that such marriage was wrong and should never be legal. Evangelicals and Muslims were the most opposed to same-sex marriage in 2011 (only 24 and 18 percent supporting it, respectively), and those declaring no religious affiliation were the most supportive (88 percent).[17] Catholics differed not at all from the Canadian average.

These dramatic changes in public opinion, on issues that have been among the most hotly contested by faith groups in recent decades, substantially narrow the room for ongoing political debate and reduce

the capacity to embrace moral traditionalism for even the most conservative leaders of the most conservative political parties – at least those with
a serious desire to win control of government at election. However,
there are several other faith-related concerns that remain unresolved in
law and public policy, and about which Canadians remain significantly
divided. We shall see that communities of faith, and particularly those
that hold traditionalist interpretations of their faith, continue to have
significant capacity for political mobilization.

We should note here that accurately gauging the size of Canada's
evangelical population is a difficult task. This is important for our purposes since evangelicals have mobilized in large numbers in opposition
to abortion and lesbian/gay rights. They are highly likely to attend church
and are more than twice as likely as the average Canadian to attach
importance to their religion. One challenge in gauging their numbers
is that many whose approach to faith is broadly evangelical still practise
their religion and formally associate themselves with denominations
that are not in any overall sense evangelical. Conversely, many who attend
more overtly evangelical denominations may hold beliefs at odds with
the official doctrines or dominant political views within those faith
traditions. As a consequence, some surveys specifically asking about
evangelical leanings have found that they constitute only about 5 percent
of the population, which differs significantly from estimates of 8 to 10
percent provided by informed observers.[18] Many other surveys do not
ask about evangelical affiliation directly, requiring those of us interested
in such questions to use a combination of denominational affiliations
widely understood to be evangelical.[19]

What about regional variations? We can see in Table I.2 a variety of
indicators that social conservatives committed to traditionalist positions
on abortion and sexual diversity are in the minority in all parts of Canada.
A 2012 Ipsos Reid poll shows that Quebeckers were more supportive of
women exercising choice over abortion; those living in the Prairies fell
below the Canadian average. This pattern is broadly replicated in the
responses to questions on abortion and sexual diversity in the 2011 and
2015 Canadian Election Studies.[20] Quebec and Alberta are once again
opposing outliers, though with regional contrasts sometimes quite
muted. Responses to a "thermometer" score question about attitudes

Table I.2   Social and religious conservatism by province and region (%)

	Canada	ATL	QC	ON	MB	SK	AB	BC
Ipsos Reid, 2012								
Abortion when woman decides	49	46	60	47	42		34	52
Canadian Election Study, 2011								
Abortion should be banned	18	30	11	19	29	29	25	13
Favour traditional values (Strongly agree)	27	23	27	24	30	39	36	23
Canadian Election Study, 2015								
Average thermometer reading for lesbians/gays	67	69	67	68	66	69	60	70
Oppose same-sex marriage	30	27	24	32	27	39	40	26
Agree on biblical literalism	35	39	24	39	34	45	39	38

Sources: Ipsos Reid, Canadian Online Omni, June 18–25, 2012; Fournier et al., 2011 Canadian Election Study, and 2015 Canadian Election Study.

towards lesbians and gays, for example, reveal only small variations. The same is also true of support for "traditional values," though there is clearly room for Quebeckers to "read" that question quite differently than other Canadians.

Confirmation that there are only modest interprovincial differences in public attitudes towards moral issues can be found in David McGrane's analysis of responses to provincial election surveys from 2011 to 2014.[21] The average "score" on a four-point index, varying from a progressive "1" to a conservative "4," varied only marginally between provinces, with, for example, Ontario at 2.51, British Columbia at 2.53, Quebec at 2.64, and Alberta at 2.71. The most conservative provincial average is in Newfoundland and Labrador, with 2.80.

What about regional differences specifically with regard to religious traditionalism? Recall that Kurt Bowen used 1997 data to explore regional variations in overall religious commitment and the proportion of conservative Protestants among them (displayed in Table I.1). Variations in the numbers of committed did not vary enormously, though there were more "very committed" in Atlantic Canada. What was more striking was the comparatively high proportion of conservative Protestants among the committed across the western provinces. The 2015 Canadian Election Study includes a question on biblical literalism, and here we find relatively high levels in Saskatchewan but general consistency in the rest of the country, except for Quebec.

The Ongoing Story of Faith-Based Conflict in Canada

Even with the enormous changes in religious faith and public beliefs over recent decades, policy debates over morality and the place of religion in the public sphere still ignite conflict, mobilize faith communities, and create or perpetuate religious distinctions in voting patterns.[22] The issues may change over time: some areas of persistent public contention recede from the partisan arena; appeals become more specifically targeted to avoid excessive publicity; new sources of disagreement are politicized. Party leaders and strategists may now largely avoid explicitly pitching appeals to particular faith communities, or raising questions about the public role of religion, but they will still often shape their messages according to what they believe will resonate with such communities. The 2015 federal election, the 2014 Quebec election, and the 2016–17 Conservative Party of Canada leadership race each threw a spotlight on the issue of public acceptance of minority religious practices, particularly those associated with Islam, all supposedly in the name of gender equality or "Canadian values." The Progressive Conservative proposal to provide funding to faith-based schools was a central issue in Ontario's 2007 election, and between 2010 and 2014 the party sided with social conservatives in opposing the provincial government's revamped sexual health curriculum. New Brunswick's long-standing restrictions on access to abortion became an issue in the province's 2014 election, ending decades of political avoidance.

The Foundations of Faith-Based Protest

The continued visibility of faith-related issues in Canadian party politics is rooted partly in the continued importance of religion for key segments of the population, even if less so than in the past. It is also based in large measure on the fact that local places of worship constitute an almost ideal grassroots foundation for the mobilization of public engagement. Conservative Protestant advocacy is in fact based overwhelmingly on local churches and networks, taking advantage of regular encounters within communities of believers. They are led by spiritual figures who have a privileged podium from which to deliver calls to action, or they include networks of co-believers that advocates can deploy. Calls to action may not be followed by all – or even most – listeners, but on the right issues, and in the right circumstances, many people will be moved to act. Social movements that rely on other institutions or networks can only dream of such an advantage. Some religious communities, most notably the Roman Catholic, also have a hierarchical clergy, which can ensure that a uniform message is delivered to all churches. Other faith communities with more independent spiritual leaders enjoy the advantage of loyal followers, who frequently have helped choose those leaders.

Religious progressives have some of the advantages that come with a network of local religious institutions, with prominent examples to be found within established Protestant denominations like the United Church of Canada, Reform Judaism, and progressive currents in other religious communities informed by principles of equity and social justice. Such religious settings have provided important voices for rethinking spiritual approaches to issues such as family and sexuality and, in more recent years, to a range of issues related to immigration, social service provision, and Aboriginal reconciliation. In decades past, such currents played an extremely influential role inside the Co-operative Commonwealth Federation (CCF), in the early years of the New Democratic Party (NDP), and in other parties across Canada. For the last several decades, however, faith-based advocacy on equality and social justice has been overshadowed by that coming from more traditionalist quarters, and certainly it is this more conservative advocacy that has troubled partisan alignments.

Adding to the leverage that is born of such traditionalist faith foundations is the proliferation of interest groups representing those views.[23] There are long-standing conferences of Catholic bishops that intervene on a variety of policy fronts, but since 1985 they have been joined by the Catholic Civil Rights League, an ostensibly independent group but effectively a political vehicle for the bishops. Such groups, and the bishops themselves, can count on the support of nominal Catholics less than ever, but the sheer number of Catholics in the general population means that even the mobilization of a modest proportion can create a loud voice in any party wishing to retain or gain Catholic votes. This applies particularly in those parts of Canada where Catholics form a significant portion of the population or where their overall numbers are large enough for protest to reach an impressive scale. For instance, Catholics constitute about 40 percent of the inhabitants across the Atlantic region, and about 30 percent in Ontario, where their potential for influence is further buttressed by the wide array of Catholic social and educational institutions firmly established in that province. (In Quebec they constitute a 75 percent majority, though very low rates of church attendance and scepticism about clerical involvement in politics substantially limit the leverage of the hierarchy.)[24]

Evangelical Protestant groups now have a stronger institutional presence than ever, particularly at the federal level. The Evangelical Fellowship of Canada (EFC) is the longest-standing of such groups, formed in 1964. It serves as a primary association for evangelical denominations in Canada and is distinguished from the Canadian Council of Churches, which brings together the Roman Catholic Church and mainline Protestant denominations, such as the Anglican, Lutheran, and United Churches. The EFC moved towards more regular political intervention beginning in the 1970s, but then expanded its size and professional expertise substantially from the 1990s on.

Focus on the Family Canada, a branch of the large evangelical American group, was formed in 1983 but at first was known mainly around its headquarters in Langley, British Columbia. It developed a national profile in the decades to follow, and, in 2006, it launched the Ottawa-based Institute on Marriage and Family in order to more directly intervene in public policy debates. In 2016, that organization left Focus on the Family and joined Cardus, a Christian Canadian think tank that had significantly increased its profile from the 2000s on. REAL Women of Canada emerged as a small anti-feminist group in the 1980s, and, although it is not expressly religious, it is now a regular and visible inter-vener on a range of issues, including lesbian, gay, bisexual, and trans-gender (LGBT) rights, alongside groups associated with the religious right. The advocacy of such groups is strengthened by Christian broad-casts on Canadian media outlets and the accessibility of American evangelical media for many Canadians. In recent years, they have also been aided by the broader institutional development on the right em-bodied in the Manning Centre, which was created by one-time Reform Party leader Preston Manning to support conservative and libertarian advocacy. Political leverage is more likely in those parts of Canada with proportionately large numbers of evangelicals, most obviously in south-ern Alberta but also in BC's Fraser Valley and in southwestern Ontario.

Cardus is one of those groups that has succeeded in bringing together conservative Catholics and evangelicals. The Campaign Life Coalition is another, having been active on the pro-life side of the abortion issue since the late 1970s. It organizes the annual "March for Life" rallies in Ottawa that have become major flash points for social conservative activism, including on the part of pro-life members of Parliament. More recently it has been joined by the Canadian Centre for Bio-Ethical Reform, though, like Campaign Life, it lacks the institutionalization exhibited by the larger multi-issue Catholic and evangelical interest groups. Specific issues, such as lesbian/gay marriage or, more recently, revisions to the sexual education curriculum in Ontario, will draw sup-port from more than one faith community, and even if they often revolve around single personalities, or last only as long as political controversy is visible in the media, they attest to sustained mobilizational capacity at the grassroots.

Social conservative advocacy campaigns have long claimed to have a broad coalition of support reflecting Canada's ethno-cultural and reli-gious diversity, but the plain truth is that these campaigns have been overwhelmingly rooted in long-established Protestant and Catholic communities – until recently. Over the last decade or so, controversies over the recognition of sexual diversity in schools have witnessed a growing profile of minority group protests working alongside or in parallel with more established white-dominated groups. This reflects a growth in size of communities such as the Sikh in British Columbia and Muslim in Ontario, and the centrality of schooling to their ambitions for retaining elements of their traditional culture. Such mobilization does not indicate that minority communities are uniformly conservative on such issues, nor that they are linked by stable coalitional links to more established conservative groups, or that the controversies around which traditionalists have mobilized shape partisan leanings. But the multiculturalization of protest around issues like schooling does mean that they have a continued potential to be noticed by party leaders. Such efforts were evident in the outreach conducted by former Conservative Minister of Multiculturalism Jason Kenney at the federal level and more recently by Progressive Conservative Party leader Patrick Brown in Ontario.

Religious minorities have also become more visibly prepared to speak out in defence of their faith and the rights associated with it. This has long been true of the Jewish community, which has a substantial network of institutionalized groups at the national and local levels. B'nai Brith Canada was formed in 1875 as a service and advocacy group. The Canadian Jewish Congress was formed in 1919 and remained a prominent voice until it merged with several other bodies to create the Centre for Israel and Jewish Affairs in 2011. Group formation among Muslims, who now constitute the largest non-Christian religious group in Canada, has been slower, reflecting the relatively recent immigration of most of that community and its cultural and theological diversity. Indeed, the Muslim Association of Canada was established only in 1997, while the more prominent National Council of Canadian Muslims was founded a further three years later.[25] Neither these nor any other Islamic advocacy group at the national or local levels have developed significant institutional capacity, but they have obtained some mainstream media visibility, and, to some extent, they can rely on a now considerable number of local mosques and Islamic centres in all of Canada's major cities. Not all parts of the country are equally likely to have sustained minority advocacy since this depends on numbers that are large enough to build institutional networks. In Atlantic Canada, adherents of non-Christian religions constituted only 1 percent of the population in 2011, while in Ontario it was 12 percent, and in Toronto 22 percent. In other major cities, non-Christians were 17 percent in Vancouver, 12 percent in Alberta, and 11 percent in Montreal.[26]

Axes of Political Contention

Three axes of contention mark faith's role in Canadian politics: the denominational divides that were prominent historically and continue to echo in a few provinces; the advocacy by social conservatives seeking to resist the secularization that has so strikingly reshaped society since the Second World War; and conflicts over how to accommodate the immigration-driven diversification of faith communities since the 1970s. Together, these divides have generated debate and conflict across a wide range of issues. Denominational tension between Catholics and Protestants (and at times among Protestants themselves) was the first to emerge and long shaped party systems in Canada – frequently intensified by French-English divisions. The second "axis" of contention, prominent in the early twentieth century and even more in the last quarter of that century, set moral traditionalists from all faiths against social progressives in struggles over questions related to gender, sexuality, and family. The third division pits advocates for the recognition of non-Christian minority religious practices against those who insist on faith being an entirely private matter and/or others who seek (often implicitly) the privileging of Christianity. We use these axes to organize the analysis presented in this book.

Conflict along these axes has not invariably pitted one party against others for, in some cases, party leaders avoid engaging them for fear of inflaming public opinion, alienating voters, or dividing their own ranks. A Liberal party may contain a strong current of anti-clericalism, as was true of the nineteenth-century federal party and the Quebec provincial Liberals throughout their history. However, such parties may also have chosen to sideline that voice for fear of either opening up wrenching internal debate or overtly challenging a once-hegemonic church. The Progressive Conservative party in New Brunswick may prosper on an electoral foundation that includes many ardently anti-Catholic Protestants but, instead, opt to balance its electoral ticket to bridge entrenched denominational and linguistic divisions. Parties in British Columbia and Ontario may fully realize that there is serious popular disagreement over how far to recognize minority faith practices and how much to eliminate specifically Christian symbols in the public sphere, but leave such issues for local institutions and courts to resolve. Parties on the right that attract disproportionate numbers of religious traditionalists may want to signal their openness to such voices but realize that boldly acting on them would lose more votes than it might win.

Denominational Conflict

For a century and a half, across much of central and eastern Canada, attachment to one Christian denomination – and not to others – mattered greatly for one's social identity, and often for party allegiance. The most prominent division separated Roman Catholics from Protestants, often enduring through periods when there were no obviously relevant policy issues at stake. In the nineteenth century, as Brian Clarke puts it, "anti-Catholicism was a frame of mind, a cluster of beliefs and emotions that organized people's perceptions of the world around them and imparted a cultural identity."[27] Through much of the nineteenth century and the first half of the twentieth, the anti-Catholic Orange Order remained a powerful social and political force in Atlantic Canada, Ontario, and parts of the west. In turn, the Catholic hierarchy emphasized the importance of supporting not just separate schools but a whole array of social institutions and associations designed to encircle the faithful and immunize them from other influences.

Tensions between Protestants and Catholics frequently exploded into violence, at times in parallel with divisions between English and French speakers. Some parties at the federal or provincial levels were dominated by adherents of one faith or the other, or were accused of being so. Other parties were divided internally by tensions between adherents of different faith communities, and, as a result, were forced to carefully consider their positioning in debates that might inflame denominational passions.

For much of the twentieth century, at the national level and in several provinces, where you worshipped remained the single strongest predictor of party preference. At the federal level, the Liberals drew significantly more Catholic voters than did Conservatives, and this remained true even as francophone Quebeckers shifted (for a time) to the sovereigntist Bloc Québécois. Outside Quebec, the Liberal preference among Catholics persisted into the twenty-first century, long after there were any federal policy issues explaining this pattern. At the provincial level, Protestant-Catholic political contention remained beyond the Second World War in several regions, most prominently in Ontario and the Atlantic region.

Conflict over the funding and control of separate school systems remained at the centre of denominational contention through much of the first century after Confederation and, in some cases, continues to this day.[28] The elimination of denominational school systems in Newfoundland and Labrador and Quebec near the end of the twentieth century, and a political "settlement" of the Catholic funding issue in Ontario in the mid-1980s, might have signalled the ultimate fading of denominational influences on provincial politics, and, generally speaking, political contentiousness has largely disappeared. Questions remain, however, about what leeway exists for state-funded Catholic schools to deviate from provincial curricula or requirements to accommodate student groups like gay-straight alliances (GSAs), and debate over such rights inevitably ignites calls for the elimination or reduction in public funding for these systems. In Quebec, New Brunswick, Manitoba, and, to some extent, Ontario, francophone interests became conflated with the defence of Catholic institutions, and language then became a more prominent source of conflict than religion itself. But even then religious differences were not swept entirely aside, and we see evidence of such even in highly secularized Quebec.

Religious Traditionalists vs. Political and Social Progressives

In recent decades, the aspect of faith-based contention that has most shaped Canada's various party systems is that driven by social conservatives collaborating across religious boundaries to resist social change. In their magisterial survey of American religion in the early twenty-first century, Robert Putnam and David Campbell talk of a political realignment that has relevance to party politics in Canada.

> In 1960, religion's role in politics was mostly a matter of something akin to tribal loyalty – Catholics and Protestants each supported their own ... By the 2000s, how religious a person is had become more important as a political dividing line than which denomination he or she belonged to. Church-attending evangelicals and Catholics (and other religious groups too) have found common political cause.[29]

Canada certainly has witnessed repeated large-scale political mobilizations in response to a perceived threat to traditional values and, specifically, efforts to counter advocacy by the women's movement and sexual minorities. Such views are often reinforced by particular, often literalist, readings of scripture. Debates over gender and sexuality have often become what Janet Jakobsen refers to as "crucial mediating points at the boundaries of religious difference."[30] This is not to say that social conservatism is always driven by religion, nor that all people of faith are necessarily traditionalist in their views. As we have already pointed out, reformist currents within a variety of faith communities have at times led the way in calling for a reconsideration of established moral stances. Even among adherents of conservative religious communities we often find pragmatic adjustment to changing social norms, especially among the young, and particularly on questions of sexual diversity.[31] But in recent decades, faith-driven intervention in political debates has been dominated by social conservatives, and it has been religious conservatives who have been in the vanguard of such intervention.

Their defensive advocacy stresses the timelessness of a particular family form in which gender roles are clear-cut and child-rearing is naturally the province of heterosexual marriage. In this moral view, abortion represents the selfish abandonment of the reproductive responsibilities that lie at the heart of marriage and the family. Homosexual activity, or any other practice that violates established gender norms or imagines changing gender identity, is a threat to this family model and, particularly, to children and young people who may still be uncertain about or experimenting with their gender identities. For this reason, schools are regularly at the centre of traditionalist concerns.

Moral conservatives will often go beyond family issues and argue for the preservation or restoration of faith practices in public institutions, such as prayers in town council meetings and public displays (such as Christmas trees) associated with religious holidays. In the area of education, they may argue that faith-based schools should receive state funding, and that such support should not compromise the schools' independence. Some will also advocate for the right to conscientious objection in the face of requests for public services that violate moral beliefs, and uphold the right to unfettered free speech in mounting faith-based interventions against those who are seen to undermine traditional values, even if some of their opponents consider these interventions to be hateful attacks.

Evangelical Protestants have often been leading advocates of these traditionalist positions. In doing so they benefit from comparatively high weekly church attendance as well as from media outlets capable of calling them to political action. On some issues, particularly abortion and sexual diversity, evangelicals often work alongside conservative Catholics who are led by bishops and archbishops informed by traditionalist teachings on such questions. There are also indications that this cross-denominational alliance of moral conservatives is being joined by traditionalists within recent waves of migration from countries in which conservative family values still prevail.

Has the religiously led or inspired mobilization of social conservatives led to the sort of political alignment we have seen in the United States? The answer must be in shades of grey. Over the course of the 1990s and 2000s, parties on the right at the federal level and in some regions did become the only plausible ally for social conservatives who prioritized the kinds of issues we are discussing. This was a direct result of such parties moving sharply right, following in the footsteps of Margaret Thatcher's British Conservative Party and Ronald Reagan's Republicans in the United States.[32] In Canada, as we shall see, this move away from the brokerage model that had so long characterized major parties at the federal level and in several provinces was driven primarily by an ideological commitment to the free market. During the 1990s, this was dramatically evident in Alberta under Premier Ralph Klein and in Ontario under Premier Mike Harris. In the early 2000s, the same radical shift occurred when the Conservative Party of Canada (CPC) was forged from the Canadian Alliance (itself the successor to the Reform Party insurgency) and the remnants of the Progressive Conservative Party (PCP).

In none of these cases were social conservative causes prioritized, and there has been no time when Canada has experienced the kind of culture war that has marked American political life. But in all these cases, and others like them, the repositioned parties on the right had a significant number of moral traditionalist supporters. Unlike their American cousins, as Sam Reimer and Lydia Bean point out, Canadian evangelicals were not developing an identity that assumed support for a particular party, and they would never be as widely or as fiercely supportive of conservative parties as white American evangelicals were of the Republican Party.[33] Nevertheless, most Canadian evangelicals tilted that way, and conservative party leaders knew that they had the potential to increase their electoral support within those communities as other parties shifted towards more progressive social policy positions. What we therefore saw was that these parties tailored their appeals to help secure the loyalty of social conservatives and religious traditionalists.

Yet, while right-wing party leaders still look for ways to signal their understanding of traditional social values, the broader process of social change has meant that the room for these leaders to manoeuvre on the hot button issues that motivate such voters has declined dramatically, and they have become increasingly more conscious of the electoral risks of siding too visibly with such groups. There is no longer any significant party in Canada, for example, prepared to explicitly oppose the equality rights of sexual minorities – one powerful illustration being the federal Conservative Party's 2016 repudiation of its formal policy opposing same-sex marriage. This development reflects not only major attitude shifts in the general public, but also a change in attitudes among many religious traditionalists, particularly the young. However, it does not mean that there are no longer any issues that provoke mobilization among social conservatives or that provide opportunities for parties on the right to engage in such signalling. Prostitution was pushed onto the national policy agenda by a 2013 Supreme Court ruling that struck down existing criminal code regulation.[34] Medically assisted suicide also became an issue at both the federal and provincial levels soon afterwards, partly because of court challenges but also due to policy shifts in Quebec. Even if the federal Conservative Party has tried to avoid debate on abortion, on both of these "new" issues, it has allied itself with the most prominent current of morally traditionalist advocacy.

Recognizing Religious Minorities

The third axis of contention, long in the background of Canadian politics but recently more prominent, is rooted in disagreement over the recognition of minority religious practices and institutions. It may seem natural to imagine sustained public and partisan conflict arising from the significant increase in immigration by ethno-religious minorities since the 1970s. After all, we can see clear evidence of anti-immigrant party growth across much of Europe and intensified opposition, among American Republicans, in particular, to illegal immigration from Mexico and all forms of immigration from the Muslim world.

There certainly has been popular opposition in Canada to some instances of minority religious accommodation, for example, in response to the RCMP's acceptance of Sikh turbans in the 1990s, and the extension to Muslims of an Ontario faith-based arbitration system in 2005.[35] In 2015, a federal Conservative policy of barring face-covering garments from citizenship ceremonies was supported by an overwhelming number of Canadians.[36] This was especially so in Quebec, where there had been years of sensationalized media focus on "unreasonable" accommodation of minority religious practices.

Some of this sentiment is based on a belief that such practices reflect a failure of immigrant or minority communities to integrate into the existing culture, though some is also directed at religious practices that deviate too sharply from those considered "normal" by the majority. Environics polling in 2016 shows that 54 percent majority of Canadians believed that "too many immigrants do not adopt Canadian values."[37] A 2014 survey conducted by Jack Jedwab for the Association of Canadian Studies indicates that 43 percent of Canadians were worried about the number of immigrants in Canada and that 40 percent agreed that "society is threatened by the influx of non-Christian immigrants."[38] This survey also shows, as do others, that Muslims have become the target of more negative sentiment than have other ethno-cultural minorities. Respondents were asked for their overall feelings towards selected groups. Immigrants as a whole elicited positive sentiments from 66 percent of all respondents, Catholics 70 percent, Protestants 68 percent, and Jews 67 percent, but Muslims only 42 percent.[39] Environics surveys indicate that, in 2010, there were about as many Canadians who favoured a ban on wearing headscarves in public places as there were opposed, significantly more than in 2006.[40]

Public concerns about and resistance to religious recognition can also result from the process of secularization. On the one hand, such opposition can be fuelled by frustration over the decentring of Christian practice in public institutions, including court rulings against the statutory designation of Sunday as a common day of pause from work and the use of specifically Christian prayers and physical symbols in public institutions. On the other, those who support such secularizing rulings may fear that the public recognition of minority religions will reopen space for religion in the public square. This fear is amplified by perceptions, broadly accurate, that people in religious minority communities are more likely to attach significance to their religion than are those who identify as Christian. This elevated religious identification of course may constitute a form of ethnic or cultural attachment, but it is also the case that faith itself is more important for those in the minority, particularly among first-generation immigrants. Warren Clark uses Statistics Canada data to show that, in 2001, attendance at religious services among foreign-born residents of large metropolitan areas was about twice the rate of the Canadian-born and that the rate among the former was holding steadily while declining significantly among the latter.[41] Reginald Bibby laments the "devastating fire" of secularism in this country but argues that the growing size of religious minority communities (Christian and non-Christian) has added new life to the old, fire-ravaged forest.[42] This is precisely what creates anxiety among those who have distanced themselves from their own religious roots, and this is especially so in Quebec.

What about party alignments? In the 2015 federal election we saw the Conservative Party use the issue of the face-covering niqab and fears over "barbaric cultural practices" in an attempt to undercut support for the New Democratic Party and the Liberals, especially in Quebec.[43] Likewise, in that province's 2014 election, the Parti Québécois (PQ) campaigned on a "Charter of Quebec Values" that preyed on anti-Muslim sentiment while claiming only to promote state neutrality and gender equity. Before that, the 2007 Ontario election hinged on contention over a Progressive Conservative promise to extend funding for faith-based schools beyond the Catholic system. But these are not typical stories. Most provincial parties across Canada have not politicized policies related to immigration and the recognition of minority religious rights, with such issues instead generally left for local institutions and the courts to resolve. When Sharia law became a focus of public controversy in 2005, the Ontario Liberals responded by shunting the issue off the political agenda and were supported in that by the two other provincial parties. British Columbia's very large populations of east and south Asians might have led to the politicization of issues related to minority recognition, but the major parties know all too well that they need to court and not repel voters in those communities. Yes, Quebec has been the only province in Canada where these issues have become the focus of sustained partisan debate. But it is worth noting that everyday accommodation of minority religious practices has become largely normalized there, as it is elsewhere in Canada. The 2017 killing of worshipers in a Quebec City mosque may also provoke thoughtful reflections on recent years of social and political contention over minority religious practices, which may in turn temper partisan debates over these issues.

The major parties at the federal level have traditionally not had major policy differences on immigration, and, more often than not, they have avoided contention over the recognition of religious minorities. This has changed to some extent since the formation of the Conservative Party of Canada in the early 2000s. While in government, even if it maintained traditionally robust levels of overall immigration, the CPC changed rules and procedures in ways that drastically reduced the acceptance of refugee claims, and, in 2015, it actively resisted admitting

Syrian refugees. And, of course, it forced women to remove face veils at citizenship ceremonies. But does this constitute a sea-changing re-alignment on such issues? Despite the Conservative's 2015 election defeat being in part blamed on its politicization of the niqab and the proposal for a "barbaric cultural practices" hotline, the issues raised in the party's 2016–17 leadership race suggest that such policies continue to be sup-ported by substantial portions of its grassroots membership. Yet at the same time, the CPC has also been quite transparently interested in ex-panding its electoral support among ethno-cultural religious minorities, recognizing that the significant growth of these populations cannot be ignored and that much of what the party stands for has at least some appeal within these minority groups. Public support for the continua-tion of Canada's comparatively high levels of immigration also remains widespread. Environics polling shows that, between the 1970s and the mid-1990s, a majority of Canadians felt that immigration levels were too high; however, by the early 2000s, an equally strong majority dis-agreed with this view.[44] In 2016, 80 percent agreed that the economic impact of immigration was positive – all this setting Canadians apart from populations in most other Western industrialized countries.

The Blurred Edges of Religious Political Contention
Compiling a catalogue of those political issues that distinguish faith communities from other parts of the population, or that mark out particular parties as appealing to particular religious communities, is not straightforward. Across the span of Canadian history, many Pro-testants have supported or acquiesced to the recognition of Catholic institutions even as many Catholics have opposed such recognition on anti-clerical grounds. In past decades, and most certainly now, oppos-ition to government funding for separate schools has been fuelled in part by those who sought a unified public school system under no reli-gious influence. The provision of state-funded and regulated child care may well be opposed by many religious conservatives but yet supported by those people of faith who have struggled to find care for their chil-dren. Restricting access to abortion or resisting the legitimation of same-sex marriage may have motivated a core of the faithful in many

distinct religious communities, but many others see reproductive issues differently or now believe that such battles are in the past. There has long been a social justice current in evangelical Protestantism, and there are certainly Canadians born of this important tradition who share little of the anti-gay preoccupations of their co-religionists during the last quarter of the twentieth century. Religious minorities invariably contain members who reject the political recognition of what might be argued to be community faith practices and resent religious leaders who claim to be the representational voice of their community. Nor is there any evidence that communities of immigrants with otherwise socially conservative views are disproportionately on the pro-life side of the abortion debate.

Law-and-order issues also must be fit into any analysis of religion and politics. There is no inherent reason that people of faith, even the most conservative among them, would support strengthening law enforcement and toughening sentences, and there are actually good scriptural reasons to oppose such an approach. On the other hand, protecting family members from criminality is woven into the belief system of many religious traditionalists, a view reinforced by a perception that the world's temptations are ever-present, perhaps especially so in a secularized and sexualized environment. The simple truth is that most religious traditionalists in North America also support a law-and-order agenda, and conservative parties in both the United States and Canada realize this. Such support is particularly strong among evangelical Protestants, and, in some respects, may be a peculiarity of the American individualism so deeply embedded in that faith current.

As this discussion of law-and-order issues demonstrates, in all cases in which particular faith groups seem to be leading the charge in policy advocacy, we must ask whether it is really faith that is driving the disagreement and any corresponding partisan attachments, whether it is a vehicle for expressing what are basically social values, or whether religious affiliation is a form of cultural or ethnic identification that stands apart from religious feeling. Classifying yourself as Catholic may be rooted in a trans-generational attachment to historic memories, or it may be more a product of language-group identity than of faith.

Muslim or Jewish identity may be much more about ethnicity or minority status than religiosity, reinforced by majority prejudice. In this way, significant currents of support for particular faith practices in the public sphere may come from an interest in preserving tradition or in protecting ethnic rights.

Causes championed by religious conservatives may attract a large number of secular supporters. Schooling issues have arisen along all the lines of contention outlined here, and there is a long history of faith communities mobilizing politically over what their children are taught, who teaches them, and who controls educational decisions. Conflicts between Catholics and Protestants, between social progressives and religious traditionalists, and between proponents and opponents of religious minority rights have all invoked educational issues. But these debates and struggles draw in a wider set of individuals concerned about how and what children are taught, and about the role that parents play in decisions about schooling. Debates about the funding of faith-based schools are also regularly lodged within broader discussions of school choice, drawing in free market advocates without any interest in supporting religious institutions.[45]

Around any episode of what appears to be faith-based contention, then, the extent to which they are driven by religious beliefs is hard to decipher. The very fact, however, that advocates of one or another position frame it in religious terms, or in coded language widely understood by co-religionists, provides evidence for the claim that religion still matters in Canadian politics generally, and party politics particularly. Association with a faith community still, for many, provides a form of social glue, a set of institutions that provides vehicles for maintaining community networks and mobilizing political advocacy, and opportunities for parties to forge local connections.

Looking Ahead

We approach the questions posed at the outset of this chapter mindful of such complexities and, in particular, of the three distinct axes of religiously inflected political contention that have at one time or another shaped the party systems in different parts of the country. Any analysis of the ways in which religious attachments and beliefs influence party systems requires attention to the faith-based dimensions of voting behaviour, and here we are able to rely on decades of federal election studies and, for more recent years, on the results of the Comparative Provincial Election Project.[46] Our analysis also tracks the policy positions adopted by parties and their candidates both during elections and when in government. In some cases, we chronicle policy change over those historical periods that we believe illuminate the central themes in particular chapters. In others, we dwell on particular incidents or periods of intense faith-based mobilization in order to decipher the positioning of parties around contentious issues, at times building on what is publicly known using insights from our confidential interviews with informants. Indeed, one reason for adopting a case study approach is that major parties do not always clarify the motivations that lie behind their policy priorities, making such interviews essential. Another is that periods of partisan contention often reveal not only party strategy but also the complex internal dynamics that may lie behind strategic calculations.

In Part 1, we begin with an examination of the federal parties. Chapter 1 looks broadly at whether the creation of the Conservative Party of Canada in the early 2000s has produced a growing policy distinction between the major parties on issues related to faith and moral traditionalism. We also examine the extent to which the parties have developed more differentiated faith constituencies in the electorate, with the faint legacy of denominational distinctions being replaced by a new cleavage that pits secular and non-religious voters together against religious and moral traditionalists from across specific faith affiliations. To further unpack these developments, Chapter 2 examines policy and legislative developments related to abortion at the federal level since the 1980s, and especially during the Harper Conservative administrations from 2006 to 2015. As a signature issue for religious conservatives, the abortion issue highlights the strategic challenges facing the federal Conservatives as they work to retain the loyalty of that constituency without alienating other elements of their "base" or the more centrist voters needed to obtain a majority government.

We follow this analysis with a series of provincial case studies that were chosen to illustrate particular themes at the intersection of faith and party politics. Provinces have considerable power in the Canadian federation, and their policy jurisdiction includes areas that have been the focus of a great deal of faith-based contention – schooling being the most obvious example. They also have party systems that in much of the country have become quite distinct from the federal system. At the same time, individual provincial parties that still use the same labels as their federal counterparts have become increasingly independent, though more so in the case of Conservatives and Liberals than New Democrats.

Part 2 explores the tenacity of denominational considerations in provincial party voting and policy making. In Chapter 3, we examine two provinces (Newfoundland and Labrador and New Brunswick) in the Atlantic region – the part of the country least affected by immigration and widely viewed as correspondingly traditional. There we find the political relevance of denominational affiliation much diminished, though the strength of pro-life sentiment among New Brunswick's Catholics translated into long-standing governmental resistance to the extension of abortion services. In both provinces, too, we find that historical patterns of cross-party accommodation aimed at reducing the temperature of faith-based discord translated into a reluctance of major parties to develop LGBT-inclusive policies that would rouse faith community opposition until such measures could secure all-party agreement. We then examine, in Chapter 4, how the long history of Protestant-Catholic differences shaped the party system in Ontario prior to 1985, focusing particularly on battles over education. This was in a party system in which Catholics and Protestants long preferred Liberal and Progressive Conservative parties, respectively, and in which policy differences between those parties were still very much at play in the early postwar period. Elements of this dynamic continued until the mid-1980s when the PC (Progressive Conservative) leadership sought to end denominational contention by extending full funding to Roman Catholic schools.

The next set of case studies (Part 3) explores the second axis of contention, that which pits social progressives against moral traditionalists of all faiths. Chapter 5 again focuses on Ontario, chronicling how the provincial parties gradually shifted in the post-1985 period from a denominational distinction to one based on conflict over "traditional family values," particularly issues related to sexual diversity. Our analysis points to the persistence of party differences on such issues up to 2015. Cross-faith alliances among religious conservatives can also be found in our two western Canadian case studies (Chapters 6 and 7).

Alberta is home to a particularly large moral traditionalist population – one consisting largely of evangelical Protestants, but also of Mormons and conservative Catholics. Our analysis chronicles this constituency's long history of influence within the Progressive Conservative Party, and its recent partial drift away from the PCs in favour of the Wildrose Party (Chapter 6). We begin with the Ralph Klein premiership and then focus on the recent period, during which the PCs have been outflanked on the right by Wildrose. Both parties now face a dilemma similar to parties on the right elsewhere in devising strategies to ensure the loyalty of religious conservatives without alienating other constituencies.

As in Alberta, evangelical Protestants and conservative Catholics in British Columbia have been able to mobilize politically relevant resources, but in this case they do so within a party system that has long been polarized between a right and left defined primarily by economic issues, and in a province in which an unusually large proportion of the population declares no religious affiliation. The moral traditionalist influence within the Social Credit was obvious when it was the dominant party on the right, but now it is the Liberals who occupy that side of the party spectrum. The obvious question for us (and the question that forms the basis of Chapter 7) is whether conservative faith groups have coalesced around the Liberals as they have around rightist parties elsewhere in Canada. Our answer is that they do to some extent, though the Liberals face a very considerable strategic challenge in luring them and keeping their attachment.

We then finish with two highly distinct case studies in Part 4. In Chapter 8, we examine Quebec, which is highly unusual in the Canadian context for the extent to which recent elections have featured highly politicized debates over the recognition of minority religious practices – the third of our axes of contention. Quebec is also distinctive in the force of its secularism, representing a particularly dramatic turning away from an earlier pattern of Roman Catholic influence over the francophone population. Our analysis goes beyond the usual interpretation of party politics in that province, which suggests a total falling away of any religious influence, by chronicling a pattern of cross-party caution in moving away from support for Catholic institutions, especially in the educational sector. What results is a complex pattern of incomplete secularism now confronting a large influx of French-speaking immigrants adhering to very different faiths and to religious practices that jar with francophone Quebeckers' evolving sense of what is appropriate in the public square.

Beyond Quebec, in Chapter 9 we focus on the North, in part because it is so little explored in Canadian politics and in part because there is so much variation from one territory to another in the political profile and influence of religion. At one extreme we find a highly secularized Yukon, while at the other we find widespread evangelical religiosity in Nunavut. Each also possesses a profoundly distinct political system, with two territories rejecting the party model found in the rest of Canada. And of course there are very substantial Aboriginal populations throughout the region. All this raises questions about how different from other parts of Canada the play of religion is in each of the territories and across the North in general.

Our provincial chapters, then, are organized in three sections. Each of them focuses on a single dimension of faith-based political contention, though our analysis of each geographic region or province also explores whether other dimensions have played a role in provincial party politics. Across all of these sections we see major variations in the extent to which, and the ways in which, religion shapes party politics – variations across time and region. We also find examples of historical voter alignments based in denominational ties persisting in the absence of substantive policy distinctions between parties. And we see instances, particularly from the 1990s and through the 2000s, in which parties have developed "family" policy positions related to gender and sexuality that are more distinct than ever but that are without as clear-cut an alignment of voters as we might have imagined. Across most of our case studies, we find parties on the right facing strategic challenges in finding ways to gain or secure the allegiance of a range of faith communities but also recognizing that many core supporters, and certainly swing voters, have little patience with policies that forge too close a connection to them.

In a country like Canada, with dramatically reduced levels of attachment to religious faith, it is not hard to understand the limited analytical attention that such questions have received. However, there are still large numbers of people with strong faith who believe that religion has a place in political life and that they have rights that are in need of protection. There are conservative Christians who advocate a retention or restoration of policies reflective of what they consider to be traditional family values, and they have repeatedly demonstrated a capacity to mobilize political resources far more successfully than have people of faith with progressive values. Ethno-cultural and religious minorities are not immune to the secularizing and individualizing forces that are so powerful in North America, and, as often as not, they have political priorities that do not align with parties supportive of traditional family values. Nevertheless, religious attachment remains a significant element in the everyday lives of minorities and newcomers, even among those who would not see themselves as particularly religious. In this sense, they help keep questions of religion in the public eye.

PART 1
Federal Politics

Conservative Faith and Federal Parties

A political earthquake reshaped federal parties in the 1990s and 2000s, upending the traditional electoral alignment of faith constituencies and establishing only one party as a natural home for social conservatives. This resulted from the gradual erosion of historic Protestant-Catholic distinctions in the electoral preferences of voters; a reunification of the right under a leader who embraced moral traditionalism alongside free market neoliberalism; the political visibility of hot button issues arousing social conservatives at the time of that reunification; and the movement of the Liberal Party and the New Democratic Party away from policies favoured by proponents of "traditional" family values.

The postwar period had, up to the 1990s, featured two centrist brokerage parties that hewed to no consistent ideological agenda, each of them including wide-ranging opinions on social issues such as abortion and gay rights within their electorates, activist bases, and legislative caucuses. The balance of forces within each major party began shifting in the early 1990s, when the Progressive Conservatives were nearly destroyed by the emergence of two new parties.[1] The Bloc Québécois (BQ) drew nationalist francophone voters from all parties but was particularly damaging to the PCs' centrist currents. The Reform Party, largely based in the western provinces, drew supporters who combined populism with a desire for less government, alongside traditional views on family, gender, and sexuality. At the same time, the Liberal leadership began to highlight its differences from Reform, including what it portrayed as a stark contrast in policy towards sexual minority rights.

In the 2000s, the new Conservative Party of Canada was forged from those Reform roots and what remained of the Progressive Conservatives. Its leadership distanced itself from the brokerage model and was instead guided by clear ideological objectives. Even if free market individualism was the most prominent core belief of the new party, the CPC's leadership knew that moral traditionalists were an important current among its voters, activists, and legislators. They needed to campaign and govern in ways that secured the loyalty not only of evangelical Protestants and traditionalist Catholics but also of what they saw to be an important strand of social and family conservatism within Canada's ethno-cultural minority communities. This would not be straightforward since court rulings and major shifts in overall public opinion had narrowed the room for policy manoeuvring on issues that, in the past, had mobilized social conservatives. However, the clearly progressive positioning of both the Liberal Party and the NDP on these traditionally contentious issues meant that the Conservatives could rely on relatively subtle messaging to signal their now-unique readiness to listen to social conservative voices.

Until the emergence of the reconfigured CPC, there had been no sustained politicization of issues associated with the recognition of non-Christian minority religions. Public opposition had certainly been voiced to some judicial rulings or institutional changes that moved towards such recognition, most notably when the RCMP allowed Sikh constables to wear turbans. But no major party had spoken out in a sustained way to align itself with such opposition. While the Conservatives' strategy of multicultural outreach would seem to have militated against any change in that avoidance, it became clear during its period in government and especially during the 2015 election campaign that the party was willing to pander to anti-Muslim prejudice and, more broadly, to popular anxieties about immigrants and refugees. Despite the unseating of Prime Minister Stephen Harper, these tactics may have produced an enduring partisan distinction centred on religious minority rights. At the very least, the sentiments lying at the heart of such campaigning are strongly represented within the party and will confront Harper's successor with the same strategic challenge that the party has faced over the persistence of social conservatism within its ranks.

In this chapter, we start by exploring changes in the religious makeup of each of the federal parties' electorates. Here we find that the longstanding tendency of Catholics to support Liberals and of Protestants to support Conservatives was slowly eliminated during the 2000s. In the place of that denominational divide we find a tendency, though uneven, for religious conservatives to gravitate towards the reconfigured CPC. We then move to an analysis of policy preferences, exploring the role of moral conservatism in shaping the policy stances of federal parties before and since the realignment of the early 2000s. Here we see that a series of political debates over the recognition of sexual diversity early in this period highlighted divisions within the Liberals and Progressive Conservatives but, later on, helped define the contrasts between the CPC and all the others. By the time that Conservatives won the reins of government in 2006, they no longer had any real prospect of reversing advances on LGBT rights, but they could appear sympathetic to those who wanted precisely that change by taking small steps to signal their support for what they would characterize as traditional family values. Finally, we look at the extraordinary 2015 federal election.

In all this we recognize that federal parties, like all political parties, are complex coalitions of groups and individuals with a variety of policy priorities. Parties that may have appeared united will sometimes fracture over particular issues or, occasionally, will witness challenges to leaders who seemed unassailable only a short time before. Contests for the leadership of a party may reveal important differences among legislators and party members that had been suppressed by past party leaders or submerged by protagonists who recognized the value of appearing united when competing for government office. On the other hand, parties in Canada are profoundly shaped by the orientations of their leaders, and it often makes sense to talk about the polarization and realignment of federal parties as though they were singular actors. Parties may not be as fully unified as this approach may imply, but, for many of our purposes, and over extended periods, it is possible to read a party's position through what its leaders campaign on. This, we find, is particularly true of leaders such as former Conservative Prime Minister Stephen Harper, who possessed both strong convictions and a willingness to impose those convictions on the rest of the party. There are limits, of course, and in the next chapter we explore in detail one policy area in which resistance to leadership preferences was particularly strong. The more usual tale, however, is one of party leaders exercising considerable influence over the policy direction of their parties and, in the process, shaping the overall pattern of party alignment.

The Voting Patterns of Religious Constituencies

For decades, indeed for more than a century, those who wrote about the role of religion in shaping party preferences in Canada focused on the divide between Catholics and Protestants. It was only well after policy challenges arose in the 1960s and 1970s from the women's movement and advocates for lesbian and gay equality that any attention was paid at all to the possibility of new electoral alignments. By that time, immigration was altering Canada's religious landscape, and secularization was thought to be reducing the overall role of faith in Canadian politics.

The Decline of Denominational Distinctions

The traditional tilt of Catholics towards the Liberal Party of Canada was eroded in the 2000s and seemed to have disappeared for good by that decade's end. This denominational distinction between voters for the Liberals and Progressive Conservatives had long maintained its standing as the single strongest "demographic" predictor of the vote, and persisted without any obviously relevant policy differences between these federal parties.

In the early 1950s, John Meisel's study of Kingston-area electors found both an extremely strong Liberal preference among Catholics, who cited long-ago federal political disputes with religious or linguistic dimensions, and a disproportionate Conservative preference among Protestants, who displayed a strong element of anti-Catholic and anti-French prejudice.[2] In 1974, using national election study data, William Irvine pointed out that, even with controlling for other factors, "the

Table 1.1 Liberal support among Catholics compared
to all voters, Canada outside Quebec, 1968–2015 (%)

	All voters	*Catholics*
1968	53	72 (+20)
1984	24	36 (+12)
1988	30	43 (+13)
1993	49	61 (+12)
2000	42	54 (+12)
2004	41	50 (+9)
2006	33	40 (+6)
2008	29	34 (+5)
2011	21	20 (–1)
2015	44	47 (+4)

Source: Canadian Election Studies.

primary line of political division is between Roman Catholics and non-Catholics," and he described it as peculiar – as a "houseguest who has overstayed his welcome."[3] Over the next three decades, Richard Johnston and other prominent scholars pointed out the persistence of this religious dimension to voter behaviour even during a time of significant secularization.[4]

Table 1.1 demonstrates this denominational divide by tracking the greater support for the Liberals among Catholics as compared to the general population.[5] The table is limited to Canada outside of Quebec because of the distinctive electoral dynamics in that province. It is worth noting that the emergence of the Reform Party and the Canadian Alliance barely disrupted this pattern. Catholics did not switch at all to those parties during the 1993–2000 period.[6] Taking the longer view, the historic allegiance of Quebec francophones (and Catholics) to the Liberal Party was successfully challenged by the PCs in the 1980s and by the BQ in the 1990s. The Liberal loyalties of most Catholics outside Quebec were then successfully undermined by the Conservatives in the 2000s. By the 2011 election, the Liberal "advantage" among Catholics overall, including those outside Quebec, had disappeared.

Table 1.2   PC/Conservative support among Evangelicals and Mainline Protestants compared to all voters, Canada outside Quebec, 1968–2015 (%)

	Party	All voters	Evangelicals	Mainline Protestants
1968	PC	32	55 (+23)	40 (+8)
1984	PC	58	73 (+15)	65 (+7)
1988	PC	45	59 (+14)	51 (+6)
1993	PC	16	13 (−3)	19 (+3)
2000	PC	13	10 (−3)	18 (+5)
2004	Conservative	41	60 (+19)	48 (+7)
2006	Conservative	45	76 (+31)	49 (+4)
2008	Conservative	49	73 (+24)	59 (+10)
2011	Conservative	47	69 (+22)	57 (+10)
2015	Conservative	30	52 (+22)	38 (+8)

Source: Canadian Election Studies.

Changes in the voting preferences of Protestants are more complex. Table 1.2 shows that the PCs had done comparatively well among both evangelical and mainline Protestants, but then lost ground in the face of the Reform surge of the 1990s, especially among the former. Not surprisingly, the new Conservative Party was particularly successful at drawing evangelical support – with well over 70 percent of evangelicals voting CPC in the 2006 and 2008 elections. This dropped significantly in the 2015 election, to just over 50 percent, though evangelicals were still much more likely to support the Conservatives than were other Canadian voters.[7]

Religiosity and Conservative Voting

To what extent have we seen the denominational distinction that for so long shaped the federal party system give way to a new alignment in which the Conservative Party becomes a pole of attraction for all Canadians who are attached to and practising their faith, no matter what their particular affiliation may be? The evidence here is mixed, acquiring none of the "clarity" of the religious divide in American politics.[8]

From the 1960s and into the 1990s, the two major parties were only moderately different from one another. The Liberals were slightly more successful than the Progressive Conservatives among those for whom religion was important – almost entirely a result of religious Catholics being more supportive of the party than non-religious Catholics.[9] The lack of a clear differentiation between the two main parties on this dimension fits with their characterization as brokerage parties.

The more recent election studies are more consistent in asking about the importance of religion in one's life, and Table 1.3 tracks the partisan preferences of those who answered that it was very important. In 2000, the PCs had lost a good many votes to the Alliance, leaving behind an unusually low proportion of religious supporters. Four years later, with the unification of the right, we see a new religious gap appearing between Conservatives, on the one hand, and all of the other parties, on the other.[10] By 2006 the Conservatives had clearly established themselves as the preferred choice of religious voters, a trend that peaked in 2011 when support for the Liberals among the most religious respondents fell to just half what it had been a decade earlier. Similar findings were obtained by a 2011 Ipsos Reid poll, which reported that 52 percent of those attending religious services once a week or more preferred the Conservatives, and by election study analysis conducted by Sarah Wilkins-Laflamme.[11]

In 2015, however, we find the Liberals and Conservatives nearly tied for the votes of those for whom religion was very important. This sharp change from 2011 may reflect the unique dynamics of the 2015 campaign, which saw the Liberals vault from third place in the polls at the start of the campaign to win a majority government on election day. Yet, as discussed further below, it also may indicate that "importance of religion" is a less effective indicator of Conservative support than moral traditionalism.

If we look at Catholics in particular, we find no real indication that the Conservatives have been particularly successful in luring the most faithful; in fact, they seem more popular among those who are less religious.[12] One reason might be that the Conservative embrace of radically individualist stances would be anathema to Roman Catholics

Table 1.3   Vote choice among those who say that religion is "very important," 2000–15 (%)

	2000	2004	2006	2008	2011	2015
Liberals	43	38	29	29	21	40
PCs/Conservatives	11	43	51	52	55	38
Alliance	34	–	–	–	–	–
NDP	7	15	14	16	19	18
BQ	5	4	5	4	2	2

Source: Canadian Election Studies, 2000–15.

shaped by their church's more collectivist philosophy. Many Catholics, too, would recognize the dependence on state support of the many social agencies spawned by their church over the previous centuries, and they might well fear that such support would be jeopardized by governments determined to cut social spending.[13] Views on such issues as same-sex marriage and abortion did not increase the likelihood of Catholics voting Conservative, possibly because Catholics as a whole have not been particularly supportive of their church's official lines on such fronts.[14] Catholics who switched to the Conservatives, then, were more likely influenced by that party's ideological approaches to lower taxation and reduced governmental authority, appealing perhaps even more strongly to the lapsed than to the faithful. Tom Flanagan cites a story that illustrates this. In 2004, a voter-contact company once used by the CPC "somehow" got a list of people who attended mass every week and then used this list to remind potential voters that the party opposed same-sex marriage. But in Flanagan's words, as a strategy, this was "not productive."[15]

Partisan Differences in Moral Traditionalism
There are stronger indications of partisan realignment on the grounds of moral or family traditionalism than on religiosity. One measure of this is the partisan sorting of those who believe literally in the Bible.[16] In 2004 and 2006, a "panel" of Canadian Election Study respondents was asked questions on this, and the results show an important shift precisely during this period when the CPC was solidifying. In 2004,

50 percent of literalists supported the party, and two years later the figure had risen to 61 percent. Another way of looking at this question is to ask what proportion of each party's supporters were biblical literalists. The 2015 Canadian Election Study found that 39 percent of Conservative voters were biblical literalists, compared to 29 percent of Liberals, 25 percent of New Democrats, and 15 percent of the Bloc.[17]

We also find evidence in response to questions about gender and sexuality. From the late 1960s through the 1980s, supporters of the Liberal Party and the Progressive Conservative Party differed only modestly on such questions, and each party faced internal divisions on them. The NDP was the outlier, influenced by the women's movement from its early years as a party and, eventually, by lesbian and gay advocacy. The 1984 Canadian Election Study asked respondents if they agreed that "the decision to have an abortion should be the responsibility of the pregnant woman," and 65 percent of New Democrats strongly did, compared to 49 percent of Liberal and Conservative supporters. The same survey asked if homosexuals could be teachers, with 43 percent of Liberals and Conservatives agreeing they could, versus 58 percent of NDPers.[18] In the 1988 Canadian Election Study, 78 percent of New Democrat voters agreed that homosexuals should have equal rights, for example, with respect to housing and jobs, along with a surprisingly robust 71 percent of Liberals and 67 percent of PCers. Chris Cochrane's analysis of voter attitudes also shows only small differences between Liberal and PC supporters on questions about abortion and homosexuality right up until the 2000 election, even though they were becoming more differentiated on economic and social welfare issues.[19]

The new Conservative Party of Canada was built to an important degree on the foundations laid by the Reform Party and the Canadian Alliance Party, and this helped create much sharper distinctions between party attitudes towards hot button social issues. Reform supporters were more clearly on the traditionalist side of these issues than were those of any other party. Not surprisingly, from 2004 on, so were the supporters of the new Conservative Party. Elisabeth Gidengil and her colleagues point out that, across the 2004, 2006, and 2008 elections, the propensity to vote for the Conservatives was 20 percent higher for those who scored highest on their moral traditionalism scale, even though

Table 1.4   Percentage of each party's supporters favouring same-sex marriage, 2000–15

	2000	*2004*	*2006*	*2008*	*2011*	*2015*
PCs/Conservatives	57	25	25	36	43	48
Alliance	36	–	–	–	–	–
Liberals	58	51	61	64	73	78
NDP	78	78	72	82	82	81
BQ	65	69	77	88	78	80
Total	55	49	51	61	66	71

Notes: In 2000, the Canadian Election Study question read: "Gays and lesbians should be allowed to get married: strongly agree, somewhat agree, somewhat disagree, strongly disagree." It was recoded to combine those strongly and somewhat agreeing. From 2004 to 2015 the question was "Do you favour or oppose same-sex marriage, or do you have no opinion on this: favour, oppose."
Source: Canadian Election Studies.

few voters regarded issues like same-sex marriage and abortion as electorally important.[20]

This sorting of voters by moral traditionalism has been most clearly evident on attitudes towards LGBT rights. Table 1.4 shows the proportion of each party's supporters in favour of same-sex marriage, and it displays what may be the single most polarized pattern that we would find on any issue.[21] By 2011, there was a significant shift towards acceptance of same-sex marriage even among Conservatives, but the gap with the Liberals from 2004 to 2015 was never lower than 25 percent. Cochrane's analysis shows that Conservative voters were at least as drawn to the traditionalist view in 2011 as they had been at the party's birth and that, in the meantime, the average Liberal was moving closer to the average supporter of the NDP and the BQ. The election results from 2015 suggest that there has been no significant change since then.

Table 1.5 shows that the partisan gap on abortion is not as large as that on same-sex marriage, but a persistent difference remains between the Conservatives and their opponents despite members of all parties shifting ever further towards a pro-choice position. Intriguingly, the 2000 survey indicates that, even among Alliance supporters, about half favoured relatively easy access to abortion. In 2004, 2006, and 2008 just

Table 1.5   Percentage of each party's supporters favouring easy access to abortion, 2000–08

	2000	*2004*	*2006*	*2008*
PCs/Conservatives	71	52	56	57
Alliance	49	–	–	–
Liberals	67	68	71	66
NDP	83	71	76	74
BQ	78	83	85	80
Total	65	65	68	66

Notes: In 2000, the question was "And now a question about abortion: do you think it should be very easy, quite easy, quite difficult, very difficult for a woman to get an abortion?" In 2004 and 2006, the question was "Do you think it should be very easy for a woman to get an abortion, quite easy, quite difficult, or very difficult?"
Source: Canadian Election Studies.

over half of the new Conservative Party's supporters also supported that position. The 2011 question asked if abortion should be banned. Here 28 percent of Conservative supporters said "yes," compared to 15 percent of Liberal supporters and 8 percent of New Democrat supporters.[22] As we see in the next chapter, this mixed view among Conservative voters stands in some contrast to the clear majority of Conservative MPs, who remained pro-life until the 2015 election.

Canadian Election Study results are reinforced by 2016 polling on moral issues analyzed by Abacus Data.[23] These results show that Conservative supporters were more than 20 percent more disapproving of same-sex relationships and abortion than were supporters of the other major parties, and more approving of the death penalty by the same margin. They were about 10 percent more disapproving of doctor-assisted suicide than were Liberals, who were only slightly less approving than New Democrats.

Minority Community Voting

The Conservative Party devoted considerable energy to drawing "ethnic minority" voters away from the Liberals, but it is not entirely clear how successful this has been or what policy appeals have been most effective.

Up to and including the 2000 election there is no doubt that the Liberals retained strong support among immigrant voters and most established ethno-cultural minorities.[24] Their success among visible minorities diminished significantly between 2000 (72 percent) and 2004 (52 percent), but more of that loss went to the NDP than to the Conservatives. Indeed, the estimated impact of social background characteristics used by Elisabeth Gidengil and her colleagues indicates that during this period visible minority status was still a strongly negative factor in explaining Conservative vote choice.[25]

The 2008 story, though, is a little different, for this time the continuing drop in visible minority support for the Liberals benefited the Conservatives more than the NDP.[26] But the change was not enormous, nor was it uniform across minority groups. Darrell Bricker and John Ibbitson show that the party's success in 2011 was pronounced among suburban-dwelling and economically established immigrants who had been in Canada more than ten years, though it was less obvious beyond that.[27] Cochrane's analysis of exit polling in that election shows that all three major parties attracted significant numbers of immigrant voters, with the Liberals doing the best of the three among those born in South Asia, the Conservatives doing best among those from East Asia, and all three parties being competitive among migrants from the Middle East and Africa.[28] This challenges any notion that there was a *massive* shift in minority vote allegiance towards the Conservatives, though there was an important one. In 2013, Michael Adams and Robin Brown pointed to evidence that immigrants in general were still less likely to vote Conservative than native-born Canadians, but that Liberal strength among them had been weakened.[29]

What success the Conservatives have had among minority voters may well have little to do with moral traditionalism or religious faith. As Adams and Brown point out, South Asian and Chinese immigrants (arriving within the last ten years) may well share the Conservatives' traditional family values, reflecting the prevailing norms in their countries of origin, but they are also more likely than other Canadians to believe in expansive government. Those groups among which the CPC has had most success, including some Asian Canadian communities, are not distinctly traditionalist on issues related to family, gender, and sexuality. The most significant minority community swing towards the Conservatives, in fact, is the Jewish vote, which does not at all support the party's social conservativism but has been swayed by its aggressively pro-Israel foreign policy.[30] The Muslim community does have a strong current of moral and family conservatism, in large measure resulting from relatively recent migration from highly traditional societies, but it would hardly have been drawn to a party that advocated a one-sided policy towards the Middle East, pandered to anti-Muslim prejudice in its high-pitched rhetoric around security legislation, and attempted to bar face-covering dress in citizenship ceremonies.

One ironic element in the Conservatives' support base is that the party is disproportionately supported by Canadians who are concerned about what they see as high levels of immigration. A 2012 Environics survey shows that 21 percent of Conservative supporters strongly agree that those levels are too high, compared to 11 percent of Liberal supporters and 10 percent of New Democrat supporters.[31] An extraordinary 49 percent of Conservative supporters strongly agree that there are too many immigrants who are not adopting Canadian values, compared to 29 percent of Liberal supporters and 25 percent of New Democrat supporters. There are also fewer Conservative supporters than supporters of other parties who believe that immigrants have a positive impact on the country, and more who believe that there are many refugees whose claims are not legitimate.

The historic attachment of minority voters to the Liberals has been loosened, but the Conservatives have not been as successful in attracting them as they had hoped. This may well be a result of minority voter perceptions that the party's welcoming stance is not whole-hearted, views reinforced by its 2015 election campaign and subsequent leadership race. The strongest faith-related distinction between federal parties is the division between moral traditionalism and more progressive sentiments, but this axis has not been driving vote switching uniformly across cultural and religious groups, and there is no evidence that it has had any gravitational pull overall in cultural and religious minority communities.

Policy Realignment

Does the record of policy disagreements between the major federal parties mirror shifts in the faith-related distinctions among their supporters? If we go back to earlier decades, we find occasional instances of Liberals distancing themselves from moral traditionalism more than the Progressive Conservatives, most famously with the Pierre Trudeau government's partial decriminalization of abortion and homosexual activity. Over the two decades to follow, however, both major parties were content to avoid such issues, not least because of a lack of internal consensus and the persistent norm of treating them as "conscience issues" that were outside the normal bounds of party whips. In the early 1990s, social conservatism was stronger in the PC caucus than in the Liberal caucus, though the Liberals remained divided and the PC leadership had no desire to prioritize advocacy on issues it still regarded as matters of personal belief or conviction.[32] These two parties were, as Ken Carty, William Cross, and Lisa Young so strikingly put it, "two great, sprawling, seemingly indistinguishable machines for vacuuming up votes," and they were both large tents on contentious issues of "moral" policy.

The question of lesbian and gay rights jostled this pattern beginning in 1993, slowly shifting the Liberals towards a progressive position and vividly displaying the new Reform Party's alliance with social and religious conservatism. As early as 1978, a Liberal Party convention had approved a resolution supporting the incorporation of sexual orientation into human rights law.[33] In 1980, however, the Liberals in Parliament were not yet ready to support the inclusion of sexual orientation in the Charter of Rights and Freedoms, helping to defeat an amendment introduced by NDP MP Svend Robinson. In 1986 and 1987, after a parliamentary committee recommended an amendment adding sexual orientation to the Canadian Human Rights Act, the Progressive Conservative Mulroney government of the day immediately encountered strong opposition within the PC caucus, enough to forestall legislative change. At that point, the Liberal caucus was still not united enough around the cause to apply forceful pressure for action.

By this time, Canada's Christian right began to acquire a political voice at the federal level outside of Parliament. The Evangelical

Fellowship of Canada had been formed in 1966, but in 1983 it appointed its first executive director, the energetic and effective Brian Stiller.[34] That same year, REAL Women of Canada was formed by Gwen Landolt, who remains a leading figure in the religious right to this day. This evangelical mobilization was spurred first by Henry Morgentaler's opening of free-standing abortion clinics and then by the alarm created by the PC government's apparent (and brief) readiness in 1986 to extend rights protections to lesbians and gay men.[35] In the years to follow, the heightened evangelical alertness to federal political developments would serve as a thorn in the side of the PC leadership but would also embolden social conservatives inside the Liberal tent.

The PCs were decimated in the 1993 election, and the Liberal government of Jean Chrétien now faced two new opposition parties: the Bloc Québécois and Reform. When it began taking cautious steps to recognize the discrimination faced by sexual minorities, it met with a wall of opposition from the Reform caucus, whose MPs gave repeated voice to the moral traditionalism that was so dominant within the party's substantial evangelical electorate.[36] Their leader, Preston Manning, had a pragmatic side, but many of his caucus members had no interest in tempering their views, with some instead marshalling the kind of extreme language deployed by the American religious right. They were backed in this by substantial extra-parliamentary mobilization in opposition to government proposals to encode rights protections for lesbians and gays.

The Liberal leadership also faced considerable opposition from moral traditionalists within its own ranks. When a government bill adding sexual orientation to the sentencing provisions in the federal hate crime statute came to a vote in 1995, eighteen Liberals (10 percent of the caucus) defied the party whip by voting "no." A year later, the government allowed a free vote on a bill that would add sexual orientation to the Canadian Human Rights Act, and twenty-eight Liberals voted against it. The ferocity of Reform opposition to these measures, however, strengthened the hand of Liberal progressives, doubly so because they and their leader Jean Chrétien could see the advantage of playing on the prejudicial claims made by Reform MPs. In later years, with Stephen Harper as leader of the Alliance and then a reconfigured Conservative Party, successive Liberal leaders regularly returned to the pattern of

highlighting the gap between the parties on moral issues and to portraying the Liberals as defenders of the Charter.

The rebranding of Reform as the Canadian Alliance in 2000, and the
selection of Stockwell Day as leader, identified the party even more
closely with family values traditionalism. The Liberals won the election
held later that year, portraying Day as a threat to women's rights and a
proponent of a broader set of moral and religious views that was at odds
with the Canadian mainstream. Some Pentecostal writers have viewed
this as part of a longer-term pattern of the Liberals alienating religious
traditionalists, though it is also hard to deny that Day's public record
– including his time as cabinet minister in Alberta and the statements
of many of his caucus colleagues over the previous seven years – left the
party open to charges of being extreme.[37] This was a lesson not lost on
Stephen Harper when he took over a languishing Alliance in 2002 and
then spearheaded the 2003 union with the PCs.

Stephen Harper's Strategy to Unite the Right

The new Conservative Party and its first leader were profoundly shaped
by the Reform and Alliance legacy. When Reform was being established,
Harper had identified himself unequivocally with the rightist challenge
to brokerage politics, though he had always prioritized its neoliberal
current over the politics of traditional morality and had only the slightest rhetorical allegiance to populism.[38] His instincts, however, favoured
moral traditionalism in broad terms, both in principle and in the light
of electoral calculation. In a 2003 meeting with Scott Brison, at the time
a Progressive Conservative MP who was concerned about the dramatic
increase in anti-gay sentiment that would come from uniting his party
with the Alliance, Harper is said to have responded: "You've got to understand that social conservatism is an important part of our support base,
and we will always have that as part of what we offer."[39]

In a now-famous 2003 speech to the conservative group Civitas,
Harper supported a version of social order that "stresses respect for
customs and traditions – religious traditions above all – voluntary
association, and personal self-restraint reinforced by moral and legal
sanctions on behaviour."[40] He attacked the left for its moral nihilism

– "the rejection of any tradition or convention of morality, a post-Marxism with deep resentments, even hatreds of the norms of free and democratic western civilization," leading to views "ranging from radical responsibility-free individualism, to tribalism in the form of group rights." Harper was, in effect, urging an alliance of fiscal and moral conservatives.

But Harper was certainly going to choose his battles carefully, avoiding the missteps of predecessors like Stockwell Day. He was not going to raise the question of capital punishment, and he was not going to lead a major charge against access to abortion. Instead, what Harper suggested to the Civitas audience were steady incremental changes such as legislatively attacking child pornography, raising the age of sexual consent, and "strengthening the institution of marriage." As Paul Wells puts it, once in office, "he would make the decisions only a prime minister can make, knowing few would be noticed, almost none would be contested, and that together they would add up."[41] Harper also recognized that a social conservative agenda would include "law and order" and increased choice in child care options, which would appeal to constituencies far beyond moral traditionalists.

The electoral and activist strength of the Reform wing of the new Conservative party, though, was going to represent a challenge to the new leader's calculations. As Tom Flanagan argues:

> The Conservative Party is now the religious party ... The religious flavour goes back to Preston and his evangelical supporters. He deliberately tried to create a secular party, and it always was in a formal sense, but he couldn't change the kind of people he attracted because of his background and his network. So clearly we started with being the party of evangelical Christians and then that got intensified with Stock [Day], who's not only evangelical but Pentecostal, and that brought in new and even more enthusiastic people.[42]

The hazards of building an electable conservative coalition were increased by the growing willingness of the Liberal Party to attack social conservatism, though this may also have increased the willingness of many Christian conservatives to support Harper's incrementalism. Again, in Flanagan's words:

> I think they realized that they had gone too far with Stockwell Day. There was this sense among religious conservatives ... of disappointment in Preston. "OK, now we have a man of God as our leader and now we're going to be able to do these things." And then they found that they couldn't and the party exploded. And Harper's view on these things had been very clear right from the beginning that he was not going to touch any of these issues. He has described himself a couple of times as a social conservative and a religious person, but right from the earliest days of Reform he would say that we've got to stay away from these issues. That's why this particular community was never keen on having Stephen as leader. Some of them gave up on politics, but others said, "well, as long as Harper shows us respect, which he does, we think it's better than being governed by the Liberals, so we'll stay involved." Stockwell Day's flame-out has a lot to do with it. They thought they could accomplish more and then they learned that Canadian political culture right now is just too secularized for them to push very hard. They are very pragmatic and realistic now about what they can expect to achieve, so they want symbolic victory and if they can get occasional policy victories they're happy. They expect the government to take their side when new issues come up. They can accept that abortion and capital punishment are past battles which they lost, but they do expect the Party to take a conservative position on new issues as they arise, like polygamy.

The 2004 election showed that this was not going to be an easy ride, and Harper knew that the party's loss that year was due, in part, to statements from Conservative candidates, primarily focused on same-sex marriage, that were all too easily labelled as extreme.[43] He of course had contributed to this by expressing his unequivocal opposition to extending marriage rights to lesbian and gay couples when the issue burst onto centre stage in 2003, and he continued to do so through the 2005 passage of Liberal government legislation on the subject. During the 2006 election campaign, he then promised to revisit the issue if elected. However, Harper was also becoming aware of the dangers of keeping this too prominently in the public eye. He talked about same-sex marriage only once, and early in the campaign. After winning office, Harper dispensed with the issue as efficiently and quietly as he could through the introduction of a resolution in Parliament calling for a re-examination of the issue. He knew the resolution, which received only the briefest of debates, would lose, and he declared immediately after the vote that the issue was settled.[44] Paul Wells puts this in a broad context: "on any day he has a choice, he can do the big conservative thing that would be the end of his career, or he can do some of the small conservative things that won't."[45] On abortion, "there were plenty of side doors into social conservatism," but Harper "kept the front door barred tight." He realized that issues like capital punishment, gay/lesbian rights, and abortion were widely perceived as "settled" and that his party would reopen them "at their political peril." About half of his caucus was conservative Christian, but he no doubt assumed that most of them would either agree with his strategic calculations or would be intimidated into acquiescence by him and his close associates.[46]

Some writers on Harper question how much this approach was purely strategic. Wells claims that "social conservatives know Harper isn't really one of them," and there are certainly evangelicals who have long been uncertain about his religious and moral commitments.[47] Chantal Hébert suggests that, with his selection as leader of the Canadian Alliance before its merger with the PCs, the party was prepared to "ditch" its social conservatism.[48] The truth lies in the ambiguous middle. The goals that were closest to Harper's heart were low taxes, unfettered markets, and a weakened federal government, all combined with a law-and-order agenda that would have broad appeal among suburbanites, rural voters, and sizable numbers of ethno-cultural minority communities. On the other hand, the Civitas speech would seem to indicate that he had a "values" agenda that aligned with much of what social and moral conservatives cherish, even if he was conscious of not endangering electoral prospects by taking on issues that would alienate too many supporters.

The Conservative Record in Power

In his time as prime minister, Stephen Harper left little doubt as to his pursuit of an ideologically driven economic agenda, even if partially sidetracked or delayed by global instability and recession. But what about the values agenda? Darrell Bricker and John Ibbitson argue that downplaying moral conservatism was part of a learning curve once he was in government.[49] This suggests, then, that the caution displayed about engagement with such issues from his first days as party leader became more pronounced once he was in office. Harper's increasingly token opposition to same-sex marriage might be cited as one example, and we see in the following chapter that his approach to his pro-life caucus colleagues is another. However, this strategic caution did not eliminate the need to retain social conservative loyalty, and, while in office, Prime Minister Harper's government regularly sent signals that it would do what it could to mark out a traditionalist image of Canadian society, incorporating a version of what Lydia Bean refers to as dog whistle politics aimed especially at evangelicals in ways that would be largely unrecognized by secular Canadians.[50] This was a constituency that had been at the core of the Reform Party insurgency in the 1990s, but the Conservatives also thought that appeals to evangelicals would attract traditionalist Catholics and what they believed was a large pool of social conservatives among Canada's cultural and religious minority communities.

Sexuality

On issues related to sexuality, the Conservative government acted quickly after being elected in 2006. Within months, it introduced legislation to raise the age of consent for sexual activity from fourteen to sixteen, an idea that had only surfaced as lesbian and gay legal victories had begun to pile up, and one eliciting only modest interest in the general public but a good deal of interest among social conservatives.[51] This was followed by other gestures. In the summer of 2006, the prime minister pointedly refused to attend a major international AIDS conference in Toronto. In 2009, the government reversed a decision to approve a tourism development grant to Toronto Pride after caucus members expressed outrage.[52]

In 2012, the Conservative caucus supported a private member's bill to eliminate the hate speech provisions of the Canadian Human Rights Code. Such restrictions had for some time been the focus of attack on the part of Christian conservatives, who argued that their faith-based right to speak freely on issues such as homosexuality was being regularly threatened by appeals to such human rights provisions.[53] The bill, which went on to receive royal assent, was supported by several senior cabinet ministers, and there can be no question that it was also supported by the Prime Minister's Office.

In 2013, all but eighteen members of the Conservative caucus voted against an NDP private member's bill that would have added gender identity to the list of prohibited forms of discrimination in the Canada Human Rights Act and Criminal Code. When combined with solid support from the NDP and Liberal caucuses, these few Conservative votes were enough for the bill to clear the House of Commons. However, it then effectively died in the Conservative-dominated Senate, and it is hard to avoid seeing the party leadership playing a role. In 2014, another NDP attempt was made to address gender identity through an amendment to a government justice bill. In that case all five Conservatives on the House of Commons Justice Committee voted against the measure, defeating it before it could return to the full House.[54]

From his first days as prime minister, Stephen Harper appointed cabinet ministers who were publicly antagonistic to LGBT inclusiveness, including Stockwell Day, Vic Toews, and Julian Fantino. However, Jason Kenney was the most enduringly influential of those cabinet ministers with a strong allegiance to religious conservatism. A devout Catholic, he has been fiercely opposed to abortion, and once co-chaired the Parliamentary Pro-Life Caucus. He also allied himself with evangelical Christians when they were attacking same-sex marriage, and he was an advocate of the view that recent immigrants and ethnic minority voters could be lured to the party, in part, by appeals to the moral traditionalism he so strongly represents.[55] It is true that the Conservative government condemned the anti-gay policies and actions of some foreign regimes, principally through statements by Foreign Affairs Minister John Baird. However, these interventions focused on policies that criminalize homosexuality – a far cry from supporting equal rights measures.

A Focus on the Family

While the Conservative government's actions on sexuality appeared to be narrowly targeted to its morally traditional base, there were other policy choices aimed, at least in part, at securing not only the loyalty of moral traditionalists, but also a broader "pro-family" constituency. Soon after winning the 2006 election, the Conservative government abandoned the national childcare strategy developed by the Martin Liberals, and instead enacted a policy of sending parents direct monthly payments of one hundred dollars per child – payments that were explicitly designed as an alternative to institutionalized child care. This strategy appealed strongly to social conservatives who favoured parental "choice" in child care and who specifically sought government support for stay-at-home mothers. It also appealed to individualist distrust of large-scale social programs and to the strategic sentiment that a direct payment program would make it difficult to introduce funding for institutionalized child care in the future.[56] Another policy similarly aimed at pleasing moral and religious conservatives, but that was also appealing to a broader audience, was the 2014 budget provision allowing income splitting for couples with children. This measure benefitted families with stay-at-home spouses and, in addition, constituted a disproportionate gain for high-income earners.

The government's legislative approach to prostitution also reflected the prime minister's willingness to choose "family-friendly" policies that would not mobilize electorally dangerous opponents. After the Ontario Court of Appeal struck down much of the criminal law regulation of prostitution in 2012, the government formulated a bill to re-regulate it by criminalizing the purchasers of sexual services. Christian conservatives were among those consulted in developing Bill C-36, and, when it was introduced in 2014, groups like the Evangelical Fellowship of Canada were prominent in publicly defending it. There was substantial opposition voiced during the Justice Committee's hearings on the bill, but there was never any realistic chance of significant political protest in defence of sex worker rights.

The Conservative government almost certainly realized that its legislation on prostitution was at serious risk of being successfully challenged in the courts. But in response to other court rulings undercutting the government's law-and-order agenda, the prime minister deployed the time-worn critique of "judicial activism," which had become a staple of Canadian as well as of American conservatism. The government took this to an extreme by launching an attack on Chief Justice Beverley McLachlin in the spring of 2014, around the time of the debate over prostitution.

Other Evangelical-Friendly Initiatives

The Conservatives also made judicial appointments that would be appreciated by evangelical Protestants. Tom Flanagan points to the example of David Brown, formerly associated with the Evangelical Fellowship of Canada, on the Ontario bench, and Dallas Miller, a supporter of Stockwell Day, on the Alberta bench.[57] The appointment of Grant Huscroft and Bradley Miller to Ontario's Court of Appeal (in 2014–15) would have been similarly applauded by evangelical policy advocates since both adhered to the "originalist" doctrine beloved of American social conservatives. This is a view, close to bizarre in a constitutional framework built so heavily on common law, that would largely preclude recognition of the rights of sexual minorities since they were not explicitly included in the 1982 Charter of Rights and Freedoms. Russell Brown, appointed to the Supreme Court of Canada just before the 2015 election call, would be welcomed by most conservative Christians because of his libertarian beliefs, his association with conservative policy networks, and his constitutional "literalism."[58]

In foreign policy there were several moves that would have found considerable favour among religious conservatives, particularly evangelicals. One was the 2011 creation of the Office of Religious Freedom inside the Department of Foreign Affairs. The appointment of an academic from a Christian college with a conservative approach to faith would reassure them of the direction to be adopted by the office. Ironically, that same year the government compromised the principle of religious freedom inside Canada by announcing that Muslim women wearing face-covering niqabs would have to remove them for citizenship ceremonies.

The government's extraordinarily tepid response to the massive flight of refugees from the Syrian civil war from 2011 onward was part of an overall policy of reducing refugee numbers, but it was hard to avoid suspecting there was a specific resistance to opening the doors to the large-scale acceptance of Muslims. When the government eventually relented, it did so by prioritizing religious minorities, such as Christians and Yazidis. As Robin Sears put it, Muslims would see this policy as excluding them, whereas "to Harper's Christian fundamentalist base, it [was] code for 'people like us.'"[59] And on a related front, the government's unqualified support for Israeli positions on Middle East questions would also have found favour among many Christian evangelicals.

Other decisions designed to reinforce support among moral conservatives, and in particular evangelicals, had a very low profile. One example is the unprecedented provision of $26 million in funding to fourteen private Christian colleges across the country, an act barely noticed in the mainstream press.[60] Grants to faith-based aid organizations awarded by the Canadian International Development Agency increased significantly after the Conservatives took office. At the same time, those organizations with missions that the government opposed saw their funding cut back – including some faith-based NGOs like Kairos (ecumenical) and Development and Peace (Catholic). These are all separate from the low-visibility concessions that the government made to pro-life advocates, to be discussed in the following chapter.

Liberals and New Democrats

When the Conservative Party assumed office in 2006, the social policy distinctions between it and the other parties around issues of family, gender, and sexuality were clear. The federal New Democratic Party was born in 1960 just as second wave feminism and then lesbian and gay rights activism were growing in strength and visibility. In some countries, the links between socialists or social democratic parties and the labour movement acted as a brake on making an alliance with such advocacy, but over the course of the next couple of decades Canadian unions were comparatively open to such influences.[61] Like the Cooperative Commonwealth Federation before it, the NDP had a social gospel current, but one oriented towards a more inclusive social justice agenda than the narrower and more exclusionary agenda that dominated the political face of Canadian evangelicism in the years to follow. This current was also weaker in the new party than it had been in the old.

By the 1980s, the NDP was resolutely on the pro-choice side of the abortion debate. On sexual diversity, the party's federal legislators did not have many opportunities to express public support for lesbian and gay rights until the next decade; but, as we have already seen, they were supportive of the 1980 attempt by Svend Robinson to add sexual orientation to the Canadian Charter of Rights and Freedoms. A late 1987 survey of partisan "elites" indicates that over 90 percent of New Democrats supported gay human rights protections. This figure was significantly higher than among Liberal and Conservative activists and legislators (61 and 56 percent, respectively), close to the average popular view.[62] An early 1990s survey by the LGBT advocacy group Egale indicated that gay rights, including relationship recognition, had strong support among federal NDP MPs, more so than among the Ontario provincial NDP caucus that then found itself in power (see Chapter 5).[63] By the mid-2000s, the NDP was more than prepared to highlight the contrast between its positioning on such issues and the Conservatives'. It also used abortion-related legislative proposals introduced by pro-life Conservatives to expose divisions within the Liberal caucus. Indeed, this whole period was marked by intense rivalry between the NDP and Liberals as each tried to position itself as the logical repository of anti-Conservative electoral support.

For their part, the Liberals had been moving steadily but unevenly towards more assertive positions on abortion and sexual diversity since the mid-1990s. On lesbian and gay rights, as we have seen, this was not always an easy shift. The late 1980s survey of Canadian partisan elites mentioned above shows that significantly fewer Liberals than New Democrats supported rights protections for gays and lesbians, and we have already chronicled the fierce opposition that Liberal Prime Minister Chrétien encountered when legislating in this area. However, staking out progressive ground on social issues helped bolster the progressive side of the Liberal brand during a period when the party was shifting right on economic issues. The visible strength of moral traditionalism in the Reform Party, the Canadian Alliance, and the new Conservative Party provided the Liberals with an incentive to toughen their stands on the issues that would most expose that social conservatism. The incentives to develop a stronger socially progressive policy profile were enhanced as evidence mounted of rapid shifts in public opinion.[64]

However, there were still Liberal MPs who dissented from this direction. One 2006 analysis, for example, suggests that about 20 percent of the caucus was pro-life.[65] The persistence of this current was evident in 2011, when Liberal leader Michael Ignatieff attempted to embarrass the Conservatives over the exclusion of abortion from the G8 Maternal Health Initiative. At the time, Ignatieff asserted: "We've had a pro-choice consensus in this area for a couple of generations and we want to hold it."[66] In response, Liberal MP Paul Szabo specifically stated that he was pro-life and that no consensus existed in the party. Several Liberal MPs then voted against a Liberal motion attacking the government's position on this issue – a major blow to Ignatieff's leadership.[67]

In 2012, a free vote on a private member's motion from a pro-life Conservative MP drew the support of four Liberals. The New Democrats' solid and "whipped" opposition stood out by comparison, and the NDP was more than prepared to highlight the contrast with the Liberals. Two years later, the newly chosen Liberal leader Justin Trudeau announced that all new candidates running under the Liberal banner would have to vote in a pro-choice fashion, though he added that he hoped that the issue of abortion was settled and would not be re-evoked.[68] In that same year, 2014, the Liberals joined the NDP in opposing the government's prostitution bill, further expanding the range of issues on which they were distinguishing themselves from the Conservatives. In so doing, they were not just recognizing that public opinion on much of this agenda had shifted, most dramatically of course on the question of LGBT rights, but also that explicitly appealing to moral traditionalists would cost the party more votes than it would gain. There was little likelihood of winning back the many evangelicals who supported the Conservatives or other voters who held conservative positions on gender and sexuality. The vulnerability that the Conservative Party had occasionally displayed in resisting the pro-life initiatives of its own MPs no doubt reinforced the shift towards clear-cut position-ing on morality policy.

The 2015 Federal Election

The Conservative leader had regularly vowed to keep contentious issues related to sexual diversity and abortion off the government's policy agenda. Nevertheless, the party had used public office to signal its social conservative sympathies during a period in which other parties were increasing their distance from such views. In policy terms, then, there was a clearer polarization between the governing party and all the other parties than there ever had been. Only a modest portion of the electorate prioritized morality issues, but those voters who used policies in this area as a guide to choosing among parties could no longer have any doubt about where each of them stood.

There were no issues evoking this division that were prominent enough to serve as campaign promises, so there was little prospect of an election in which this alignment would be at centre stage. On the other hand, there were Conservative strategists in Ottawa who believed that a wave of protests in Ontario, mobilized in the spring of 2015 against a new school curriculum on sexual health education, would benefit them in the upcoming election. They would not have wanted a high-profile attack that could easily be construed as anti-gay, and, in fact, during the campaign they disowned one of their Toronto-area candi-dates for attacking Liberals who marched in Toronto's Pride Parade. But there could be no mistaking the delight they felt at watching the prov-incial Liberal government being besieged on the sex education file, and they were tempted to use low-visibility local campaigning to remind voters of the party's family values. In the words of one close observer of the party: "it gets translated into dirty, micro-targeted flyers on wind-shields at faith-based organizations, and targeted mail drops of disgusting pieces of literature, left completely out of the broader campaign."[69]

The Conservatives were also mindful that the sex education protest wave was led not only by white evangelical Protestants but also by a strikingly diverse array of activists emerging from minority communities – an important component of the Conservatives' coalitional ambitions. This would seem to encourage the use of a framework of traditional family values in building or solidifying support in urban areas with large concentrations of visible minority voters. And, in fact, there was some local campaigning that reflected this micro-targeting approach. Flyers distributed in the Punjabi- and Cantonese-speaking communities in the Greater Vancouver and Toronto areas warned that a Liberal victory would result in "illegal drug injection sites" and "brothels" in people's neighbourhoods.[70]

However, the election campaign ended up turning more publicly on a completely different axis – one centred on religious minority rights, ethno-cultural integration, and refugee policy. As we see in Chapter 8, party contention over religious minority practices had arisen in Quebec provincial politics since the mid-2000s, but, up to now, there had been nothing like this in federal elections. Going into this campaign, things seemed little different, with the Conservatives appearing to be planning for a focus on economic management and on the unreadiness of Liberal leader Justin Trudeau to assume high office.

Yet, while in office, the Conservatives had adopted policies that played on public anxiety about the cultural and religious "other," particularly Muslims. At the same time, they drastically restricted the flow of refugees and warned against the constant danger of queue jumping in seeking entry to Canada. True, they did maintain a cross-party consensus on comparatively high levels of points-driven immigration, although they also placed a two-year restriction on some forms of family reunification – a restriction that seriously affected many immigrants already in Canada and played into subterranean fears of large minority group families burdening the welfare state. As we have already seen, Jason Kenney instructed citizenship court judges to prevent the wearing of face-coverings in citizenship ceremonies in the face of clear indications that this would not pass constitutional muster. The Conservative government also passed legislation allowing the revocation of citizenship for dual citizens convicted of major crimes (including terrorism), effectively creating two classes of Canadians, the more vulnerable of which was populated almost entirely by immigrants. Throughout their years in government, the Conservatives had regularly resorted to the drumbeat of fear over the domestic threat posed by Islamic extremism. In the same vein, they justified their reticent approach to the Syrian refugee crisis by focusing on the potential risk entailed in allowing large numbers of immigrants into Canada without proper security checks.

In the election itself, it was no particular surprise that there were Conservative candidates who were prepared to take advantage of public anxieties. Dianne Watts, a star Conservative candidate in Surrey, BC, campaigned locally with a flyer that warned of jihadi terrorism, quoting an Islamist fighter as proclaiming "you will not feel safe in your bedrooms," and suggesting that the migration of Syrian refugees was being "orchestrated" by ISIS.[71] A suburban Toronto candidate campaigned against allowing a flood of Muslim refugees by warning that Saudi Arabia had funded two hundred mosques in Germany alone as part of an agenda to change Europe: "something I certainly don't want to see happening in Canada."[72]

What was more striking was the decision by Prime Minister Harper to focus his party's campaign so much on fear, and to play so starkly on anti-Muslim prejudice and, to some extent, on anxieties about high levels of immigration. This placed minority religious communities in the cross-hairs of a debate over values in which the Conservatives, despite all their minority outreach, situated themselves on the side of those who feared the "other."

A September court of appeal decision rejecting (on procedural grounds) the government's 2011 denial of Muslim women's right to wear the niqab while taking their citizenship oaths provided a vehicle for the Conservatives to enhance the visibility of a stand that had widespread popular support. This was most dramatically true in Quebec, and the Conservatives saw an opportunity to undermine the NDP's large seat count in that province by attacking its leader's unequivocal opposition to the ban. Restricting niqab use also had appeal beyond that province, with Ontarians only slightly less supportive of a face-covering ban than Quebeckers, and polls briefly showed a boost in Conservative support.[73] Because this was an issue that had particular resonance among Quebec francophones and in the Quebec media (see Chapter 8), Harper kept expanding his use of this wedge, speculating about the introduction of legislation that would ban face coverings for federal public servants and for those receiving governmental services.[74] The Bloc Québécois served as the Conservatives' willing partner, using the leaders' debate and ominous TV ads to portray the New Democrats as siding with Islamists. The Conservatives also revived pre-election fears about the threat to Canadian values posed by "barbaric cultural practices" when they announced plans for a new RCMP tip line allowing Canadians to report such things to the police. This measure was unquestionably directed at immigrant and religious minority communities, once again with Muslims being the most visible target.[75]

The Liberals and NDP had opposed the Conservative government when it introduced legislation or enacted regulations on such issues prior to the election, and they continued to attack it during the campaign. The NDP was particularly wounded by the niqab issue in Quebec, and it tried to recoup by arguing that the prime minister's wedge politics was an attempt to distract voters from the reality that the government's economic record was clearly weaker than it was proclaiming. The Liberals moved from the particular to a more general "values" campaign, accusing the Conservatives and the Harper government of playing to fear and dividing Canadians against one another.[76] Trudeau's emphasis on optimism and inclusiveness dovetailed with his attempt to present the Liberals as significantly more progressive on economic issues than the Conservatives (and the Liberals of the recent past) and more prepared than the NDP to incur short-term deficits in the interest of economic stimulus.

In the end, the Conservatives' politicization of immigration and minority religious recognition did not win them the election. Their vote declined from 40 percent to 32 percent, and they won a majority of seats only in Alberta and Saskatchewan; nowhere else did they come close to a plurality. The NDP vote declined from 31 percent to 20 percent. Both shifts benefitted the Liberals, who won a legislative majority and increased their vote share from 19 percent in 2011 to 40 percent. Whether the new government will be significantly more progressive on economic issues than previous Liberal governments is open to question, but the caucus that emerged from that victory was almost certainly less influenced by moral traditionalism than any Liberal caucus in history.[77]

This outcome cannot be explained by evidence that the Conservatives were out of touch with Canadian opinion on a number of the specific issues upon which they preyed. The polling evidence on restricting the niqab is particularly clear, showing that support for the Conservative position was almost as high among immigrants as it was among the native born. However, as Jaime Watt reports, many of those who were willing to side with the government on restricting the niqab did not like the social divisiveness that the use of this issue entailed.[78] There seemed to be some version of this response within a range of immigrant communities, who began to see that the fear-mongering deployed by the Conservatives could be used against all minority communities. There also seemed to be a growing sense that the Conservatives' targeting of dual citizens in the name of national security was demeaning. The Muslim community was for the most part already outside of the Conservatives' tent, but now it was speaking publicly of being unfairly stigmatized and was mobilizing to get out the vote. Even though polls during the campaign showed the Conservatives as having more support from immigrants than from native-born Canadians, their success among newcomers was somewhat lower than it was in 2011, and it probably slipped further in the last days before voting.[79]

Another contributor to the Conservatives' losses may have been a degree of disillusionment among some evangelical Protestants and other traditionalist people of faith who once saw the Conservative Party as their natural home. The many pro-life advocates among them would have been more than a little disappointed at Stephen Harper's opposition to any attempt to restrict access to abortion and the party's relative silence on the question of physician-assisted suicide. But in the view of evangelical Christian broadcaster Lorna Dueck, the Conservatives' campaign would have disturbed many people of faith in other ways as well.

> The Tories' response to the global refugee crisis was the shot over the bow that came to be interpreted as a party who no longer cared about their faith base ... Hundreds of churches are trying to process refugee sponsorship, and finding nothing but frustration ... The harsh stance on the niqab, the government hotline for barbaric cultural practices ruse, sent even an "ultra" conservative Hutterite woman public with

shaming the Conservatives. Welcome for the stranger and love of neighbour are the bedrock in faith communities. It was impossible to square that conviction with what came to be digested as the Tories' campaign of fear.[80]

As we have already seen, voter surveys provide evidence for this view. The proportion of evangelicals supporting the Conservatives declined from about 70 percent in 2011 to just over 50 percent in 2015. The party's "edge" among evangelicals, as compared to other voters, was still 20 percent and therefore in line with the 2011 figures, but this still shows a decline in enthusiasm. This reinforces the analyses of Samuel Reimer and Lydia Bean, respectively, that, in Canada, evangelical identity is less bound up in a particular partisan attachment than it is in the United States.[81]

Conclusion

How do we answer the opening core question of whether there has been a faith realignment in Canadian federal politics? There can be no doubt that, after the formation of a united right in 2000, the Catholic-Protestant division that once shaped federal politics is no longer a major factor when it comes to differentiating Liberal Party and Conservative Party preferences in the electorate.

To what extent, however, has this denominational "axis" been replaced by one that distinguishes parties according to their response to advocacy on the part of religious and social conservatives? Added to this is the question of whether the 2015 election campaign and the Conservative Party leadership race that followed suggests a new axis of contention focused on the recognition of religious minorities. If we look at policies around which social conservatives and religious traditionalists have mobilized, there is now a clear polarization between the Conservatives, on the one side, and the tightly clustered Liberals, New Democrats, and Blocistes, on the other. This persisted despite the Harper government's attempts to keep the moral policy preferences of its legislators in check. But this was also a period during which the Conservative leadership repeatedly used a number of policy tools in ways that signalled its sympathies with religious and moral conservatives.

Many of the most outspoken social conservative MPs left electoral politics in 2015, and the overall demographic strength of religious traditionalists has been in decline, but this current remains an important component of the Conservative Party's electoral and activist coalition. The fact that the Liberals have moved towards the New Democrats and the BQ in rejecting the policy preferences of the religious right on issues of sexuality and reproduction means that those who adhere to traditional family values positions have no other party for which to vote. If there is any doubt about the accuracy of this statement, the new Liberal government's 2016 legislation on physician-assisted suicide, even if impelled by a Supreme Court ruling, reinforces it. So does the government's replacement of the Office of Religious Freedom with a new agency that has a broader human rights mandate, along with the raising of an LGBT Pride flag on Parliament Hill in June 2016 and other measures acknowledging past and continuing discrimination against sexual minorities. Conservatives may not have wanted to prioritize opposition to such measures, but they would also have known that the possible emergence of a new Reform-like party that would forcefully represent moral traditionalism would have disastrous consequences for the Conservative Party.

However, things became more complicated when attempting to locate this socially progressive/moral traditionalist divide in survey data. Tom Flanagan talks of the Conservatives becoming the party of religious people – "not of Muslims, or of those who interpret their religion as social gospel – but the party of most religions."[82] The evidence provides a clear indication of this in the concentration of evangelical Protestants in the Conservative Party, though we should remind ourselves that, up to 2011, this still accounted for no more than 70 percent of that constituency. Recall, too, that Catholic voters who have shifted from Liberal to Conservative voting are not distinctly attached to their faith. The Conservatives have quite recently had some success in drawing votes among Asian minorities and relatively established immigrants, but here, too, there is no evidence that it was the party's often subtle pitch to moral and family traditionalism that did the trick. What is clearer is a sharp distinction in moral policy attitudes between supporters of the Conservative Party and those of the other parties. Even as the

Conservative Party tries to distance itself from anti-gay policy stances in the post-Harper period, the contrast between party supporters on such issues is dramatically and persistently evident, as it is in attitudes towards abortion.

It is plausible to argue that these partisan distinctions will have less and less political relevance, mostly because the portion of Canadians resolutely opposed to abortion and LGBT rights, particularly the latter, has been steadily declining. As elaborated further in the next chapter, it is no surprise that the Conservative Party's leadership has recognized the electoral risks of being too closely associated with social conservatism, and this pattern will remain firmly in place regardless of future party leadership. It is also worth noting that there are more and more spokespeople from what might still be characterized as conservative faith communities who are speaking out about poverty, Aboriginal marginality, foreign aid, and environmental degradation, and who are putting some of the old battles behind them.

But this does not eliminate the strategic challenge of retaining the votes and activist energy of people with relatively traditional or conservative views on family, gender, sexuality, and the end of life. As we have seen with prostitution and euthanasia, they are still able to mobilize enough political energy to influence the Conservative Party. To some extent, the party leadership can keep the Conservative coalition loyal by focusing on issues of lower taxes, greater individual responsibility, more social service "choice," and law and order. But, repeatedly, we have seen that moral traditionalists are not always content to have the issues around which they have traditionally mobilized be sidelined, and, in the following chapter, we see how true this has been with regard to abortion. The growing difficulty they have in finding vocal champions in Parliament, coupled with declining religiosity in the general public, may easily intensify their interest in wielding influence within the Conservative Party.

What of the possibility of there being entrenched distinctions over immigration and minority religious recognition? The defeat of the Conservatives in 2015, in part over their campaign of fear and division, may well have weakened that party's temptation to politicize such issues, and most party strategists realize that no party realistically aiming for

Canadian federal office can ignore the large and growing population of visible and religious minorities. However, Canadian public attitudes are mixed enough to create the potential for contentious debate over questions related to the recognition of minority religious practices and whether immigrants have adapted sufficiently to what are thought to be Canadian norms. We also know that the Conservative Party's base includes a disproportionate number of Canadians who favour immigrant assimilation and who worry about the country shifting too much in favour of those whose cultural and religious practices are unfamiliar. When Kellie Leitch, a candidate for the party leadership in the wake of Stephen Harper's resignation, suggested screening for immigrant adherents to "Canadian values," a Forum Research poll found that 67 percent of Canadians and 87 percent of Conservative supporters agreed.[83] A late-2016 poll by the same firm showed that 40 percent of Conservatives had "unfavorable feelings" about Muslims, compared to 23 percent of Liberals and 19 percent of New Democrats.[84] Repeated polling results (discussed in the introduction) indicating that Canadians still support relatively high levels of immigration, and that they still disagree with more general statements about immigrants not adapting Canadian values, potentially act as a brake for the translation of such sentiments into Conservative Party policy. Yet there are still grounds for concern that more negative sentiments will influence how that party's leadership responds to new issues that arise.

Faith matters in federal politics, then, in complex ways. A new Conservative coalition with an unequivocal ideological commitment to lowering taxes and reducing the role of government also contains an important current that adheres strongly to traditional family values, as well as a current that either resents or fears the social changes that come with high levels of immigration from regions of the world that seem so different from Canada. These are essential elements of the party base, and this means that even leaders who do not prioritize them will feel pressured to demonstrate sympathy for them in both symbolic and substantive terms. The federal parties have already sorted themselves in policy terms on both these dimensions – that is, the moral traditionalist, on the one hand, and minority rights, on the other – to a degree that many observers fail to fully appreciate, and their electorates are more distinct than they have been in the past. At present, it is hard to say whether either the "morality" or the "minority" divide between the Conservatives and other parties will endure over the long term and whether either one will retain any capacity to significantly affect policy outcomes. The federal party realignment in policies and electorates does not even come close to the culture-war polarization of American party politics. But elements of that sort of contentiousness are audible in Canada's federal party system. The politicization of religious minority rights, so evident in the 2015 election and in statements by several Conservative leadership candidates since then, reflects strong currents of opinion within that party that will not soon disappear.

Abortion Politics and Federal Parties

2

Canadian federal leaders have largely avoided engaging the politics of abortion. This is in stark contrast with the United States, where reproductive rights have played an ongoing and divisive role in partisan politics since the 1970s. To be sure, Canadian federal party distinctions are as clear as they ever have been in the policy preferences of legislators and voters on this issue, with Conservatives much more likely to favour restricting women's reproductive choice than those allegiant to other federal parties. In fact, the Liberals under Justin Trudeau have moved officially to embrace a pro-choice position, increasing the likelihood that pro-life advocates would see the Conservatives as their only possible ally in federal politics.

But as much as in any area that has a history of mobilizing religious conservatives, debate over abortion, at least domestically, is one that the federal Conservatives have aimed to avoid. During the 2011 federal election, Prime Minister Stephen Harper restated his long-standing position that a Conservative government would not legislate on this issue, announcing that "as long as I am Prime Minister, we will not reopen the debate ... we will leave the law as it stands."[1] This did not preclude pro-life activism among his party's candidates and backbench MPs, and, in the Conservatives' early years in government, the leadership seemed prepared to flag its sympathy with such initiatives. However, the prime minister and his closest advisors quickly realized that such support risked undermining their attempts to widen the party's electoral appeal, and they began opposing any further advocacy. Over time, the very determination of pro-life Conservatives to keep the issue visible intensified the party leadership's determination to move it to the margins, while at the same time pursuing lower-visibility strategies designed to remind pro-life electors that the Conservatives were their only hope.

The abortion file gives us a specific lens through which to explore the strategic challenge facing the Conservative Party of Canada as it seeks to hold together its coalition of fiscal and moral conservatives. In particular, it allows us to consider in detail the Conservatives' attempts to retain the loyalty of moral traditionalists in ways that did not endanger their electoral prospects. Here we are specifically interested in pro-life advocacy within the Conservative's parliamentary caucus and how the party leadership has reacted to the significant number of pro-life supporters in its ranks. We also examine whether the long-term policy record and the voting patterns of MPs on abortion reinforce or modify the analysis of party realignment in the previous chapter. In exploring this complex terrain, we take an especially close look at the advocacy stance adopted by a sizable minority of Conservative backbenchers during their party's time in power and what we see as increasing prime ministerial discontent with such activism.

Party Struggles over Abortion from 1988 to 2006

Canada is unique among advanced industrial countries in that it lacks any legal framework governing the provision of abortion services. In its 1988 judgment in *R. v. Morgentaler*, the Supreme Court of Canada struck down the existing provision of the Criminal Code that had made abortion illegal unless performed in a hospital and only after a committee of three doctors certified that the procedure was medically necessary. The Court found that these restrictions violated women's right to security of the person under the Canadian Charter of Rights and Freedoms.

The question of abortion did not play a significant role in the 1988 federal election, but pro-life advocates within the Progressive Conservative caucus and in the broader public pressured the government of Prime Minister Brian Mulroney to fill the legal vacuum.[2] Mulroney knew that this would be complicated by serious divisions within the party. On one side was cabinet minister Jake Epp, a devout Mennonite from Manitoba, who believed that life began from the moment of conception, while on the other was Barbara McDougall, the only woman on the cabinet's priorities and planning committee, who advocated freer choice for women. In 1989, the government presented Bill C-43 to establish new legal restraints on women's access to abortion. While the prime minister imposed a disciplinary whip on cabinet ministers, he followed long established practice in treating abortion as a "conscience" issue for backbenchers, leaving them free to vote according to their personal beliefs.[3] In the end, the House of Commons narrowly passed C-43 at third reading by 140 votes to 131, with twenty-six MPs abstaining. However, despite clearing the House, C-43 went on to be defeated in the Senate on a tie vote. Since that time, no Canadian government has attempted to introduce a new abortion law.

Social movement advocacy directed at restricting abortion access has been a recurrent feature of federal politics, especially since 1988. Groups such as the Campaign Life Coalition, the Canadian Centre for Bioethical Reform, and the Association for Reformed Political Action draw the majority of their activist energy from Catholic and Protestant faith communities, and they have demonstrated a capacity to mobilize significant numbers of pro-life supporters. The Campaign Life Coalition, for example, organizes large annual "March for Life" rallies at the Parliament Buildings – in recent years attracting as many as twenty-five thousand people. While not translating into formal party commitments, there are backbench MPs who regularly give these marchers a warm welcome.

Throughout the 1990s, pro-life MPs could be found in the Liberal, PC, and Reform/Canadian Alliance Parties. At several points these MPs worked across partisan lines through the all-party Parliamentary Pro-Life Caucus, building up their ties with pro-life groups, and working to coordinate legislative strategy. The Campaign Life Coalition in particular played a role in re-establishing the caucus in the late 1990s, at which point it was said to have close to fifty members. One 2004 estimate was that the caucus had seventy members: two-thirds Conservative, one-third Liberal.[4] Care was also taken to ensure inclusive leadership across party lines, with its co-chairs in the late 1990s being the PCs' Elsie Wayne (a Baptist), as well as the Reform's Jason Kenney and Liberal Tom Wappel, both Catholics. Over the following years the caucus was co-chaired by Liberal Paul Steckle and Conservative Maurice Vellacott, both Mennonites.

Abortion and the Liberal Party of Canada

During its time in office from 1993 until 2006, the Liberal Party took no steps to change Canada's abortion law. The Liberal caucus, however, did include a significant minority of pro-life MPs, reported to have been as high as 40 percent in the 1980s. In addition, the party's internal pressure group "Liberals for Life" had for years been assisting pro-life candidates in nomination races, though during the run-up to the 1993 election, Jean Chrétien used his leverage over candidate nominations to limit further gains by pro-life candidates. As Carty, Cross, and Young argue, Chrétien's actions "did not reflect a deep commitment to reproductive freedom on the part of the Liberal Party; rather, it was motivated by the party's need to maintain its ability not to take a stand on this potentially divisive issue."[5] Even then, several pro-life candidates, such as Dan McTeague, Paul Szabo, and Paul Zed, still managed to win their nominations and then their constituencies in the 1993 Liberal victory. Others, such as John McKay, followed in 1997. With few exceptions, these pro-life MPs never held senior positions within the Chrétien or Paul Martin governments, but their caucus presence was a continuing brake on the Liberals developing an unequivocally pro-choice stance. The fact that the Liberals still drew a disproportionate number of Catholic voters may also have helped to embolden pro-life Liberal legislators during this period. At this time, most of the more outspoken pro-life Liberal MPs at this time were Catholic, including McTeague, Szabo, and Zed.

Abortion and the Conservative Party of Canada

The addition of Canadian Alliance Party members meant that the newly created Conservative Party of Canada started out with an even larger portion of pro-life MPs than were contained in the former Progressive Conservative Party.[6] Indeed, the Alliance's first leader,

Stockwell Day, a devout Pentecostal, had been quite open about his pro-life views, and the new party would depend on maintaining the loyalty and energy of those who shared his stance.

In its early years, the CPC adopted a number of formal policy positions favoured by social conservatives, including opposition to same-sex marriage and a pledge to impose restrictions on abortion. The leadership ranks of the new party included not only Day but other pro-life evangelical MPs such as Monte Solberg and Chuck Strahl. This social conservative influence was also evident in positions adopted by Conservative MPs in the House of Commons, where patterns of voting on issues of concern to social conservatives (related to reproduction and sexual diversity) showed sharper party distinctions than ever before.[7]

Yet, as we saw in Chapter 2, Stephen Harper had already warned against excessive focus on issues that would arouse accusations of a hidden moral agenda. With the formation of the CPC in 2003, the party leadership was keener than ever to temper the social conservative image that had been so firmly tied to the Reform Party and the Canadian Alliance. One dramatic illustration was the party's convention vote in 2005 to remove the policy handbook provision on tightening restrictions on abortion, replacing it with a resolution stating: "a Conservative government will not initiate or support any legislation to regulate abortion."[8] This commitment was reiterated during the 2006 election campaign when Harper stated: "a Conservative government will not be bringing forward, will not be supporting, and will not be debating the abortion laws in the country." He again made this point in the 2008 campaign, declaring:

> I have been clear throughout my entire political career. I don't intend to open the abortion issue. If I haven't in the past, I'm not going to in the future, and I simply, I simply have no intention of ever making that a focus, the abortion question a focus, of my political career.[9]

Crucially, however, the party maintained its policy that parliamentary votes on moral issues would be unwhipped, leaving MPs free to vote with their conscience on issues like abortion and, presumably, to introduce their own motions on the subject.

This effort to position the CPC as officially agnostic on the issue of abortion was part of a calculated attempt to broaden the party's appeal without alienating social conservatives. Although there seemed little risk of social conservatives moving to the Liberal Party or the NDP, given their recent support for same-sex marriage, the Conservative leadership would have known what damage had been inflicted on major parties of the right or centre right by small parties pitching explicitly to moral traditionalists in federal and provincial elections. The Christian Heritage Party (CHP) has not been viewed as much of a threat in federal politics and has accepted that it has little chance of forming government, but its very persistence as "Canada's only pro-life party" serves as a reminder of the potential for partisan breakaway over an issue such as abortion.[10]

Funding for Abortion through Canada's Foreign Aid Spending

Two related policy developments appeared to contradict Harper's stated goal of avoiding debate on abortion, suggesting instead a strategy of catering to social conservatives in less visible ways. One was the 2010 decision to block funding for abortion services in the government's centrepiece initiative on maternal and child health launched at the G8 meetings in Muskoka, Ontario. The second was the government's long delay in funding the overseas development work of the International Planned Parenthood Foundation and, ultimately, a substantial reduction in federal financial support for the organization.

The G8 Muskoka Initiative

The Muskoka Initiative was originally proposed in a letter to the prime minister written by a coalition of civil society organizations, including UNICEF Canada, Save the Children, CARE Canada, and World Vision. Since the Canadian government was hosting the G8 and G20 meetings, the coalition members believed that the proposal would be politically appealing to Harper as a legacy project, both domestically and internationally. As one strategist close to the file put it, "if it was true that his support base was largely male, largely interested in hard security issues, [then] a maternal and child health piece would allow him to speak to another side of the potential support base – so appeal to women, appeal to mothers."[11] Internationally, there was widespread recognition of the gap between international commitments on maternal health (such as contained in the Millennium Development Goals) and programs actually implemented. A literal "motherhood" initiative therefore had the potential to appeal to other governments and to soften Canada's increasingly hard image on the world stage.

When the Muskoka Initiative was unveiled in January 2010, no statement was made as to whether abortion services would be supported. Within days of the announcement, the opposition Liberals began to ask if abortions would be covered, with party leader Michael Ignatieff saying, "If we're going to improve maternal health and child health around the world, women need access to the full gamut of reproductive health services."[12] He added: "We've had a pro-choice consensus in this area for a couple of generations and we want to hold it."[13] For nearly a month, the Conservatives remained silent on the issue, until the then foreign minister, Lawrence Cannon, stated that the G8 Initiative would "not deal in any way, shape or form with family planning."[14] Civil society groups and opposition politicians interpreted the statement to mean that the government planned to exclude funding not just for abortions but for contraceptives as well. The next day, however, the prime minister quickly backtracked, clarifying that, while the CPC would not rule out condoms, the initiative was not intended to open the abortion debate and Canada would not support any programming that included abortion.

Ignatieff sensed an opportunity to embarrass the Conservatives and continued to press the question of abortion funding. However, this move sparked frustration among the remaining pro-life MPs within the Liberal caucus, with long-serving Liberal MP Paul Szabo publicly stating both that he was pro-life and that no consensus existed in the party. Despite such internal dissent, the Liberals introduced a parliamentary motion that called on the government to ensure that the G8 Initiative included a "full range of family planning, sexual, and reproductive health options, including contraception."[15] The motion also called on the government to "refrain from advancing the failed right-wing ideologies previously imposed by the George W. Bush administration in the United States, which made humanitarian assistance conditional upon a 'global gag rule' that required all non-governmental organizations receiving federal funding to refrain from promoting medically-sound family planning."

Some Conservatives were unsettled about the motion, in part, of course, because this was increasing the visibility of an issue that the party leadership had wanted to avoid and, in part, because they had only a minority in the House. Yet, in the end, the members of the CPC caucus reached the decision that they could safely oppose it on the grounds that it was "anti-American." And so, in the House, they unanimously voted against it.[16] They were joined by three pro-life Liberal MPs, and enough other MPs stayed away to ensure the motion's defeat.

The prospect of the G8 Health Initiative including restrictions on abortion elicited condemnations from the governments of both the United States and Great Britain. Canadian aid agencies also vigorously protested the move, despite being advised by pro-choice Conservative Senator Nancy Ruth that they should hold their fire and hope for openings in the final G8 communiqué. All this provided fuel for media coverage. Ultimately, the final text of the initiative allowed for leeway on funding for abortion among the various donor countries. Until its defeat in 2015, however, the Harper government maintained a Canadian ban on international funding for abortion services.

The exclusion of abortion services from the Muskoka Initiative appeared to be custom-made to appease social conservatives. Indeed, the response was enthusiastic among anti-abortion activists, and the government's policy was lauded at the annual March for Life. There is some doubt, though, that it had in fact been deliberately planned to that end. One close observer has argued that the question of abortion was simply not discussed in the early planning stages and was then addressed haphazardly only after the process was under way.

> I think their original plan when the PM rolled out the expanded programs hadn't thought this one through, how this would tie into abortion ... I think when they rolled out maternal health care – whoever was handling this issue had no grasp of the abortion politics on either side. Someone put a proposal [forward], it would have

looked good, and they said, "Ah, backdrops of the PM and Third World children, you know – Third World stuff, how Canada cares."[17]

Once the government was pressed on the issue, it had little room for manouevre, especially in light of the strength of feeling among pro-life advocates within the party. The prime minister and his strategists might well have thought that controversy over restrictions on abortion in a foreign aid program would not have the same staying power as would attempts to limit abortion domestically.

Canadian Funding for the International Planned Parenthood Federation

Government funding for the International Planned Parenthood Federation (IPPF) had already been targeted by anti-abortion social conservatives in Canada, as it had been by their US counterparts. In November 2009, Conservative MP Brad Trost, a Mennonite, launched a petition calling on the government to stop any support for the organization, which, at the time, was seeking a renewal of its funding from the Canadian International Development Agency (CIDA). This campaign seemed to have had some impact, since the funding proposal submitted by the IPFF in 2010 lingered for an extended period with no response. During the 2011 federal election campaign, Trost claimed to his supporters that the IPPF had been "defunded" by the government. The Prime Minister's Office quickly responded that Trost was mistaken and that CIDA was still reviewing the file. However, when Bev Oda, the minister responsible for CIDA, signed an order renewing the IPPF's funding several months later, the level of support had been drastically cut from $6 million per year to $2 million and came with severe restrictions. Government money was limited to non-abortion related projects and was targeted to a set of countries in which abortion was illegal.

IPPF funding, however, had become such a categorical litmus test for pro-life advocates that they were not satisfied with the government's response. They believed that any support for the IPPF would indirectly support pro-abortion activity and that this decision stood in

sharp contrast to the Conservative government's willingness to completely cut support for a variety of other aid groups that had been
critical of its policies – for example, on the Middle East. As Brad Trost
put it, "The battle over [the IPPF] continues. Pro-Life politicians have
been taught a lesson. The government only responds to Pro-Life
issues and concerns when we take an aggressive stance. We will apply
this lesson."[18]

In fact, the government may well have learned from this episode
that it was becoming increasingly difficult to develop policy or funding
decisions that at least partially acknowledged social conservatives' views
on the abortion file without attracting broader public attention. If
there were to be additional gestures on this file, and it was not at all
clear that there would be, they would have to be even less likely to appear in media headlines.

Conservative Backbench Restiveness on Abortion and Fetal Protection

Private members' business gives those MPs who are not in cabinet an
opportunity to shape government policy by allowing them to introduce
either bills or parliamentary motions. Private members' bills cannot
require government spending, but otherwise they have the same force
of law as government legislation. Motions simply express the views of
the House of Commons on a particular issue and are not binding on
the government unless they relate to a particular aspect of parliamentary organization, such as the creation of a legislative committee. At the
beginning of each session, a lottery is held to determine the order in
which private members' initiatives will be considered. Although MPs
can introduce an unlimited number of draft motions or bills for placement on the list of parliamentary business, they must select a single
initiative to put forward for debate when their turn comes up.

A small number of pro-life MPs have repeatedly attempted to use
private members' initiatives to restrict abortion services, recognize fetal
rights, or create legal protections for health professionals who refuse to
provide abortions on the basis of conscience. All told, at least twenty-
three separate measures along such lines were introduced in the House
of Commons between the Supreme Court's 1988 ruling in *Morgentaler*

and the 2006 election that brought the Conservatives to power. During this period, however, there was a marked shift in the party affiliations of the MPs introducing them. Between 1988 and February 1996, all of the private members' initiatives relating to abortion came from one of four Liberal MPs: Don Boudria, John Nunziata, Tom Wappel, or Ralph Ferguson – the first three Catholic, the last a Presbyterian. From that point on until the 2005–06 election, all such motions came from four MPs representing either the Reform Party, the Alliance, or the CPC: Garry Breitkreuz (a Baptist), Maurice Vellacott (a Mennonite), or Keith Martin and Jim Pankiw (both Catholic).[19] It was during this second period that the Liberal leadership also began to use the moral conservatism in those parties against them, while, at the same time, curtailing pro-life activism within its own ranks.

Between 1988 and the 2005–06 election, just a handful of abortion-related private members' initiatives were actually debated, and only one ever came to a vote. M-83 was introduced in March 2003 by then Canadian Alliance MP Garry Breitkreuz, and it called for the Commons Standing Committee on Health to investigate whether abortions were necessary to promote health or prevent disease, and to compare the health outcomes for women who underwent abortions to those who carried their fetus to full term. The motion went on to be defeated in October 2003 by a vote of 139 to 66. It had support from three-quarters of the Alliance caucus, one-quarter of the PCs, and just under 10 percent of the Liberals.

The Conservative Minority Period, 2006–11

Given that private members' bills are not government legislation and, therefore, not matters of confidence, votes on such measures have usually not been subject to tight party discipline. As Haussman and Rankin point out, private members' bills would therefore appear to provide an excellent way for individual Conservative MPs to pursue their personal desire to restrict access to abortion while not violating the commitments by their party (and party leader) not to legislate on the issue. For a time, this may have been approved by the party leadership as a vehicle for signalling an affinity with socially conservative electors. Indeed, writing about one private member's bill, Haussman and Rankin argue that the government's main strategy for "keeping its pro-life caucus majority happy" was to give backbenchers leeway to introduce measures but then to ensure that they did not pass.[20]

The first private members' initiative relating to the protection of fetuses came soon after the Conservative victory in January 2006 (see Table 2.1). Leon Benoit won second place in the ballot for private members' business and used the opportunity to bring forward Bill C-291, which would have imposed punishments on offenders who harmed a fetus during an attack on a pregnant woman. In this instance, the House of Commons Subcommittee on Private Members' Business ruled the bill to be unconstitutional and therefore non-votable since it would impose penalties even if the offender did not know the woman was pregnant. Some pro-life activists contend that the discussion of constitutionality was just a way for the government to bury the bill.[21] Notably, just minutes before an appeal of the subcommittee's ruling was heard by the Commons Committee on Procedure and House Affairs, the committee received a rushed letter from Justice Minister Vic Toews, which supported the view that the bill was unconstitutional.

The next private members' bill on fetal protection to come up for debate initially received a much more supportive response from the government. Outgoing Conservative MP Ken Epp's Bill C-484 (the Unborn Victims of Crime Act) was similar to that brought forward by Benoit but limited the offence of harming the fetus only to those instances in which the offender knew the victim was pregnant, and it specifically excluded "conduct relating to the lawful termination of the pregnancy."[22] When the bill came to a vote at second reading in March 2008, it received massive support from the Conservative caucus. To the cheers of pro-life activists in the House of Commons gallery, all of them voted yes except for four who voted against and two who abstained.[23]

However, the government's support for C-484 quickly evaporated. Despite being referred to committee for study, no hearings were held before Parliament's summer recess began. In August 2008, the bill became a political issue in two Quebec by-elections, with women's groups and some doctors arguing that it could introduce a slippery slope towards the criminalization of abortion. Similar statements were also made by then Liberal leader Stéphane Dion, who challenged Prime

Table 2.1 Private members' initiatives relating to abortion under Conservative governments, 2006–15

Title	Sponsor	First reading	Issue	Progress
C-291	Leon Benoit (CPC, Catholic)	May 2006	Impose "on a person who injures or causes the death of a child before or during its birth … the same punishment that the person would have received had the death or injury occurred to the mother."	Deemed non-votable
C-388	Paul Steckle (Liberal, Mennonite)	June 2006	Make it an offence to procure an abortion after 20 weeks gestation, with certain exceptions.	Not debated before 2008 election
C-484	Ken Epp (CPC, Mennonite)	November 2007	Create an offence for those who deliberately harm a fetus in an attack on the mother.	Passed only second reading before 2008 election
C-537	Maurice Vellacott (CPC, Mennonite)	April 2008	Create legal protection for medical professionals who chose not to conduct procedures that violate their conscience.	Not debated before 2008 election
C-510	Rod Bruinooge (CPC, unknown)	March 2010	Make it an offence for someone to coerce or attempt to coerce a female person to have an abortion.	Defeated at second reading

Title	Sponsor	First reading	Issue	Progress
M-312	Stephen Woodworth (CPC, Catholic)	February 2012	Create a committee to review Subsection 233(1) of the Criminal Code, which states that a child only becomes a human being at the moment of complete birth.	Defeated
M-408	Mark Warawa (CPC, Mennonite Brethren)	September 2012	Calls on House to condemn discrimination against females occurring through sex-selective pregnancy termination.	Deemed non-votable
M-476	Stephen Woodworth (CPC, Catholic)	November 2013	Calls on House to affirm that every law must be interpreted to recognize the "equal worth and dignity of everyone who is in fact a human being."	Denied unanimous consent
M-482	Maurice Vellacott (CPC, Mennonite)	December 2013	Create a committee to study Supreme Court rulings pertaining to children before birth and to recommend how Parliament and/or the government could address negative impact of these decisions.	Not put forward for debate
M-483	Maurice Vellacott (CPC, Mennonite)	December 2013	Create a special committee to study what protections Canada should provide to children before birth under the provisions of the United Nations Declaration on the Rights of the Child.	Not put forward for debate

Minister Harper to publicly state his own views on abortion. This unnerved the government, and during the week after Dion's statements Justice Minister Rob Nicholson held an "unusual, quickly arranged press conference," at which he announced the government would pre-empt C-484 by introducing its own legislation.[24] What resulted was much tempered, making pregnancy an aggravating factor in sentencing rather than creating a separate offence for harm to the unborn. Nicholson then restated the prime minister's commitment not to reopen the abortion debate.

The period of the Conservatives' first minority government also saw the introduction of two other private members' bills related to abortion. The first, C-388, was brought forward by Ontario Liberal MP Paul Steckle. This was the first private members' initiative on abortion by a Liberal in a decade, and it would be the last. The bill would have banned abortions performed after twenty weeks of gestation unless the procedure was medically necessary to prevent the death of the mother. Steckle's bill failed to get its turn for debate before the 2008 election, and it died on the order paper when Parliament was dissolved. The second bill, C-537, was introduced by Conservative MP Maurice Vellacott, a longtime pro-life campaigner, and it once again sought protections for health professionals who chose not to perform an abortion due to their personal beliefs. However it, too, failed to get debating time before the 2008 election.

The Conservatives won the election that year with another minority government, but it was not until the spring of 2010 that the next abortion-related private member's measure was debated in the House. Bill C-510, also known as "Roxanne's Law," would have made it an offence to coerce someone to have an abortion. It was sponsored by Rod Bruinooge, Conservative MP and co-chair of the Parliamentary Pro-Life Caucus, and was named for Roxanne Fernando, who was murdered by her boyfriend after she refused to terminate her pregnancy. However, unlike C-484, Bruinooge's measure was actively opposed by the government, which argued that the proposed offence was already covered by the Criminal Code. This opposition reflected not only the negative public reaction the government had received following its support for C-484 but also the awkward timing of the debate, which occurred during the lead-up to the G8 meeting in Muskoka and shortly after the government had announced the prohibition on abortion funding in its maternal health initiative. As a result, the government appeared to be more sensitive than ever about appearing to reopen the abortion debate at the domestic level. The bill went on to defeat at second reading.

Going into the 2011 election, then, social conservatives were left with a mixed message on abortion. On the one hand, the CPC had moved to exclude abortion services from the Muskoka Initiative despite receiving widespread criticism both in the media and from its international allies; on the other, the government was becoming more steadfast than ever in its resolve to block any effort to change the status quo on the issue within Canada itself.

Backbench Conservative Initiatives, 2011–14

The abortion issue surfaced during the 2011 election, as we saw earlier, when MP Brad Trost claimed to have succeeded in his campaign to have the IPPF defunded by the government. This prompted a quick denial from the party, providing one more indication of the party leadership's growing unease and impatience with the advocacy of pro-life MPs. It was in this context of frustration that Conservative MP Stephen Woodworth introduced his private member's motion, M-312, in February 2012. The motion called for the House of Commons to establish a special committee to "review the declaration in Subsection 223(1) of the *Criminal Code* which states that a child becomes a human being only at the moment of complete birth." The reaction from the party's front bench was remarkably harsh. Chief Conservative whip Gordon O'Connor personally spoke against the motion in the House, giving what one journalist described as "one of the most amazing defences of abortion rights that I've heard in the Commons ... It just took the wind out of the place."[25] Likewise, Paul Wells argues that O'Connor's intervention was deliberately staged to put a decisive end to activism on the part of pro-life MPs:

> This was the clearest possible message to anti-abortion Conservatives. They were out of luck with this prime minister. MPs who wanted to

do anything that had even a whiff of pro-life sentiment to it could abandon any hope of getting it past Harper. They had been waiting for a majority. Now he had sent his chief caucus enforcer to tell them they could wait longer than that. Until the hell in which many of them sincerely believed froze over, say.[26]

Following this, the prime minister issued a private warning in a party caucus meeting that "if anyone raise[d] this issue of fetal rights again, he [would] use every power that's in his possession to stop it."[27]

Even in the face of such extraordinary pressure, ninety-one Conservative MPs voted in support of Woodworth's motion when it came to a vote in September 2012, and these ranks included several cabinet ministers. Four Liberals also voted "yes," illustrating the persistence of the party's small but determined socially conservative wing. The New Democrats' unified opposition to the motion stood out by comparison, and they were more than prepared to highlight the contrast with the Liberals.

Rather than settling the matter, the defeat of Woodworth's motion only sparked further pro-life activism. Just one day after the vote, Conservative MP Mark Warawa introduced another abortion-related motion, M-408, which called on the House to "condemn discrimination against females occurring through sex-selective pregnancy termination."[28] Once again, this provoked strong opposition from the prime minister, who instructed cabinet to vote against it. Before it could be debated, however, in March 2013 the House of Commons Subcommittee on Private Members' Business ruled the motion non-votable on the grounds that health was a provincial jurisdiction and that the issue of abortion had already been discussed during the debate on M-312.

Warawa responded by filing an appeal to the full House of Commons Committee on Procedure and House Affairs and suggested that the subcommittee may have been subject to outside interference. More dramatically, however, he also attempted to publicly complain about his treatment during the fifteen-minute time slot for members' statements that is set aside each day before Question Period. Each statement is a minute long, and, since the 1980s, the standing convention has been for parties to provide the Speaker of the House with a list indicating which of their MPs are scheduled to speak each day. Warawa was initially given a spot on the CPC list but was removed before he could speak. To protest this treatment, Warawa then took the unprecedented step of raising a question of privilege to the Speaker on the grounds that his rights as an MP had been violated by his own party. Conservative whip Gordon O'Connor stood firm, arguing that parties were like teams, with the party whips being able to decide which MPs to call on at which time. However, the Speaker ultimately ruled in late April 2013 that the party whips do not have control over members' statements; instead, MPs unable to obtain a spot on their party's list would be able to stand and be recognized directly by the Speaker. Warawa soon took advantage of this new opening, rising on May 9 – the day of the 2013 March for Life – to denounce the practice of sex-selective abortions and to call for government action.

Contention over the abortion issue continued in the fall of 2013 with a spate of activism by pro-life CPC members. In early November, the annual Conservative Party convention adopted a resolution sponsored by Warawa's riding association that condemned the practice of sex-selective abortions. The resolution was passed "clearly and easily" by the plenary and received enthusiastic support from senior cabinet minister Jason Kenney. In case there was any ambiguity about the purpose of the vote, Conservative MP Rob Anders said the outcome showed that the prime minister could not ignore the party's social conservative wing.

The following month, media stories shone a spotlight on an initiative by the Campaign Life Coalition to sell Conservative Party memberships in the Ottawa area in the hopes of supporting pro-life candidates for CPC nominations. Campaign Life was even prepared to oust sitting pro-choice Tory MPs, and the group's chair, Jeff Gunnerson, was also blunt about his desire to replace Harper with someone more receptive to the pro-life cause: "The good thing is he won't be leader forever ... We still have to work for that day."[29]

Pro-life MPs also continued to introduce measures in the House. In November 2013, Stephen Woodworth introduced yet another abortion-related motion, M-476, which called for the "House of Commons [to] affirm that every Canadian law must be interpreted in a manner that recognizes in law the equal worth and dignity of everyone who is in fact a human being.["][30] Soon after, two further motions were put forward by MP Maurice Vellacott. M-482 took direct aim at the Supreme Court, calling for a special committee to:

> (a) study the decisions of the Supreme Court of Canada since 1988 related to children before birth in order to understand what the Supreme Court has said about Parliament's responsibility with respect to resolving public policy questions in this area;
>
> (b) propose options that the House and/or the government could take to address any negative impact these decisions of the Supreme Court of Canada may have had, directly or indirectly, on women, men, children and Canadian society.[31]

The second, M-483, called for the creation of a special committee to investigate "what legal protections Canada ought to provide to children before birth, in accordance with the United Nations Convention on the Rights of the Child ... which states that 'the child ... needs special safeguards and care, including appropriate legal protection, before as well as after birth.'"[32] However, neither Vellacott's motions nor Woodworth's were ever debated, bringing an end the string of abortion-related private members' initiatives by Conservative backbenchers – at least during the time their party controlled the government.

The Evolution of Party Responses to Pro-Life Caucus Advocacy

Pro-life Conservative MPs have followed what they see as an incremental approach to abortion. None of the private members' bills discussed above have actually sought to recriminalize abortion; instead, these measures raised issues related to abortion without tackling the question head on. The potential legal impact of each successive initiative has also tended to be smaller than those that came before it, a move that may have made it easier for the initiatives to gather broader public support.[33] For instance, Mark Warawa's M-408 called on the House of Commons to condemn a practice (sex-selective abortions) that had already been heavily criticized by the medical community, including in an editorial published in the *Canadian Medical Association Journal*.[34] There was also a trend away from bills in favour of motions proposing committee studies or non-binding declarations. All this fits with what Paul Saurette and Kelly Gordon point to as a systematic shift in pro-life discourse, reflecting changing activist frames in the United States.[35] Religious justifications had already been largely jettisoned by the US movement in the 1980s, and the same was evident in Canada by the 1990s. More recently, there has been a shift away from attacking women's supposed irresponsibility in seeking abortions and towards a view claiming to protect women against physical or psychological risks.

However, while the initiatives themselves came to be framed in more qualified language, the response from the CPC leadership became less tolerant. The party's growing opposition was undoubtedly designed to end accusations that it harboured a hidden socially conservative agenda, particularly after the media attention given to its initial support for Ken Epp's Unborn Victims of Crime bill (C-484) in 2007, and the resurfacing of the abortion issue in the 2008 Quebec by-elections. The readiness of the media to spotlight even those measures conceived by their proponents as cautious and limited came in large part because they were being put forward by MPs known to have policy objectives grander than the small steps they were proposing. After all, there had been decades of similar steps by pro-life advocates in American state legislatures.

Changing MP Voting Patterns on Abortion

The Conservative Party's efforts to suppress backbench activism were accompanied by important shifts in the distribution of MPs' preferences across parties. Within the Conservative caucus this was driven, in part, by front-bench determination to marginalize pro-life advocates, but it was also a reflection of change in the composition of the caucus itself and of shifts in public opinion. The responses of MPs in other parties during this time similarly reflected shifts in party strategy as well as changes in legislative ranks and public opinion. We see important changes in Table 2.2, which displays the votes cast by MPs from the major parties on the four private members' initiatives relating to abortion to be considered by the House from 2003 until the 2015 election. The first was debated in the final months of the third Chrétien Liberal majority, while the others all came to a vote after the CPC came to power

Table 2.2 Voting record of MPs on private members' initiatives relating to abortion, 2003–15

Motion	Party	In favour (%)	In favour (n)	Opposed (%)	Opposed (n)	Did not vote (%)	Did not vote (n)
M-83							
October 2003	Cdn. Alliance	73	46	5	3	22	14
(Liberal majority)	PC	27	4	40	6	33	5
	Liberal	9	15	60	96	30	48
	NDP	0	–	64	9	36	5
	BQ	0	–	96	24	4	1
C-484							
June 2008	Conservative	95	118	3	4	2	2
(CPC minority I)	Liberal	27	27	55	54	18	18
	NDP	3	1	83	25	13	4
	BQ	0	–	100	47	0	–
C-510							
December 2010	Conservative	61	87	34	49	5	7
(CPC minority II)	Liberal	13	10	71	55	16	12
	NDP	0	–	89	32	11	4
	BQ	0	–	87	47	13	6
M-312							
September 2012	Conservative	53	86	45	74	2	3
(CPC majority)	Liberal	11	4	80	28	9	3
	NDP	0	–	96	96	4	4
	BQ	0	–	100	3	0	–

Note: Percentages of affirmative and negative votes are of the entire caucus, including those not voting. Some MPs not voting undoubtedly abstained deliberately to express sympathy with the motion under consideration, while others may have been absent for other reasons.

in 2006. Each vote under the CPC was separated by a general election, making it possible to track how opinions within the caucuses have evolved over time as new MPs arrive and old ones depart.

It is dangerous to extrapolate a trend from just four divisions, particularly since each vote was on a somewhat different issue. Nevertheless, these data point to important shifts over time. The BQ has been the most consistently unified party on the abortion question, with none of its MPs ever voting for a pro-life measure. The NDP comes a close second, with just one MP (Nova Scotia's Peter Stoffer) voting in favour of one bill. The proportion of Liberal MPs who were prepared to explicitly support pro-life initiatives actually rose when the party moved from government to opposition, with 27 percent supporting C-484. Nevertheless, pro-life MPs were clearly still a minority in the party, and each subsequent vote saw their strength fall.

At first, the post-merger CPC closely resembled the Canadian Alliance in MP voting patterns. This was clear in 2008, when 95 percent of CPC members voted in favour of C-484 versus just 3 percent against. However, either for electoral calculations or pro-choice convictions, subsequent votes witnessed a massive rise in CPC opposition to abortion-related initiatives, with 34 percent voting against C-510 and 45 percent opposing M-312 (see Figure 2.1, which charts the proportion of each caucus voting against each initiative). Turnover is undoubtedly a factor. Of the 22 Conservative MPs who retired or were defeated in the 2008 election, all but one had supported C-484. Likewise, M-312 was supported by nearly two-thirds of CPC MPs elected in 2006 or earlier, but just one-third of those first elected in 2011. As the CPC sought to move away from any identification with pro-life advocacy, and as its hold on power seemed more secure, the MPs recruited by the party became correspondingly less socially conservative, or at least less willing to vote in a socially conservative fashion.

The Persistence of a Determined Social Conservative Constituency
Parliamentary voting patterns make it absolutely clear that by 2012 it was only the Conservatives who had a visible and determined pro-life presence large enough to shape party policy. While the proportion of social conservatives within the CPC caucus appeared to be in decline,

Figure 2.1   Proportion of each party caucus voting against private members' initiatives relating to abortion, 2003–12

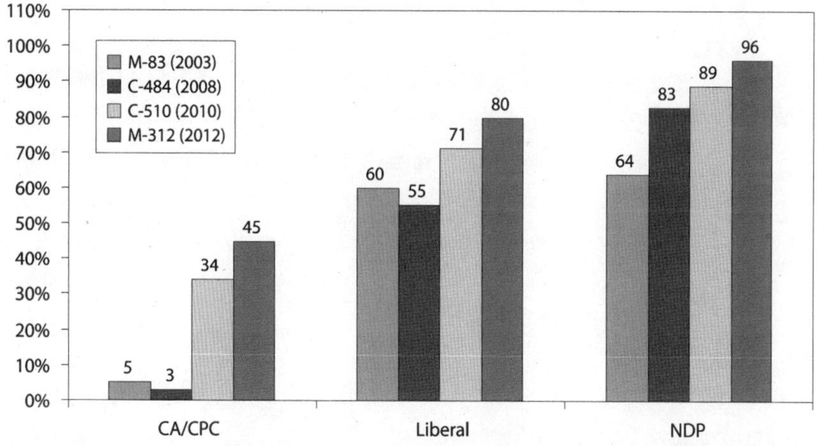

Source: Parliament of Canada, *Hansard.*

there were still ten to twenty MPs in the party so highly committed to the pro-life cause that they would be willing to incur the anger of the party leadership in order to pursue their advocacy. Most of these were broadly evangelical in their religious backgrounds and driven by personal faith. (This includes a notably visible contingent of Mennonites – a faith current that includes churches that have taken more moderate or progressive positions on other issue fronts than have many other evangelical churches.)[36] These committed activists had sympathizers among a broader range of morally traditional MPs (there were, after all, eighty-six Conservatives who voted for M-312) as well as what one MP called a "huge chunk of [Conservative Party] rank-and-file membership [who were] pro-life."[37] This connection between the CPC's anti-abortion grassroots and its MPs means that the abortion debate is not going to go away, a reality vividly demonstrated in the policy resolution on sex-selective abortion adopted at the party's convention in November 2013. In the words of one backbencher:

> In a party where really the rank-and-file majority are socially conservative, you're going to have a friction between the leadership that isn't

and the membership that is. The MPs are sort of half-way between the two, so naturally you're going to have friction. Even if they want to, Harper doesn't have the votes, the ability, the strength, the political clout to stop this issue. He just doesn't. What's he going to do? Go against the majority of his caucus? Go against the majority of his National Council? Go against the majority of his membership? He doesn't have the political strength to do that. Everyone has their political boundaries of what they can and cannot do. And this is an issue, no matter how much he wants to try to shut it down, he doesn't have it. You get 15-20 MPs who decide they want to do something different, what's he going to do?[38]

MPs determined to keep up pressure also draw strength from CPC official policy. As one MP argued:

Our policy statements are very clear as a party – in fact it's one of the reasons I agreed to run as a Conservative candidate – that on issues ... like life, abortion, marriage, we have the right to vote our conscience. That's clear in our policy statements. So, while there can be varying degrees of pressure brought to bear, in my opinion the policy statements are clear, and there are a large number of us within the Conservative caucus that will continue to be sure those policy statements are honoured.[39]

Indeed, at the end of 2013, the stage seemed to be set for a prolonged period of contention over abortion in Parliament and, particularly, within the Conservative Party. The March for Life rally in May, which had been attended by thousands of supporters and twenty-two Conservative backbenchers, demonstrated that there was a significant core within the CPC dedicated to keeping the abortion issue on the public agenda, no matter the cost. Activists of varying approaches then seized the opportunity at the party convention in November to push forward the resolution against sex-selective abortions. It was in this context that Stephen Woodworth and Maurice Vellacott brought forward motions that seemed poised to throw the House of Commons into further debate over whether Canada should implement any measures to protect infants before they are born.

In the approach to the 2015 election, however, there seemed for a time to be a de-escalation of the open conflict between pro-life back-benchers and party leaders. One possible factor is that the party's leadership may have finally convinced pro-life MPs to restrain themselves, particularly in the lead-up to an election in which the Conservatives were destined to have a difficult fight on their hands. Fatigue may also have played a role. In the spring and summer of 2015, over thirty sitting Conservatives announced that they were not seeking another term, and among them were several pro-life advocates who had originated in the Reform and Alliance periods. Some were retiring simply because of the length of their service, but at least one veteran – Maurice Vellacott – suggested that he was frustrated at not being able to make more difference on the Reform Party's "core social agenda."[40] Vellacott was particularly pointed in his criticism of those inside his party and across the parliamentary aisle who blocked debate on Mark Warawa's motion on sex-selective abortion, calling it "shameful and cowardly." Rod Bruinooge also decided not to run again, despite being comparatively young (forty-two) and first elected only in 2006.

And yet, after all this, the Harper government still seemed to recognize that it had to engage in at least minimalist signalling to social conservatives that they were a valued part of the Conservative coalition. There was always a chance that the strength of personal convictions among pro-life advocates within the party could provoke defection to an insurgent party on the right.[41] Almost as damaging, their disillusioned withdrawal from the party could become more widespread. Even pragmatic pro-life advocates who had long recognized the strategic difficulties of engaging the abortion issue were increasingly disappointed by the Harper government.[42] In May 2014, Prime Minister Harper announced that Canada's support for maternal and child health programs in developing countries would continue to exclude funding for abortion on the grounds that the issue was "extremely divisive."[43] That same year, he responded to Liberal leader Justin Trudeau's announcement that future Liberal candidates would need to be pro-choice by declaring that pro-life individuals were welcome in the Conservative Party. In doing so, he repeated his intention not to reopen the abortion debate but stressed that the CPC would respect the views of its MPs, stating: "the reality is [that] in public life there are issues that engage peoples' moral views, engage their faith, engage their most deeply held beliefs." He then added, "it's our party's view that on those issues you cannot impose views on people."[44] This would have been only small comfort to pro-life advocates, who had hoped for so much more from the Harper Conservatives, but they and many others would now see that the other main parties in Ottawa were definitively on the other side of the debate.[45]

Delaying the Approval of RU-486

While receiving less attention than the various private members' initiatives, another major issue relating to abortion access was also unfolding in the run up to the 2015 election. Since 2011, Health Canada had been evaluating the drug RU-486 (known as mifepristone). It can terminate a fetus in the first seven weeks of pregnancy, making it much more effective than the so-called "morning-after pill." As such, RU-486 can greatly increase access to abortion services, especially in rural areas, giving it much support among reproductive health advocates. The drug has been licensed for use in over fifty countries, dating back to the late 1980s, and, in October 2011, its manufacturer, Linepharma International, applied for approval in Canada. In response to Health Canada's request for further documentation, Linepharma then resubmitted the application in October 2012.[46] The application was strongly opposed by social conservatives, who made it the focus of the 2014 March for Life.

No parliamentary debate was required as part of the approval for RU-486, and no backbencher attempted to use a private member's initiative to introduce one. It is no surprise that Prime Minister Harper would not have wanted a parliamentary debate on RU-486, perhaps all the more so because of the highly visible social movement advocacy. What is a surprise, however, is that pro-life Conservative MPs did not campaign against its approval in Parliament. Instead, with the exception of a single petition to disallow the drug introduced by Conservative MP Harold Albrecht, a former pastor in the Brethren in Christ Church, all mentions of RU-486 in parliamentary proceedings after the licensing process began were from by opposition MPs calling for its approval.[47]

Health Canada dragged out its initial evaluation of the drug from the resubmission of the application in October 2012 until January 2015, twice the usual time required by officials. And then, in early 2015, Health Canada announced that it required still further safety data from the manufacturer before the full assessment could be completed.[48] This extraordinary request for additional information, years after the drug's approval in so many other countries, is hard not to link to arguments from anti-abortion campaigners on the drug's side effects. At the very least, senior officials in the health ministry knew full well the government's wish to avoid controversy on the abortion file, and administrative delay was one of the arrows in their quiver. Indeed, pro-choice researchers who supported Linepharma with its application for RU-486 reported that Health Canada officials seemed hostile to the application. One international expert who was involved in the process put it this way: "There seemed to be a lot of negativity toward this drug in some of the meetings I attended ... I've been in a lot of regulatory meetings and the Canadian one was unusual in that people were attacking in a way I wouldn't have expected in a regulatory meeting."[49]

Recognizing the exceptional circumstances, the *Globe and Mail* published an editorial in early 2015 calling on Health Canada to explain the further delay:

> The drug's success in other countries, and the benefit it would bring to women here, is turning Health Canada's unusual slowness into an issue of a woman's right to an established medical treatment. This, in turn, is exacerbated by the complete secrecy that Health Canada maintains around its approval process ... The longer regulators dither in this unaccountable manner, the more people will wonder if there is more going on than meets the eye.[50]

These delays and roadblocks may well have convinced pro-life MPs that their restraint was appropriate. By staying largely silent, Conservative MPs may have hoped to create sufficient political space to allow the government to delay the application on technical grounds. Voicing strong opposition would attract public attention and could have actually reduced the government's space to act.

In the end, the drug was approved in the same quiet fashion as was the reduction in the Planned Parenthood grant, with Linepharma being notified on July 29, 2015, that its application was successful. The approval came when the Conservatives were just days from launching a federal election campaign, so there was obviously some need to manage this announcement so as to keep abortion from being a campaign issue. Two Conservative MPs quickly attacked the Health Canada ruling. David Anderson condemned it, stating that "Health Canada scientists have failed Canadian women and children," while Harold Albrecht, who had presented the sole petition against RU-486 in the House of Commons, also called for Health Canada to reconsider.[51] As expected, strong criticism also came from pro-life civil society groups. In an editorial on Lifesitenews.com, Mike Schouten, director of the WeNeedaLAW.ca campaign, was particularly scathing, arguing that the approval was further proof of the Conservatives' failure to act on pro-life concerns:

> That the approval of a drug which expands access to abortion occurs under the watch of a Conservative government is not surprising. This government has an abysmal record of advancing pre-born human rights. Even with a majority of MPs in the House of Commons, the Conservatives have refused to pass anything close to a regulation on abortion.[52]

Conservative Health Minister Ambrose distanced herself from the decision, saying, "It's out of my hands, and the decision is final."[53] This resigned acceptance stood in contrast to the sharp criticism she had levelled at Health Canada in 2013 after it approved the use of prescription heroin for a drug treatment program in Vancouver, a move that she argued worked against the government's drug control policy.

There were also some pro-life activists prepared to give the Conservatives pre-election slack. The Campaign Life Coalition did not even mention RU-486 in its federal election overview, focusing instead on the officially pro-choice policies adopted by the Liberals and the NDP:

The election of either the pro-death NDP or the abortion-loving Justin Trudeau would almost certainly mean bad things for preborn children, and for the elderly and disabled who are the targets of euthanasia. We would see an increase in "abortion access" and abortion funding with Canadian taxpayer dollars, both at home and abroad ...

Although Prime Minister Harper has himself been rated pro-abortion by CLC, the Conservative caucus is home to about 100 pro-life or pro-life leaning Members of Parliament. Many of these speak out routinely against the barbaric practice of abortion, including MP Stephen Woodworth (Kitchener Centre), MP Brad Trost (Saskatoon-Humboldt) and many others. The pro-life presence is alive and well within the Conservative caucus. The same cannot be said for the NDP or Liberal parties.[54]

Post-Election Revival of Debate

The Conservatives' defeat in the 2015 election and Stephen Harper's resignation as party leader reignited internal debate over the party's direction, the breadth of its "tent," and the place of social and religious conservatives within it. The new Liberal government's decision to formulate legislation on physician-assisted suicide elicited a wide range of opinions across the political spectrum. The Conservatives were far from united on the issue, but it was within that caucus that the strongest dissent emerged, including a scathing attack from veteran pro-life MP Brad Trost. In the meantime a new Conservative MP, Cathay Wagantall (a Baptist), introduced a private member's bill (C-225) proposing the creation of a new offence for violent criminals who knowingly injure or cause the death of a "pre-born child" while committing an offence against a pregnant woman. When C-225 came to a vote in late 2016, seventy-six Conservative members supported it, including most of the declared candidates for the party leadership, and only two opposed.

The vote on that measure demonstrated a complete reversal of Conservative MP's wariness of the party's increasing moderation on abortion-related private members' initiatives during Stephen Harper's tenure as leader. As shown in Figure 2.1, this trend reached its peak when 45 percent of Conservative MPs had voted against M-312 in 2012. The nearly complete Conservative support for C-225 suggests that the shifts we observed in earlier years were not a sign of moderation among Conservatives MPs, but of pressure from the party leadership. Indeed, it is notable that while Stephen Harper had voted against M-312, Rona Ambrose, the Conservative's interim leader during the vote on C-225, had supported it. Ultimately, this most recent vote was a stark reminder to any future Conservative leader of the challenges ahead in moving the party closer to the centre on social issues.

Realignment Complete: The Pro-Choice Liberal Party?

In May 2014, a little over a year after taking over as leader of the Liberal Party, Justin Trudeau announced that all new Liberal MPs would be expected to be pro-choice. As part of this commitment, the party would screen potential candidates based on their views on the issue to ensure that they would vote according to party policy. Sitting MPs would be given some dispensation so they could stay in the parliamentary caucus but would still be expected to adopt a pro-choice position on any legislative vote that might arise. The data on parliamentary voting presented earlier demonstrate that the Liberals were already moving strongly towards a pro-choice consensus even before Trudeau became leader. Of the twenty-seven Liberal MPs who voted for the Unborn Victims of Crime Act in 2008, just five were still in Parliament for the vote on M-312 in 2012, and only three supported the motion. The party's convention in January 2012 also adopted a new policy that specifically upheld a woman's right to choose.

Trudeau's 2014 declaration did not go unchallenged. Ontario Liberal MP John McKay was secretly recorded criticizing Trudeau and referring to the new policy as a "bozo eruption" – a term usually used to describe politically controversial comments made by social conservatives. At first, long-time PEI MP Lawrence McCauley, a Catholic, argued that pro-life MPs would be allowed to continue to vote their conscience, but he came to accept the new policy after meeting with Trudeau. Even McCauley's pro-choice PEI colleague, Wayne Easter, expressed concern that the announcement might "narrow the breadth of opinion that is within our party on the various issues."[55] A group of seven former Liberal MPs published an open letter criticizing the move on the grounds that it eroded the freedoms of conscience and expression, undermined the capacity of Liberal riding associations to nominate their preferred candidates, and set a dangerous precedent for further edicts by party leaders on moral issues. Trudeau, however, stood firm, determined to move the party squarely into the pro-choice camp along with the BQ and the NDP. This was clearly aimed at ensuring that neither of those parties would be able to claim that the Liberals were still soft or internally split on abortion or any other issue that had historically roused social conservatives.

There might have been a time when the Liberal Party's electoral success among Catholics, including those outside Quebec, would have strengthened the voices of pro-life Catholics in the federal caucus. And, of course, there were Catholic bishops who were more than ready to apply public pressure to Catholic legislators, including threats to deny communion to those who supported abortion or failed to back pro-life legislative initiatives.[56] But, as we saw in Chapter 1, the Liberal "advantage" among Catholics had essentially disappeared by the time that Trudeau became leader, and there was no clear indication that party strategists believed that there were electoral gains to be made with appeals targeting moral conservatives in general and/or Catholics who opposed abortion in particular. Most of the Liberal legislators who vocally supported pro-life positions, or abstained for reasons of conscience when private members' initiatives came up for a vote, were older veterans such as John Mackay or Lawrence MacAulay, and this, too, may have diminished their influence within a party aiming for an image of youthful reformism.

Trudeau's announcement reverberated at the provincial level, and particularly in the two Atlantic provinces that had retained comparatively restrictive policies on abortion. Within days of Trudeau's announcement, a group of three Liberal MPs wrote to federal health minister Rona Ambrose asking her to investigate whether the restrictions on abortion access in New Brunswick (then governed by the Progressive Conservatives under David Alward) violated the Canada Health Act's requirement for medical services to be easily accessible. They noted that the province's refusal to fund the Morgentaler clinic meant that it would soon be closing, which would greatly reduce access to abortion services. During New Brunswick's election campaign in the summer of 2014, provincial Liberal leader Brian Gallant seemed to follow Trudeau's example by saying that all Liberal MLAs would be expected to support a woman's right to choose, and then added a pledge to improve access to abortion. Gallant won that election, and although the policy ultimately introduced fell substantially short of what pro-choice advocates had expected, his government did broaden access somewhat (as we see in Chapter 3).

In the fall of 2014, Trudeau himself raised questions about PEI's compliance with the Canada Health Act after it emerged that the provincial government had put a stop to plans to provide abortion services on the Island. This time, however, the government in office was a Liberal one. During the Island's spring 2015 election campaign, Trudeau tempered his language, saying: "[I have] full confidence in the premier to make sure that women in Prince Edward Island have their rights respected, and that's something I'm reassured is in the capable hands of the premier right now."[57] The provincial Liberals, under a new leader, the openly gay Wade Maclauchlan, went on to be re-elected, and, as again discussed in Chapter 3, with a government cautiously moving to allow the provision of abortion services on the Island.

To ensure that the federal Liberals' socially progressive credentials remained intact during the 2015 election, the party platform included a provision on the Muskoka Initiative that declared a commitment to policy "driven by evidence and outcomes, not ideology" – one that would cover "the full range of reproductive health services."[58] This was in a campaign in which the Liberals tilted left on a range of policy fronts, all designed to draw votes away from the NDP across Canada and, especially, in Quebec, where pro-choice sentiment is strongest. Following the election, the government made good on its pledge, removing the restrictions on funding abortion services overseas.[59] When the pro-life-motivated Bill C-225 was voted on near the end of 2016, all Liberal MPs present in the House of Commons voted against it.

Conclusion

The changing federal politics around the issues of abortion and fetal rights helps illustrate the faith realignment that has taken place between the major parties and also displays the limits of social conservative influence. What is clear is that all but a few social conservatives now find their home within the Conservative Party of Canada – something that is especially true in Parliament. When a pro-life contingent was more visible in the Liberal Party, it was made up mostly of Roman Catholics, which is not surprising in view of the comparative importance of Catholic voters to that party until the 2000s. This pro-life current is now smaller, and less vocal, with MP John Mackay (a Baptist) being the most important exception.

Within the Conservative Party, most pro-life advocates are now rooted in Protestant denominations broadly associated with evangelical Christianity. These evangelical MPs are highly committed, with Mark Warawa, for example, willing to file a complaint with the Speaker of the House to secure the right to raise the issue of gender-selective abortion. It was also a Mennonite, MP Brad Trost, who led the advocacy against the funding of abortion services through Canadian foreign aid. Yet, at the same time, the number of Conservative MPs willing to publicly pursue socially conservative stances on initiatives relating to abortion has declined. As dramatically evident in the 2016 vote, broadly pro-life sentiment within the Conservative caucus is much stronger than pro-life opinion in the general public, but, even in caucus, outspoken social conservatism is a minority view. There is a stronger contingent whose privately held views are broadly sympathetic with pro-life advocates, but many are resigned to keeping such sentiments away from the light of campaign rhetoric and legislative debate.

In the first several years after the formation of the Conservative Party of Canada, backbenchers were prepared to take advantage of their party's formal commitment to respect the rights and conscience of individual MPs. They also believed that the party's own leadership was prepared to adopt a subtle incrementalism on abortion, even while denying its interest in doing so. Indeed, the 2010 Maternal Health

Initiative seemed to illustrate an approach that pro-life backbenchers were prepared to emulate (even if that policy emerged haphazardly).

However, the watchfulness of political opponents and of the mass media, compounded by the negative publicity associated with the Muskoka Initiative and Bill C-484, shifted the Conservative leadership towards greater unease over backbench advocacy. Private members' initiatives on abortion-related questions soon became politically hazardous for the Conservatives, and the leadership reacted with increasing harshness towards persistent steps to keep the issue before parliamentarians. The intensity of this response was especially evident after the 2011 federal election and, if anything, increased in response to the persistent activism of pro-life MPs.

After reaching a boiling point in 2013, internal strife seemed to dissipate. MPs with unassailable pro-life credentials started sidestepping opportunities to present abortion-related private members' motions and bills. In the face of an election apparently destined to be close, some may have realized how much worse they and their cause would fare with a Liberal or NDP victory. Yet others may have been convinced that the party's leaders were still prepared to take steps in the direction they favoured but that they would only do so if the visibility of the issue within the caucus disappeared.

However, pro-life activism has certainly shown no signs of disappearing in the party's grassroots. In 2015, one Ottawa-area CPC nomination contest pitted a comparative moderate, backed by former cabinet minister John Baird, against Andy Wang, a Chinese Canadian social conservative endorsed by the Campaign Life Coalition, and it was the latter who won.[60] Likewise, in the BC riding of Peace River-Westlock, the Conservative nomination went to Arnold Viersen, the treasurer of the local chapter of the Association of Reformed Political Action and a self-described "social conservative."[61] While Wang was defeated in the 2015 campaign, Viersen won his seat and went on to speak at the 2016 March for Life. On announcing his retirement, Maurice Vellacott also pointed to a number of young MPs utterly devoted to social conservative policies. Commenting on the party's loss of the 2015 election, influential Christian broadcaster Lorna Dueck argued that many people of faith, and particularly evangelicals, had become disillusioned with the Conservatives not only because of the heartlessness of their response to the Syrian refugee crisis and the government's targeting of minority faith communities but also because of the marginalization of pro-life voices.[62] Even if most such voters ended up voting disproportionately for the party they had supported so strongly over the past decade, Dueck was pointing to an important loss of enthusiasm. Only time, and particularly the outcome of the Conservative leadership race triggered by Harper's resignation, will tell whether such enthusiasm can be regained or whether religious conservatives will seek out alternative political vehicles, such as the Christian Heritage Party.

The strategic dilemma facing the party, therefore, is not disappearing. The Conservative leadership still recognizes the need for social conservative signalling, even on a file as electorally risky as abortion. This is more likely, of course, where the steps to this end are less visible (or less significant) to the wider public, but it is made more challenging by the readiness of the media, and pro-choice activists, to highlight the slightest of measures that appear to be sympathetic to pro-life advocacy.

PART 2
Persistent Denominationalism in Provincial Politics

Religion in Atlantic Provincial Politics: The Special Cases of Newfoundland and Labrador and New Brunswick

3

It is in Atlantic Canada that the politicization of Protestant and Catholic affiliations was most tenacious. From the early nineteenth century until late in the twentieth – and in some areas beyond – belonging to one or another denomination shaped your partisan affiliation or your sense of who within a particular party represented your interests. These four easterly provinces are not unique for witnessing episodes of bitter denominational conflict over, for example, Catholic schooling. But much of the region is distinctive for how long denominationalism was institutionalized in the political order and how strongly it was reflected in people's partisan identity and in those of their political representatives.

Crucial to the longevity of such patterns was the fact that school systems remained denominationally segregated either in law (as in Newfoundland and Labrador) or in practice (in the three other provinces) until quite late.[1] Indeed, it was conflict over schools, as much as over any other policy area, that not only politicized denominational ties but also impelled so many party leaders to pursue forms of political accommodation that entrenched denominational "consciousness" so deeply within Atlantic region politics.

The persistence of such consciousness and political caution over religiously contentious issues also reflects an unusual demographic "continuity" in the region, which has been much less affected than other regions by immigration from outside Canada or from other parts of the country. The high proportion of the population with local and regional roots helped to foster a political culture dominated by traditionalism and caution and, in turn, contributed to a comparative resistance to policy change that deviated from established family norms.[2] As a result, contention over gender and sexuality issues was for some time met by even more political avoidance than was found in other regions of the country. Such inaction reflected the socially conservative consensus in the various provinces' political classes. In addition, the habit of political accommodation that had developed to temper denominational conflict, especially in the second half of the twentieth century, was applied to such potentially controversial issues as abortion and the rights of sexual minorities.

The modest scale of migration has also meant that the region's non-Christian minorities are comparatively small. Religious minorities have therefore not come close to the sort of critical mass that would enable them to press significant claims. While ethno-racial issues have been prominent in Nova Scotia, they are primarily centred on the historic marginalization of the Halifax area's black population and have not invoked religious differences.

Despite these general trends, each Atlantic province has its own distinct history at the intersection of faith and politics. In this chapter, we focus on two of them – Newfoundland and Labrador and New Brunswick. On the one hand, Newfoundland and Labrador retained denominationally segregated schools longer than did the other three Atlantic provinces, a reality that was an important flashpoint in an often-conflictual history of Protestant-Catholic division, though in a party system in which it was the Progressive Conservatives who attracted the most Catholic votes. On the other, New Brunswick is the Atlantic province in which religious and linguistic divides most strongly overlap, yet its politics are also characterized by a pattern of cross-party accommodation that has been practised almost continuously over the last half century. This unwillingness to rouse faith-based or linguistic passions translated into an extraordinarily cautious approach to a range of policy questions and, especially, to the provision of abortion services.

What, then, are the roots of religious differentiation and accommodation in these two provinces? Why did denominational factors continue to influence party alignments as long as they did? And to what extent has denominational difference given way in the face of secularizing pressures? Does religion still matter in the provincial politics of the region? And, if so, along what dimensions?

The Entrenchment of Denominationalism in Newfoundland and Labrador

Across the twentieth century and into the twenty-first, Newfoundland and Labrador was populated with about one-third Roman Catholics, one-third Anglicans, and one-third "non-conformist" Protestants, this last group increasingly diversified by evangelical expansion. Immigration to Newfoundland in the late eighteenth and early nineteenth centuries was mostly from Ireland and the west of England, and the early settlers brought their religious divisions with them.[3] The English dominated the economy and held a firm grip on political power before the arrival of responsible government, in the face of what was then an Irish Catholic majority. As Gertrude Gunn puts it, for Irish Catholics, "'racial' and religious animosities against the English smouldered ... for conditions in the new land fostered memories of wrongs in the old."[4] Intensifying the animosity between communities was the fact that they settled in quite distinct geographic areas. Even in 1945, most communities outside the Avalon peninsula were overwhelmingly Protestant, and, among the 265 communities on that peninsula with more than 50 people, 96 of them were almost completely Protestant and 97 were Catholic.[5]

Still today, Newfoundlanders are distinctive in the small number of them who claim no religious affiliation (3 percent, compared to a Canadian average of 24 percent). This reflects the depth of earlier conflict between Protestants and Catholics, the mobilization of religious communities in the divisive debates over Confederation, the extent to which denomination was cemented into constitutional arrangements in 1949, and the persistence of formal denominationalism in schooling until the late 1990s. In the contemporary period, too, the ranks of Protestants still include religious currents strongly linked to moral traditionalism, with

7 percent identifying as Pentacostal and the same percent affiliated to the Salvation Army, compared to 1 percent for each in the Canada-wide census.

In policy terms, denominational conflict almost always centred on schooling. English authorities had long favoured non-denominational elementary education (even if implicitly built on Protestant assumptions), and soon after the installation of representative government, the Education Act of 1836, reflected just that. Strong opposition, and the dominance of religiously based schools in the colony's early history, resulted in a new act in 1843, which conceded the denominational principle by mandating the establishment of Catholic and Protestant boards in each school district, and the allocation of public financial support in proportion to the population of each faith group.[6]

New education acts in 1874 and 1876, respectively, further entrenched this pattern, apportioning Protestant grants among several denominations. At the provincial level, this legislation created three "Denominational Superintendents" for Roman Catholics, Anglicans, and Methodists. Each of these was given twenty-four school districts, with additional concessions given to the Free Church of Scotland (two districts), the Kirk of Scotland (one), and the Congregationalists (two). Religious conflict in the lead-up to these measures, particularly evident in the 1861 election, had also led to agreement across partisan lines that denominations be proportionally represented in political office. This arrangement was secured, in part, by drawing constituency boundaries so that one or another religion would be unquestionably dominant. This political expediency, as Gunn puts it, produced a rigid sectarianism that became "the permanent rule of political life."[7]

These accommodative policies did not eliminate conflict. The implantation of the anti-Catholic Orange Order in the 1860s, and its rapid spread into the early decades of the twentieth century, helped ensure that tensions remained.[8] In Harbour Grace, a violent sectarian clash in 1883 left seven people dead. At the same time, new waves of evangelizing were crossing the island, with the Salvation Army prominent at first, then Pentecostalism. These new faiths sharpened the divide with Catholics and provoked further adjustments in school organization and funding.

Some tentative steps towards non-sectarian education came through government bills early in the twentieth century, allowing the creation of amalgamated schools in underpopulated areas, and through the 1925 opening of Memorial University College. However, school legislation in the 1920s and 1940s perpetuated denominationalism as the dominant principle by creating separate administrators in the Department of Education for Anglicans, Catholics, the newly formed United Church, and the Salvation Army. During the period of direct British rule (Commission Government) in the 1930s, proposals that would reduce the power of denominational authorities in education were met by furious (and effective) hostility from both Catholic and Anglican hierarchies.

The late 1940s debate over Confederation was deeply divisive along religious as well as social class lines.[9] The Roman Catholic archbishop of St. John's campaigned vigorously against union with Canada, advising Catholics to vote against it on the basis of fears that union would threaten Newfoundland's denominational school system. This provoked Protestant reaction, led by the province's many Orange lodges, and stoked by pro-Confederation champion Joey Smallwood. Even if the final vote cut across religious lines more than this suggests, Protestants voted disproportionately for union with Canada and for Smallwood's Liberal Party. Catholics were more likely to vote against union and for the Conservatives.[10]

By the 1960s, there was growing recognition that schooling denominationalism was inefficient and that it may have compromised the quality of education. The province eliminated many of the smallest of the 270 school boards and consolidated many schools. In 1967, the Royal Commission on Education and Youth recommended significant further changes, including a reorganization of the Department of Education on functional rather than denominational grounds, and a consolidation of school districts.[11] Predictably, the commission's proposals were resisted by Catholics, Pentecostals, and Seventh Day Adventists. Fortunately for these communities, Premier Smallwood had no interest in any fundamental change to the status quo, and the commission's recommendations went largely ignored. The Progressive Conservative administrations of the 1970s and 1980s were also just as reluctant to upset this system, with Premier Brian Peckford supporting the insertion of Section 29 in the new Charter of Rights and Freedoms to help buttress denominationalism in the school system.

Eliminating Publicly Funded Denominational Schools

By the 1980s there was even more evidence that Newfoundland and Labrador school students were not performing well, if they were attending at all.[12] Declining birth rates, population loss from outmigration, and depopulation in rural and small town coastal areas were reducing the student-aged population and amplifying inefficiencies in the existing school system. The rise of neoliberalism across much of the Western world, starting in the mid-1970s, affected Newfoundland politics by politicizing the cost of public services, particularly in the face of economic hardship.

The province's Royal Commission on Employment and Unemployment reported in 1986 and sought, as Phillip McCann put it, to "put aside any idea of a return to a 'mythical past' of independent, subsistence-based fishing outports, or to 'lost industrial dreams', and boldly go forward to 'a post-industrial society.'"[13] This vision suggested an educational system able to train "a flexible workforce with an entrepreneurial outlook suitable to the new economy." Moreover, it dovetailed with a wave of educational reforms across the continent highlighting the importance of efficient delivery aimed at preparing students for the workforce.

The province was also not immune to the forces of secularism that affected so many industrialized societies from the 1960s on, a trend accelerated by urbanization. Newfoundland may not have experienced anything quite like Quebec's Quiet Revolution, but, as McCann points out, in the 1970s it was shifting dramatically: "If in 1949 Newfoundlanders could be considered localized, frugal, God-fearing, and socially conservative, by the 1990s they had become urbanized, secular-minded, better educated members of the consumer society."[14] Galway and Dibbon have a similar view, arguing that, in the 1970s and 1980s, societal values moved significantly away from a "religious-communal" orientation towards individualism.[15] Church attendance declined in most denominations, as did the number of candidates for ministry and the preparedness of people to treat religious leaders as the source of unquestioning moral guidance.[16] In 1989, the sexual abuse scandal at the Catholic-operated

Mount Cashel orphanage exploded into view, accompanied by growing evidence of this being widespread in the church far beyond the shores of Newfoundland and Labrador. Investigations of abuse had been launched in 1975 and 1982 but became more public as evidence emerged of sustained failures by the police, the provincial Ministry of Justice, and the church itself to take allegations seriously. The damage to the Catholic Church's reputation was lasting and continued long after the government closed Mount Cashel in 1990.

The election of Clyde Wells's Liberals in 1989 provided an opening for more fundamental change than had been contemplated before, and, in 1990, another Royal Commission on education was appointed under the leadership of Len Williams, a former president of the Newfoundland Teachers Association and a known reformer. The commission's own surveys indicated that, by this time, 60 percent of the province's population supported a single non-denominational system, even if most also favoured the teaching of religion in schools and the protection of church rights.[17]

The 1992 Williams Commission report recommended that the denominational system be replaced with an "inter-denominational" one, combined with a provision that, where numbers warranted, students would be provided with opportunities to participate in religious activities and instruction in their own faith.[18] The government embarked on an extensive consultation with church communities, but it was soon evident that agreement would be difficult. The Roman Catholic Church soon placed ads in newspapers supporting Catholic education, and other voices raised the alarm about "godless" schools.

The Wells government, re-elected in 1993, formulated a complex proposal leaving room for separate denominational schools where numbers warranted. The government put the plan to a referendum in 1995, prompting a widespread campaign against the changes by Catholics, Pentecostals, and Seventh Day Adventists, who stoked fears that school prayer and Christmas celebrations would be banned. Both political parties were divided, and the Progressive Conservative leader tried to broker internal differences by opposing the government proposal on what might be called the peripheral ground that it did not do enough to eliminate religious discrimination within the school system.[19] In the end, only 55 percent of referendum voters supported the proposal, and six Liberal assembly members went on to vote against the enabling legislation brought forward by their own government.[20]

The new order turned out to be administratively complex, producing turmoil that was compounded when Catholics and Pentecostals were successful in demanding a court injunction.[21] The issue was bounced back into the hands of the new Liberal government of Brian Tobin, who was elected in early 1996. This time, however, the premier was emboldened by the absence of sustained popular opposition to the elimination of denominational schools during the election campaign. Tobin moved ahead with a more sweeping schooling reform than his predecessor had dared to present, and this time he had the full support not only of his caucus, including prominent Roman Catholic and Pentecostal members, but also the Progressive Conservative and NDP opposition.

Another referendum was called in 1997 based on the question: "Do you support a single school system where all children, regardless of their religious affiliation, attend the same schools where religious education and observances are provided?" This was a clear recognition of the continuing popular support for some form of religious practice in the schools, but it would sweep away a century-and-a-half-old denominational system. This time, the popular approval jumped to 73 percent. A formal constitutional amendment was then encoded in provincial and federal legislation, and the new regime was inaugurated in 1998. Opposition from Roman Catholic quarters continued, but attempts to reverse the move through court action finally ran out of steam (and judicial support) in 2001.[22]

Persistent Denominational Differences in Voting for Liberals and Conservatives

This educational reform reflected a major reduction in the political influence of denominational distinctions, though not their complete elimination. In so much of the post-Second World War (and post-Confederation) period, Liberal success in Protestant areas and PC success in Catholic ones was locked in by an electoral system still designed to elevate religious representation above all other factors, even if attempts to draw district boundaries to differentiate Catholic, Anglican, and

Methodist/United Church electorates had already become more difficult in practice than they appeared in theory.[23] In fact, sectarian distinctiveness persisted through long periods without any obvious religious conflict over substantive issues, and, indeed, party leaders shared a strong interest in keeping such contention out of politics. However, religious divisions were reinforced by the infusion of denominationalism into all manner of political appointments and by everyday segregation. Writing in the 1970s, Susan McCorquadale pointed to the fact that "they go to the same schools, they play sports together (and against other schools which are at the same time other denominations), they inter-marry and they inter-dine."[24] It was also kept in place by memories of conflict over schools, never so far in the past that they could not be vividly recalled. Analyses of the 1972 election by McCorquadale and Mark Graesser show that religion was still the most powerful predictor of party choice at the provincial level.[25]

Yet McCorquadale also points to change, for example, in the religious make-up of provincial party caucuses. Across the first two postwar decades, the PC caucus had been 80 percent Catholic, and the Liberal caucus only 26 percent. In 1976, however, the PC caucus was only 43 percent Catholic, and the Liberal 35 percent.[26] Frank Moores, who won the Premier's Office in the 1971 election, was himself an unusual Progressive Conservative leader, being a Protestant from outside St. John's. The collapse of the cod fishery in the 1990s, and the discovery of offshore oil, contributed to the gradual erosion of the kind of personalistic and clientelistic politics that had kept party alignments relatively stable.

Still, Graesser observes strong denominational influences on partisan sorting in the 1989 election, even in a period without discernible policy differences reflecting denominational affiliation.[27] Since then, this pattern has continued, though with increasingly muted tones. In the 2011 election, as Table 3.1 shows, Catholic voters still disproportionately favoured the Progressive Conservative Party – and shunned the Liberals – even if there were no indications that religion was playing a significant role in the nomination of local candidates or the selection of party leaders.[28] As such, the tenacity of the denominational differentiation of parties seems more the result of antique subcultural habits than of contemporary political disagreements. It is also worth noting that, in

Table 3.1   Vote choice within religious groups in Newfoundland and Labrador, 2011

	Liberals (%)	PCs (%)	NDP (%)	Total (n)
Denomination				
Roman Catholic	10	60	29	191 (100%)
Mainline Protestant	22	55	23	258 (100%)
Evangelical	19	59	22	27 (100%)
Other	34	26	40	62 (100%)
Unaffiliated/atheist	10	36	55	104 (100%)
Total	17	52	30	642 (100%)
Importance of religion				
Very important	22	61	17	152 (100%)
Somewhat important	21	54	25	265 (100%)
Somewhat unimportant	12	45	43	108 (100%)
Very unimportant	14	40	46	117 (100%)
Total	17	52	30	642 (100%)

Note: "Other" category includes Muslims and Jews.
Source: Jared Wesley et al., Canadian Provincial Election Project, http://cpep.ualberta.ca/.

response to a survey asking respondents to place themselves on a 10-point moral traditionalism scale, with 1 as the conservative pole and 10 the progressive, PC and Liberal supporters were almost indistinguishable, at 5.8 and 5.7, respectively. Only New Democrats were noticeably different, averaging 7.2, and, not surprisingly, they attracted a much higher proportion of supporters who score the lowest on our measures of religiosity.

The Relative Absence of Conflict over Abortion and Sexual Diversity

One might have expected that the gradual weakening of religious segregation in Newfoundland and Labrador society, and that the slow but uneven decline of denominational "sorting" into different political parties, would have created room for the kind of faith realignment we have seen in federal politics – one in which moral and religious trad-itionalists gravitate to one party over issues such as reproduction and sexual diversity. In fact, though, it did not. The 2011 provincial election study found that both the Liberals and the PCs drew disproportionately from those who saw religion as very important in their lives, while such voters were much less likely to support the NDP. Likewise, while the sample of evangelicals in the study was small enough to warn against precise interpretation, the numbers suggest a tilt towards to the PCs, but with the Liberals retaining some strength among them. This does not suggest as strong a voting concentration in one party as we have seen at the federal level and that we will see in some other provincial party systems.

The political management of the divisiveness associated with repro-duction and sexual diversity was long sustained by a socially conservative two-party consensus among the Liberals and Progressive Conservatives. It was conservative first in the sense that established restrictions on abor-tion and exclusions of sexual minorities from legal recognition were not seriously challenged. It was also conservative in the reluctance of the major parties, which alternated in political power, to support policy changes that would risk mobilizing religious constituencies around hot button issues. When changes did come, they had usually been suffi-ciently delayed that they were accomplished without much cross-party contention.

In Newfoundland and Labrador, women's access to abortion re-mained very limited after federal legislation partially decriminalized it in 1969. After 1988, when the Supreme Court of Canada struck down the restrictive regulations still in place, the Newfoundland and Labrador government, like other Atlantic provincial governments, maintained as much resistance as it could. This provincial defiance led to another court ruling in 1993 that effectively ended such resistance. Even so, full fund-ing for the two hospitals and single free-standing clinic with abortion services was provided only in 1998, at which time public opinion in the province was roughly in line with prevailing views across Canada.[29]

The abortion issue surfaced briefly during the lead-up to a Progres-sive Conservative Party leadership convention in early 2014, when the front-running candidate assured voters that his own strong pro-life views would not be imposed on provincial policy making. Reactions from Liberal and NDP leaders made clear their parties' respective adherence to a pro-choice position, and there was every indication that most PC legislators had no interest in reopening political debate on the issue.[30] In response to increasingly intense protests around abortion clinics, the government announced in mid-2016 that it would establish a protest-free bubble zone modelled on earlier legislation in British Columbia.

A similar pattern played out in the area of lesbian and gay rights. Like the other Atlantic provinces, Newfoundland and Labrador was slow to incorporate sexual orientation into its human rights code, generally the first significant LGBT issue to arise within provincial jurisdiction.[31] Advocates of equity began ramping up pressure for change in 1985, and in 1988 they won the support of the provincial Human Rights Commission. But the PC government pointedly left sexual orientation out of amendments to the code in 1988, by which time there was significant momentum for change in other Canadian provinces. The 1989 election brought a new Liberal government, but even then Premier Clyde Wells, though widely seen as influenced by Pierre Trudeau's views on rights, resisted arguments that the Charter would eventually be found to prohibit discrimination based on sexual orientation. His justice minister worried about lesbian/gay teachers and child care workers, this in a time when revelations of abuse at Mount Cashel orphanage were surfacing. Not surprisingly, the provincial Conservatives were disinclined either to raise the issue or to support a change if introduced.

In 1993, the Human Rights Commission extended rights protections to lesbians and gays by reading sexual orientation into the province's Human Rights Code, and two years later its right to make the change was upheld in court against a government challenge. Only after Liberal Brian Tobin took over as premier was legislation passed, with the support of all parties, to explicitly amend the code in 1997. In 2000, the government brought in changes to family law in response to the Supreme Court of Canada's 1999 ruling, *M. v. H.*, which prohibited discrimination against lesbian and gay couples, though it would be another two years before it took additional steps that included adoption rights. From then on, resistance to change pertaining to LGBT rights seemed to recede, making policy moves relatively uncontentious. In contrast to the situation in New Brunswick, the Progressive Conservative government of Danny Williams made it clear, once marriage rights were legislatively encoded in 2005, that marriage commissioners could not refuse to officiate. In 2013, Conservative Premier Kathy Dunderdale's government brought forward legislation to add gender identity and expression to the province's Human Rights Code, again without much controversy.

Neither abortion nor sexual diversity, then, became a source of partisan differentiation between Liberals and Progressive Conservatives when pressure for change arose either from social movement advocacy or court rulings. By the time, following the 2011 election, that the NDP temporarily became a force in provincial politics, an accommodative pattern had emerged that reduced or eliminated opposition to reform from within the other two parties. As a result, neither of the two major parties provided an enduring set of signals that it was the natural home of moral traditionalists.

The Intermingling of Religion and Language in New Brunswick

New Brunswick has the largest proportion of Roman Catholics in the Atlantic region, constituting about 50 percent of the population. This community is itself evenly divided between francophones and anglophones, and the province is unique in the region for the extent to which language-group divisions gradually became more prominent than religiously based divisions, even if religious sectarianism was not eliminated. The 2011 census found that, while only 2 percent of New Brunswickers classified themselves as evangelical, 10 percent were Baptist, a denomination that, in its social conservatism, has been broadly allied with evangelicals. Only 8 percent declared no religious affiliation, considerably lower than the 24 percent Canadian average.

For the first three-quarters of the twentieth century, little appeared to have changed in the province's political life. As P.J. Fitzpatrick wrote in 1972:

> Provincial politics in New Brunswick might best be described as parochial, stagnant, and anachronistic – reminiscent, in some ways,

of politics in nineteenth-century Britain before the reform movement. The Liberal and Progressive Conservative parties dominate the political environment ... traditionally sustained by gerrymandering, patronage, and constituencies with hereditary political loyalties kept intact by ancient ethnic and religious antagonisms.[32]

In describing the depth of partisan attachments and antipathies, he adds: "to a British Protestant New Brunswicker of United Empire Loyalist stock ... the idea of voting Liberal might well be unthinkable, an act of cultural treachery equivalent to conversion to Roman Catholicism."

Catholic-Protestant opposition had been prominent since well before Confederation. Linguistic issues arrived later, becoming central to the province's politics from the 1910s on and continuing as such until the 1980s. Parties sometimes played on these divisions, though, by the late nineteenth century, a pattern of shaky compromise had developed on schooling. From the 1960s on, accommodative approaches, especially to language tension, became more continuously applied within both the Liberal Party and the Progressive Conservative Party, even though this did not completely eliminate contention or the lingering influence of ancestral attachments to one party or another.

Religion, Schooling, and Party Attachment
The Orange Order planted itself in the pre-Confederation colony early and powerfully, fuelling religious tensions sufficiently to provoke riots in Woodstock and St. John in 1847 and 1849. In the decades to follow, separate school issues became more than ever a focus of political contention. As in Newfoundland and Labrador, conflict intensified during the 1860s and 1870s, particularly in the wake of the Common Schools Act, 1871, which established a single public system and prohibited religious instruction. The system became the focus of the 1874 election, prolonging tension between Catholics and Protestants and between Acadians and anglophones. In 1875, deadly riots in Caraquet arose from the clash between Catholics opposed to government intransigence and Protestants fearful of population growth among Acadians and Catholics.

Sobriety returned long enough for the government to add two Roman Catholics to the cabinet in 1876. An unofficial compromise was developed, where particular public schools were known to be Catholic or Protestant and allowed to remain as such. In fact, in Catholic-dominated areas, schools could be rented from the church, which was involved in the selection of teachers and delivering religious instruction (after hours). This approach was similar to that put into place in Nova Scotia and PEI, but many Protestants vehemently opposed the arrangements, and, in 1890, Orange lodges attempted to make the system an election issue. The effort, however, was unsuccessful, with the governing Liberals remaining in power. The party then once again prevailed in the 1895 election with a campaign advocating cooperation across religious lines against an opposition promoting unequivocal Protestant domination.[33]

By this time, the Liberals had forged an alliance that rallied the great majority of Acadian votes, along with significant numbers of English-speaking Catholics and moderate Protestants. Protestants not only remained dominant in the provincial Conservative Party but also continued to be a formidable extra-parliamentary force well into the twentieth century. The Orange Order grew rapidly in the last two decades of the nineteenth century, rising from eighty-five active lodges in 1880 to 119 in 1900, and continued its expansion into the 1930s. In the late nineteenth and early twentieth centuries, Protestant activism beyond these lodges had also been mobilized in favour of restricting alcohol and gambling, with evangelicals in the lead. An 1898 national plebiscite on prohibition then amplified Protestant-Catholic divisions. As Edmund Aunger points out, the New Brunswick Baptist Convention characterized the debate over temperance as pitting "moral law-abiding Christian citizens" against "the saloon keeper, the brewer, the fallen inebriate and Rome."[34]

Aunger, however, also emphasizes the accommodationism in New Brunswick politics. He describes the 1875 Caraquet riots as having a lasting impact, and he highlights the victories of political moderates in elections that featured Protestant majoritarian demands. Local controversies, over language in particular, endured through most of the twentieth century, but at the provincial level he suggests that schooling stopped being a major source of political controversy in 1935. The Catholicism of the Liberal Party leader had become a major issue in the election of that year, but this had not prevented the Liberals from winning.

From the 1960s on, the same kind of school reorganization and consolidation that was applied in other parts of Atlantic Canada also reduced the capacity to retain religious distinctions as a tool for political mobilization. By as early as the mid-1970s, enrolment in Catholic-rented buildings, the mechanism that had long secured de facto Catholic schools, had declined to 4 percent of total provincial enrolment. As in Newfoundland and Labrador, the increase in publicity around abusive patterns in Catholic orphanages had a lasting impact on Catholic feelings towards religious authorities and weakened their religiously based loyalty to Catholic institutions.

The Emergence of Divisions on Language and Culture

From the late nineteenth century on, the axis of political division in New Brunswick began to shift in the direction of language issues, propelled in part by an Acadian "national awakening" in the 1870s and 1880s. Starting in the 1890s, nationalist focus was on increasing the use of French in the church. In this the Acadians frequently clashed with Irish Catholics as well as with a hierarchy that remained English speaking and resistant to the use of French until the 1920s.[35]

In the first two decades of the new century, Acadians also mobilized to increase the teaching of French in public schools. As in Ontario, this led to significant resistance, enough that a 1925 government proposal to establish bilingual schools was withdrawn after protest, with the issue left for local school districts to resolve. Orange Order Protestants, not surprisingly, opposed any official recognition of French.

Ethnic contention seemed to have abated after the Second World War, helped by a decline in the political influence of the Orange Order, but tensions arose once again in the 1960s. Nationalist revival in Acadia (alongside that in Quebec) was increasing demands for French language recognition in schooling and provincial government administration, and these were being met by increasing anglophone resistance in the general public. Such divisions were reinforced by geographical and economic segregation between the Acadian-dominated north and northeast, which was comparatively disadvantaged, and the anglophone-dominated south and southwest, which was economically better off.

The province's 1960 election saw the defeat of the incumbent Progressive Conservative government and its replacement by the Liberal Party, which was led by the Acadian Louis Robichaud. During Robichaud's decade in office, the Liberal government secured the approval of an official languages act, which, in part, responded to schooling demands, and an "equal opportunity" program aimed at significantly improving the economic standing of Acadians. These victories for the Acadian population intensified backlash among some of the province's anglophones. During this decade, too, there were Progressive Conservative Party legislators who were willing to play to such sentiment, particularly from 1966 to 1970, under the leadership of Charles Van Horne. But the party itself had not formally opposed official linguistic equality. This response was perhaps informed by the accommodationist instincts pointed out by Aunger, but it was also affected by the growing recognition in federal politics that language group tension, and francophone nationalist discontent, required political attention. This was much more evident when Progressive Conservative Richard Hatfield took over the Premier's Office in 1970. He continued governmental support for official bilingualism and secured passage of stronger language guarantees in 1981 and 1982, respectively.[36] He also worked to shift his own party away from its traditional demographic moorings and to broaden its appeal to francophones, an approach that paralleled the policies of Ontario Progressive Conservatives under John Robarts. New Brunswick's Progressive Conservatives (as well as Liberals) tried to select local candidates who reflected the ethno-religious character of their constituencies, making for only rare contests in which anglophone and francophone candidates opposed one another. Such accommodation was not altogether new, but it was now more stable and was accompanied by an even greater preoccupation with avoiding public discord on ethnoreligious lines.

This accommodationism may well have been reinforced by the visibility and stridency of the public resistance to official bilingualism.

During the 1960s and 1970s, for example, Moncton mayor Leonard Jones garnered national news for his vitriolic opposition to the recognition of French. In the mid-1980s, similar bitterness greeted a provincial inquiry into the impact of the province's language legislation. When the commission reported that there was little real bilingualism in New Brunswick's central provincial administration, and that French language services had to be extended, anglophone mobilization increased. The strength of anglophone resentment was also made evident in the 1991 provincial election when the Confederation of Regions Party (CoR) scored an "astonishing breakthrough" to become the official opposition. The party won 21 percent of the popular vote and 8 seats, largely on the promise not to modify but to abolish official bilingualism.[37]

These linguistic divides contributed to internal divisions among Progressive Conservatives, and even among Liberals, reflected in clearly distinguishable language group differences in support for leadership hopefuls. For example, in the 1997 Progressive Conservative leadership race, Bernard Lord (the victor) was supported by 67 percent of francophones voting in the first ballot and only 26 percent of anglophones.[38] Yet, despite the persistence of this pattern, the leadership of both parties remained committed to relatively accommodationist policies. Liberal premier Frank McKenna, serving from 1987 to 1997, stuck firmly to an expansion of French language services. Bernard Lord handily won the 1999 election for the PCs, extended official bilingualism in the health sector, and worked in other ways to move his party beyond its traditional English-speaking Protestant base.[39]

Denominational and Language Differences in the Electorate

William Cross argues that the traditional ethnic and religious electorates of the two parties remained largely intact until about the time that Lord took over the PC leadership, despite attempts by other leaders of both parties before him to broaden their appeals.[40] And, in the view of Jacques Poitras, the 2003 campaign seemed to suggest a significant reduction in the ethno-religious distinctiveness of each major party's electorate: "Maybe, just maybe, that old diagonal line cutting across the centre of the province would no longer determine the outcome of elections."[41]

Table 3.2 Vote choice within religious groups in New Brunswick, 2014

	Liberals *(%)*	*PCs* *(%)*	*NDP* *(%)*	*Total* *(n)*	
Denomination					
Roman Catholic	59	32	9	181	(100%)
Mainline Protestant	36	49	15	89	(100%)
Other	46	31	24	51	(100%)
Unaffiliated/atheist	37	27	36	92	(100%)
Total	47	35	18	413	(100%)
Importance of religion					
Very important	42	46	12	115	(100%)
Somewhat important	45	40	15	135	(100%)
Somewhat unimportant	55	25	20	99	(100%)
Very unimportant	33	23	45	123	(100%)
Total	43	34	23	472	(100%)

Notes: Only supporters of the three major parties are included. Only 1.5 percent of the total sample declared non-Christian religion. The low number of evangelical respondents resulted in large differences between the raw results (75 percent support for the PCs) and those obtained when the data were weighted by region (60 percent support for the NDP). As such, the evangelical respondents are excluded from the analysis.
Source: Jared Wesley et al., Canadian Provincial Election Project, http://cpep.ualberta.ca/.

Does this suggest that Protestant-Catholic distinctions have essentially disappeared in provincial politics – if it is even possible to fully disentangle them from language? Joanna Everitt argues that Protestant and Catholic affiliations still count in shaping the Liberal and Progressive Conservative identifications of many voters: "Divisions are weaker than they were in the past, but they are far more obvious now here in New Brunswick than they ever were in Ontario thirty years ago."[42] Indeed, as Table 3.2 shows, there are clear signs of a continued preference for the Liberals among Catholics and for the PCs among mainline Protestants.

However, a more detailed examination of the results of the 2014 provincial election study shows that the denominational differences separating PCs and Liberals now appear to be primarily a function of language. The Liberals received the support of 62 percent of francophone

Catholics in 2014, contributing to that party's retention of a majority of Catholics overall, whereas only 24 percent supported the Progressive Conservatives. But the Liberals drew just 27 percent support among English-speaking Catholics, versus 39 percent for the PCs – exactly the same proportion of English-speaking Protestants who voted Progressive Conservative.

The Persistent Political Influence of Religious Conservatism

Table 3.2 indicates that religiosity has only a modest impact on preference for the two major parties, though the Conservatives do fare disproportionally well among those for whom religion is relatively important. Here, as in Newfoundland and Labrador, New Democrats are quite distinct. One factor militating against a sharper contrast among the two major parties is that Progressive Conservatives in New Brunswick, and more generally in the Atlantic region, did not swing to the free-market ideological pole in the way that rightist parties did in Ontario and western Canada from the 1990s on. They retained a form of centrist toryism that still supported, for example, a significant role for state authority.[43] And at the same time, both of New Brunswick's major parties remained hesitant to alienate moral traditionalists in a province with Canada's highest rural population.

New Brunswick was until very recently one of the two provinces in which major restrictions on access to abortion remained in place (PEI being the other). Pro-life activism in the province was strong enough to narrow access to abortion within its borders during the 1980s and to ensure that the government continued to limit abortion services after the Supreme Court of Canada struck down the 1969 Criminal Code restrictions on access. In 1982, Henry Morgentaler announced that he would open free-standing abortion clinics across Canada. That same year, the New Brunswick Right to Life Association mustered thirty-three thousand signatures for a proclamation published in all five New Brunswick dailies calling for absolute respect for all family life. Among the signatories were 119 of the province's eight hundred medical doctors.[44] For some time, pro-life advocacy was reinforced by the Knights of Columbus, which poured considerable resources into the struggle.[45] Such pressure was sufficient for the Moncton Hospital, which had been performing two-thirds of the operations in the province, to suspend the service for six months in 1982, restoring it only after 98 percent of hospital staff voted in favour of doing so. Between 1980 and 1984, the number of hospitals with therapeutic abortion committees, required under the partial decriminalization enacted by Parliament in 1969, declined from seven to three and, in subsequent years, slipped to two.

In 1984, Richard Hatfield's Progressive Conservative government easily secured passage of legislation prohibiting abortions outside hospitals and requiring the agreement of two doctors (in writing) that the procedure was medically necessary.[46] The Liberal government of Frank McKenna, elected in 1987, continued its support for that law. In 1989, a year after the Supreme Court of Canada struck down the Criminal Code restrictions on abortion, the Liberals responded to Morgentaler's efforts to ease access to the procedure for New Brunswick women by reinforcing those restrictions. Resistance to change continued even after 1995, when New Brunswick's Court of Appeal upheld a lower court ruling that the province had no right to restrict abortions to hospitals and when the federal government threatened to withdraw Canada Health Act transfers.[47] A free-standing clinic was opened in Fredericton in 1994, but the government remained firm in its resolve to not fund abortions performed at it, with Premier McKenna promising Henry Morgentaler "the fight of his life."[48] His government and successor administrations, both Liberal and PC, then used every possible tactic to delay the resolution of a court challenge fought by Morgentaler until his death in 2013. By then New Brunswick was one of just two provinces officially denying funding for free-standing clinics (again, PEI being the other) and the only one that deployed the policy specifically for abortion clinics. Writing in 2012, Rachael Johnstone was struck at the political silence surrounding the issue, reinforced by what one clinic volunteer maintained was the prevalence of "religiously motivated, socially traditional views."[49]

This silence was broken in 2014, when the Morgentaler clinic announced that financial difficulties were forcing it to close its doors. At about the same time, a Liberal Party policy convention had approved a resolution that proposed an easing of access to abortion. Soon after both developments, Liberal leader Brian Gallant declared his personal view that the existing provincial policy was too restrictive and urged Progressive Conservative premier David Alward to review it.[50] Gallant claimed that he was not imposing his views on the rest of the caucus, and soon after, in May of that year, five of the thirteen Liberal MLAs appeared at a pro-life rally.

Unsurprisingly, NDP leader Dominic Cardy sided with pro-choice advocates and was fully prepared to point out divisions inside the Liberal tent. The PC premier declared his party's continuing opposition to change. But, with an election coming up that September, Gallant decided to harden his stance by following in the footsteps of federal Liberal leader Justin Trudeau and declaring that the party's candidates would be expected to support pro-choice governmental policy on the matter.[51]

The Liberals won the election, which had mostly centred on economic development issues even though it was stalked by the abortion question. The new premier had promised no concrete steps towards reform, though party insiders talked of dealing with the issue "swiftly and cleanly" so that it did not to continue to haunt the policy-making process.[52] In November, the government eliminated the requirements that two doctors approve the procedure and that it be performed only by specialists. There was no change, however, in the government's refusal to fund abortions at free-standing clinics, and talk of expanding hospital access in the end produced only one additional institution in a city (Moncton) that was home to one of the only two hospitals that was already providing service. These two were in the French hospital network, and the additional service was to come from the only institution in the English network willing to take it on. There had been discussions of offering service in Fredericton and St. John as well as Moncton, but hospital administrations there dropped out, partly because staff "safety" concerns had increased cost estimates. There was also particular worry in St. John about reactions from its "significant Irish Catholic community."[53] Even faced with the modesty of the change ultimately delivered, the health minister made clear the government's refusal to fund abortions outside hospitals. A new clinic did open in the former Morgentaler site, providing abortions as well as health services explicitly targeting the LGBT community, but it was still going to face the financial challenges produced by the provincial policy.[54]

The Liberals' caution undoubtedly came from continuing differences within the party itself as well as from public uncertainty. A 2011 survey showed that support for banning abortion was somewhat higher (32 percent) in New Brunswick than across Canada (25 percent).[55] Polling in 2015 revealed that just under half of New Brunswickers (48 percent) supported abortion being available in the first three months of pregnancy, up only modestly from 42 percent in 2008.[56] On the other hand, the 2014 provincial election study shows that 70 percent of New Brunswick respondents (and almost the same percent of Roman Catholics) believed that the government should make abortion services more accessible to women, 41 percent strongly agreeing.[57] By the time of the election the Liberals had fairly strong support for change in their own electorate. Fifty-five percent of Liberals strongly supported increased accessibility, higher even than the 37 percent of New Democrats and much higher than the 22 percent of PCs. Conversely, agreement came from only 8 percent of Liberals and a full third of PC supporters. Prior to this election, there would have been no strong incentive for pro-life voters to gravitate towards the PCs, but the Liberals' positioning on abortion may well have contributed to some reshuffling in the faith composition of the major party's electorates.

Consensual Caution on LGBT Rights
The story of the policy response to lesbian and gay advocacy is somewhat different from that of abortion policy, with change coming late and gradually enough to reduce conflict between the Liberal and Progressive Conservative parties.[58] It was the Liberal government of Frank McKenna that took the first significant steps towards inclusive policy after winning office in 1988. By that time, LGBT advocates had begun significant mobilization, and so had opponents. The Confederation of Regions Party, riding a wave of opposition to official bilingualism, was more than eager to ally itself with religious conservatives in opposing any initiative recognizing lesbian and gay rights. A bill adding sexual orientation to the province's human rights code was finally introduced and voted on in 1992. The measure was supported by the PCs as well as the New Democrats, with only CoR's MLAs opposing. The PCs' willingness to support the bill may well have been motivated in part by the

dangers they saw in the polarizing debate over bilingualism fuelled by CoR and the aversion to such divisiveness among Liberals and PCs alike.

This non-partisan incrementalism was also evident on most other fronts related to LGBT rights. The government extended provincial civil service benefit plans to include same-sex partners in 1993, at a time when tribunals were clearly prohibiting their exclusion. It resisted granting full parental rights until obliged to do so in a 2004 human rights challenge, years after other court rulings had made the unconstitutionality of such discrimination crystal clear. The province's Human Rights Commission has issued guidelines that provide some protection against trans discrimination, but no government has so far advanced legislation to provide a more comprehensive response. Birth certificates in the province continue to use gendered categories in asking for parental information.[59]

There were more adventurous policy change in 2014, though here, too, only when cross-party consensus was attained. While the Progressive Conservatives were still in government, the Department of Education implemented a policy that assured students the right to form gay-straight alliances (GSAs) in schools, and it worked with Egale Canada and the provincial Pride in Education Group to create training materials for teachers.[60] This followed contentious debates in Ontario and Alberta over GSAs and a growing chorus of criticism aimed at educational authorities for their insufficient response to homophobic and transphobic harassment. Compared to changes on other fronts, these reforms were not as slow to emerge in New Brunswick as they were in some other jurisdictions, and they were facilitated by the absence of opposition from any of the established parties. The reluctance of the PCs in particular to side with moral traditionalists was central to this process.

Such reluctance is especially notable in light of the results of the 2014 election study, which found that PC supporters were significantly less likely (29 percent) to support progressive positions on such issues as sexual diversity and abortion than were other partisans (65 percent of Liberals and 72 percent of New Democrats).[61] The relatively moderate position of the party leadership, then, would seem to have come from the accommodationist pattern that had largely shaped that party since the 1960s, even with evidence of the provincial PCs attracting a dispro-portionate number of supporters with morally traditionalist views.

Conclusion

As recently as the late 1980s, Reginald Bibby argued that Canada's most prominent Bible belt was the Atlantic region, but, in fact, the evidence for this is now mixed.[62] Kurt Bowen's 1997 survey shows that the pro-portion of the population that counted as "very committed" religiously in the Atlantic region was 26 percent, only slightly higher than Ontario (at 22 percent) and the Prairies (at 23 percent).[63] David Eagler tracked changes from 1986 to 2008, suggesting that Atlantic Canada had moved towards the secularized average in English Canada, primarily a result of a dramatic decline in Roman Catholic church attendance. Protestant church attendance remained stable across the region at around 13 percent, but Catholic church attendance plummeted from 41 to 13 percent.[64]

Public opinion polling on abortion and sexual diversity now shows little significant difference between the Atlantic region and the rest of the country. Back in 2002, when a Gallup Poll asked whether respondents personally believed that abortion was morally acceptable or wrong, 57 percent of Atlantic region respondents thought it wrong, the highest disapproving number of any region in the country, and significantly higher than the 40 percent Canadian average.[65] However, a 2007 survey finds that disapproval was lower in the region than in Canada as a whole, while another in 2012 shows little deviation from the Canadian average, with 46 percent of Atlantic Canadians supporting abortion "whenever a woman decides she wants one," compared to a Canadian average of 49 percent.[66] Across the region, 64 percent supported same-sex marriage as equal to conventional heterosexual marriage, just above the 62 percent support across the country.[67]

Overall, it appears that, throughout most of the twentieth century, traditionalist attitudes did have more hold in the Atlantic provinces than in most other parts of Canada, which may help to explain the slow pace of change in the stances taken by most of the region's major parties. Yet much has changed in the region over the past twenty years, includ-ing in Newfoundland and Labrador and New Brunswick, virtually eliminating the political relevance of age-old denominational affiliations even if they retain faded empirical traces. In both places, the attitudes that once helped mobilize religious conservatives across Canada have also been changing, and they now sit at about the Canadian average.

In this chapter we focus on two provincial stories rather than imagining a single regional narrative. In Newfoundland and Labrador we could see just how tenacious denominational considerations were in provincial politics and also how resistant both major political parties were to policy change on schooling and sexuality. In New Brunswick, denominational differences were overtaken by discord over language, and even if Catholic and Protestant identification still matters socially, it seems to have left no important traces in either of the major parties. Language does, certainly, but it now seems almost entirely stripped of religious baggage.

For decades, Liberals and Progressive Conservatives in both these provinces maintained a political order that institutionalized distinctions between Protestants and Catholics, especially in Newfoundland and Labrador. Patterns of denominational accommodation that were put into place as a result of bitter nineteenth-century conflict, in other words, secured denominational recognition in the life of each of the major parties in the two provinces, once again, especially in Newfoundland and Labrador. Economic change, rationalization in government administration, the need for efficiencies in public education, and declining religiosity all contributed to the slow reduction in these patterns.

Memories of religious contention (and, in New Brunswick, language-group conflict) helped develop forms of accommodation and pragmatism that in some ways perpetuated denominational consciousness in provincial politics. Such patterns also helped create a cross-party consensus among Liberals and Progressive Conservatives on avoiding issues that would mobilize religious traditionalists. The comparative weakness of the NDP, except sporadically in Newfoundland and Labrador, meant that a potential source of reformist pressure on one or another of the dominant parties was limited. On abortion in particular, resistance to change in New Brunswick might be partly explained by the substantial size of the Roman Catholic population. We know that most Catholics are not regular mass attenders or faithful adherents to church doctrine, but, in parts of Atlantic Canada, the voice of bishops has been augmented by evangelical voices – including Baptists in New Brunswick, and Pente-costals and Salvation Army followers in Newfoundland and Labrador, and the many social conservatives in mainline Protestant churches across the region.

The traditionalism that so slowed the response to changes in legisla-tion on reproduction and sexual diversity has been fed until quite re-cently by low rates of economic growth and by ongoing population stability. Immigrants to Canada, for decades, have chosen other parts of the country over the Atlantic region, with Halifax a very partial excep-tion. All this reinforces traditionalism as a pervasive thread in the region's political culture.

The new morality politics of the post-1960s period seems to have had very little impact on party alignment in Newfoundland and Labrador, but it does seem to have made visible a difference between Progressive Conservatives and Liberals in New Brunswick. This may have been in progress for some years, but, until 2014, party leaders avoided adopting positions significantly at odds with one another, continuing the accom-modationist pattern that has been such a hallmark of that province's major political parties. By and large, the tradition of pragmatic centrism and conflict-avoidance evident across the Atlantic region has dominated Liberal and Conservative parties here as well as in Newfoundland and Labrador.

Ontario's Progressive Conservatives and Tenacious Denominational Politics, 1943–85

4

Ontario's postwar history vividly illustrates the tenacity of denominational distinctions in the electorates of the province's major parties. Until the mid-1980s, that history also provides ample evidence of persistent Catholic-Protestant contention and its capacity to differentiate partisan appeals. All of this was in a period marked by dramatic secularization and by a party system characterized by pragmatic centrism, which, yes, reduced the capacity of denominational contention to inflame electoral politics. But conflict persisted over the long-vexed question of Catholic school funding, an issue that still surfaces in Ontario provincial politics today.

This chapter highlights the place of religiously based conflict in a period of transition from a society in which Christian faith was taken for granted to one in which religious faith was in dramatic decline and being visibly reshaped by waves of non-Christian immigration. It focuses on the Ontario Progressive Conservative Party, primarily because it was the governing party in Ontario from 1943 until 1985 and because its postwar history illustrates the influence of its traditional strengths among Protestants. Near the end of its unbroken period of governance, at which point PC premier William Davis dramatically proposed a "resolution" of the school funding issue, the religious right was becoming a political presence in provincial affairs. However, Davis's disinclination to focus on the hot button issues that most energized the moral conservatism of American Republicans helped keep such questions off the legislative and electoral agenda, and the opposition parties did not aggressively seek a confrontation on them. In Ontario, then, the politicization of faith was until the 1980s an almost entirely denominational affair.

Our analysis starts by tracking the recurrent political conflicts centred on schooling issues from the nineteenth century through to the 1980s. This analysis ends with PC premier William Davis reversing his party's long-standing resistance to extending full funding to Catholic schools and overseeing its gradual acquiescence to the elimination of religious instructions in public schools. After the endless rancour over denominational schools, all parties wanted to put aside any policy position likely to arouse the religiously based passions that had so persisted on that axis.

The Context of Postwar Contention

Like the Atlantic region, Ontario has a sizable Roman Catholic population – 31 percent of the total – giving it the potential for electoral influence. There is also a substantial number of francophones among those identifying as Catholic, and even if demands for the right to French-language education have often been voiced by those with no particular allegiance to Catholic education as such, their advocacy has more often than not reinforced claims made to secure the separate school system. An additional source of political leverage has come from the fact that the province's Catholic population has been regularly fuelled by non-francophone immigration. From the mid-nineteenth century on, huge numbers of Irish Catholic immigrants settled in Ontario, and, over the course of the twentieth century, and particularly after the Second World War, waves of immigration from Italy, the Iberian peninsula, and Poland added significantly to the province's Catholic ranks. Later in that century, newcomers from the Philippines and Southeast Asia added even more visible diversity to Ontario's Catholic population.[1]

Debates over school funding have been shaped by the constitutional guarantees of funding for separate schools that were already established by the time of Confederation. The Protestant majority in Ontario's colonial-era predecessors, Upper Canada and Canada West, would almost certainly never have agreed to this arrangement had it formed a separate colony. However, the pragmatic requirements of maintaining a governing coalition while Canada West was joined together with Canada East (present-day Quebec) required acquiescence to denominational schooling in both jurisdictions.[2]

The education system that Ontario inherited from the pre-Confederation period was centred on public elementary schools that were formally non-denominational but characterized by "a vague sort of Protestantism."[3] Catholics could withdraw their support from public schools and direct their taxes towards a separate school, which would be eligible for provincial grants. This arrangement was locked in by the British North America Act, but inequities remained. The division of local taxes between school systems favoured the public since institutional property taxes (including businesses) went overwhelmingly to that side. The guarantee of Catholic schooling also applied only to the elementary level, and, as educational expectations rose in the decades to follow, so did the volume of demands for an extension of funding beyond those years. At the same time, in the late nineteenth and early twentieth centuries, the Vatican was calling for a more proactive development of distinct Catholic institutions to provide insulation from what it saw as the corrosive forces of liberalism and socialism.[4]

The Protestantism of Prewar Conservatives

The "denominational" alignment of Ontario's party politics was nourished for more than a century by the recurrent opposition to Catholic school funding given voice by the Conservative Party, and it was reinforced by an Orange Order that had become deeply entrenched in Ontario in the nineteenth century, remaining so well into the post-Second World War period. This entailed standing firmly against moving an inch beyond the funding guarantees established at Confederation and, at times, expressing regret at those.

Debate over educational funding was bound to intensify with the 1871 extension of the "common school" system to secondary education.[5] It did so particularly in the 1880s, and from that point onward a partisan divide opened up that would see the Conservatives siding with Protestant antagonism towards separate schools. In that decade, they accused Liberal premier Oliver Mowat and his government of being too "subservient to Rome." The irony here is that this was the same charge that was being levelled against Canada's Conservative Prime Minister John A. Macdonald, and it is doubly ironic given Mowat's roots in Upper Canada's distinctively anti-Catholic party, the "Clear Grits."[6] Despite the ferocity of opposition, the re-elected Liberals approved a provision allowing separate as well as public elementary schools to add what amounted to Grades 9 and 10, making them eligible for funding (though at the elementary levels of support rather than at the higher rates for secondary schools). Earlier in the decade, a storm of controversy had arisen over the government's dissemination of a book containing a selection of scriptures for religious instruction in schools.[7] Because the scriptural selections were thought by Protestant leaders to have been influenced by the Catholic archbishop of Toronto, the link between the Liberal Party and Catholic interests persisted in the mind of the broader Protestant electorate.

By the late 1800s, a network of lodges associated with the Protestant Protective Association (and the Orange Order) had sprung up in Ontario, driven by an interest in maintaining "sectarian political warfare."[8] In 1860, Toronto already had twenty lodges, and by 1895, it had fifty-six. Members of the Orange Order dominated the Office of Mayor of Toronto from this period until 1954, and the office of the premier from 1919 to the Second World War.

From the late nineteenth century on, franco-Ontarians' demands for the right to education in their own language intensified. They had few political allies, though, and the reluctance of any party to promote French-language educational interests was reinforced by the fact that the English-speaking majority among Catholics was ill-disposed towards providing space for the French language.[9] In 1912, a Conservative government approved the draconian Regulation 17, which severely restricted instruction in French, though over time both Conservative and Liberal governments gradually lightened the enforcement of the ban.

The partisan divide on Catholic school funding persisted through the interwar period. The 1934 victory of the Liberal Mitchell Hepburn was attributed, in part, to the strength of Catholic support for his party and his willingness to address the question of more equitable funding. When, in 1936, his government secured passage of legislation intended to address the distribution of corporate property taxes, the Conservatives were vehemently opposed, a move applauded by Orange Order lodges across the province.[10] A by-election called that year quickly generated what Peter Meehan calls "a maelstrom of sectarian bigotry."

> Determined to make a singular issue out of the "school tax question," the Conservatives assembled a Protestant alliance that laced speeches throughout the riding with a steady volume of anti-Catholic invective. What should have been a routine by-election ultimately marked the greatest political challenge of Mitchell Hepburn's career.[11]

Opposition was bolstered by growing recognition that the new law was difficult or impossible to administer. In a year it was repealed, and the anti-Catholic reputation of the Conservatives was cemented.

Postwar Alignments

What emerged following the Second World War was a party system characterized by continued Progressive Conservative governments on the centre-right squaring off against divided opposition parties on the centre and left of the political spectrum. The left-leaning Co-operative Commonwealth Federation (CCF) came close to winning in 1943, with the PCs forming a minority government. However, beginning with the 1945 election, the PCs won a string of eight consecutive majorities under four different premiers. For most of this period the Liberals were the primary opposition, shifting slightly from centre right to centre left and back. The Liberals' failure to seize the reins of government was in large part due to the ongoing presence of the CCF and later its successor the NDP, which continued to split the opposition vote. The Conservatives were eventually reduced to minority status from 1975 to 1981, and, after a brief return to majority, were finally removed from power in 1985 when the Liberals formed a minority government with NDP support.

The Progressive Conservatives thus dominated Ontario politics throughout the period under examination here. During almost all of this time, they remained either firmly opposed to expanding support for Catholic schools or unwilling to tackle the most significant of the remaining inequities. Writing in the mid-1970s, Walter Pitman asserts: "no issue has had a more pervasive influence on the politics of Ontario than the controversy over the role of the separate school system."[12]

George Drew's Assertive Protestantism

During the Second World War, the Conservatives elected a new leader, George Drew, who was destined to lock in for some time his party's reputation as representing an assertively Protestant constituency. Despite overseeing the change in the party's name from "Conservative" to "Progressive Conservative" in 1943, in Joseph Schull's words, "Drew was a man of old central Ontario."[13] "He disliked separate schools, opposed the claims of the French and was inclined to stand on familiar Protestant grounds." After becoming premier in the 1943 election, he talked of the public school's importance in preserving a citizenship that emphasized loyalty to the Empire, support for military strength, and Christian values.[14] This may not, in itself, have been a radical break for, as Robert Vipond reminds us, the official provincial statement of educational philosophy issued in 1937 held that schools had obligations for "preparing children to live in a democratic society which bases its life upon the Christian ideal" and that the curriculum "should be pervaded by the spirit of religion."[15] But Drew's party seized on the issue in a way that ensured confrontation.

For decades there had been calls from religious leaders for schools to assume more responsibility for moral and religious education, spurred by concerns about lowering rates of Sunday school attendance and what many reformers saw as a decline in the influence of the home in transmitting moral values. As Robert Stamp argues, the Second World War intensified such worries, "with fathers in the armed forces, and mothers flocking to industrial jobs as never before."[16]

In 1944, provincial regulations were amended to require religious instruction in elementary schools, with two half-hour class periods devoted to scriptural study each week. Passages were ostensibly nonsectarian, but it was widely assumed that they would be entirely Christian. Religious exercises had already been common in the province's schools, but now Drew was moving Ontario's schools into unprecedented terrain by, as Vipond puts it, "making the teaching of Christianity a core, compulsory subject in every public school."[17] Boards could ask for exemption from the requirement, as could individual parents, but only forty of five thousand boards did so, and few parents. In the 1945 election, Drew presented himself as a defender of Christianity, accusing the Liberals of wanting to take religious instruction out of schools. The issue of funding for Catholic schools remained a backdrop to such contention, and there was no doubt whatever that the PCs would oppose any expansion. The CCF leadership was well aware of the explosiveness of these issues and seemed largely to avoid the subject.[18] Drew won the election in a landslide.

The Centrism of Frost, Robarts, and Davis

In 1949, the more accommodating Leslie Frost replaced Drew as PC leader and premier. From this point through to the middle of the 1980s, the Progressive Conservatives retained power on the basis of a centrist and pragmatic approach to governing. PC success in election after election helped secure the relative centrism of the two opposition parties and the avoidance of controversy all the way around. Ontario was still a very Protestant place during the Frost years. In the early 1950s, serving alcohol was banned on Sundays, as was the playing of professional sports. Toronto's largest public events were the Santa Claus Parade and, on July 12th, the Orange Parade. Premier Frost, however, lost little time in declaring that his government had no interesting in provoking "religious animosities," and he took his distance from a Drew-appointed commission that, in effect, recommended a reduction in Catholic school funding.[19] No other party was prepared to challenge the status quo, thus allowing the government to leave the question of separate schools to one side and to increase grants to all schools to help keep discontent to a minimum.

There were signs of change in the 1960s and increased restiveness among Catholics. In 1962, by which time John Robarts was PC leader and premier, Ontario's bishops submitted a brief to the government calling for a revision of financial support arrangements, the extension of funding beyond Grade 10, a role in curricular planning at the provincial level, and the creation of separate institutions for teacher training.

Two years later, Robarts moved significantly on the question of inequitable funding, introducing a new tax plan for schools that brought the separate system "within reasonable reach" of the levels of support for public boards, though resisting the bishops' other demands.[20] By now both Liberals and NDP supported more equitable financing, so the plan encountered no difficulty from the legislature. Perhaps because the whole educational system was expanding at this point, the increased funding for separate schools elicited little response from "even the most virulent anti-religious school critics," though some protests did come from what NDP leader Donald MacDonald described as militant Protestant supporters of the public system.[21]

Only at the end of the 1960s were the Liberals and New Democrats prepared to support the full funding of Catholic high schools. As Fleming points out, both were influenced by a wave of educational reformism, most dramatically embodied in the Hall-Dennis Report issued in 1968, which called for a reduction in the rigidity of school structure and an enhancement of the continuities in student experience from the earliest to the most advanced grades.[22] This highlighted the rupture represented by Catholic students needing to transfer schools (and school systems) to proceed beyond Grade 10.

By now, pressure was being mobilized on both sides of the funding issue. In 1968, Catholic educational groups mounted a very public campaign, culminating in a rally that packed Toronto's Maple Leaf Gardens.[23] This was mobilization unprecedented in its scale, and it succeeded in rallying a very large number of Catholics across the province. By the following year, however, opposition to any extension of funding was also being organized by, among others, groups with representation from the full range of mainstream Protestant denominations. One of the tools deployed by opponents involved arguing that extending Catholic funding would provoke all private schools to claim government support. Indeed, in 1971, the Ontario Alliance of Christian Schools coupled its support for Catholic funding with a request for provincial grants for Christian and Jewish schools in addition to Catholic.[24]

Around the same time, the Progressive Conservative leadership began shifting on the question of French-language education. Soon after the 1967 publication of the first report of the federally appointed Royal

Commission on Bilingualism and Biculturalism, the Robarts government announced that French-language high schools would be created in the public school system. This weakened the movement for extending Catholic school funding to all high school years since it opened up the prospect of significant numbers of French-speaking Catholics transferring to the public system. Indeed, the political palatability of the move was based, in part, on its being applied only to the public system.[25]

The Progressive Conservatives' pragmatic reformism, then, did not lead to support for systematically expanding separate school funding. During the 1971 election, in fact, the party declared its firm opposition to it, with Premier Davis claiming that it could not be limited to just some faiths.[26] This stance no doubt reflected his own awareness of the strength of feeling within the PCs' electoral and activist base and the need to solidify his position soon after narrowly winning the party leadership. It may also have come from his recognizing that the two opposition parties were themselves divided internally on the question.[27] The PCs were elected in 1971 with a strong majority, and it was unlikely that any of the provincial parties would raise the funding issue for some time. To the extent that there was contention over schooling among educators, parents, and the broader public, it was centred on French-language schooling, and the continuing debate over this was not framed much – if at all – in denominational terms.

"Settling," for Now, the Catholic Funding Issue

In June of 1984, close to the end of his years as premier, William Davis surprised a great many in his own party, even his own cabinet, by declaring his government's intention of extending support to Catholic high schools. The response from all parties in the legislature that day was a standing ovation, though many within his own caucus (and inner circle) were unsupportive.[28] Davis knew from his own party's polling that the intensity of Protestant opposition to the move, though still substantial, was declining. The Catholic population of the province was also increasing, fuelled largely by immigration, and the electoral risks for the PCs in retaining opposition to school funding were mounting. One disputed account suggests that a few years earlier Davis had promised Cardinal Emmett Carter that the issue would be addressed within the life of the current government and that the head of the Ontario Church had warned that a failure to keep that promise would result in an outcry from every Catholic pulpit in the province.[29]

Davis certainly knew the move would be controversial, and he outlined a proposal with compromises that he hoped would take the edge off that controversy. Teachers who lost their jobs in public high schools because of the growth in the Catholic system would be guaranteed jobs in the latter, whatever their religious affiliation. Catholic high schools would also be open to non-Catholic students. These measures may have helped secure a degree of peace within the opposition parties, though the premier kept delaying the introduction of a bill.

Opposition from outside the legislature came swiftly enough. Though mostly framed as support for a single integrated system, a significant portion of this opposition, particularly outside major cities, came from Protestants angry at the expansion of the Catholic system. Such antagonism was rooted partly in anti-Catholic sentiment and partly in fears about the risks to local public schools whose students were being siphoned off. Some evangelical Protestants and adherents to minority faiths, Jewish in particular, were also disturbed that this move was coming without any nod to the needs of other faith-based schools, an argument thought to have a sympathetic ear in parts of the Davis cabinet.

Even if all parties were now formally on the same page, "the stage was set for the most divisive conflict over an educational issue in Ontario since the middle decades of the nineteenth century."[30] The opposition parties had displayed public unity, according to one close observer of the period, only because "they didn't think it would happen." School populations were contracting and an expanded Catholic system would risk the loss of even more teaching positions in the public system than were already predicted. The Liberals' electoral reliance on Catholic votes might have made the issue less complex for them, but party insiders at the time were not convinced that the province's Catholics were overwhelmingly in favour of the extension of denominational school funding, and more than a few worried about public reaction to the transfer of public schools to the separate system. Former Liberal leader Robert Nixon furiously argued that the announcement was "pre-meditatively divisive."[31] Within the NDP, there was significant unease at the prospect of weakening the public system, especially since denominational school rights included the right to discriminate religiously in hiring teachers.

An election was anticipated later that year or in 1985, and Davis was widely expected to step down as leader. Many Progressive Conservatives were concerned about going into an election under an untried leader with such an explosive issue in the air.[32] When Frank Miller replaced Davis in early 1985, and then called an election within a few months, the PC fears about the risks of this issue were realized. During the campaign, Anglican archbishop Lewis Garnsworthy angrily attacked the extension of Catholic school funding, drawing an enormous amount of media attention and making this the keystone issue of the election.[33] Polling indicated that the Davis declaration was costing support among Protestants, while the party's previous resistance to it was keeping most Catholic voters within the Liberal fold.[34] There were other causes of PC decline that were more important than this one for, after all, the three parties formally had the same policy on full funding for separate schools. But PC activists who were discontent enough to wait this election out certainly did not help.[35] Miller himself blamed the PCs' significant losses in that election on the separate school issue, and he indicated (for a brief time) that he was prepared to reverse the party position on it.

The Progressive Conservatives won the most seats in the election, but were soon out of office, replaced by David Peterson's Liberals with support from the NDP. The new government was committed to carrying through a version of the Davis commitment, but it could have had no illusions that it would be an easy ride. After introducing legislation to enact the change in funding, it may have wished for a limited set of public committee hearings, but, in fact, they lasted longer than any in provincial history and received almost nine hundred submissions.[36] The Liberal leadership managed to contain dissent among its parliamentarians, who realized that they would not benefit from prolonging debate. NDP leader Bob Rae had to face some opposition within his own caucus and the broader party, especially with unionized public school teachers favouring a merger of the two publicly funded systems. Rae managed to secure majority support among his legislative colleagues and delegates to the annual NDP convention, but there was no guarantee that the issue would be easy for the party to navigate.

Within both parties on the government's side, the resistance to full funding that remained was driven less by Protestant sectarianism than by secularist opposition to state support for faith-based schooling and by concerns about the threats posed to the public system by having a fully funded second system alongside it. Even within the Progressive Conservatives, opposition to full funding was now coming from a range of sentiments, though admittedly with a current of anti-Catholicism that was especially persistent in rural Ontario. The new (and moderate) PC leader Larry Grossman would not have wanted any association with such feelings, and even with his own misgivings about full funding he managed to get support for the bill from a majority of his caucus.[37]

After some manoeuvring on amendments, especially those dealing with guarantees for redundant public system teachers, the Liberals secured passage of Bill 30 in 1986. The new regime would open Catholic high schools to non-Catholic students, who would be able to abstain from religious education. After a decade, too, Catholic school boards would no longer be able to require that newly appointed teachers be Catholic. This seemed to put an end to more than a century of sectarian conflict, and there were no significant pressures within any of the parties, including the Progressive Conservatives, to revisit the issue.

Funding Faith-Based Schools beyond the Catholic System

The issue of Catholic school funding had kept state support for other faith-based schools almost entirely out of partisan political debate. True, there had been a long history of campaigning for such funding. In 1968, the Ontario Alliance of Christian Schools had put the case for provincial support to Premier Robarts, without success.[38] In 1974, Roman Catholic, evangelical Protestant, and Jewish community members had formed the Ontario Association of Alternative and Independent Schools to press the case for provincial funding, encouraged by the direct or indirect government support being provided to private schools in a few other provinces. (Saskatchewan, Alberta, and Quebec had all done so in the second half of the 1960s, British Columbia in the 1970s).[39]

But no party at Queen's Park was firmly on board. If the governing Progressive Conservative Party was reluctant, other parties at Queen's Park were even more so. The intensity of conflict over funding Catholic schools, and the overlapping controversy over French-language instruction, had reinforced the desire across the partisan spectrum to avoid further entanglements with schooling. Political avoidance was aided by the Supreme Court of Canada's 1996 ruling in *Adler v. Ontario*, which denied provincial obligation to fund non-Catholic private schools. And, as James Farney points out, most faith communities were divided between those who favoured state support and those who feared the loss of autonomy that would accompany it.[40] The Jewish community was less split than others, though its negotiations with the province failed in 1977 when the proponents decided against acquiescing to government insistence that schools operating under a new Jewish board would have to be open to any students within their territories.[41]

Religious Instruction in Public Schools

By this time, the question of religious instruction in schools had seemed to largely disappear as a partisan issue and as a source of extra-parliamentary contention. The 1944 requirements for religious instruction remained on the books, but in an increasingly secular period they were gradually seen to be incongruous. In the late 1960s, the Progressive Conservatives had seemed prepared to take up the issue, appointing the Mackay Committee to examine religious education more generally. It received briefs in support of the existing requirements, at times in the name of recognizing the province's heritage. But the committee's 1969 report called for the elimination of the Drew requirements, which it described as out of touch with prevailing educational emphasis on children formulating their own value judgments.[42] At the time, though, the PC government of the day took no action, and neither of the opposition parties championed the recommendations, perhaps for fear of fuelling mobilization among the minority of Ontarians for whom religious instruction in schools still mattered.

In any event, in the years leading up to and following the report, there were more and more schools that simply ignored the Drew requirements and an increasing number of boards that were seeking an exemption for all their schools.[43] In 1990, the Ontario Court of Appeal ruled in *CCLA v. Ministry of Education and Elgin County* that mandating the teaching of a single religious tradition was unconstitutional. This decision did not prohibit all faith-related practices, but it did require that no one religion (Christianity, for example) be privileged in schools. This reflected a broader jurisprudential wave that ruled against public policies favouring just one faith – for example, those requiring Sunday closing.[44] No provincial party was particularly intent on speaking out against such decisions, and, to some extent, this reflected widespread public indifference. Sunday closing remained a controversial issue for a time as an NDP government wrestled with ways of securing a day of rest for employees – in other words, casting it as an issue not of faith but of labour relations.

There was more extra-parliamentary opposition to a 1988 Court of Appeal ruling in *Zylberberg v. Sudbury Board of Education*, which struck down the requirement that school days in Ontario open or close with the Lord's Prayer, an issue, of course, that had been a source of continual discordant political debate in the United States. In Ontario, evangelical Protestants voiced enough opposition to be noticed at Queen's Park.[45] Vocal discontent, however, was not sustained, in part because it lacked the support of Catholics whose school system still had the right to retain a Catholic spirit. None of the major parties had much incentive to express a view.

Conclusion

For decades, stretching back to the nineteenth century, Ontario's Progressive Conservatives articulated policies reflecting the outlook of their sizable Protestant electorate, even during the postwar decades when they were led by pragmatic centrists. Catholic school funding was the faith-based issue that most dogged provincial governments. William Davis's change of course on this issue, at first, resurrected contention in the general population. However, because it was a shift from historic PC policy opposing such an expansion, the move served more to create internal divisions within the parties than it did to reinforce the antique sectarian distinctions between them. And, by that time, the heatedness of debate over such conflicts had been lowered by more openness to ecumenism among religious leaders and by overall secularization. The electorates of the Liberals and PCs would continue for some time to reflect Catholic preference for the latter and Protestant for the former, but the fading of policy disagreement would create the potential for the dissolution of that electoral cleavage.

There were other schools issues that could have led to party differences, such as the provision of state funding to faith schools beyond the Catholic system, but all three major parties avoided seizing any large initiative on them – at least during the period covered by this chapter. The same was true in response to growing opposition to obligatory religious instruction in the non-Catholic public system. The Progressive Conservatives might have been seen as an ally by those who supported such instruction, but that party's leadership was unprepared to take yet another religious issue on board. And in the absence of PC engagement, no other party had any reason to pronounce itself.

Party differences remained after the George Drew premiership, but his successors were more drawn to centrist pragmatism that suggested avoiding those issues most likely to be contentious in the general public. This pattern endured into the period after the mid-1960s, when social movement activism increased challenges to prevailing norms related to gender and sexuality. No PC government was prepared to take dramatically reformist steps in response to feminist or lesbian and gay pressure, and, up to the mid-1980s, neither of the opposition parties was willing to prioritize the most contentious of the issues raised by such advocacy.

As we see in the following chapter, the Progressive Conservative Party began to be the natural home of the constituencies mobilized by religious traditionalists. But for the period under examination here, the centrist leadership of the party was content to avoid the issues most likely to provoke them. It was the federal government that was most targeted by social movement activists on abortion, and all of the provincial parties seemed ready to leave it that way. There were other provincial governments that enacted regulations to limit women's access to abortion after partial decriminalization in 1969, but the Ontario government did not. Even in the mid-1980s, when pro-life pressure was mounting in opposition to Henry Morgentaler's Toronto abortion clinic, PC leaders largely avoided comment.[46] Party representatives were more outspokenly allied with religious conservatives on questions related to sexual diversity and, specifically, in rebuffing demands that sexual orientation be added to the provincial Human Rights Code. However, until the mid-1980s, neither of the opposition parties, not even the NDP, was prepared to assertively side with such demands.[47] In the next chapter we see more clearly than ever evidence of a faith realignment in the provincial party system, though we also see that issues related to Catholic schooling had not completely lost their capacity to provoke public contention and anguish for party leaders.

PART 3
Religious Conservatism and the Partisan Right

Sexual Diversity and the Mobilization of Faith Communities in Ontario, 1986–2015

Of all Canada's provinces and territories, Ontario is distinctive in the extent to which the party system shifted away from alignment based on Christian denomination to one in which the primary axis of religious contention pitted moral traditionalists against progressive reformers. This became clearer over time in the policy positions adopted by the three major parties and also, to some extent, in the electoral support given to each. But, as we have found at the federal level, this was no replication of an American-style culture war. Even as the Progressive Conservative Party shifted radically right at the end of the 1980s, it avoided the abortion issue – one of the hot button issues around which religious conservatives had mobilized. And, by the 2000s, the party's room for political manoeuvring on questions of sexual diversity had been substantially narrowed by court rulings and changes in public opinion. Nevertheless, we find recurrent instances in which this party made a point of siding with moral traditionalists and in which the Liberals and New Democrats were internally split by waves of opposition spawned by the religious right. For this reason, Ontario's party system realigned enough to make the PCs the only logical home for social conservatives, as has been true of their federal Conservative counterparts.

What we see, then, is a long arc of change in policy positions from 1985 until 2015. The Progressive Conservatives had long been dominated by moral traditionalists, but, as they shifted more radically to the neoliberal right under Mike Harris, they became more distinctly a champion of that constituency. In the mid-1980s, Ontario's New Democratic Party had already been clear in representing a pro-choice position on reproductive rights, but now it was more willing than it had been in the past to articulate progressive policy on basic lesbian and gay rights, though it would take more than another decade to solidify support for other causes related to sexual diversity. The Liberal Party had an even more tortuous route towards social progressivism, and the controversy over sexual health education in 2010 revealed its persistent uncertainty when facing the prospect of mobilization by religious conservatives. It was only in the period from 2012 onward that the party seemed ready to declare itself firmly on such issues and to sharpen its political distance from the Progressive Conservatives.

This new faith alignment seemed largely irrelevant in the first decade of the new millennium, especially because policy questions related to abortion and the recognition of lesbian and gay relationships were widely regarded as politically settled. It is worth adding that denominational distinctions in voting for Liberals and PCs were declining, and there was no sign of policy disputes re-inflaming debates over Catholic schooling. But then, beginning in 2010, heated controversies over the recognition of sexual diversity in publicly funded schools reinforced the PCs' alliance with social conservatives and distanced the other two parties more than ever from that constituency. This contentiousness over sexuality again raised questions about Catholic schooling – both in the funding provided to it and the leeway given for its religious instruction. By late 2015, conflict over such issues had once again receded and the PCs were avoiding policy positions that publicly allied them with social conservatives.

In the meantime, there was no indication that the recognition of minority religious rights was being systematically politicized. All three parties in Ontario had an interest in drawing in voters from minority religious communities, so, by and large, none was prepared to forge policy platforms that catered to public anxiety about high rates of immigration or enhanced institutional recognition of minority rights.

Does this mean that faith no longer matters at all in Ontario's provincial politics? Not necessarily. Even if religious conservatives constitute a declining portion of the province's population, they remain an important part of the PCs' electoral and activist core, enough to help secure the leadership of Patrick Brown in 2015. Party strategists may have finally learned the lesson that catering too obviously to social conservatives loses more votes than it gains, but the period since 2010 illustrates the mobilization capacity of moral traditionalists to shock the political system and influence policy, even in a region, and country, with declining rates of religious practice and an increasing consensus on the separation of "church" and state.

We start this analysis of faith realignment in Ontario with an outline of the religious demographics of the province, the religiosity of its people, and the attitudinal distinctions between supporters of the three major parties. Following this, we examine shifts over the last three decades in the policy positioning of each of Ontario's major parties on issues that have roused religious communities. We take a particularly close look at the 2010–15 period – a lens through which to explore the persistence and, in some respects, the sharpening of partisan differentiation on these issues until at least 2015.

Religion and Morality in Party Supporters

Ontario's religious landscape is as complex and diverse as that of any region in Canada. It has a relatively large Roman Catholic population of about 30 percent of the province that is itself highly diversified in ethno-cultural terms. Catholics also have access to a fully funded separate school system, providing their religious communities with an important institutional buttress. Ontario also has the highest proportion of non-Christian religious minorities in Canada, with the 2011 census showing that Muslims were 5 percent of the population, Hindus 3 percent, Jews 2 percent, and Sikhs 1 percent. Many members of these religious minorities are also first-generation immigrants, and overall 29 percent of the province's population was born outside of Canada.[1]

Ontario does not have a comparatively large number of people identified as evangelical or as linked to denominations most likely to be conservative on gender and sexuality issues. The 2011 provincial election study shows that 4 percent of the population identified as evangelical, though this may undercount those who identify with specific Protestant denominations but who share the conservatism of evangelicals. Kurt Bowen's 1997 data show that 17 percent of those whom he classifies as "very committed" religiously were conservative Protestant, slightly less than the 21 percent Canadian average.[2] A 2011 Ipsos Reid poll indicates that 16 percent of Ontarians attended religious services at least weekly, somewhat above the 13 percent cross-country average. The 2011 provincial election study indicates that 20 percent of respondents saw religion as very important, close to the average across Canada.

What evidence do we have of public attitudes on the issues most likely to have mobilized Christian conservatives – abortion rights and the public recognition of sexual diversity? On both these fronts, Ontarian beliefs seldom stray noticeably from the Canadian average, more conservative than those in British Columbia and Quebec, more reformist than those in the Prairie provinces or Atlantic regions. As we see in the Introduction to this volume, Ontarians were slightly more disapproving of abortion than was the typical Canadian in 2007, but, by 2012, what differences there were had disappeared. A 2012 Ipsos Reid poll shows that only 6 percent of Ontarians opposed abortion under all circumstances, and only 28 percent supported legal limits on when a woman can have an abortion.[3] The same poll shows strong support for same-sex marriage, with Ontarians responding similarly to Canadians as a whole, and only 18 percent believing that such marriage was wrong and that it should never be lawful.

Partial Faith Realignment

The 2011 and 2014 provincial election studies allow us to examine the extent to which the traditional denominational distinction between Liberal and Progressive Conservative supporters has been replaced by a new faith alignment. As we see in Tables 5.1 and 5.2, though the PCs retain a disproportionate number of Protestant supporters, the Liberal advantage among Catholics has disappeared. In fact, in 2011 a slightly

Table 5.1   Vote choice within religious groups in Ontario, 2011

	Liberals (%)	PCs (%)	NDP (%)	Total (n)	
Denomination					
Roman Catholic	40	42	19	157	(100%)
Mainline Protestant	31	43	26	246	(100%)
Evangelical	24	57	19	31	(100%)
Other	42	29	29	114	(100%)
Unaffiliated/atheist	48	23	30	252	(100%)
Total	39	35	26	801	(100%)
Importance of religion					
Very important	39	37	25	161	(100%)
Somewhat important	33	39	28	252	(100%)
Somewhat unimportant	36	41	23	153	(100%)
Very unimportant	47	25	28	228	(100%)
Total	39	35	26	794	(100%)

larger proportion of PC supporters were Catholic (23 percent) than of Liberal supporters (20 percent).[4] The number of evangelicals in the two studies is small enough to require caution, but the results suggest that nearly 60 percent or more lean to the PCs, similar to the proportion of Canadian evangelicals who support the federal Conservatives.

On questions tapping overall religiosity, there are indications of a growing contrast between the PCs and other parties. The party has a comparatively low number of supporters who declare no religious attachment or who say that religion is completely unimportant. This is more evident in 2014 than in 2011. The differences are not radical, though it is likely that many of those mainline Protestants for whom faith is important and who are also religiously traditional gravitate to this party.

How distinct is each party's electorate on questions of abortion and sexual diversity? Here we see indications of a clear distinction between the PCs, on the one hand, and the Liberals and NDP, on the other. The

Table 5.2   Vote choice within religious groups in Ontario, 2014

	Liberals (%)	PCs (%)	NDP (%)	Total (n)	
Denomination					
Roman Catholic	46	36	18	188	(100%)
Mainline Protestant	33	55	12	203	(100%)
Evangelical	13	65	21	38	(100%)
Other	56	17	27	108	(100%)
Unaffiliated/atheist	51	24	25	268	(100%)
Total	44	36	20	805	(100%)
Importance of religion					
Very important	37	50	13	161	(100%)
Somewhat important	42	39	19	253	(100%)
Somewhat unimportant	43	32	26	153	(100%)
Very unimportant	51	27	22	228	(100%)
Total	44	36	20	806	(100%)

Note: Half of the "other" denominational category comprises Muslim, Jewish, Buddhist, and Hindu respondents.
Source: Jared Wesley et al., Canadian Provincial Election Project, http://cpep.ualberta.ca.

question from the 2011 provincial election survey that is most relevant here is the one that asks respondents to rate themselves on a 10-point scale, where 1 represents traditional values in respect to issues like abortion, homosexuality, and euthanasia, and 10 the least traditional. Supporters of the Liberal Party and the NDP averaged 7.4 on this scale, close to the progressive end. PC supporters averaged 5.7, not especially traditional but a significant distance from the other two parties. The 2014 election study used the same device, and produced even more dramatic results. The average PC supporter score was 5.3, with the Liberals even further towards the less traditional end, at 8.0, and the NDP at 7.5. This echoes the analysis of David McGrane, who places supporters of the PCs significantly to the right of the other two parties on a "post-materialism" scale as well as on a scale measuring attachment to "market liberalism."[5] William Cross and his colleagues find a similar pattern of differentiation on a left-right scale.[6]

What these numbers suggest, then, is that there are important religious and values distinctions across party lines, with the Liberals and NDP looking increasingly similar in faith terms. The differentiation is not radical, but it is clear and undoubtedly persistent. The drawing power of moral traditionalists to the PCs may have roots going back to the party's historic strength among Protestants, but it now appears to have no denominational colouration. As we move into a discussion of the policy stances adopted by the provincial parties since the late 1980s, and in particular the clear positioning of the PCs on the right, we see that this electoral "sorting" makes sense and may well persist beyond the availability of specific issues around which moral traditionalists rally.

1985–90: An Emerging New Divide between Liberals and Progressive Conservatives

Until the early 1980s, it would have been difficult to distinguish the Liberals from the PCs on the issues that matter to moral conservatives. In fact, from the 1950s to the mid-1970s, the Liberals' positioned themselves broadly to the right of the governing PCs and, for the next decade, moved only slightly towards the centre.[7] The Liberals had strong support in rural and small-town western Ontario as well as in parts of eastern Ontario that were also known for their social traditionalism, and party leaders were more than ready to avoid marking out clear positions that challenged such views. When, for example, proposals to add sexual orientation to the province's Human Rights Code surfaced prior to 1986, few Liberal MPPs were ready to support them.[8] The New Democrats had established a clear position on abortion long before this but were reluctant to appear as advocates for lesbian and gay rights, and, in 1981, party leader Mike Cassidy declared that the prohibition of discrimination based on sexual orientation was not a priority. This reluctance, of course, made it easier for both other parties to avoid the issue.

Amending the Human Rights Code in 1986

During the 1980s, the Liberals slowly increased their recruitment of city-based candidates with reformist credentials: before the 1985 election, more than half the Liberals' caucus came from outside cities.

Writing of that period, Rosemary Speirs argues that the party was aiming to "grab the social conscience role from the NDP, and to appeal to ... urbanites, women, youth, and ethnic organizations."[9] After the Liberals gained office with a legislative minority in 1985, Premier David Peterson named high-profile ministers who were very progressive by provincial Liberal standards, most notably Attorney General Ian Scott. They were, in turn, given extra leverage by the government's dependence on NDP support for its legislative survival.

The shift to reformism was evident to some extent on the abortion file. The Liberals were in government when the Supreme Court struck down Criminal Code restrictions on women's access to abortion in 1988. Leading party figures like Ian Scott were not sympathetic to pro-life advocates, so the natural path for the government to follow was to do nothing to circumvent the court ruling. It helped that previous PC governments had followed a cautious path, avoiding provincial restrictions on access or funding when abortion was partially decriminalized in 1969.[10] The government's room for manoeuvre was increased by public revulsion at an attempted fire-bombing of Henry Morgentaler's Toronto abortion clinic in 1983 and by the Roman Catholic hierarchy's increasing unease with the militant tactics adopted by pro-life protesters.[11]

The rights of lesbians and gays were more difficult. Soon after the 1985 election, it seemed possible that an amendment adding sexual orientation to the Human Rights Code might gain traction, in part because of growing agreement in constitutional circles that sexual orientation was an equity ground analogous to those that were explicitly named in Section 15 of the Charter of Rights and Freedoms.[12] The NDP caucus, too, was more firmly supportive of such a move than it had been five years earlier, and LGBT advocates within and beyond the party were better organized.

There was no doubt that the Liberal leadership would have preferred to avoid the subject, but through the course of the first half of 1986, the attorney general was convinced that this amendment was supportable. When the issue came to a committee vote in May, all four Liberals on the Justice Committee voted in favour of it, even if there was still substantial opposition to the change within the Liberal caucus.

That fall, a tidal wave of opposition mobilized by religious conservatives broadened the unease within the caucus, and especially among those members from outside the province's large cities, such that about half would have voted against the amendment if left to their own devices.[13] The Premier's Office and the attorney general lobbied hard and mollified some caucus members by underlining the limited nature of the measure. When the crucial vote on the amendment came in early December, 39 Liberals supported it, with 4 opposed and 6 abstaining. The New Democrats remained firmly supportive of the measure despite the weeks of massive religious right mobilization. Even if some caucus members were nervous about openly siding with lesbian and gay advocates, all twenty-one NDP members who cast votes supported the amendment, with only three abstaining.

In contrast, the Progressive Conservative caucus was overwhelmingly opposed to recognizing lesbian and gay rights. Many caucus members angrily prolonged the legislative debate and provided a vehicle for the anti-gay extremism used by so many of the amendment's religiously conservative opponents. When the vote on the sexual orientation provision of the government's bill came up, only four of the fifty-two PCs supported it. However, this included party leader Larry Grossman, a centrist in the Robarts and Davis tradition. His vote helped prevent the issue from becoming a campaign focus in the next election (1990), even though, by that time, he was no longer leader.

The 1990s: The Religious Right Re-Energized

The decade began with the New Democratic Party under Bob Rae defeating the Liberals and Progressive Conservatives to form a majority government, surprising itself and everyone else. Perhaps even more significant for the solidification of faith realignment was the PCs' choosing Mike Harris as leader in that same year. The NDP's front bench was very different from past cabinets, dominated by economic and social reformers. The new government was severely hampered by a significant economic downturn and by overwhelming media and business opposition to its attempt at a Keynesian-style expansionist budget in the first year of its mandate. But, on other fronts, the government was open to a comparatively progressive agenda. In 1993, for example, when abortion-related activism was centred on free-standing clinics, the government established a demonstration-free bubble zone around three of them across the province.

Lesbian and gay rights, however, were not so simple. Claims for the recognition of same-sex relationships were now a priority for activists, but it was not until relatively late in its mandate that the NDP government was persuaded to introduce legislation comprehensively recognizing such relationships. No provincial government had attempted such a move, and public opinion was still divided – particularly on the question of adoption. Legislation was introduced in 1994, and it was soon clear that the party's caucus was deeply divided.[14] The legislative debate over the bill was now regularly in newspaper headlines across the province and, to some extent, the country, and it was seen as a major challenge to the NDP's unity. The premier responded by allowing a free vote, and the twelve NDP members who sided with the opposition were enough to defeat the bill in an episode that produced even more front-page headlines. While court rulings made this moral conservative victory short-lived the memory of the episode would long remain vivid both inside the party and among LGBT advocates.

This legislation also revealed the fragility of the Liberals' shift to social reformism. Lyn McLeod, who became Liberal Party leader in 1992, had at first expressed some sympathy with the NDP government's proposal, but had to back down in the face of overwhelming opposition from within her caucus – opposition that was reinforced by the party's loss in a by-election contest fought partly on that issue. The fact that the PCs were willing to attack the NDP government and the Liberals on their real or imagined support for the recognition of lesbian and gay relationships was an essential factor in heightening resistance. Whether by resignation or defeat, losses in the 1990 election had also stripped the Liberal caucus of some of its strongest progressive voices. When the measure came to a vote in the legislature in 1994, PC opponents were joined by thirty-two of the thirty-five Liberals who voted that day.[15]

The Progressive Conservatives' Common Sense Revolution
Despite this resurgence of moral conservatism within the Liberal party,
Mike Harris's leadership ultimately made the Progressive Conservatives
the only natural choice for social conservatives across denominational
boundaries.[16] On the surface, the policy program around which the PCs
rallied – the "common sense revolution" – had very little to say about
morality issues. It was preoccupied with reducing taxes and spending,
and not in any obvious way tied to conservative faith. In fact, according
to John Ibbitson:

> Unlike many American neo-Conservatives, Mike Harris and his advis-
> ers have steered away from espousing what are called "family values"
> ... and with good reason ... Harris and his advisors believe, philosoph-
> ically, in keeping the state out of both the boardroom and the bed-
> room. Furthermore, family values conservatives oppose premarital,
> adulterous, and homosexual relationships, yet [the PC leadership]
> knew full well that all three could be found in the government.[17]

Yet at the same time, the party's leadership was given more than
one reminder that it had to think carefully about how to attract or
retain the support of religious traditionalists. Party insiders partially
attributed their 1990 election loss to the NDP to right-wing fringe
parties that drew away enough PC support to cost them up to sixteen
seats.[18] The Christian Heritage Party had been formed in 1987 in response to what religious conservatives believed to be the "social liberalism" of Brian Mulroney's federal PCs, but it would have been noticed
by the provincial party as an indication of discontent in the religious
right.[19] The 1993 federal election then produced another shock, with a
strong showing by Reform Party candidates in Ontario. The provincial
PCs' individualistic distrust of government would have appealed to
many Reform-tilting provincial voters, but there was no doubt that such
voters were also attached to moral traditionalism. During the period of
centrist pragmatism, there was little incentive and few opportunities
for the PC leadership to explicitly mark itself out as a pole of attraction

for social conservatives, even during the 1986 conflict over lesbian and gay rights. Now the Harris PC government had a vehicle to be clear about where it stood, and it ferociously attack the NDP's bill recognizing same-sex relationships.

The party's election campaign in 1995 concentrated on reduced government taxation and spending, but, as Geoffrey Hale argues, it also clearly positioned the PCs as "the party of social conservatism ... in sharp contrast to the socially liberal, urban-oriented Toryism of the Davis years."[20] There were lessons available from Margaret Thatcher's British Conservatives and Ralph Klein's Alberta PCs that one way of doing this was to mark out conservative positions on LGBT rights (see Chapter 6).

After winning that election, the party had few opportunities to translate these views into action, even if there was no doubt about where the party's leadership and caucus stood. Neither the Liberals nor the NDP had any interest in reviving debate on same-sex relationship recognition. Court rulings also narrowed the room for manouevre on this front, especially with the 1999 Supreme Court of Canada ruling against exclusionary provisions in Ontario family law in the case of *M. v. H.* This left the provincial PCs no choice but to introduce a bill amending sixty-seven provincial statutes. They signalled their grudging approach to the issue by the use of the term "partner" rather than "spouse" to describe same-sex relationships, language that Attorney General Jim Flaherty argued would help retain "the traditional values of the family."[21] But then, in late 1999, the government cooperated with other party house leaders in the legislature to ensure the fastest passage imaginable. When the Ontario Court of Appeal opened the door to lesbian and gay marriage in 2003, the provincial Progressive Conservatives (now with Ernie Eves as premier) remained quiet, leaving their federal counterparts to carry the torch for "traditional" marriage.

The Harris government stayed away from abortion, again following in the footsteps of Britain's Conservatives and Alberta's PCs. Despite pressure from pro-life advocates, Harris took no action to undo the court injunction creating a protest-free "bubble zone" around Henry Morgentaler's Toronto clinic, and he did not "de-list" abortion for health insurance purposes.[22] On another front, however, the PCs were prepared to adopt policies that would shore up support among religious conservatives. In 1999, the Harris government announced a tax credit for private school tuition, in the name of school "choice," to be phased in over five years. The primary beneficiaries of this were faith-based schools, and it was from among their supporters that pressure had been applied on provincial authorities. The pledge, therefore, reminds us that the PCs were still concerned about retaining the loyalty of social conservatives.

2003: Religious Right Declines as Liberals Return to Power

When Dalton McGuinty replaced Lyn McLeod as Liberal leader in 1996, it seemed as though the party was embracing a form of pragmatic "blandness."[23] Though known to be broadly pro-choice, McGuinty had voted against the NDP's legislation on same-sex relationships, and those around him knew that restoring the electoral strength of the party depended on retaining at least some rural and small-town support as well as shoring up strength among those Catholic and ethno-cultural minority voters who had traditionally voted Liberal. In the 1999 election, they significantly increased both their vote share and seat count but still lost, and so they could take none of their traditional voting blocs for granted.

The Liberals won the 2003 election, but by that time the sorts of issues that had aroused moral traditionalists in Ontario seemed relegated to the past. McGuinty had opposed the Harris government tax credits for private schools at the time they were introduced, and his government quickly eliminated them.[24] The one faith-related issue that provoked controversy after the Liberals' return to power was not one that distinguished the parties clearly from one another. In 2003, an Islamic group announced its intention to establish family dispute resolution processes in line with 1991 legislation that allowed for faith-based arbitration.[25] The government responded to growing controversy over Sharia law by asking former NDP minister Marion Boyd to report on the matter, and, in late 2004, she responded with an affirmation of the appropriateness of voluntary recourse to tribunals using religious frameworks, including Islamic law. Dissent had been growing inside the Liberal caucus, however, enough to convince Premier McGuinty to come out in opposition to all religiously based family arbitration. The NDP had no common view on this question, and it was eager enough to see it disappear from political debate. Throughout this process, the PC leadership remained largely mute.

The PCs, however, had not stopped thinking of ways to shore up the social conservative support of their party. In 2004, the party membership had elected John Tory as party leader, and, in doing so, they seemed to revert to pre-Harris centrism. Tory was more moderate on fiscal issues than were the common sense revolutionaries, and he had even less affinity to moral conservatism. He also had stronger connections to the pragmatic PC dynasty of the postwar era than to the Harris administration, and he had once served as principal secretary to former premier Bill Davis.

However, for precisely these reasons, Tory was never fully supported within his own party, and, in a sense, this might have moved him to shore up his rightist credentials. In the 2007 election, he resurrected the school funding issue by championing government support for private schools. This promise on schools, like the earlier Harris tax credits, dovetailed with neoliberal talk of school choice, but it also seemed aimed specifically at conservative Protestants and religious minorities. The PCs lost that election, badly, and post-mortem analysis focused on the ill-advisedness of the promise on faith-based schools. Tory had lost his own riding and then resigned as party leader after failing to win a 2009 by-election.

The Liberals' 2007 victory was based on an electorate and legislative caucus more urban than ever, with the PCs having made gains in areas that once were Liberal strongholds. This did not eliminate the party's concerns for retaining and even regaining some of the more centrist or even centre-right support it once had, but in the meantime the caucus leaned towards social progressivism.

In contrast, the PC leadership race provoked by John Tory's 2009 resignation resulted in a victory for Tim Hudak and a return to the unchallenged ascendance of the Harrisites. Hudak was not the candidate most favoured by religious conservatives (MPP Frank Klees was), and he borrowed the lines used by federal Conservative leader Stephen Harper in saying that a government led by him would not reopen the abortion issue.[26] Neither he nor his party could afford to ignore the party's social conservatives, but there was no obvious issue to deploy resources to that end.

2010–12: Renewed Contention over Sexual Diversity

Any attempt to increase the inclusive recognition of sexual diversity in public schools would have had the potential to be politicized, and, indeed, at the school board level that had regularly been the case. Despite considerable opposition from religious conservatives, in the early 1990s, Toronto's public school board became the first in the country to take significant steps to respond to LGBT demands for greater inclusiveness.[27] Over the following decade, other boards (e.g., in Ottawa, the Peel Region, London) developed policy responses, often using school safety and bullying as the primary "wedge."

Until 2008, however, provincial governments of various partisan stripes had avoided engagement with such issues, leaving them instead to local school boards. The provincial Ministry of Education was not alone in this, for none of its provincial counterparts had adopted significant policies that recognized the challenges facing sexual minority students, teachers, and parents. But pressure for change was building, not least because of increased evidence that most schools remained profoundly unwelcoming of sexual diversity.

Under the Liberals, the incentives for the ministry to adopt a more assertive profile on this front were enhanced, particularly with the 2006 appointment to the education portfolio of Kathleen Wynne, who came from the relatively progressive side of the party and had a specific interest in equity and diversity. The Safe Schools Act passed under Mike Harris's Progressive Conservative premiership had come under regular criticism for its exclusive focus on punishment and the large number of racialized youth expelled under its provisions. In the meantime, more public attention across North America was being paid to school violence and to the harmful impact of bullying and harassment.

After the 2007 election, Wynne directed an already-created Safe Schools Action Team to examine violence and harassment based on gender and sexual diversity. The team's 2008 report (*Shaping a Culture of Respect*) recommended comprehensive preventive measures, including revisions to school curricula.[28] In 2009, the government secured passage of Bill 157 (The Keep Our Kids Safe at School Act), which increased obligations on educators to report serious incidents of bullying and harassment (explicitly including sexual orientation and gender identity).[29] Importantly, none of these steps provoked measurable controversy from religious or political conservatives.

The 2010 Explosion over Sexual Health Education

In 2007, consultations began over the preparation of a new health and physical education (HPE) curriculum, which was to replace one developed a decade earlier. This was a routine process through which all school curricula were renewed. This particular subject area warranted unusually elaborate consultation with stakeholders and experts, driven by widespread agreement on the need for major change in addressing physical, psychological, and sexual health awareness at the elementary school level.[30] At the end of 2009, the new HPE curriculum was ready for distribution to school boards across the province. There were, as promised, more specific guidelines for teachers responding to student questions related to sexuality and sexual diversity. This was in the form of teacher "prompts" for subjects on which teacher uncertainty and hesitancy were widely acknowledged. The document did not break radically new ground but, rather, reflected curricular developments in provinces as different as Alberta, Saskatchewan, Manitoba, and New Brunswick.[31] It also indicated that teachers should inform parents about the content of the curriculum, and stipulated that parents could withdraw their children from particular lessons. The new document was distributed in January 2010, almost innocuously. Coincidentally, on the day that the new curriculum was sent to school boards, Premier McGuinty announced a cabinet shuffle that moved Kathleen Wynne from education to transport, replacing her with Leona Dombrowsky, who had been chair of the Roman Catholic School Board in a rural and small-town region of eastern Ontario.

There was a minor sign of protest from a pro-life source in early March, when the socially conservative online newspaper LifeSiteNews accused the Ministry of Education of attempting "to instill a sense that homosexuality and transgenderism are perfectly normal."[32] However, the piece did not arouse widespread alarm among social conservative circles. But then, an April 15, 2010, story on the new curriculum in the *Hamilton Spectator*, which had been triggered by local school board controversy over the development of policy on sexual orientation, came to the attention of evangelical activist Charles McVety, president of both Canada Christian College (a seminary) and the Canada Family Action Coalition.[33] McVety did not always have amicable relations with other evangelical advocates, but he had been a vocal anti-gay crusader for years and had an extensive contact list of co-religionists and journalists.[34] Shielding young people from positive messages about sexual diversity had long been a preoccupation of religious conservatives and had featured prominently in Canadian religious right advocacy since the 1970s, so McVety recognized that the new curriculum would have mobilizing potential.

At 9:00 am on Tuesday, 20 April, McVety widely distributed a press release headed by the denunciating line: "Mr. McGuinty, Withdraw Explicit Sex Ed for 8 Year Olds." He then quoted himself as saying "it is unconscionable to teach 8-year old children same-sex marriage, sexual orientation and gender identity ... it is even more absurd to subject 6th graders to instruction on the pleasures of masturbation, vaginal lubrication, and 12 year olds to lessons on oral sex and anal intercourse." That very morning, when a reporter asked if the claims in McVety's press release were accurate, Premier McGuinty appeared unprepared, responding only by vaguely expressing confidence in the educators who had developed the curriculum. So convinced were the party leaders' advisors that this new curriculum was uncontroversial, and/or that the province's religious right was now politically marginal, that no one had provided the premier with any background.

On Wednesday, Toronto's major newspapers had front-page headline stories on the issue, of course framing it as "controversial."[35] The absence of any strategic government communications meant that media reporters and commentators shaped the story (perhaps more than they realized) in ways that dovetailed with the McVety press release. In the first day or two, the impulsive draw to controversy then led reporters to seek out "outraged" parents, even if some reports also cited more reasoned voices.[36] And, with stories that regularly discussed curricular guidelines related to sexual activity alongside those tied to increasing awareness of

LGBT diversity, the media coverage contributed to precisely the conflation of the two that McVety sought.

In Wednesday morning's legislative question period, Progressive Conservative leader Tim Hudak vowed to "stand with moms and dads across the province of Ontario," and accused the government of listening only to "so-called experts and elite insiders."[37] Prominent Liberals like Wynne fought back, but there were party strategists and rural caucus members who feared that an issue such as this could unseat the Liberals at the next election (slated for 2011). That afternoon, the premier absent-mindedly brought Catholic schools into the discussion by indicating that the new program would apply to students in all publicly funded schools, later clarifying that the Catholic system had the right to adapt the curriculum. But this was enough to provoke the ire of conservative archbishop Terrence Prendergast of Ottawa, who encouraged Catholics to voice their concerns.

By Thursday morning, unease was building inside the Premier's Office. The government had faced rough seas over other issues, and those responsible for managing the next election campaign were determined to get rid of this one. That afternoon, just fifty-four hours after Charles McVety sounded his alarm, the premier announced that the sex education segments of the new curriculum were being withdrawn for a "rethink."[38] No one was anticipating this review to be completed before the election expected for the fall of 2011.

A year and a half later, during the campaign in that election, the PCs attacked the Liberals on this issue. Tim Hudak argued that it was parents' responsibility to teach young people about discrimination and tolerance, and he accused the Liberal government of wanting to teach "adult concepts" to youngsters.[39] He also backed a local PC candidate in Brampton who distributed flyers widely perceived as prejudicial towards sexual minorities in their scare mongering over the elementary school curriculum.[40] All this elicited an overwhelmingly negative reaction from the media, but this was, in part, because the Liberals were able to say that they had withdrawn the parts of the curriculum being argued as objectionable. In the end, the Liberals lost more than a dozen seats, but still managed to win a minority government. Their success in holding off the PCs was helped by popular distaste for the latter's starkly neoliberal campaign, but that party's pitch to social conservatism was also widely seen as contributing to its loss in an election it was widely expected to win. At the very least, as William Cross and his colleagues point out, the sex-ed issue drew Hudak off his economy-focused messaging and into moral traditionalist terrain in the crucial last days of the campaign.[41]

Gay-Straight Alliances

The election may well have emboldened the McGuinty Liberals to sharpen the contrast between their policies and those of the PCs, in line with the federal Liberal Party's increased willingness to attack their Conservative opponents on issues related to sexual diversity and abortion. In the fall of 2011, the Liberals introduced Bill 13, the Accepting Schools Act, which aimed at further strengthening school responses to bullying. It addressed the full range of discrimination grounds, but placed unusual emphasis on sexual minority students and their right to establish groups combatting prejudice. The specificity of the references to sexual diversity came, in part, from front-page coverage in October of the suicide of openly gay Ottawa student Jamie Hubley, the son of an Ottawa city councillor, who had been targeted by homophobic bullying after trying to start a gay-straight alliance.[42] The LGBT advocacy group Egale Canada had also been campaigning specifically on GSAs, emphasizing their importance in responding to prejudice and harassment. There was no doubt about NDP support for the measure, and since the Liberals had only a minority in the legislature, such support was vital.

In the meantime, there had already been some resistance to pressure from students wanting GSAs in the Catholic system, and earlier in the year explicit bans were enacted by at least two Catholic boards. Ontario's bishops and many school trustees argued that student groups addressing a wide range of equity issues were welcome, but not if they used the word "gay." When the government introduced Bill 13 in November, it in fact created some wriggle room for Catholic boards by allowing them to avoid approving groups with the specific GSA label.[43] Despite this, however, the Ontario Catholic School Trustees' Association attacked the legislation as constituting "an adult mandate being pushed on young people who are minors, who may still not know where they're going in life."[44] In late March 2012, a group called Concerned

Catholic Parents of Ontario organized a rally in front of Queen's Park protesting Bill 13 that attracted two thousand supporters. They were joined by Charles McVety, who portrayed the premier as a totalitarian radical engaged in a "bizarre social engineering experiment" and claiming that this new measure was "a front for radical sex education."

In the meantime, the Progressive Conservatives set themselves squarely against the government bill. They introduced their own alternative, Bill 14, which avoided any provisions for student group formation and redeployed the disciplinary framework of the Harris governments Safe Schools Act.[45] Not surprisingly, official Catholic sources expressed support for the PC option.[46] This had the unintended consequence of focusing public attention on the separate school system and linking Catholic opposition to the strident language still being used by evangelical Protestants.

In much contrast to the 2010 sex education controversy, the government's response this time was to toughen its stance, apparently relishing an opportunity to once again paint the PC as having a moral agenda antithetical to most Ontarians. In late May the Liberals amended their own bill to eliminate any wriggle room by requiring all publicly funded boards – including the separate school system – to recognize student groups that wished to use the GSA label.[47] PC leader Tim Hudak once again placed himself firmly on the side of religious conservatives, accusing the government of using Bill 13 to "pick a fight" with Catholics.[48] Ironically, Catholic opponents were starting to pull in their horns, seeing polls that showed that a majority of Ontarians now opposed state funding for separate schools.[49]

When Bill 13 came to a vote in early June 2012, the party divisions were stark. The PC leader's office had already made it plain that any dissent from the official party position would not be tolerated, and all thirty-six PC votes cast were in opposition to the Liberal bill.[50] A Liberal caucus that may well have been divided on such a measure in earlier years was now firmly supportive of it, backed up of course by the NDP. This would not signal an end to resistance within the Catholic system, and there continued to be signs that individual schools were putting roadblocks in the way of GSA formation. But it did end partisan debate over the issue.

Less than a week after the Liberal win on the GSA measure, a private member's bill introduced by NDP MLA Cheri DiNovo to add gender identity and expression to Ontario's Human Rights Code came to a vote in the Legislative Assembly, passing by voice vote with the support of all three provincial parties.

2013–15: Liberals Shift Left and the PCs Avoid Social Conservativism

From 2013, it seemed as if there was no major party ready to openly ally itself with moral traditionalists. The New Democrats had long forsaken any interest in a current of opinion that, up to the 1990s, had still seemed to matter to them, particularly in rural Ontario. The Liberals chose a new leader, Kathleen Wynne, who seemed to embody a shift towards social reformism that would have held little prospect of appealing to moral traditionalists. And the Progressive Conservatives seemed finally to have learned the lessons of recent elections that catering to the religious right had more risks than benefits.

On the Liberal side, Premier Dalton McGuinty stepped down in late 2012 in the face of growing scandal around the cancellation of two power plant contracts. The party's leadership contest in early 2013 resulted in victory for Kathleen Wynne, the first openly lesbian or gay premier in a Canadian province, and a Liberal more clearly associated with the party's reform wing than any previous leader. From the outset, she was unhesitating in expressing progressive views on issues that had roused religious conservatives. One example is her clear opposition to federal Conservative legislation on prostitution and her favouring of approaches that prioritized the safety of sex workers.[51] It now looked as though the members of the Liberal leadership accepted that conservative evangelicals were largely lost to the Progressive Conservative Party, and that most of their Catholic constituency would support the positions they were championing, whatever stances were taken by their bishops. They also appear to have decided, on grounds of principle or electoral calculation, that they could profitably play on the Progressive Conservative willingness to associate with religious right causes.

The PCs went into the 2014 election with high expectations and seemed, this time, to be determined not to undercut their campaign with diversions into what Jonathan Malloy refers to as the "bright shiny objects" beloved of religious conservatives.[52] And there was no indication from any of the local campaigns that the party's candidates were making anything of the Liberal leader's sexual orientation. After years of signalling to moral traditionalists, including Catholic conservatives, that theirs was their natural party preference, the PCs seemed now to be recognizing that more harm than good was coming from the stances they had been defending. But, once again, they campaigned on a hard-right economic platform, enough to rescue the Liberals and lead them to a majority government. Tim Hudak announced his resignation has PC leader, and many observers assumed that any new leader would lean closer to the centre.

The Return of Sex Education and the Diversification of Protest
Even under Kathleen Wynne's premiership, there was still no indication of quick action on the sexual health education curriculum. Caution may well have been reinforced by media coverage of child pornography charges laid against Benjamin Levin, a member of Wynne's transition team and a former deputy education minister from 2004 to 2007.[53] Even though Levin had nothing to do with the reform of the sex education curriculum, conservative commentators were more than prepared to forge that imaginary link.

However, the pressure on the government to update sexual health education was not letting up, and, in the fall of 2014, the government signalled that it would begin a new round of consultations. The education minister in charge of this project was Liz Sandals, who had led the task forces reporting on school bullying during the McGuinty period. Flanked by Premier Wynne, she emphasized that extensive new consultations would be conducted with parents and educators.[54] Four months later, on February 23, 2015, the new curriculum was very publicly announced, broadly similar to the earlier revision, though with new discussions of the risks associated with young people's use of social media.[55] In announcing that the new program would be in schools by the start of classes in September, Sandals made a point of vowing not to cave in to pressure from religious conservatives. When reminded of the government's withdrawal of reforms in 2010, her response was: "I was disappointed that didn't happen, but you can rest assured that I will make sure it happens now."

The PC leadership race was now under way, and the candidate most favoured by the Christian right, MPP Monte McNaughton, was quick to attack the government, arguing, "it's not the Premier of Ontario's job, especially Kathleen Wynne, to tell parents what's age appropriate for their children."[56] This personal attack provoked the premier into delivering a blistering response in the legislature, one that made absolutely clear the homophobic subtext of McNaughton's remarks. Media coverage seemed for a time to treat opposition to the curriculum as anachronistic, and even very conservative political commentators were saying that an updated curriculum was essential.[57]

Protests, however, were becoming more widespread, and this time there was a wider array of opponents. To be sure, evangelicals were prominently involved, including Charles McVety and Gwen Landolt, the central figure in the anti-feminist REALWomen of Canada. So too were conservative Catholics, coming out of groups like the Campaign Life Coalition and the schools-focused group Parents as First Educators, though the Catholic educational system's right to refract the curriculum through its own lens muted Catholics response overall.[58] This time, however, much more activism emerged beyond this predictable core, with mobilization in Chinese Christian, Muslim, Sikh, and Hindu communities constituting what one writer describes as "a multicultural army of social conservatives who are angry, energized and eager to test their political power."[59] There had been some signs of this earlier on. In 2012, the group Public Education Advocates for Christian Equity had staked out a public profile by encouraging Christian and Muslim parents to withdraw their children from classes that would touch on questions of faith and morality, and their long list of objectionable topics included sex education (from the old curriculum) and any teaching suggesting that homosexuality was normal or healthy.[60]

Almost immediately after the release of the new curriculum, highly visible protests emerged from ethnic minority communities. In Brampton, an area with a large South Asian population, long-time community activist Jotvinder Sodhi had organized a town hall meeting on the subject just before the curriculum was released in February, accusing its proponents of encouraging students to "experiment with homosexuality."[61] He then introduced Monte McNaughton as the "star speaker" who "stands for us." Chinese Canadian evangelical Christians were also in the forefront of the growing opposition movement, and they helped to essentially shout down Liberal MPPs who tried to inform their local constituents about the new curriculum. They formed the Parents Alliance of Ontario, which quickly grew to three thousand members. It prepared a petition letter for parents and friends, which led off with the claim that the new curriculum was directed by "the convicted child pornographer Benjamin Levin."[62] On April 14th, it booked twenty-five school buses to get supporters to a large Queen's Park rally that was a turning point not only for its size but also for the media attention it garnered.

In late April, protesters announced a plan to encourage parents to withdraw their children from school for a week in early May. The government was concerned enough about the scale of protest that, on April 29th, Premier Wynne met a group of protest leaders in her office. The group included Jotvinder Sodhi, Feras Marish (from the Muslim Dar Foundation), Christina Liu (from Parents Alliance), Gwen Landoldt (from REAL Women), and Lorraine La Vigne (from Parents as First Educators).[63] They were uncompromising in their demands, and the meeting did nothing to slow the protest wave.

The parent and student "strike" began on Monday, May 4th. In the Toronto District School Board there were about twenty thousand more absentees than would have been normal for that day – more than double. Even though the overall protest had a large evangelical presence, absenteeism was most dramatic in schools with large Muslim concentrations. In Toronto's Thorncliffe Park, for example, public school absenteeism ranged from about 50 to 90 percent. The chair of the Thorncliffe Park Parents Association was quoted as saying: "There's an agenda of promoting the LGBTQ community and, although we know this is a secular society, please don't come into my home with this ... it means we're indoctrinating children with a minority lifestyle."[64]

The multicultural dimension to the protest wave might have given the Liberals pause, but they had developed the view that opposition to the curriculum was driven either by prejudice or misinformation.[65] This was not a difficult conclusion to reach, given many of the claims about what was in the new curriculum, the virtually constant evocation of homophobic language in the voices of the opposition, and the unrealistic expectation that parents could fully protect themselves from what they saw as objectionable messages about gender and sexuality. The government response was to develop an information campaign in several languages, seconded in some cases by school board measures to address what were perceived as myths.

The opposition persisted into the new school year that fall, with renewed calls for students to be pulled out of school. Once again, over half of the students at Thorncliffe Park Public School were absent on October 1st, the day of protest, though apart from that one day, only about one-tenth of students had stayed away. Parental unease at this one school was sustained enough that the principal came to an agreement with parents that students would have the option of enrolling in a class that offered a slightly amended version of the new Grade 1 curriculum, which 40 percent opted to take and which significantly reduced overall absenteeism. Outside of this particular area in Toronto, schools across the province saw very few unusual absentees, with one analysis estimating that a provincewide total of two thousand students had been withdrawn from the public system in favour of home schooling by parents upset over the new curriculum.[66] By then, extra-parliamentary supporters of the new curriculum had made a point of creating multicultural alliances. When an information guide was developed by the Peel District School Board, which has a very large South Asian student population, it was endorsed by groups like the Hindu Federation of Canada and the World Sikh Organization.[67]

Change in the Progressive Conservatives' Leadership

In the spring of 2015, in the midst of protests over the new sex education curriculum, the PCs selected Patrick Brown as their new leader. He had long been regarded as a dark horse candidate, but was strikingly successful in signing up thousands of new party members, many of them within ethnic minority communities. His past record while a federal Conservative MP clearly placed him in the social conservative camp, and in his run for the provincial leadership he had courted social conservative support. As part of this effort, Brown had also associated himself with curriculum protesters and promised that, as premier, he would go "back to the drawing board."[68] He then told a February rally that "teachers should teach facts about sex education, not values ... parents teach values."[69] When Monte McNaughton withdrew from the PC leadership campaign because of weak support, he urged his followers to throw their weight behind Brown, arguing that he was the only candidate who would work to eliminate the new sex-ed curriculum. When Brown won in May, the congratulatory messages he received included one from Charles McVety and another from the Campaign Life Coalition.[70]

In addition to helping Brown's leadership campaign, there was also speculation that the sex-education issue could be advantageous to the federal Conservatives in the upcoming national election scheduled for October, 2015, especially in the crucial ethno-culturally diverse regions around Toronto. Senior federal strategists had already been predicting that the party's campaign would emphasize that immigrant values aligned with the party and that Prime Minister Harper believed that parenting should be left to parents.[71] It was also reported that, as a reaction to the Ontario provincial curriculum, the federal Liberals were experiencing a drop in public support among ethno-cultural minorities in Toronto's western suburbs. (In the end, the Trudeau Liberals took nearly all of those suburban seats, though few imagined that concern over the sex education issue had disappeared.)

The federal election results indicated that pitching to social conservatives might produce more vote losses than gains. And indeed, even before the PC leadership race was over, there were signs that Patrick Brown was rhetorically distancing himself from family traditionalism. After winning the leadership he was asked about the sex-ed curriculum issue, and he responded: "That's not a significant issue for me."[72] In early June, no Progressive Conservative MPPs voted against an NDP private member's bill banning "conversion therapy" for sexual minority young people, a frontal attack on a "remedy" long promoted by evangelical Christians.[73] The party also did not have any public response to the Liberal government's announcement that it would expand access to sex reassignment surgery, and, at the end of June, Brown marched in Toronto's Pride

Parade as part of a sizable contingent organized by a newly formed group known as LGBTories. When the legislature resumed sitting in the fall, Brown announced that he would serve as his own education critic, but he insisted that he had no interest in "revisiting social issues" and reminded reporters that he had marched in Pride.[74] At the federal Conservatives' policy convention in the spring of 2016, he expressed support for the campaign to remove the official party policy opposing same-sex marriage, despite having sided with social conservatives in favour of a 2006 Conservative parliamentary motion aimed at rolling back recently won marriage rights.

However, neither the sex education issue, nor Patrick Brown's strategic challenges in managing social conservatives, were destined to stop there. During a late-summer by-election in 2016, local PC campaigners widely distributed a letter from the party leader's office that promised to "scrap the controversial changes to sex-ed introduced by Premier Wynne." Within days Brown disavowed the letter, claiming to have strong support for a sex education curriculum to "combat homophobia and raise important issues like consent, mental health, bullying, and gender identity," and signalling his determination to lead a party that was "modern, inclusive, pragmatic, and that reflects the diversity and values of our province."[75] This reversal was the mirror image of former Liberal Premier's flip-flop six years earlier. Furious evangelical leaders, including Charles McVety, then reported on conversations from the leadership campaign in which Brown had assured them of his social conservative beliefs, citing his long-standing opposition to abortion and same-sex marriage.[76] Christian conservatives then flexed their muscles by helping to secure the PC nomination for one of their own, nineteen-year-old Sam Oosterhoff, in Tim Hudak's old riding of Niagara-West Glanbrook. In the nomination race, Oosterhoff edged out the establishment candidate, Rick Dykstra, who was a former federal Conservative MP, the sitting President of the PC Party, and a personal friend of Patrick Brown. Oosterhoff went on to win, and during the campaign declared his unequivocal opposition to the sex-ed curriculum, same-sex marriage, and abortion. Soon afterwards, Patrick Brown stated that "if your reason for going to Queen's Park would be to push a divisive social issue, then that would be unwelcome."[77] On the other hand, federal Conservative Party of Canada leadership contestant Brad Trost cited the case as illustrative of the fact that "social conservatives are alive, they're important, and they need to be included in all conservative parties all across Canada."[78]

More than ever, the PC leadership was in a difficult position, relying significantly on a religiously traditional base but now also wary of making this alliance explicit with religiously conservative stances. Yes, the reduction in number of people who protested against the sex education curriculum reduced the issue's overall attractiveness to the party. Conservative Catholics seemed to be becoming less visible in pressing Queen's Park for exemptions, even if there were school trustees who continued to offer up resistance.[79] As a result, there seemed to be little room to signal the party's understanding of a constituency that remained vital to it in hotly contested elections. Developments in late 2016, however, indicated that such issues were still contentious within PC ranks and would continue to present the party's leadership with strategic and policy dilemmas.

The Persistence of a Partisan Divide on Social Conservative Issues

By 2010, it appeared highly unlikely that any party in Ontario would attempt to secure electoral advantage by seizing a faith-related policy issue. Important shifts in public attitudes towards abortion and sexual diversity, reinforced by constitutional rulings in the courts, suggested that many more votes could be lost than gained by promising to roll back the clock on "morality" policy. We then saw that the threat of mobilization by evangelical Protestants and conservative Catholics over what young people were taught in schools was sufficient to draw the Progressive Conservatives into an explicit defence of traditionalist values and to force a Liberal premier to reverse course on sexual health education.

There seemed to be a shift in mid-2015. Even in the face of renewed and more broadly based protest against the sex education curriculum, PC leaders were now increasingly distancing themselves from openly expressing support for their social conservative constituency. The Liberals stood firm in their policy initiatives, in part because of troubling memories of 2010 and now also convinced that they could benefit from painting the PCs as having a traditionalist moral agenda. It appeared reasonable to conclude that the faith realignment that had positioned the PCs as the only natural home for social conservatives no longer had policy relevance and might eventually go the way of the historic de-nominational distinction between Liberals and PCs.

Developments in late 2016, though, require us to be cautious about this, not least because few observers would have predicted that religious conservatives would be influential in 2010. Few, too, would have pre-dicted that the Christian right's message would be so significantly strengthened by the kind of widespread political mobilization in ethno-cultural communities that we witnessed in 2015. The multiculturaliza-tion of protests against a revised sex education curriculum that was so evident in the spring and early fall of that year gives pause to any assertion that the Progressive Conservatives in particular, can fully sidestep such issues over the medium term.

The Mobilizing Resources of Religious Conservatives

Religious conservatives, in Ontario as well as in other parts of Canada where they form a critical mass, have mobilizing advantages in their local networks and in their regular contact with faith leaders whom they trust. This is true of evangelical Protestants and, to some extent, of conservative Catholics, who are now more ethno-culturally diverse than they were in the past. It is also true of traditionalists within at least some religious minority communities that are substantially represented in urban Ontario. This does not automatically translate into the poten-tial for political mobilization, but the 2015 protest wave aroused by sex education in schools showed that minority communities have robust networks that are able to rally significant numbers.

Evangelical Protestants constitute less than 10 percent of Ontario's population, and they have not formed provincewide groups that consist-ently press their policy concerns in provincial affairs. However, national groups such as the Evangelical Fellowship of Canada and Cardus have a presence in Ottawa, and they have both staff and members from across Ontario. For decades, going back to the 1970s, there have also been individual Christian leaders in the Greater Toronto Area who have mobilized provincewide evangelical opposition to liberalized abortion and the public recognition of sexual diversity. The first major wave of evangelical political mobilization in Ontario occurred during the 1986 debate over adding sexual orientation to Ontario's Human Rights Code. And, even if the groups taking the official lead were small and not particularly skilled, church communities across the province galvanized an unprecedented volume of phone calls and written messages to politicians. This mobilization happened again in 1994, though this time the coordination was more sophisticated. On those and other occasions, evangelical political leverage has been aided by media vehicles representing this perspective, amplified by the access that Ontarians have to US Christian broadcasts, which have long attended to what have been viewed as alarming developments in Canada.[80] A preparedness to listen to such warnings is maintained, in part, by comparatively high rates of attendance at religious services (over 50 percent among evangelicals compared to the provincial average of between 15 and 20 percent).

Evangelical protests against abortion and LGBT rights have regularly been combined with Catholic mobilizing. Decades of conservative rule in the Vatican ensured that bishops across Ontario and archbishops seated in Kingston, Toronto, or Ottawa were conservative on questions of reproduction and sexual diversity. In their attempts to influence public policy they are assisted by the Toronto-based Catholic Civil Rights League (formed in 1985) and, at the local level, by chapters of such groups as the Knights of Columbus. Catholic schools can also be used as vehicles for generating activism on selected issues. The sheer size of the Roman Catholic population in the province means that calls to activism delivered by clerics can mobilize a sizable response, and the threat of such calls to action can, under certain circumstances, still give pause to politicians nervous about marginal seats. There can be no doubt that this leverage has declined in recent decades, evidenced in the church's "loss" in the GSA debate and its comparative silence in the renewed debate over sex education in 2015. The vast majority of Catholics do not attend mass regularly, and many of those who do take exception to church teachings on the issues that have been most contentious in recent decades.[81] Still, we have found in recent years that conservative Catholicism continues to provide an important fuel for political mobilization.

The large number of immigrants who arrive in Ontario each year have helped to reinforce the ranks of morally conservative Catholics and evangelicals, even if there are no grounds for assuming the ubiquity of such conservatism among immigrant groups and ethnic minorities. In the Greater Toronto Area particularly, churches from both Catholic and evangelical traditions are increasingly multicultural, and this was on full display at the multi-coloured protests against the sex education curriculum in 2015.

One contributor to the continuing political leverage of moral traditionalists has been the common cause forged by evangelical Protestants, Catholics, and conservatives in other faith communities. The Muslim community is now significantly the largest such minority, and, even if it is not politically conservative on most issues, it does have a strong current of moral or familial conservatism.[82] The same applies to the first-generation migrants in other minority groups from regions of the world in which sexual diversity is repressed. Minority faith groups have had little profile in pro-life organizing, but they have become more visible in protests against the public recognition of LGBT rights. In earlier periods of contention, their participation was largely tokenistic, but now their own numbers and confidence have been swelled by immigration and by the focus on schooling.

The Specificities of Schooling

The room for manoeuvre available to those who protest the public recognition of sexual diversity has substantially narrowed over recent decades, but it is no accident that its extension to the question of schooling still has the capacity to inflame. This is a policy area that affects parents very directly, and it also raises complex questions that have never been fully resolved anywhere in Canada. Public uncertainty and anxiety are amplified when childhood sexuality is at play or when any serious challenge to gender norms arises. This is at least as true among more recently arrived members of ethno-cultural minority communities as it is among more established communities of faith, concerned as they are about both integration and cultural retention.

Among the issues that retain important elements of irresolution are whether schools should convey values that have traditionally prevailed in society or encourage questioning of dominant ideas; whether they should emphasize commonalities in Canadian society or factors that differentiate them; whether they should protect childhood "innocence" or deliberately expose students to the world as it is; and whether educators should defer to parental authority, particularly when moral perspectives are in question.

There is no doubt that most religious conservatives across all faiths come down clearly on the side of reinforcing tradition and protecting "innocent children" from "confusing" ideas – for example, about gender and sexuality. However, there are broader publics who are also uncertain about the role of schools in general, and who also have anxieties about childhood sexuality and gender. Many in this broader population know little about what schools actually teach in such areas, and are therefore susceptible to distorted campaigning. These concerns may be especially obvious in small towns and rural areas as well as in urban communities whose members have migrated from countries dominated by comparatively traditional family norms.

In reality, traditional gender constructs are deeply set in Canadian schools, reproduced and policed by peer pressure, media portrayals, and, indeed, by parental behaviour. As Epstein and Johnson argue, "attempts to educate students about sexuality take place in a context complicated by the homophobia of many students, the macho performances of many boys, the wish of many girls (and boys) to be desired, the official taboos on talking about sexuality in school, and the need to made the sex education classroom a (relatively) safe place in which all their students can talk about sexuality."[83] For decades, teachers have often avoided talking about both sexuality and sexual diversity, in part because they anticipate resistance from students or their parents.[84]

Many opponents of reform in sexual health education basically support such avoidance and the reinforcement of established gender norms. Advocates of reform who talk about how much information on sexuality is available to young people outside of school (for example, over the internet) simply fuel the determination to protect children from nontraditional messages. The most devout may seek to send their children to private schools, though the absence of state funding means that this is not an option that many parents can afford, leading some to turn to home-schooling as an alternative. Many non-Catholic parents will also send their children to Catholic schools, sensing (or hoping) that they are more disciplined and more traditional in their teaching on gender and sexuality.[85] Still, there are many traditionalists who continue to send their children to public schools, and they are deeply concerned about the prospect of their children getting taught lessons with which they profoundly disagree.

Circumstantial Facilitators

While there have been several instances of impressive mobilization by moral traditionalists in Ontario, their influence has varied significantly. Indeed, on those occasions when mobilization has been effective in defeating legislative initiatives or delaying reformist policy, there have often been specific circumstances that augmented its leverage. In 1994, conservative Christians advocacy against the NDP's bill to recognize same-sex relationships was aided by the unprecedented and sweeping nature of the legislation, and particularly by the fact that it included adoption – an issue that many Canadians found difficult to accept at the time – as well as by the tenuous hold that the NDP had on government.

In the 2010 sexual health education controversy, the Liberal government's unpreparedness for controversy contributed to a flat-footed early response to an attack from a lone-wolf evangelical activist. There was also a degree of media sensationalizing of the issue, which further amplified the volume of Charles McVety's accusations. The Liberal Party's uncertain fate in the upcoming election made it wary of the electoral consequences of alienating some of the Catholic base that it still held, along with the moral traditionalists among the new Canadians who were still part of the Liberal coalition. When a Liberal government under new leadership reintroduced curricular change on sexual health education, it was much better prepared. It also knew that one more attempt by the Progressive Conservatives to take the traditionalist side posed electoral risks from which Liberals could benefit. Patrick Brown's climb down from association with religious conservatives following his leadership campaign seemed to reinforce the views of Liberal Party strategists that they could ride out the storm. The PCs still had a noteworthy constituency of social conservatives in their ranks, and Brown's victory in the party's 2015 leadership race was built in significant measure upon a core of supporters from among evangelical Protestants, conservative Catholics, and traditionalist currents in several ethnic and religious minority communities. But for the time being, they were exercising little policy leverage.

The Absence of Sustained Partisan Distinctions on Religious Minorities

When discussing the role of faith in Ontario provincial politics, we find one axis of contention largely missing – that based on conflict over minority religious rights and practices. There has certainly been no public consensus supporting, for example, RCMP constables wearing turbans or Sikh students carrying kirpans. There was sufficient public opposition to broadening family arbitration to include Sharia law that the Liberal government of Dalton McGuinty announced an end to official recognition of all religiously based arbitration. By and large, however, public contention over minority recognition cases in Ontario has been muted. Party leaders have generally avoided politicizing court rulings and institutional policy changes that de-privilege Christianity or enhance recognition of other faiths.

The dramatic increase in numbers of minority religious communities – more so in Ontario than in any other Canadian region – has given all three major parties an interest in either retaining minority voters or capturing more of them. Minority voters have traditionally supported the Liberals in Ontario, as they have at the federal level, but the contemporary provincial party knows that it cannot take such support for granted. The federal Conservative Party transparently adopted a policy of appealing to minority communities, in part on the basis of free market entrepreneurialism but also on the basis of traditional family values. The provincial PCs have been slower to adopt an explicit goal of doing the same, but the party's campaign in the 2011 election clearly targeted ethnic minority communities in the Greater Toronto Area by using the sex education issue. This effort was unsuccessful, but Tim Hudak's willingness to side with religious conservatives in the year following that election still owed something to a belief that minority voters could be swayed by such positioning. And, of course, Patrick Brown's leadership of the party owes a great deal to an electoral coalition that very much includes ethno-cultural and religious minority voters.

The point is that no party in Ontario has an interest in systematically marginalizing any large religious minority. True, the McGuinty Liberals' opposition to the PCs' 2007 campaign promise on private school funding played, in part, to public fears about Muslim schools. And individual politicians might well have sounded off locally about going too far to accommodate religious minorities. But no party has shown signs of systematically marshalling such sentiment or playing to it. And none shows any indication of being tempted in that direction. The by-now long history of leaving such issues to local resolution, or to the courts, seems to appeal to the strategies and leaders of all three major parties and to virtually all of the serious contenders to their leadership.

Conclusion

In Ontario's party system, denominational differences now seem entirely relegated to history in policy terms and in distinctions between the electorates of the PCs and the Liberals. The full public funding provided to Catholic schools remains contentious for many Ontarians, and the resistance of some parts of the separate system to the recognition of sexual diversity has helped keep that issue in the public eye. But it is a muted conflict rooted almost entirely in the belief that two fully funded school systems is no longer appropriate and not at all anchored in denominational animosity.

The faith alignment that has most influenced the province's parties has been that between religious, moral, and family traditionalists, on the one hand, and progressive reformers, on the other. From the mid-1980s onward, the Progressive Conservatives became the only party willing, recurrently, to support policies favoured by social conservatives. The other two parties had their ups and downs on the road to adopting policies that were on the progressive side of this divide, particularly with respect to sexual diversity. While the NDP got there by the end of the 1990s, it took the Liberals until the middle of the 2010s. By then we were seeing strong indications that the influence of traditionalist constituencies was waning.

Since the mid-1980s, social conservative mobilization has generally failed to stop changes in law and institutional practice, but we have seen that, in recent years, controversies over schooling suggest that we should not completely discount the political influence of moral conservatives, including communities of evangelical Protestants and Catholics still prepared to take advantage of well-established networks. The large proportion of Ontario's population that is constituted by first- and second-generation immigrants might well be a source of new fuel for religious conservatism, even though these are not populations that are generally supportive of the political right. Much of this conservatism is derived from the traditionalism on such issues found in countries of origin, and so we anticipate substantial intergenerational change.

None of this means that there is much potential for a multi-faith coalition among religious conservatives. Continuing links between faith communities that are very different and that agree on little are very difficult to build and sustain. Cooperation between Catholics and evangelical Protestants can be tenuous enough, and this type of cooperation becomes much more challenging in broader coalitional attempts. Chinese evangelicals with significant roots in the Greater Toronto Area and first-generation Muslim traditionalists may have been able to mobilize in parallel with conservative Sikhs and Hindus to protest revisions to the sex-ed curriculum, but this is not an easily replicable phenomenon.

Also, to be successful, the religious right requires support from at least one of the major parties at Queen's Park. Until 2015, the Progressive Conservatives consistently demonstrated their willingness to do just that, even while prioritizing public service cuts and tax reduction. None of that party's past leaders, from Mike Harris through to Tim Hudak, talked in any sustained way about faith or "traditional family values," and yet it is they who aggressively opposed LGBT-positive policy. In this way, the PCs positioned themselves as representing the only party defending moral and family traditionalism. Even as late as 2015, when the Progressive Conservative Party of Ontario finally seemed to realize that its rhetorical alliance with social conservatives was electorally ill-advised, this current within the party was sufficiently large to propel little-known Patrick Brown into the leadership. By and large,

Brown has been clear about avoiding the hot button issues championed by moral traditionalists and has repeatedly denied his own social conservatism, but he knows better than most that the social conservatives within his party are an important and restive constituency.

While far less important in the twenty-first century than it was in the late twentieth, faith still matters in electoral alignments, in party positioning, and in the capacity of religious conservatives to mobilize their grassroots. Denomination no longer matters much, if at all, in differentiating parties from one another or in provoking widespread public contention. The institutional recognition of minority religious practices has, until now, not provoked sustained public mobilization and has not seriously divided parties one from another. But social conservatism remains a vocal part of the province's citizenry, particularly within the Progressive Conservatives, and this will continue to confront that party with the same strategic dilemma faced by the federal Conservative Party of Canada and by provincial parties on the right in western Canada – how to retain the loyalty of that current within the electorate without alienating other voters. Most importantly, questions over what students get taught in school will remain contentious among new and old Canadians. These concerns have the potential to rouse anxiety as well as opposition within a broad range of communities, including those of very different faiths and those without strong religious attachment. To imagine that this no longer has the power to intimidate politicians is unwise.

The Declining Influence of Conservative Faith in Alberta since 1971

The election of Rachel Notley's New Democrats in May 2015 was one of a series of events suggesting that religious conservatism has rapidly declined as a source of political influence in Alberta. During the 2015 election, evangelical voices were entirely marginalized – this in a province widely seen (and accurately so) as having Canada's most significant "Bible belt." This silence extended to the Wildrose Party, which had provoked outrage in its 2012 election campaign when one of its candidates was found to have previously condemned homosexuality as leading to eternal damnation in a "lake of fire."[1] These developments represent a real change, drastically reducing whatever was distinctive to Alberta in the play of religious conservatism, even if not eliminating that current from the province's partisan right.

For decades, moral traditionalism had been an important current within the perpetually governing Progressive Conservative Party, even during the long periods in which that party's leaders seemed to have little sympathy for policies most strongly advocated by the religious right. Political nods towards the religious right persisted through the end of the opening decade of the twenty-first century. Much like their counterparts in Ontario, the PCs had governed from the pragmatic centre upon forming government in 1971. However, the Alberta PCs also inherited the mantle of the political right from the Social Credit

Party, which had been unequivocally associated with evangelical Protestantism. The PC turn to the neoliberal right under Ralph Klein in the early 1990s simply reinforced the party's logical attractiveness to moral and religious traditionalists.

Since its birth as a province, Alberta has had an unusually large evangelical population. From the mid-1930s, when the Social Credit Party won its first election, through almost all of the period of the Progressive Conservative Party's electoral dominance, a religiously infused current of conservatism was an important part of the electoral coalition maintained by Alberta's governing parties. Denomination mattered much less than did adherence to traditional notions of faith and morality.

But, over time, things changed. The 2010 election of Naheed Nenshi as Calgary's mayor reinforced talk of a "new Alberta." In 2011, Alison Redford was chosen PC leader and the province's first female premier, seeming to mark out a new direction for the party's approach to the role of government and "morality" policy. This was a time when the Wildrose Party was mounting an increasingly threatening challenge on the right, but its selection of Danielle Smith in effect downplayed moral traditionalism and highlighted libertarianism.

The Redford victory in the 2012 provincial election strengthened the argument that politics had fundamentally shifted, especially as the Wildrose loss was seen as coming in part from public reaction against vocal expressions of views associated with the Christian right. The 2015 victory of the NDP, a party with almost no links to traditionalist faith communities, further cemented the idea of an Alberta that was no more conservative than were other Canadian regions. The Wildrose Party put up a strong fight in that election, under a leader with conservative Christian roots, but within its ranks, too, there now seemed an aversion to talking about faith in the political realm.

However, the dramatic and important developments of recent years do not eliminate the sizable constituency of religiously conservative voters. Until the Progressive Conservatives' defeat in 2015, every party leader, Redford included, reacted with caution and hesitation on issues related to sexual diversity. Neither they nor the NDP government, which won office in that year, was prepared to significantly challenge the variety of ways in which public funding supports a school system uniquely tailored to the needs of faith communities – including evangelical Christians. And however much the Wildrose leadership would like to keep faith-based voices on the margins of that party, its electorate is still heavily tilted towards them. This reality has presented that party with dilemmas aplenty in the last half decade, and it will continue to do so. At the same time, the Progressive Conservative leadership recognizes that winning back public office will probably require some degree of respectful recognition of moral conservative voters, alongside modest policy gestures towards such recognition – a pattern we have seen in the federal Conservative Party and that we will continue to see in the Progressive Conservative Party of Ontario.

In this chapter, we begin with an exploration of the roots of moral traditionalism in Alberta and then provide an analysis of the strength of that current within the Progressive Conservative Party since the early 1970s. The discussion of Ralph Klein's premiership chronicles the response of his government to sexual diversity issues and the development of school "choice" at the provincial and local levels. As we focus on the period since 2011, we examine the Wildrose Party's capture of most of the moral conservatives who once supported the PCs, and the strategic dilemmas occasioned by that shift, not only for that party's leaders but also for Progressive Conservatives hoping to lure them back. The chapter ends with a consideration of the current influence of religious conservatism, cautioning against over-hasty conclusions about its disappearance from provincial politics, particularly in areas related to education and social policy.

The Cultural and Historical Roots of Alberta's Moral Traditionalism
Analyses of Alberta history point to early white settlement that fuelled a religiously distinctive political culture. Nelson Wiseman sets Alberta apart from the Loyalist and later British migration that dominated other parts of the country by pointing to the formative influence of immigration from the midwest great plains of the United States. What came with these migrants was a radical form of individualism, mixed with "religiously-infused moral conservatism."[2] Clark Banack suggests that the

impact of evangelical Christianity on the province's politics lies primarily in support for populist anti-statism and opposition to economic "collectivism."[3] These views find their roots in particular currents of American evangelicism and in the politics of such early Alberta premiers as William Aberhart and Earnest Manning.

In recent decades, the prominence of evangelical Christianity in the province's political life has been visible in the careers of several prominent politicians, among them one-time provincial treasurer and federal Conservative cabinet minister Stockwell Day, as well as Reform Party leader and now elder statesman Preston Manning. The central role that Albertans played in the development of the Reform Party and the Canadian Alliance during the 1980s and 1990s, and the significant participation of religious conservatives in those parties, seemed to reinforce the argument that the province had a stronger and more politically visible Bible belt than did any other part of Canada. Well into the twenty-first century, Progressive Conservative politicians at the provincial level in Alberta were prepared to make policy statements and adopt measures that symbolized their sympathy with moral traditionalists. And, where possible, they have pursued policy initiatives in areas such as school choice, which appealed both to social conservatives as well as to fiscally conservative neoliberals. During the period we examine here, evangelical concerns were never central to Alberta political discourse and were often at the losing end of policy debates, but they continued to have influence.

Over recent decades, several analysts point to the relative conservatism of Alberta politics but emphasize either anti-state or populist attitudes rather than faith. Examples include Rand Dyck as well as David Laycock in his analysis of the Reform Party and the Canadian Alliance Party.[4] Jared Wesley does not address the issue directly, but in his extensive exploration of the core messages of party campaigns in Alberta he finds that moral traditionalism is almost entirely marginalized by the themes of populism, individualism, and a sense of alienation from centres of power located elsewhere in the country.[5] On the other hand, while Linda Trimble's analysis of the politics of gender in Alberta deals very little with religion, it argues that, from the 1970s through the 1980s, traditional family values had a stronger hold on government policy and public beliefs here than elsewhere in Canada.[6] By the time she published this analysis in 1992, she could see changes occurring across all parties, including the governing PCs, although she had no illusions that Alberta's distinctiveness on this front had been eliminated.

This emphasis on one or another form of regional distinctiveness is not universally embraced, however. David Elkins and Richard Simeon argued decades ago that regional differences in Canada were both exaggerated and diminishing.[7] Ailsa Henderson has adopted a view that is fully compatible with this, pointing to "regions" as more shaped by urban-rural differences than by provincial and territorial boundaries.[8] In the introduction to their 1992 volume on Alberta politics, Allan Tupper and Roger Gibbins cite trends in public opinion and government policy in arguing that the province is not particularly distinct from other parts of Canada.[9] This, they argue, is the unsurprising product of urbanization, immigration, and globalization.

Writing in 2004, Mark Lisac challenges the "hackneyed" stereotypes of "maverick" and self-sufficient entrepreneur and the belief that this generated a distinctive approach to government:

> In reality, Alberta is a highly conformist society in which complaints about the federal government or Eastern (actually Central) Canada make up the only accepted displays of opposition to authority. And the reality of the self-sufficient business owner ... is compromised by the equal reality of agricultural and resource-extraction industries that depend heavily on government regulation, government subsidy, government-provided infrastructure, and government financial aid during periods of low prices or other disasters.[10]

Lisac points out that, in some domains, the government has become a big spender and a controlling presence steadily removing the capacity of local governments and institutions to deviate from provincial policy. Lisac spends little time on questions of religious faith, but he talks about the "remnants of William Aberhart's and Ernest Manning's Bible Belt" surviving in small towns, "with small posters in [shop] windows advertising evangelical meetings."[11] In any event, he argues that, under

PC governments, rural Albertans in effect "provided a salt-of-the-earth cover for urban ideologues."

There are elements of truth in all these portrayals. Highly individualistic evangelicism has made a mark on Alberta provincial politics, and, until very recently, it has done so quite visibly. But there is no question that the moral traditionalism so assertively represented in the parties that governed the province until 2015 is no longer the force that it once was. Alberta politics have changed, though it has been an extraordinarily slow evolution.

The Progressive Conservatives' Neoliberal Preoccupations, 1971–2011

The long period of Progressive Conservative rule that began with Peter Lougheed's stunning election victory in 1971 did entail an important change in the role of faith-based politics. The Social Credit Party, in power until then, was transparently infused with evangelicism, but the PCs were different. In the words of one observer:

> If you arm wrestled on the political right, the libertarians would win out against the social conservatives – they do every time ... Everyone listened to [Premier "Bible Bill"] Aberhart's broadcasts on the radio – you could walk down the street without missing a word. Ernest Manning, as a concession to human weakness, did allow liquor to be sold in this province, but it was with a very, very tough regulatory body. I think it just embarrassed people that they were governed by this preacher who would get on the radio every Sunday morning. This was the kind of paternalism from which [Peter] Lougheed's Conservatives rescued Albertans so they could be modern.[12]

Lougheed never demonstrated any particular affinity for religious conservatism. His focus was on the provincial economy, on oil and gas particularly, and on asserting provincial rights. As Peter Smith argues, the rise of the Progressive Conservatives in the early 1970s signalled an increase in the political influence of – and PC attentiveness to – the "new urban middle classes."[13] In the 1980s, economic issues along with federal-provincial relations dominated the party and government agenda. By this time, the PCs held near-absolute control of the province's rural ridings, effectively forging an alliance between rural interests and the oil and gas capital of Calgary. But there was little doubt that the party's preoccupations remained with retaining the confidence of business, particularly in the resource-extraction sectors.[14]

When Don Getty took over the party's leadership in 1985, there was little indication of a fundamental change in direction. Recession and falling oil prices had hit the province hard, producing what Smith calls a "new politics of scarcity and conflict."[15] This crisis increased the party's dependence on the rural electorate, which had already been an influential part of its winning coalition. But Getty had worked in the oil industry when he left government in 1979, and the party's strategic pitch to rural Albertans focused primarily on support for small business, enhanced farm loan programs, and better roads.

Premier Ralph Klein's Agenda

Ralph Klein became PC leader in 1992 and turned the party to the free-market right, promising to eliminate the sizable provincial deficit by 1997.[16] David Stewart, Anthony Sayers, and Mark Lisac warn us against over-stating the shift towards smaller government, pointing to levels of government spending that were substantially above the Canadian provincial average and to continuing patterns of centrally controlled government regulation. Nevertheless, most writers see the early Klein years as embodying a form of neoliberalism that was more radical than anything else in Canada at the time and that served as a prototype for both the Mike Harris Progressive Conservatives in Ontario and the Stephen Harper Conservatives in Ottawa.

To what extent was this neoliberal shift accompanied by an embrace of social conservatism? Klein's record as Calgary mayor during the early years of the AIDS epidemic, in fact, suggested that he was not drawn to the anti-gay politics of the religious right or to moral regulation on other fronts.[17] In the 1980s, for example, he supported funding for AIDS Calgary at a time when most city councillors were opposed. In 1995, while in provincial office, a sizable group of his caucus members advocated measures to stop funding abortions, and Klein publicly argued that the government should stay out of the debate on the issue.

In 1999, Klein addressed fifteen hundred delegates meeting in Ottawa to discuss the formation of the "United Alternative" – designed to bring together supporters of the federal Progressive Conservative and Reform Parties. He warned that their efforts to create a united right would fail if they adopted policies seeking to legislate morality.

> We cannot declare ourselves to be the party of minimum interference in the everyday lives of everyday Canadians, and then propose to interfere in the most personal of all decisions – those decisions that are matters of conscience, those issues that present a moral dilemma, those things of so personal a nature that the decision becomes one between an individual and his or her God.[18]

These remarks received only polite applause, but Klein was undeterred in pressing the point in other settings and at other times. He and other government insiders were becoming increasingly concerned that the province not present itself to outside investors as a socially conservative, reactionary backwater. In the premier's view, economically powerful decision makers contemplating a head office in Calgary were unlikely to be impressed by narrow-minded prejudice.

Ed Stelmach's five-year stint as premier, from 2006 to 2011, saw little major shift from the Klein approach, though he came into politics with "small-c" values of family, community, and order. He did not steer the government away from the prioritization of neoliberalism, and he governed during a time when most Albertans would have seen the most controversial moral issues – related to sexual diversity and reproduction – as settled, for better or for worse. Moral traditionalism was playing second fiddle to economic priorities and, more than ever, was seen as a hindrance in governmental attempts to market the province to investors.

The Persistence of Religious and Moral Conservatism under Ralph Klein

However, even if the PCs pursued an agenda dominated by neoliberalism (though not always followed through in practice), the party needed to retain the support of the morally traditional base that it had pulled away from Social Credit. As Peter Smith points out, rural and small-town Albertans became an even more important core of the party's governing majority after the early 1980s recession made provincial elections more competitive.[19] This current within the party was never powerful enough to push favoured leadership candidates into the Premier's Office, but it was large enough, representing, as it did, an important electoral constituency, to exercise influence.

Ralph Klein depended as much on this coalition as had his predecessors, both in gaining the party leadership and in winning provincial elections. In the early 1990s, he could see the growing appeal of the Reform Party, and there were polls indicating that, in 1993, a provincial version would have attracted 43 percent of Alberta votes, many more than his own party. In 1994, another survey indicated that 55 percent of PC provincial support came from Reform supporters.[20] The principal effect of this threat from the right may well have been to sharpen the appeal of a shift to more radical fiscal conservatism, but it would also have emboldened supporters of traditional family values. In his first election in 1993, Klein supported colleagues who talked up family values and who specifically favoured weakening the province's Human Rights Commission, an issue of particular significance to religious conservatives.[21]

Klein's first term as premier was in fact almost entirely dominated by a neoliberal agenda. But then, after the 1997 election, pressure from social conservatives intensified. In 1995, in the lead-up to a provincial PC convention, pro-life forces had mobilized enough of a campaign to produce about one hundred letters a day in the Premier's Office, and petitions containing about twenty thousand signatures were tabled in the legislature. This was not enough to sway the PC leader, who made it clear that the government would not eliminate health care coverage of the costs of abortion.[22]

On sexual diversity, however, social conservative mobilization had some leverage. More than any provincial government in Canada, Progressive Conservative governments in Alberta resisted taking any steps to officially recognize lesbian and gay rights. At crucial times when equity advocates pressed for more inclusive policy, prominent PC politicians marshalled language on LGBT rights issues that, in most other parts of Canada, would have been regarded as extreme. This rhetoric was matched by a preparedness to enact medium- or low-profile policies that reflected sympathy with the religious right's distaste for sexual difference and its portrayal of LGBT rights as a threat to family values.

Resisting the Prohibition of Discrimination Based on Sexual Orientation[23]

From the 1970s until the end of the 1990s, the central "moral" issue in the province was the addition of sexual orientation to the Individual Rights Protection Act (IRPA). Alberta's Human Rights Commission had begun recommending such a change in 1976 to no effect, despite slowly increasing public support. In 1990, the government's refusal to act came at a time when polling showed that 57 percent of Albertans favoured the addition of sexual orientation to the Act.[24]

Half of Canada's provinces had taken this step by the end of 1992, and courts were leaning strongly in the direction of interpreting the Charter of Rights and Freedoms as prohibiting anti-gay discrimination. But Ralph Klein's 1992 victory as party leader was unlikely to change PC resistance, since he won, in significant measure, on the strength of his support among rural voters. After the 1993 election, too, the fifty-one-person-strong PC caucus probably contained only four or five who favoured adding sexual orientation to the IRPA, and, by this time, the fears about the Reform Party's popularity in the province were at their peak.

Meanwhile, a constitutional challenge to the exclusion of sexual orientation from provincial human rights law was working its way through the courts. Launched in 1991 by Edmontonian Delwin Vriend, the Charter challenge was upheld in a 1994 court ruling. This was reversed by the Alberta Court of Appeal in 1996, but then, on April 2, 1998, the Supreme Court of Canada delivered a stinging rebuke to the Alberta government – "reading" sexual orientation into the IRPA. Anticipating such a defeat, Christian conservatives had already begun mobilizing supporters to press the government to invoke the "notwithstanding" provision of the Charter of Rights and Freedoms, which allows provincial or federal governments to circumvent a court ruling. They were emboldened by Premier Klein publicly musing about precisely this step.

The government was already planning to hem in such a court ruling, but by the time the Court's decision was released, Klein was delivering mixed signals. On the one hand, he told his caucus that he would not circumvent the Court ruling and that discriminating on the ground of sexual orientation was morally wrong. On the other, he reserved the right to limit such advances as gay adoptions, pension benefits, and same-sex marriages. He then encouraged mobilization on the part of Christian conservatives by publicly declaring that he wanted to hear from Albertans. This appeal produced a huge wave of letters and phone calls directed at legislator offices. The premier's own office received nine thousand calls, more than on any other issue during Klein's tenure up to that point.[25] Groups like the Canada Family Action Coalition, the Alberta Federation of Women United for Families, and the Alberta Civil Society Association (led by Calgary politics professor Ted Morton, who would eventually seek the leadership of the party) helped to mobilize a campaign that also had grassroots support in church halls. In the words of one gay activist:

> That week when the decision came down and [the government] announced that they would not respond to it – was just hell here. It was like they had unleashed the dogs of war; it was open season. On Sunday the fundamentalist Christian pastors stood up across the province and said "no," and so the Christians went on the air and the media. It was everywhere: people were constantly talking about it. You couldn't get away from it, and the media was just blowing it up. It was the most unsafe I have ever felt.[26]

Even Klein seemed shaken by the wave of hatred that he had helped generate, characterizing many of the calls and faxes he was getting as "sickening."

> I abhor discrimination. We have people writing letters that quite frankly make your stomach turn. [The Court's ruling] is a very narrow decision giving people the right to go to the Human Rights Commission on issues like residency, employment and services. It's been the law for almost a week now and the world is still standing.[27]

The premier and his core ministers then did take a few steps towards removing the most odious of governmental discrimination based on sexual orientation – for example, by slowly opening up room for lesbian/gay fostering and adoption. Klein and most of the party leadership recognized that public support for basic LGBT rights was increasing, with one late-1998 poll showing just over half of Albertans favouring the extension to same-sex couples of benefits that were already available to co-habiting heterosexual couples, and two-thirds supporting the government's decision to abide by the Supreme Court's *Vriend* decision.[28]

The story, however, does not end here. The Progressive Conservatives' right flank was as determined as ever to resist the recognition of sexual diversity in Alberta law, and observers were talking about how this episode had caused more serious internal divisions in the party than had been seen for the entirety of Klein's hold on the leadership. It can hardly be accidental, then, that in the following year or two, several legislative measures that might have included recognition of same-sex common law couples pointedly excluded them. The government also announced that, in the future, it would invoke the notwithstanding clause to prevent same-sex marriage, a commitment that bordered on the constitutionally ridiculous because jurisdiction over the definition of marriage is federal. In March 1999, when a PC cabinet committee reported on what measures should be adopted to limit the impact of the *Vriend* decision, Klein also offered assurances that sexual orientation was not included in any part of the provincially approved school curriculum, that parents could exempt their children from sex education classes, and that provincial policies aiming to ensure tolerance and understanding in the selection of instructional materials did not include sexual orientation.

Klein, then, was steering a complex path that held social conservatives close to the party while acquiescing to those policy changes that were constitutionally required. According to a veteran PC politician:

> It's a characteristic of the Klein government that they would find some kind of middle ground so that the issue goes below the water. In the end he welcomes the courts helping him set the policy framework. He does not honestly think he can prevent any of this stuff

from happening, so he puts out press releases that give an interpretation that is very nebulous and vague, and he tells people that he's neither giving nor taking away rights in these areas, except the only thing I am going to do is not allow them to call it marriage.[29]

The firm stand on marriage was the most prominent of the bones thrown to his moral and religious traditionalist supporters. After a 1999 Supreme Court of Canada ruling in *M. v. H* that swept away the discriminatory treatment of co-habiting same-sex couples in family law, the Alberta legislature approved in principle a private member's bill aimed at ensuring that same-sex marriage would never be legal in the province, with only two PC members dissenting.[30]

In mid-2003, after the Ontario Court of Appeal ruled that the exclusion of same-sex couples from the definition of marriage was unconstitutional, Alberta's premier stood alone among provincial and territorial leaders in promising to fight any attempt to encode same-sex marriage in law. Klein eventually gave up his crusade on marriage, but after the federal marriage bill cleared Parliament in 2005, he declared his government's intent to "protect" those marriage commissioners who objected to same-sex marriage as well as his readiness (once more) to invoke the nothwithstanding clause if that should become necessary.[31]

Klein's record in office, then, was filled with contradictions. As premier, he recurrently conceded the inevitability of accepting legal protections against anti-gay discrimination. But he regularly pandered to the many social conservatives in his caucus and in the party's rural grassroots, often using language inflaming precisely the prejudice he decried. At times he was highly sensitive to shifting public opinion on issues related to sexual diversity, but he could also apply governmental brakes to policy change in the pursuit of quixotic crusades that reinforced his standing among rural Albertans.

Enhanced Support for Faith-Based Schools

Beyond this erratic record on the recognition of sexual diversity, we also find additional indicators of the PCs shoring up moral conservative support in their schooling policy. The development of a paradigm of school "choice" has very strong support among evangelicals and other moral traditionalists, though its political saleability also comes from its support among fiscal conservatives who dislike state control or believe that competition improves outcomes.[32] It is impossible to disentangle these sources of pressure, particularly in a province in which individualism is such a strong current among evangelical Protestants. What can be said, however, is that religious conservatives have been active for decades in pressing for state funding for faith-based schools and home schooling, and for creating as much leeway as possible in what students are taught.[33] Here we are dealing primarily with evangelical Protestants since Alberta has long provided full funding to a separate Roman Catholic school system. As Alison Taylor points out, the shifts we chronicle here have parallels in Britain, the US, and New Zealand, but Alberta has moved further than has any other Canadian jurisdiction.[34]

The "choice" framework that evolved in Alberta has four key components. One is increased public funding for private schools, most of which were (and are) faith-based. Another is the creation of space for alternative schools *within* public boards and for the incorporation of faith-based schools under this rubric. A third is the relatively generous support provided to home-schooling families, who are allowed to register with any board willing to accept them. And a fourth is the creation of charter schools – publicly funded independent schools operating under charters established by the provincial education ministry and therefore operating outside school board jurisdictions.

Early Policy Shifts

The provision of public funds to support private schools began in 1967 under a Social Credit government, though at a modest level. When the Progressive Conservatives came to power in 1971, they faced intensified pressure to expand such support, and, in 1974, they increased funding to 33 percent of the per-student operating grant provided to public schools (boosting it to 40 percent two years later) and made it easier to meet eligibility requirements.[35]

In 1976, the Edmonton Society for Christian Education submitted a brief to the minister of education calling for such funding to be incrementally increased to 80 percent and then vigorously lobbied PC MLAs, ministers, and government officials in support of this proposal. The government soon declared this high level of support as an eventual goal, justified, in part, by the full funding accorded to Catholic schools.

By this time, the PC government had also stated its support for further expanding school choice and had developed an "umbrella" concept that envisaged private schools receiving full funding by coming under the jurisdiction of public boards.[36] They amended the School Act in 1975 to allow for alternative schools, following a government-commissioned report that called for increased options and experimentation in the public system. In Calgary, the Board of Education incorporated two existing Jewish private schools into the public system as alternative schools, and, within a few years, others followed, including a Christian school operated by the Logos Education Society. The first Logos Christian school began operations as part of the board in 1979 with three hundred students, and a year after that the Logos group asked for a second school site.

Within a few years, opponents of faith-based alternative schools were organizing, and they supported a slate of candidates in the 1983 Calgary elections.[37] A majority of the trustees (seven of nine) were replaced in an election framed as pivoting on the question of faith-based alternative schools. To no one's surprise, the new board cancelled the contracts of the two Christian and two Jewish schools in their system. In an odd twist, the Catholic school board then took in the two Jewish schools, a step obviously approved by the provincial ministry and one that might provide a precedent for later "shopping" between boards by faith-based schools.

In the late 1970s, additional "flexibility" was introduced in response to a human rights challenge launched by a Mennonite school that was employing uncertified teachers. It won at trial on the basis of religious freedom, and, rather than appealing, the government chose to establish a new category of private schools that could use uncertified teachers but that would not be eligible for the government funding for private schools described above. Those in this new category would eventually be referred to as "registered" schools, distinguished from those referred to as "certified" or "approved."

From 1980 to 1987, the Progressive Conservatives increased government support for private schools at a rate 50 percent faster than that for
public schools, and, not surprisingly, enrolment in the former more
than doubled (reaching 3 percent of the total school population in the
latter year). Then, in 1988, changes to the School Act further widened
"choice" by making clear that alternative schools within public board
jurisdictions could be based on language, culture, subject-focus, or religion, and by providing support for home schooling. Funding for private
schools was also increased, and the government resisted calls for greater
ministerial oversight on what was taught, providing room to manoeuvre
that was particularly important for faith-based schools.

The Klein "Revolution"

Under Ralph Klein's premiership (from 1992 until 2006), school choice
became more firmly and elaborately placed at the centre of the PC policy
agenda.[38] On the one hand, the province reduced the power of school
boards by centralizing funding controls, and, on the other hand, it enhanced the power of individual schools and strengthened school councils in the name of parents' rights. The government also opened the
door to charter schools, making Alberta the first province to follow in
a path developed during Margaret Thatcher's premiership in Britain.
These schools could not be faith based, but, as Taylor points out, the
capacity to create charter schools "increased pressure on other public
schools to respond to parental demands for religious and other kinds
of alternative programming."[39]

Albertans for Quality Education (AQE) was a group widely seen as
influential in policy circles, and, as Taylor points out, "[it] had developed
a conservative alliance united around a notion of choice that included
parents concerned about morals and pedagogy alongside representatives of the private sector."[40] The provincial educational policy that
emerged more clearly than ever in the 1990s was a successful pitch to
both currents within the AQE as well as within the Progressive Conservative Party itself.

It was during this period, when the provincial government's push
for school choice was at its peak, that developments in local school

boards most dramatically opened up options for faith-based schools. The Edmonton School Board was one of the first to expand the number and range of alternative schools following the backlash mobilized against the Calgary board's short-lived foray into supporting faith-based schools. Edmonton's small set of alternative programs included a Hebrew language school, and then, in 1995, the board was ready to accept a proposal for Christian Logos programs in five existing schools. It also agreed that the Logos Society would be involved in the selection of school staff, and the Christian schools were effectively given considerable leeway in using Christian curricular materials.[41]

According to Taylor, by 2000, at least eight school districts across the province had Christian programs or schools under the public board umbrella, and, by the decade's end, Calgary was the only board still resisting. Even there, however, a route circumventing the public board had been developed. When three private Christian schools facing difficult financial challenges were turned away by the Calgary public board, they got a "yes" in 2006 from the nearby Palliser school board, which saw nothing in the Schools Act that limited its jurisdiction to schools within a fixed territory.[42] The provincial government had no interest in challenging this and was not averse to snubbing the Calgary board. And, while all of this expansion of alternative schools in the public system was happening, provincial support for private schools also continued to increase, up to 70 percent in 2009. As much as ever, the government was supporting "flexibility" and rejecting what it saw as "one-size-fits-all" approaches.

Controversies over Sexual Diversity in Schools

In Alberta and across North America, controversies over the public recognition of sexual diversity have invariably invoked school issues. We have already had a taste of that in Premier Klein's assurances that the constitutional prohibition on discrimination based on sexual orientation wouldn't threaten schools. Here and elsewhere, religious conservatives and educational traditionalists oppose any school experience that presents homosexuality or transgenderism in a positive light, and they routinely play on fears beyond their own core constituencies about "exposing" young people to ideas that would "confuse" them about gender and sexual norms.

In the 1997–98 period, opposition specifically targeting school programs or materials on homosexuality surfaced at least twice. In late 1997, Calgary's public school board removed library books (pending investigation) that had been the subject of complaint on the part of the advocacy organization Parents' Rights in Education. This conservative group was systematically searching all school libraries for books with homosexual or "pornographic" material. Its leader, Tom Crites, was quoted as being concerned that "the gay rights movement [was] trying to teach children to be gay is fine," without alerting them to the risks of the gay "lifestyle."

The provincial PCs were acutely aware of the support for such views among many of their supporters, and this extended beyond the transition from Ralph Klein to Ed Stelmach in 2006. The new leader was a compromise candidate, receiving most social conservative votes from party members who had supported Ted Morton before his elimination from the ballot. After becoming premier, Stelmach was pressed by moral conservatives (including Morton) to limit the authority of the province's Human Rights Commission – an issue of persistent concern for religious conservatives. Offering a kind of consolation prize to such voices, the government delivered two swipes at sexual minorities. It refused to recognize gender identity in a package of human rights amendments, and it "delisted" gender reassignment surgery from those services provided in the public health care system, effectively denying transgender people access to a vital health procedures.

More importantly, in 2009, the government also pandered to the schooling concerns of its social conservative constituency by enacting Bill 44, the Human Rights, Citizenship and Multiculturalism Amendment Act. This explicitly added sexual orientation to the IRPA (symbolically encoding the Supreme Court's *Vriend* ruling) but added a stipulation that schools had to notify parents when classes were to engage "subject matter that deals explicitly with religion, sexuality or sexual orientation" and that parents could have their children excluded from such classes.[43] The inclusion of this provision in the Human

Rights Act expanded the remedies for parents who believed that their rights had been infringed and, thereby, increased the pressure on teachers to avoid these subjects entirely. As Pamela Dicky Young argues, the legislation was an "olive branch" to religious and conservative voters, signalling to them that the addition of sexual orientation to human rights law "did not mean that the Government of Alberta had all of a sudden changed its mind on the matter of appropriate sexualities and begun to treat members of sexual minorities as normative citizens."[44]

Even if the push for such legislation came from only a minority of PC legislators, the party leadership knew that religious conservatives were vital to its electoral success. According to a 2008 post-election survey of Alberta voters, a large minority of PC supporters indicated that they considered the Bible to be the literal word of God.[45] Not surprisingly, then, the party's supporters overall were more socially conservative than were supporters of the main opposition parties, averaging .38 on a scale from "0" to "1," where 1 is the most conservative possible response. In contrast, the average Liberal supporter was .20, and the average NDP supporter .17.

Social Conservatives Abandoning the PCs in the Early 2010s

During their four decades in power, PC premiers and most cabinet ministers have been wary of the electoral risks that come from seizing on moral issues in ways that align the party too closely with the Christian right. As we have seen, however, moral conservatives were plentiful in the caucus, and there were always a few prominent cabinet ministers drawn from their ranks. In policy terms, as one former MLA observes, "if a particular issue was seen as bringing along a particular constituency, the party was glad to do it."[46] Contributing to this was the growing fragmentation of the party in the post-Klein period, which left room for individual policy entrepreneurs. As a close observer of provincial politics puts it, "Lougheed and even Getty were very, very strong – with them as leader the caucus was a whole cloth – [but] the caucus now is nothing but a shifting kaleidoscope of fragments."[47] Anti-gay manoeuvring over Human Rights Code amendments in 2009 was, for him, the product of sometimes quite small clusters of MLAs who were prepared to insist on their point of view and who eventually prevailed even over the objections of the minister of education. "It was pushed through by a small number of people, some say as few as three or four, who insisted that this was a hill they were going to die on."[48]

Alison Redford's Leadership

Alison Redford's victory in the 2011 leadership race was as sharp a break from the past as could be imagined. Her candidacy seemed a long shot, in part because she was a centrist "red tory" but also because she was a woman in a province in which women's place in the political arena had been comparatively late to secure and slow to expand.[49] More important, she had only been elected to the legislature in 2008 and had no real policy record.[50] Veteran cabinet minister Gary Mar was already working to claim some of the moderate ground that Redford had staked out, and he had significant support in caucus. Ted Morton was running once again from the right.

Redford's campaign strategy, however, helped to distinguish her candidacy in a crowded field of six. In taking some positions that distanced her more than the others from previous government policy – for example, by calling for increased spending in health care and education – she was reaching out to new areas of support. In the midst of the campaign, she took part in Calgary's Pride march, and, a week later, she talked about the creation of a respectful environment being "a fundamental principle."[51] She had also hired as campaign manager the man who had helped elect Naheed Nenshi as Calgary's surprise new mayor.

Redford won the race in early October 2011, drawing in large numbers of new party members from among public-sector professionals and others who would normally have voted for other parties. She trailed far behind Mar in the first ballot but secured enough second choices to edge out the other leading candidates. Ted Morton, the candidate most clearly on the right, and most favoured by moral conservatives, received 12 percent, less than half his support in the 2006 leadership race – a clear sign of how many moral traditionalists had already abandoned the PCs for the increasingly popular Wildrose Party.

Many commentators remarked that Redford's selection signalled a sea change in the province's political life. As journalist Josh Wingrove put it, "Booming Alberta is a changing Alberta – younger, more urban and less homogeneous ... and its politics has caught up."[52] There was no indication of Redford raising fundamental questions about the government's relationship to the oil and gas industry or its support for school choice. But it did seem clear that she would move public policy away from expressions of moral traditionalism. Within a week of her leadership victory she talked about changing the provisions of the 2009 human rights law, which had been such an obvious concession to moral conservatives resistant to LGBT rights.

The challenge facing the new leader on this and other similar issues, as we shall see, was that, even before her selection, moral conservatives now had Wildrose to go to – a party that was well to the right of the PCs. She also inherited a caucus with significant fracture lines, and it could hardly be insignificant that she had so little support from it during the leadership race. Much of her ability to rein in caucus extremes would depend on her first general election test in 2012 and on the pattern of competition for the votes of moral traditionalists that came with the emergence of an alternative.

The Wildrose Surge

The Wildrose Alliance (the name was later changed to the Wildrose Party) was born of a 2008 merger of two small parties – Wildrose and Alberta Alliance. Rural evangelicals had been prominent among the 1 percent of voters that each of these had previously attracted. By the 2008 election, when support for the merged party had increased to 7 percent, Stewart and Sayers estimated that 57 percent of its voters were Christian conservatives.[53]

When Paul Hinman stepped down as party leader in 2009, one of the two front runners to replace him was Danielle Smith; the other was Mark Dyrholm, a Calgary chiropractor with strong connections to religious conservatives (Mormons in particular). The Dyrholm campaign was said to have characterized Smith as someone "who's going to take our province swiftly to the left," and who supports both homosexuality and abortion.[54] In fact, Danielle Smith was a laissez-faire conservative with ties to the Canadian Federation of Independent Business and the Fraser Institute. According to Tom Flanagan:

She was a pro-choice libertarian who had no problems with gay marriage, whereas the party membership had a heavy representation of religious and social conservatives. She squared this circle by being candid about her own views, while also vowing to stand up for the freedom of speech of social conservatives.[55]

The strength of her candidacy was primarily a function of the large current of neoliberal dissatisfaction with the PCs. As David Climenhaga puts it:

Key components of its membership include the perpetually disgruntled Alberta social conservative super-right, rank and file Alberta Conservatives who for one reason or another didn't approve of Premier Ed Stelmach, a subset of the Calgary oil industry that wanted to punish Stelmach for daring to contemplate higher royalty rates, and economic market fundamentalists not particularly interested in social conservative issues.[56]

Supporters such as these viewed the Wildrose Party as a vehicle for getting a new right-wing government in the province, though they would need to move it from one based strongly in social conservatism to one focused on fiscal conservatism.

Smith won the leadership in October 2009, and, soon afterwards, while addressing a breakfast gathering attended by major business interests in Calgary, she made clear her aim to sideline moral issues like abortion and gay marriage: "the divisive issues that tear us apart are not ones that are going to be on our election platform."[57] As party policy was slowly articulated, party leaders were clearly preoccupied with ensuring contentment in the oil and gas sector, increasing choice in health care, containing government spending, and addressing discontents over property rights in rural areas. However, the party was also aiming at a populist image, calling for the election of the province's representatives in the Canadian Senate and for more free votes in the legislature. These commitments would appeal to most moral conservatives, with the reference to free votes potentially serving as a coded message for them. The same dual appeal would come with promises to equalize schooling options by having funding "follow the student" even more than it already did. By year's end, polls were showing that Wildrose was now a serious competitor for office, never far behind the PCs and sometimes ahead.

But this support was destined to be insufficient. The party was in fact becoming a natural pole of attraction for many social conservatives who wanted more explicit attention to measures designed to protect what they saw as the traditional family. With this base, it turned out to be impossible to keep moral issues completely on the margins. Smith realized that winning office would require shoring up support among moral traditionalists who had already been voting Wildrose as well as among those of them who had until then been supporting the PCs. As Flanagan put it in 2011:

> Danielle realizes and we all realize that there is a religiously motivated element of the vote in Alberta and we're not going to alienate them. So Danielle consciously takes positions that she believes that the religious conservatives could endorse even if it wouldn't necessarily be their first choice ... It's true of Danielle, and it may be true of any effective leader anywhere on the political spectrum, that you have to craft political positions that can appeal to broad coalitions.[58]

In fact, during her leadership race, she had written to a socially conservative magazine that the government should not be funding abortions (even if on libertarian grounds rather than on the basis of moral disapproval). In the words of a party insider:

> We messaged ourselves for all of the things that a libertarian would have in common with a social conservative ... Although she spoke about defunding abortions only once on a Christian radio show, it is something that most Wildrosers want to see happen because you've got your libertarians who view it as an issue of self-responsibility, and you have your so-cons who view it as a morality issue.[59]

Smith also made statements critical of the Human Rights Commission, an obvious touchstone for the religious right. As one party member puts it:

> Social conservatives are deeply concerned that it will be human rights commissions that drive us towards American-style banning of anything quasi-religious in schools. Social conservatives are deeply concerned that the human rights commissions will enact by fiat things that parliamentarians would never have the balls to bring forward in Parliament. And it also fits very nicely with the small government message: there is no way that when a street preacher writes a letter to the editor that it should become an issue that the government is spending your tax dollars on.[60]

At the same time, the party was training candidates to be careful about what they talked about, particularly with respect to morality politics. Candidates who were known to be socially conservative were counselled to be realistic about what can be achieved.

Heading into the 2012 election, Wildrose strategists had an interest in spinning out some policies that would appeal specifically to social conservatives, while remaining as ambiguous as possible on the most explosive of such issues. In this respect the party was broadly similar to the federal Conservatives, which is no coincidence, given that there were prominent federal Conservatives active in Wildrose behind the scenes. Indeed, there seemed significantly more in common between the CPC and provincial parties than there was between the federal and provincial PCs, even more so once Alison Redford was chosen as PC leader.

The 2012 Election Turning Point

A provincial election was called on March 26, 2012, with voting day set for April 23. From the outset, there was no doubt that it would be a race between Redford's PCs and Smith's Wildrose. Liberals, New Democrats, and the relatively new centre-left Alberta Party would be effectively on the sidelines. Early polling showed that Wildrose was leading the PCs and benefiting from a legislative scandal that highlighted age-old patterns of PC entitlement while casting doubt on Redford's promise of change.

The Wildrose campaign routinely characterized Redford as a closet Liberal intent on turning Alberta into a "big government nanny state," though with no reference to traditional hot button social issues.[61] Not surprisingly, though, the PC campaign team considered Wildrose as vulnerable to charges that it was willing to cater to prejudice. So in early April, Redford criticized Wildrose support of "conscience rights" for health care professionals and, potentially, other provincial employees – a commitment outlined in the party's *2011 Member Approved Principles and Policies* and repeated by Smith in the previous summer. Encoding such rights would allow marriage commissioners to refuse to perform same-sex marriages, and it certainly looked like it would allow doctors and nurses to refuse to perform procedures or prescribe medications of which they disapproved on religious grounds. Smith was now trying her best to portray herself as neutral on the subject and asserted: "we don't have positions on contentious moral issues." She also tried to characterize criticism of the party's stance as fear-mongering – a common strategy of "Eastern Canada and Eastern Canadian critics."[62]

Abortion funding was another issue that seemed never to fully disappear. In early March, Alberta Pro-Life had launched a campaign seeking to make defunding abortions an election issue.[63] At first it had little traction, but the issue then surfaced recurrently enough to impel Wildrose to issue a statement saying that it "ha[d] absolutely no intentions" of defunding abortion. Adding fuel to this particular fire was the publication of an e-mail from a leading party organizer promising that Wildrose would immediately introduce legislation allowing citizens to put issues like abortion to a citizen initiated referendum "to let the government know what they believed was important."[64]

Wildrose Candidates Fuelling Fears of Extremism

Soon after a televised leaders debate, and now in a period when public interest in the election had sharpened significantly, controversial remarks by two Wildrose candidates surfaced in the media and in so doing dragged the party's campaign more dramatically off message than anything up to that point. The first flare-up occurred over a 2011 blog posting by candidate Allan Hunsperger, a Pentecostal minister. It had been written as a response to the release of Lady Gaga's song, "Born This Way," and in it Hunsperger had this to say about homosexuality: "you can live the way you were born, and if you die the way you were born then you will suffer the rest of eternity in the lake of fire, hell, a place of eternal suffering."[65] The story was quickly picked up by the provincial and national press on April 15, and went viral on social media.

Smith did not want to force Hunsperger out of the party, fearing that she would threaten party cohesion by turning away from her commitment to allow party members to state their views. With about one-quarter of Wildrose candidates broadly sharing Hunsperger's moral conservatism, the question of unity was not easy. So, when pressed on the issue, Smith refused to condemn the comments, saying, "it was a year ago when he was talking in his capacity as a pastor. He now understands, we've spoken, we've communicated on this, that we will not be legislating on contentious social issues. He understands that. He accepts that."[66] This statement did nothing to dispel media scrutiny, and it fuelled anxieties about whether the party was ready to govern. And then, the very day that this statement was issued, Smith stirred controversy on another front when, in an online debate, she said that "the science isn't settled" on climate change. This caused outrage among environmentalists and provided another argument for PC portrayals of Wildrose as extreme.[67]

Another candidate controversy erupted almost immediately after Smith's climate remarks. Ron Leech, like Hunsperger an evangelical, told a Calgary radio station that, even in his ethnically mixed constituency: "I think as a Caucasian I have an advantage. When different community leaders such as a Sikh leader or a Muslim leader speak, they really speak to their own people in many ways. As a Caucasian, I believe that I can speak to all the community."[68] The pressure grew on Smith to say more in response to this misstep, and the earlier Hunsperger remark, but she still equivocated, trying to portray her and her party as victims.

> Let me be perfectly clear – a Wildrose government will not tolerate discrimination against any individual based on their ethnicity, religion, beliefs, background, disability or sexual orientation, period ... The Wildrose candidates and supporters in this room and all over Alberta know the truth. They know the stereotypes are bogus, and often used by liberal political parties when they feel threatened by conservatives.[69]

The ambiguities in a statement that many reporters expected would be clearer kept the matter firmly in the spotlight during the crucial final stretches of the campaign, helping to sow doubts in more voters' minds about what this comparatively new party stood for.

There was much vote switching in the final two or three days of the campaign, and it looked as though there was something of a swing to the PC camp. Still, it was an immense surprise to most Albertans that election day delivered a PC majority government, with the party taking 44 percent of the popular vote and 61 seats, as compared to 34 percent and 17 seats for Wildrose. PC candidates won the overwhelming majority of the city vote, electing 20 of 25 MLAs in Calgary, and most of those in Edmonton. Wildrose won only 2 seats in Calgary, so most of its caucus was based in rural areas. However, while far short of its hopes (and most pre-election polling), this result still represented at dramatic improvement for the party, which had won just seven percent of the vote and no seats in the 2008 election. In contrast, Liberal support collapsed from its 2008 levels in the midst of a competitive race that pitted a clearly right-wing alternative against a governing party that had shifted noticeably to the centre, and it dropped from about one-quarter of the popular vote to just 10 percent, yielding 5 seats. The NDP saw modest improvement, taking 10 percent of the vote and doubling its seat total to four. The Alberta Party earned just one percent of the vote and was shut out of the legislature.

Distinguishing Party Supporters

Vote Compass data gathered during the 2012 campaign period shows that the set of beliefs that most clearly set Wildrose supporters apart from others were in the area of morality policy.[70] They were much more

Table 6.1   Vote choice within religious groups in Alberta, 2012

	PCs (%)	Wildrose (%)	Liberals (%)	NDP (%)	Total (n)
Denomination					
Roman Catholics	48	35	10	7	127 (100%)
Mainline Protestants	46	41	9	5	217 (100%)
Evangelicals	28	63	3	7	70) (100%)
Other	33	34	14	19	122 (100%)
Unaffiliated/atheist	39	27	19	16	241 (100%)
Total	40	37	12	11	777 (100%)
Importance of religion					
Very important	31	51	9	9	224 (100%)
Somewhat important	46	34	10	10	202 (100%)
Somewhat unimportant	44	36	12	8	135 (100%)
Very unimportant	42	25	17	16	211 (100%)
Total	40	37	12	11	772 (100%)

Source: Jared Wesley et al., Canadian Provincial Election Project, http://cpep.ualberta.ca.

likely than others to agree that "there should be no government funding for abortion," and most favoured "scrapping" the Human Rights Commission, a position opposed by the great majority of supporters of other parties. They were also distinctly more conservative on economic issues, Canadian multicultural funding, and environmental regulation, but it was on the traditional hot button issues on which religious conservatives had mobilized that they were the most distinct.

We can see this pattern in the 2012 provincial election study, extracts of which are displayed in Table 6.1. Evangelicals were much more drawn to Wildrose than to any other party, and the same was true among those for whom religion was very important. The PCs still held noticeable constituencies with each of these characteristics, and, not surprisingly, the Liberals and NDP fared significantly worse. Fully 40 percent of Wildrose supporters said that religion was very important.

David McGrane's analysis of provincial voters in this particular election displays with great clarity the new polarization of Alberta politics, with Wildrose supporters further to the right of those who favoured most of Canada's other right-wing parties, and the PCs under Redford left of most provincial Liberal parties across the country.[71] On the provincial election study's "market liberal" values scale, PC supporters (at 2.30) were closer to the provincial NDPers (1.86) than to Wildrosers (2.95).

Media analysis and insider commentary on the PC victory regularly highlighted the candidate controversies and especially Hunsperger's condemnation of homosexuality in starkly colourful language. More than any other election in Alberta's recent history, the outcome of this one was interpreted as a repudiation of moral conservatism. Smith herself seemed to agree with these analyses, admitting: "there are certain policies that clearly Albertans didn't want to see implemented."[72]

Some weeks after the election, Tom Flanagan mused that the formula used by Smith to retain party unity – appeasing religious conservatives through support of free speech and personal responsibility – worked inside the party but did not work when exposed in the heat of the campaign: "Danielle allowed herself and the party to be manoeuvred into appearing to be prejudiced."[73] He elaborated with this bit of advice: "stop flirting with issues such as abortion and gay marriage, over which past generations of social conservatives have done battle and lost; those battles are over, and voters don't want to hear about them again." In the words of another, the Hunsperger comments, "reflect what you would have heard from a Social Credit politician in the 1950s, so it was very much sending the message that this was the old Alberta. Whatever has happened in the last ten or twenty years, 'we're just not there anymore.'"[74]

Continuing Struggles over Social Conservative Support

For months after the election, Danielle Smith seemed to be struggling to position her party in ways that would not see a repeat of the election missteps. In June, she attended a Pride event in Edmonton, clearly aiming to build bridges. She reiterated that Hunsperger's comments did not represent her or her party's views, describing them as "strident" and "offensive."[75] At the Wildrose annual general meeting in November, she spoke of the need for more care in selecting candidates, asking local constituency associations to ensure that people running for public office declare their beliefs "in a way that is respectful of all Albertans."[76] She also referred to the need for a review of the party's policies in light of the election results, including those related to the province's Human Rights Commission and conscience rights. At the same time, she insisted that her party would still offer a voice to moral conservatives and those with strong religious beliefs. Referring to the Conservative Party of Canada as an example, she talked of the possibility of allowing private members' bills and citizen-initiated referenda as outlets for such views.

At first, the PCs weren't in nearly as complicated a position as was Wildrose. The election outcome seemed, for a time, to bolster Premier Redford's chances of shifting the party definitively away from any dalliance with moral conservatism. A number of veteran PC MLAs had not run at all or had been defeated, so that the nineteen re-elected PC members who had served three terms or more were now outnumbered by twenty-three rookies (in a sixty-one-person caucus). Senior staff in the Premier's Office were also largely unconnected to previous provincial leaders. When faced with an assertion that there were still social conservatives inside the PC tent, one senior party official responded with: "Really? Not anymore! The PCs lost everything outside the cities except the rural North, and the rural North is not Southern Alberta."[77]

Giving credence to this view was the new PC government's decision, early on, to relist gender-reassignment surgery as an insured procedure, with Redford telling a *Swerve* magazine interviewer that this was "fundamental ... to people's physical health, their mental health, their social identity."[78] In June, she also participated in Edmonton's Pride festivities – the first Alberta premier to do so.

However, the Redford government's record was mixed on schooling issues. A new education bill introduced before the election had been designed to combat bullying, in part by requiring schools and boards to promote respect for difference and to pass codes of conduct prohibiting discrimination on grounds protected by the Charter of Rights and Freedoms and the Alberta Individual Rights Protection Act. But Christian conservatives loudly opposed it primarily for its recognition of sexual minorities, and supporters of home schooling were particularly resistant to the notion that they would be subject to the same requirements. The bill was delayed long enough to die with the 2012 election, and when re-introduced that fall (2012), the requirements for home schoolers had been removed, and the government meekly claimed that anti-bullying rules were already in place and that the Human Rights Act would constitute sufficient protection. Redford also showed no interest in reducing taxpayer support for private schools, and, apart from wanting an overall increase in educational spending, she appeared to have had no philosophical objection to the existing regime.

Another PC Leadership Change

Alison Redford did not last long as Alberta's premier and was basically forced from her office in March 2014. Restiveness within her own caucus was intensified by complaints about what was said to be her non-consultative leadership style and by a sense of scandal surrounding her expense claims. None of the background to Redford's departure suggested that there was a significant ideological backlash against her leadership. However, the dramatic slippage in her approval ratings was benefiting Wildrose and, thereby, providing ammunition to those who sought to pull away from some of the reformism that Redford seemed to represent – a shift from the centre back to the party's traditional centre-right position.

Anxieties about the party's right flank were made visible only a few weeks after Redford's resignation. A vote in the legislature was held on a motion introduced by Liberal MLA Laurie Blakeman urging (not requiring) school boards to develop policies supportive of students wanting to establish gay-straight alliances in their schools. It was no surprise, even within clear memory of the 2012 election, that all eight members of the Wildrose caucus who voted on the measure voted against it. More interestingly, two-thirds of the PC caucus also voted "no."

The Progressive Conservative leadership contest was one-sided once Jim Prentice, a former federal cabinet minister, announced his intention to run. He was in some respects a safe bet, not known to be on either the radically neoliberal side of that party or the reformist side represented by Alison Redford, and entirely comfortable in the company of Calgary's corporate directors. He had much support both within the Alberta PC caucus and among the party's insiders, and in September 2014 he won 77 percent of the votes cast for the leadership.

Prentice's cabinet appointments were clearly intended to portray the PCs as a large tent, and extended well into the right-wing terrain captured by Wildrose. Three ministers were thought to be associated with moral conservatism, among them, Education Minister Gordon Dirks, who, like the premier, would have to win a seat in a set of four by-elections slated for late October. Dirks had been an evangelical pastor, a senior administrator of a local evangelical Bible college, and a one-time Calgary school trustee who advocated school choice. Now he was in charge of a portfolio that for decades had been the target of pressure from moral traditionalists and supporters of faith-based schools. Premier Prentice also wanted to include progressive voices, but in doing so he made clear his determination not to talk about issues (including anything related to sexual minorities) that would provoke conflict with religious conservatives.

The new government improved its standing in the polls, and voting in the four by-elections swept the premier and his education minister into legislative seats. These victories were widely read as a serious blow to the Wildrose opposition. A few weeks later, the new government's throne speech clearly indicated an attempt to further undercut Wildrose support by prioritizing legislation on property rights (a major issue in the Wildrose's rural heartland) and on accountability.

As the new government laid out its carefully calibrated program, its standing was further boosted by a growing sense of internal disorder within the Wildrose Party. Just before the throne speech, a majority of Wildrose convention delegates defeated a motion that would have enshrined a new party policy that recognized human rights on a wide range of explicitly named grounds, including sexual orientation. The retention of more generic language stripped of specification was widely seen as a slap in the face of Daniel Smith, who had worked so hard to portray her party as no longer prey to narrow-mindedness and intolerance. One week later, the Wildrose caucus reinforced its socially conservative credentials by its vehement opposition to a revived Laurie Blakeman bill on gay-straight alliances, which this time would force school boards to allow them and also remove the requirement that parents be notified when sexuality was to be discussed in the classroom. The measure was barely presented when Wildrose immediately introduced amendments designed to undermine the bill by focusing on parental rights and religious freedoms.

The notion that Wildrose was unravelling became even more widespread in November 2014 when two caucus members defected to the PCs amidst growing talk of political fissures ripping the party apart.[79] Then, in December, Daniel Smith and eight of her colleagues declared that they were switching to the PCs. This defection left the party with just 5 of the 17 seats won in 2012, leading almost all informed observers (prematurely) to see the end of a serious Wildrose challenge to the governing PCs.

The PC government, however, did not have long to savour the moment. Now it was its turn to face internal divisions fomented by social conservatives. The party leadership knew that the caucus was split on the Laurie Blakeman bill and that this division would be laid bare in a free vote in the legislature. To head this off, the government hastily drafted a clumsy alternative bill that effectively allowed schools to ban GSAs from school property. The government bill drew praise among social conservatives but also provoked a flurry of objections, including those from three PC MLAs. It was, in the words of *Edmonton Journal* columnist Paula Simons, a "vile and hateful piece of legislation."[80] Facing what now seemed a media firestorm, the premier soon withdrew the entire measure, saying he wanted to hear more from Albertans before proceeding. Soon after that, Calgary's mayor, Naheed Nenshi, told a Chamber of Commerce gathering that the debate was "damaging and hateful" and that the passage of the government's bill would have drawn international attention "toward what kind of hillbillies we are."[81]

When the legislature reconvened in early March, the education minister immediately presented a new bill that represented a complete about-face on the issue, obliging all schools to recognize GSAs when requested by students, eliminating the parental notification requirement for discussions of sexual orientation, and adding gender identity and expression to the provincial human rights law. The government steered the bill through passage with tight reins, virtually eliminating any time or space for significant mobilization against it among politicians or extra-parliamentary groups.

The 2015 Election

In a widely anticipated move, on April 7, 2015, Jim Prentice asked the province's lieutenant-governor to call an early election for May 5. The previous week the government had presented its new budget, which was greatly shaped by low oil prices and a looming deficit. Notably, that week had also seen Danielle Smith lose her bid for the PC nomination in the Highwood constituency to a little-known candidate – a setback for the government that may have signalled more voter discontent with the PCs than the leadership seemed to recognize.

The election came at a time when the much-diminished Wildrose Party was choosing Brian Jean as its new leader. He was a former Conservative MP, and his education at a Christian university led to understandable assumptions about his religious conservatism. But, in early March, when the leadership race was on, he immediately answered "no" when asked if he was a social conservative. When reminded of the harm done by Wildrose candidates in 2012, he responded with extra-ordinarily strong language:

> There are nuts in every party ... What do we do with them? Well, at first, we can try to manage them and then we get rid of them. That's the truth of it. Albertans need to be able to trust us. When they see our reaction it will be quick. It will be ruthless. It will make sure Albertans know they can continue to trust us and know we're not some little gang of crazies. I understand the Charter of Rights and the Constitution and that is ultimately the law of the land. I will not let anybody in the party under my leadership that believes other-wise. That means all Albertans are treated equally and all Albertans are governed equally. It doesn't matter what colour you are or your sexual orientation. We are there for all Albertans.[82]

Jean soon had a test of those views. In mid-April, Russ Kuykendall, a Wildrose candidate running in Calgary, was discovered to have posted comments in 2007 virulently attacking gay activists as part of a blog operated by the *Western Standard* magazine. As reporter Paula Simons remarks, this was not "lake of fire" material, but it was strikingly evocative of that moment in the 2012 election campaign.[83] Within hours of the issue going public Kuykendall was removed as a candidate. Later in the campaign, Jean reiterated his determination to avoid a "social agenda."

> I don't think that's what governments are for. Governments are for making a better quality of life for people, and I think I should stay out of their personal business ... That sort of thing only splits Albertans, splits Canadians, and there's no benefit in it.[84]

Over on the Progressive Conservative side, the embarrassment that the government had faced over GSAs similarly increased that party's determination to marginalize social conservatism. And, of course, the NDP had not even attempted to create an electoral coalition broad enough to include moral traditionalists. The result, then, was that there was no major party leader left in Alberta who was prepared to publicly sympathize with moral or religious conservatism. Both Wildrose and the Progressive Conservatives were interested, in principle at least, in retaining the image of a broad tent but, at the same time, in avoiding candidate statements that expressed support for a religious conservatism now widely thought to be out of tune with the new Alberta.

Remarkably, election polling immediately showed a close three-way race between the PCs, the Wildrose, and the New Democratic Party under its dynamic leader Rachel Notley. Both opposition parties appeared to have been buoyed by the budget, with the NDP benefitting from discontent over expenditure cuts and the Wildrose from anger over increased taxation. Both also profited from cynical public reactions to an early election call by the very party that had previously secured legislative approval of fixed election dates. The mass Wildrose defection of the previous December had also left a bad taste in many voters' minds – a reminder of the kind of backroom deal-making that scraped against populist sensibilities. Jim Prentice may have assumed the leadership of the party with the benefit of appearing as an outsider to provincial politics, but such manoeuvres lost him that brand.

The New Democrats also benefited significantly from the tarnishing of the PCs' reformist credentials. Alison Redford's 2012 victory owed much to supporters of the NDP and, especially, the Liberal Party who were prepared to strategically oppose Wildrose. But the continuing visibility of the PCs' traditionalists, especially during the Prentice period, could not help but increase scepticism of the party's commitment to social reform. Wildrose was as fiscally hawkish as it had been from its beginnings, so centrists had no reason to lodge their protest at PC rule in that direction.

Vote switching towards the NDP was also made easier by its campaign, which tilted more than ever towards the political centre. The party made few dramatic commitments, covering its proposals for greater government spending with equally modest proposals for increased taxation on corporations and high-income earners. It was able to avoid sexual diversity issues entirely, in part due to the former PC government's acquiescence to progressive legislation on schools and also, of course, because both the PCs and Wildrose wanted to stay away from any causes favoured by religious conservatives.

By the campaign's final days, the NDP was consistently in the lead, and voters then gave the party, and more specifically Rachel Notley, a stunning majority of 53 seats and 41 percent of the vote. The NDP had never before won more than 16 seats in the legislature, which it did in 1986. Now, in 2015, it had won all of the Edmonton-area seats and most of Calgary. In terms of the popular vote, the PCs finished second, with 28 percent support. However, these voters were more dispersed than those of the other major parties, leading the PCs to finish third in terms of seats with ten. Most of its constituencies were in Calgary, with only two rural seats left for a party that once dominated the Alberta countryside. Outgoing premier Jim Prentice resigned immediately, both from his own legislative seat as well as from the party leadership.

The Wildrose vote share dropped to just 24 percent of the popular vote from 34 percent in 2012. However, the concentration of the party's support in rural areas allowed it to actually improve its presence in the legislature, taking 21 seats (compared to 17 previously), placing it ahead of the PCs in legislative standings. The Liberal vote collapsed further to just 4 percent, with party leader David Swann receiving its only seat. Support for the Alberta Party increased to two percent, with its leader, Greg Clark, winning a seat in Calgary.

Table 6.2   Vote choice within religious groups in Alberta, 2015

	PCs (%)	Wildrose (%)	Liberals (%)	NDP (%)	Total (n)
Denomination					
Roman Catholics	25	21	11	44	131 (100%)
Mainline Protestants	24	30	5	41	154 (100%)
Evangelicals	31	36	3	30	59 (100%)
Other	12	36	1	50	133 (100%)
Unaffiliated/atheist	11	20	5	64	215 (100%)
Total	18	27	5	50	692 (100%)
Importance of religion					
Very important	14	43	1	43	198 (100%)
Somewhat important	48	35	10	37	156 (100%)
Somewhat unimportant	23	21	3	53	143 (100%)
Very unimportant	9	19	7	65	193 (100%)
Total	18	27	5	50	690 (100%)

Source: Jared Wesley et al., Canadian Provincial Election Project, http://cpep.ualberta.ca.

Table 6.2 provides data on the party leanings of various religious groups, and, if we focus on the differences between Wildrose and the PCs, we find some elements of continuity, though we should keep in mind that the population of evangelicals is small enough to warrant interpretive caution. The 2015 survey indicates that Wildrose and the PCs did comparatively well among evangelicals but that Wildrose was significantly more successful among all those for whom religion was very important. Fully 46 percent of that party was, by that measure, highly religious, about twice the proportion of supporters for the PCs and NDP. The data also show that the 2015 surge of the NDP was striking in its inclusion of a sizable number of evangelicals and of the highly religious, even if they constituted a much lower proportion of the party's total ranks (one-quarter).

Once again, Wildrose formed the official opposition and assumed a prominent role in attacking the new government. And once again, the

Wildrose leadership faced the dilemma that had dogged the party under Danielle Smith: trying to focus on a neoliberal agenda but with an electorate and grassroots membership still containing a significant evangelical current and a populist element that did not always take kindly to discipline. Brian Jean's evangelical credentials helped retain their loyalty, but the party had clearly learned the hard lessons of the 2012–14 period, and no one was yet forgetting the lake of fire.

As the new government was taking shape, there was yet another wave of media stories and commentaries about how much the provincial politics of Alberta had caught up with social change. It was no longer more conservative than the rest of the country, having a younger, more educated, highly urbanized, and culturally diversified population fuelled by high levels of immigration. These assessments may have been premature.

Reshuffling Cards on the Partisan Right

Two developments in the aftermath of the 2015 election illustrated the continuing relevance of moral conservatism in Alberta politics. In early 2016, controversy resurfaced over the recognition of sexual diversity in Alberta schools. The province's education minister had required that school boards and private schools submit draft LGBTQ policies by the spring of 2016, encountering resistance (and refusals) from some private faith-based schools. That summer, the minister distributed an open letter to students pointing out that they had rights relating to sexual orientation and gender identity – including the right to establish a gay-straight alliance, which had been authorized by the previous PC government.[85] The NDP government, then, was not breaking radical new ground.

And then there was the race for the Progressive Conservative leadership, dominated from the outset by Jason Kenney, a prominent former Conservative MP and federal cabinet minister under Stephen Harper, and also an outspoken social conservative. Kenney had been a high-profile opponent of same-sex marriage when it was being debated in Ottawa and was unequivocally pro-life. During the campaign, he may well have focused on the tax-cutting and deregulatory priorities of Harper's federal governments, but he was entirely prepared to signal its sympathies with social conservatives, for example, airing grievances against any attempt to modify school curricula to be more accepting of sexual minorities.

Policy debates at a November 2016 PC conference provoked one leadership contender to cite "dog-whistle" talk of limiting abortion access, stopping inclusive school reform, and weakening public education. What had been a five-person leadership race was down to three following that convention, with the only two women and "moderates" dropping out. One, MLA Sandra Jansen, said her decision resulted from the harassment and bullying she received during the campaign, and she subsequently crossed the floor to the NDP – a move that attracted even more hateful messages. All this, in the view of political scientist Duane Bratt, was evidence of significant polarization.[86]

While the PC leadership race differed in many ways from the electoral politics practised in the United States, there were certainly observers, and PC moderates, who cited parallels between the rhetoric used in Alberta and that employed by US Republicans, in general, and Donald Trump, in particular. At the time, the PCs were ahead in the polls, and there was no doubt that a Kenney leadership would lure back from the Wildrose Party many of the social conservatives who had once been an important part of the PC base.

The Remaining Influence of Conservative Faith in Modern Alberta

Mark Lisac argues that only modest remnants of the Bible belt are left in Alberta, and these are mostly in rural areas.[87] As we saw in the Introduction to this volume, most indicators of religiosity have placed Albertans very close to Canadian averages. By Kurt Bowen's late 1990s estimate, 18 percent of Albertans were "very committed" religiously compared to 19 percent for Canada as a whole.[88] Brenda O'Neill and Warren Clark both show that, in 2000, Albertans were slightly less likely to attend religious services monthly or more frequently (33 percent and 31 percent, respectively) compared to Canadians as a whole (39 and 32 percent, respectively).[89] Clark also demonstrates that attendance in the Calgary metropolitan area (29 percent) and Edmonton (30 percent) was lower than it was in Toronto (38 percent) during about the same time period, and only slightly higher than in Vancouver (28 percent). According to Statistics Canada, a full 32 percent of the province declared themselves unaffiliated on religion in 2011, significantly more than the 24 percent Canadian average.

However, what always distinguished Albertans is the comparatively high proportion of evangelical Protestants. In Bowen's analysis, the proportion of the "committed" who were members of conservative Protestant denominations (i.e., not mainline) was 38 percent, significantly higher than in any other region in the country (with the rest of western Canada just under 30 percent and Ontario at 17 percent). And it is evangelicals, as well as the sizable Mormon population in southern Alberta, who have been at the forefront of politically mobilized social conservatism.

Faith-Based Political Organizing

Has the comparative strength of evangelical Protestantism in Alberta translated into sustained and effective political organizing? The lessons we draw from provincial politics from the early 1970s on are mixed. On issues related to sexuality, we saw recurrent waves of mobilization led by religious conservatives, often on a sufficient scale to eliminate any chance that Progressive Conservative governments would legislate in favour of sexual minority rights. On educational policy making, Christian-led groups have been able to significantly boost the case for a regime of school choice that has provided extraordinary support for faith-based options. Their legislative backers were sometimes only a minority in the PC caucus, but even then they had the capacity to extract concessions from premiers who had no particular sympathies with the religious right. When lesbian and gay rights became front-page news in 1998 and 1999, evangelically dominated groups like the Canada Family Action Coalition (based partly in Calgary) and the Alberta Federation of Women United for Families launched formidable campaigns against adding sexual orientation to the province's Human Rights Code. None of these groups was ever a particularly large organization, but they could build on local church networks – the key to evangelical political leverage.

Alberta's Roman Catholic bishops have issued strong statements on moral issues, with the very conservative Bishop Frederick Henry of Calgary having been particularly outspoken in policy discussions related to sexual diversity. Pro-life politics would seem to be a unifying factor among religious conservatives, though the Catholic hierarchy has opposed the use of graphic imagery employed by groups such as the Canadian Centre for Bio-Ethical Reform. Alberta's Mormons have been a notable political force on the side of conservative family values. But, while they have taken positions on moral issues that are close to those adopted by most evangelical Christians, stable coalitional links have been difficult since many, and probably most, evangelicals do not regard Mormons as Christian. Still, this combination of religious conservative forces has had the capacity to influence the Progressive Conservative Party and the Wildrose Party, even if that they do not constitute a particularly united block. When courts forced change, the religious right was ultimately unsuccessful in convincing PC governments to side with the draconian measures it favoured, but recent electoral volatility has come in part from the restiveness of social conservatives looking for a partisan home.

Liberalizing Public Opinion on Morality Issues

Writing before the dizzying changes in party fortunes witnessed in the 2015 election, David Stewart and Anthony Sayers used survey evidence to argue that Albertans in general are not as conservative, by almost any measure, as the usual view would suggest. In economic terms, their 2008 data found that "a strikingly consistent three-quarters of respondents favoured government action to ensure decent living standards (76 percent) and adequate housing (78 percent)."[90] Nor is Alberta's conservatism evident in a comparative perspective. David McGrane's analysis of provincial election studies between 2011 and 2014 includes province-wide "scores" on attachment to free market liberalism, which range from low (1) up to high (4). While finding that Albertans (and Manitobans) were more adherent to free market values (scores of 2.43) compared to Ontarians and British Columbians (scores of 2.25), the differences were not at all large.[91]

Stewart and Sayers's survey includes questions tapping moral traditionalism, and here, too, they find a less conservative populace than many would expect. Asked if abortion was a matter between a woman and her doctor, 76 percent of Albertans agreed. Once again, Alberta also fails to stand out in comparative terms, with the 2011 Canadian Election Study finding that one-quarter of Albertans supported a ban on abortion, almost exactly the Canadian average.[92] On same-sex marriage, Stewart and Sayers in 2008 and Ekos in 2010 similarly show clear majority support, with the province's numbers little different from those for Canada overall.[93] However, as we have seen, the minority in Alberta who disagree on such questions of morality tend to have exceptionally strong views and significant willingness to take political action on the issues. This is a current of opinion with a distinctive history of political intervention in Alberta, and a regular capacity to surprise.

Conclusion

Despite Alberta's early immigration waves and the character of its political life until the 1970s, by the time that Alison Redford took over as leader of the PCs and as premier of the province, Alberta had become less distinct in terms of the intensity of religious faith and of its explicit role in provincial politics. Until then, voices representing religious and moral conservatism had been vocal and at times influential – enough to push PC leaders and the Alberta government towards resisting change on LGBT rights. And while religious conservatives were not the only source of influence on the governing party's schools policy, they contributed to making Albert's educational system more accommodating to faith schools than any other jurisdiction in the country.

The comparatively large population of conservative evangelicals, and the not-inconsiderable minority of conservative Catholics, were unable to convince PC governments to make abortion a provincial issue. Moral traditionalists eventually did lose ground on the political recognition of lesbian and gay rights in the face of court rulings and major shifts in public opinion. And yet, over and over again, PC governments retained policies or limited reform in order to placate such currents within the caucus and the party's grassroots. They also marshalled language that gave religious conservatives at least enough recognition to retain their loyalty. Leaders like Ralph Klein, with no obvious animus towards sexual minorities, provided political space for the public expression of hatefulness and regularly used language signalling his anxieties about or opposition to recognizing their constitutional rights. On every single policy front related to sexual diversity, the province of Alberta was a laggard until the 2010s.

From 2011 through the momentous election of 2015, the political influence of religious and moral conservatives was dramatically reduced. If there had already been recurrent indications that gender and family traditionalists were engaged in a rear-guard action, the pace of change now quickened. The Progressive Conservatives became a more urban party, and, for a time at least, most social conservatives moved to the Wildrose Party. In a pattern reminiscent of Ontario's PCs during this same period, the 2012 election campaign brought to light the enormous risks involved in giving visible expression to that current. Allen Hunsperger's "lake of fire" post was endlessly cited as the single most important factor leading to Wildrose's defeat in that election. By the time of the 2015 election, both the Wildrose Party and the PCs were treating any potential expression of moral conservatism as electorally toxic – an unprecedented development in the province.

But Alberta's large population of religious conservatives has not simply gone away. They remain numerically large, and recent history has shown that they can still mobilize politically. What we have seen here is that they were able to generate caution in the Redford government and to convince the Prentice government, for a time, to propose school legislation that blatantly pandered to social conservatives. During the 2016–17 PC leadership race, the powerful candidacy of Jason Kenney was not based entirely on social conservatism, but it did demonstrate the continuing attractiveness of appealing to that side of the party's traditional base. Controversies over school recognition of sexual diversity, amplified by the Kenney campaign, illustrate the continuing potential of religious conservative political mobilizing, particularly in response to educational reform. Moral traditionalists in Alberta would be the first to admit that they have lost the major battles they fought over abortion and the public recognition of sexual diversity, but they attach huge importance to the gains they have helped secure, alongside free-market advocates of school choice, over the education of their children. And a devoted core are still keen to re-ignite debate over the hot button issues on which they lost ground in recent decades.

For years, there have been academic and popular commentaries on how much has changed in the outlook of Albertans, accurately pointing out that they are no more religious or morally conservative than are other Canadians. The province is highly urbanized, much like the rest of the country, and its major cities have had distinctively forward-looking leadership. Its population has grown significantly from in-migration, and dramatically diversified in ethno-cultural terms. Still, religious conservatism remains an important part of Alberta's culture and a very important current on the right side of Alberta's party system. Moral traditionalism also remains an important factor in Ontario politics, as we have seen, and the same can be said of party politics of Saskatchewan and, to some extent, Manitoba. So in this sense Alberta's one-time distinctiveness may well have been eliminated. But, as in much of the rest of the country, the differences between the worldviews espoused by moral traditionalism and social progressivism, respectively, still constitute an important component of the distinctions between left and right in Alberta, even if no one now wants to talk about it.

Schooling, Sexuality, and Religious Conservatism in British Columbia Politics

7

In the summer leading up to the closely contested 2013 provincial election – as the BC Liberal Party was trailing the New Democratic Party and facing what seemed a newly resurgent BC Conservative Party – premier Christy Clark agreed to appear on the most prominent evangelical Christian talk show in Canada, *100 Huntley Street*. During her interview, she talked of finding lessons on leadership from the Bible in order to make "tough" decisions.[1] These comments built upon earlier public statements about her own Anglican faith, one of them during the Liberal leadership campaign when she talked about her faith being "very personal" and that it was "consistent with [her] desire to want to make a difference in the world."[2] She and her party had also been publicly endorsed by Stockwell Day, who had long been a prominent representative of conservative Christianity in federal politics as well as in BC and Alberta. All this was in a campaign widely perceived as focusing exclusively on economic and resource-related issues and in a province generally seen as devoid of enduring religious divisions. In recent times, in fact, BC's faith landscape is distinctive precisely because of the comparatively high number of people who declare no religious affiliation whatsoever – 44 percent in 2011.

Here we argue that, even if religious differences are less influential than they were in the past, they have remained an important source of political mobilization in BC provincial politics since the emergence of the Social Credit Party in the 1950s. While overtly religious politics have never been prominent in BC as an independent source of alignment, divisions along faith lines have reinforced the left/right party divide. BC's socially conservative faithful, including its prominent evangelical community, have long been an important constituency of the province's right-wing provincial parties, including the Progressive Conservatives, the Social Credit, the Reform Party of BC, and now the BC Liberals. Conservative Christians have recurrently demonstrated the capacity to mobilize large enough numbers of British Columbians to intimidate provincial politicians, particularly on education policy. To this day right-wing parties recognize the need to court religiously traditional voters, who are crucial buttresses to the "free market" coalition they assembled to keep the New Democratic Party out of power. It was no accident that, before and during the 2013 election campaign, Premier Clark went further in displaying her faith and appealing to religious communities than almost any other leader of a right-wing or centre-right Canadian party in recent memory, even if there were no campaign promises explicitly tied to demands or expectations from evangelical Christians or conservatives in other faith communities.

The provincial Liberals in BC behave quite differently from parties using the Liberal label in other parts of Canada, drawing significant support from what was once the provincial Reform Party, the remains of Social Credit, and those who cast their federal votes for the contemporary Conservative Party of Canada. At the same time, they retain a current of centrist voters who are socially progressive but economically conservative. The BC Liberals are, therefore, a very wide coalition in a system within which two strong parties are often in close competition and within which neither party can afford to lose any votes to any disaffected splinter movements. This means focusing on the economic growth and the creation of a pro-business environment and sidelining as much as possible those issues that open up internal fissures.

This approach is coupled with often subtle displays of keeping an ear open to religious communities. This may mean framing economic growth as essential to maintaining strong families. It also means holding on to policies that have solid appeal among traditionalist faith communities, such as government funding for faith-based and other independent schools. In a polarized party environment, moral conservatives need little convincing that a leftist NDP government would be worse than one led by centre-right Liberals, but they need reassurance that they are being listened to.

This chapter starts with an overview of BC's religious make-up, which is unique in the low levels of religious identification, the comparatively small Catholic population, and the substantial numbers belonging to non-Christian minority religions. Next, we point to the importance of faith groups in the postwar history of the major provincial parties. Then, in documenting the rise of the BC Liberals, as well as their time in government since 2001, we point to their outreach to faith groups as a key factor in their electoral success. We conclude by taking a close look at BC's education policy as a site of contestation that has been particularly important for social conservatives.

Religious Context

British Columbia has as many people who declare no religious affiliation (44 percent) as declare themselves Christian (2011 figures). A 2013 survey by the BC Humanists Association shows an even higher percent (64) who said they did not practise a religion or faith.[3] This would include significant numbers from minority faith communities who might declare a religious affiliation on ethno-cultural grounds but without adhering to those communities' spiritual beliefs. On the other hand, various other indicators of religiosity – weekly attendance at religious services and declarations on the personal importance of faith – indicate that BC is close to the pan-Canadian average.[4]

Just over one-quarter of British Columbians declare an affiliation to mainstream Protestant denominations and only 15 percent to Roman Catholicism. During the formative years of colonization, BC's white population was overwhelmingly British and Protestant. With a comparatively small Roman Catholic population, no extensive Catholic school system was established, and none with the constitutional guarantees associated with separate schools found in most other provinces. Catholic schools have emerged, but they operate as faith-based independent schools, and, as we shall see, this helps strengthen a cross-denominational alliance in favour of governmental support for private schools.

Evangelical Protestants were prominent in provincial politics during the 1980s and 1990s, though election studies suggest that they constitute just over 5 percent of British Columbians.[5] If our interest lies in gauging the extent of conservative forms of Christianity, however, we must look beyond these numbers. There are Christians who attend churches that are not affiliated with any of the theological currents widely associated with that term but who share much with evangelicism in terms of biblical literalism, moral traditionalism, and individualism. There are also significant numbers of church-goers in ethno-cultural minority groups whose religious views coincide a good deal with those of evangelicals. In 2011, approximately 22 percent of the Chinese community identified as Christian, and many of these adhere to relatively traditional values on issues around which evangelicals have mobilized. The same is true for the 64 percent of Korean Canadians who identify themselves as Christian.[6] Among Filipino Canadians, a full 95 percent identified as Christian, mainly Roman Catholic, and here, too, we find a leaning towards family traditionalism. These communities have their own social networks, such as the Canadian Alliance for Social Justice and Family Values Association, a Chinese Canadian group that, among other issues, has campaigned against the legalization of same-sex marriage and the inclusion of homosexuality in the sexual education curriculum.[7]

Kurt Bowen's 1997 analysis of religiosity indicates that of all Canadian regions, BC had the highest proportion of conservative Protestants among those he classifies as religiously committed (38 percent).[8] Evangelicals are heavily concentrated in the Fraser Valley, which is home to the head offices of Focus on the Family Canada and Power to Change Ministries (formerly Campus Crusade for Christ), as well as to Trinity Western University, Canada's largest private Christian university. Focus on the Family has frequently played a significant role in relation to moral issues at the federal level, including debates over the recognition of same-sex marriage and the decriminalization of abortion. In the wake of policy losses on moral issues in the early and mid-2000s, Focus on the Family made significant investments in federally targeted lobbying through the creation of the Ottawa-based Institute for Marriage Family (now part of Cardus). In 2002, Trinity Western University also established a new leadership development program in Ottawa to better equip Christians to engage in public affairs. However, this nucleus of evangelical institutions in the Fraser Valley, close to Vancouver, suggests a strong network available for episodic mobilization around BC-specific campaigns.

High levels of immigration from non-Western countries over the last several decades have dramatically increased BC's religious pluralism. The province is home to Canada's largest Sikh community (5 percent), concentrated in the Vancouver area and the Fraser Valley (Abbotsford in particular). Large waves of Chinese, Southeast Asian, and Japanese immigration have given the Vancouver area one of Canada's largest Buddhist populations (2 percent). The Muslim population is not as large as Ontario's, but at 2 percent it is still a visible presence in and around Vancouver. Hindus comprise about 1 percent of the population, and the long-established Jewish community makes up half a percent. Overall, non-Christian religious minorities constitute 11 percent of the province's population. The much-touted "highway to heaven" in the Vancouver suburb of Richmond is a three kilometre stretch of No. 5 Road that is home to Buddhist and Sikh temples, mosques, and a variety of churches that largely cater to immigrant communities.

Sikhs in particular have become prominent players in provincial and federal party politics. One prominent example of this is Ujjal Dosanjh, who became premier under the New Democratic Party label in 2000 and then entered federal politics as a Liberal. Traditionalist currents within a few religious minority communities have been visible in protest movements in which they find common cause with evangelical Protestants and conservative Catholics, though there is no indication of sustained mobilization of this sort and no indications of stable links between social conservatives across faith backgrounds.

Provincial Party Polarization

The distinctive polarization of BC's party system is long-standing, solidified by the 1940s ascendance of the Co-operative Commonwealth Federation on the left and the early 1950s surge of the Social Credit

Party as the dominant pole on the right. The period of NDP rule in the 1990s was accompanied by the slow emergence of the provincial Liberal Party as the dominant party on the right and inheritor of the free-market legacy of Social Credit. This "recolouration" of the right did not, however, disrupt the sharp left/right divide that makes BC's party system the most "ideologically shaped and driven" in the country.[9]

Prior to the Second World War, there were no significant traces of the denominational influences on party voting that were so powerful in Ontario and the Atlantic region.[10] Roman Catholics, as we have seen, were a small enough minority to have no major weight in provincial party development, and none of the mainstream Protestant denominations were able to secure privileges that would rankle. The Second World War did not alter this pattern, though evangelicals would become a recurrent source of influence on provincial party politics.

The Rise of Social Credit

The end of the Second World War saw a significant realignment of the province's parties, a growing ideological polarization, and the beginnings of a disentanglement from the federal parties. According to Donald Blake and his colleagues, left/right polarization began under the wartime coalition governments as a rhetorical tool to keep the CCF from power, but other factors also encouraged these divisions. The particular character and importance of resource extraction produced a strong and militant labour movement, bolstering the CCF. Economic migration brought significant numbers of expatriate Albertans, who brought with them both the individualistic and evangelical traditions of their home province as well as their allegiance to the Social Credit movement.

The BC Social Credit Party was founded in 1935 as part of a protest movement aimed at the power of Vancouver as an economic centre and at the established political parties, though it soon shed the controversial fiscal theory associated with its Alberta founders.[11] Like its Alberta sibling, the new party had a fundamentally Christian character and included in its constitution a clause stipulating that one of its priorities was "to foster and encourage the universally recognized principles of Christianity in human relationships."[12] In fact, BC was developing a polarization along faith lines. Burkinshaw argues that the strength of both evangelicism and secularism in the postwar period resulted from the transient nature of the population, institutionally weak Christian denominations, the province's geographic and cultural isolation, and the "spirit of materialism" that pervaded a province built on economic migration.[13] Over time, the religious/secular divide would become increasingly associated with the province's right/left split: evangelicals voted for the Social Credit, while those without faith, or whose faith prioritized social justice, voted for the CCF/NDP.

BC's first Social Credit government was as much an accident as a reflection of the province's changing political environment. Alarmed at the increasing popularity of the socialist CCF, a Liberal-Conservative coalition government attempted to head off political defeat in the 1952 provincial election by changing its voting system from one based on a plurality of votes to one based on ranked ballots. Officials in the governing parties incorrectly assumed that voters would rank the coalition's two parties as their first and second choices, thus solidifying the anti-CCF position. Instead, many British Columbians picked Social Credit as their second choice, resulting in the decimation of the Liberal and Conservative ranks, and launching Social Credit from a fringe party with no seats into a minority government with a slim one-seat lead over the CCF. Shortly after the election, the Social Credit caucus elected W.A.C. Bennett, a former Progressive Conservative MLA, as its leader and provincial premier.

Burkinshaw attributes this remarkable turn of events, in part, to a growing evangelical presence.[14] In one study conducted by W.E. Ellis during this period, 72 percent of evangelical church ministers supported Social Credit, in contrast to 8 percent of mainline Protestant ministers.[15] While the majority of Social Credit MLAs in 1952 and 1956 were mainline Protestants, 23 percent were evangelical. Throughout his long term as premier, W.A.C. Bennett regularly marshalled religious rhetoric in demonizing the CCF and, later, the NDP. In his farewell speech, following the victory of Dave Barrett's NDP in 1972, Bennett described his work in maintaining his anti-NDP coalition in power as "a holy crusade." He implored the party: "[Do not] rest until this foreign philosophy of extreme state socialism is done away with ... Go out and get enough members for Social Credit and victory will be yours."[16] On the other hand, Social Credit maintained power by attracting supporters all across the right and even from the centre, supporting social programs in a manner broadly similar to trends established in the rest of Canada. Indeed, the party provided a useful vehicle for those supporting the federal Liberal and Progressive Conservative Parties to "support a pragmatic and development-oriented government." As Daniel Gawthrop observes:

> Although the party maintained a strong level of support among Protestant evangelicals, most Socred power brokers knew that a religious platform of any kind did not translate into broad, popular appeal in a province like BC. Thus, while the party maintained its fringe element of religious eccentrics ... not even W.A.C. Bennett, a devout Protestant himself, was willing to adopt the missionary zeal of Alberta's Social Credit mentor, William "Bible Bill" Aberhart.[17]

Social Credit, now led by W.A.C's son Bill Bennett, was less prone to the kind of religious rhetoric used by Bennett's father, though his government needed evangelical voters. Donald Blake's study of the 1979 provincial election finds that, while their numbers were relatively small at 5.5 percent of the electorate, approximately 83 percent of the community voted for Social Credit during a period in which elections were closely contested.[18] It could have been no accident then that the Bennett government gave Trinity Western University the right to grant bachelor degrees and extended limited funding to independent schools, both significant gestures to the evangelical constituency.

The younger Bennett's third mandate, beginning in 1983, marked a sharp turn further to the right, with "massive budget cuts and a comprehensive program to reduce the size and scope of government."[19] This provoked sustained extra-parliamentary opposition and more extreme party polarization than the province had ever seen. This period did not see any significant discussion of issues likely to rouse particular religious constituencies, and the premier displayed no distinctive affinity for the moral traditionalists within his party. But when he stepped down in 1986, the leadership contest to follow illustrated the deep divisions within the party and the continuing strength of social conservatism within it. Bill Vander Zalm, a devout Catholic, won the leadership against the "establishment" candidate Brian Smith on the fourth ballot.[20] Vander Zalm was an avowedly pro-life and pro-family leader who offered "hope and optimism" to moral conservatives.[21]

Vander Zalm went on to win a majority government in 1986, in part because of this energized conservative religious base. In contrast to his predecessors, Vander Zalm was entirely prepared to extend partisan polarization into the realm of morality politics. Speaking before the Christian Business Men's Committee in Trail, BC, Vander Zalm claimed the difficulties of welfare recipients and single mothers would be eased "if we [could] somehow help them to get to know Jesus Christ."[22] The premier adamantly refused to countenance any public recognition of sexual diversity during a time when AIDS was spreading rapidly in the Vancouver area. Though the BC Centre for Disease Control and Vancouver public health officials spearheaded progressive initiatives to respond to the epidemic, the premier and his health minister, Peter Dueck, did everything they could to avoid prioritizing AIDS or to encode human rights protections for sexual minorities.[23] In response to calls for the inclusion of AIDS information in the province's sexual education curriculum, Vander Zalm talked of his Catholic beliefs, adding: "I think people elect others to represent them basically on what they stand for, which includes, certainly, their moral values."[24] According to Gawthrop, issues related to sexual diversity were added to the mixture of polarized policy positions that would demarcate left and right:

> Throughout the 1980s, the political culture in BC was such that homophobic Socred ministers could afford to make bigoted remarks about gays and lesbians without fear of reprisal from their premier ... Gays and lesbians aren't real British Columbians, the reasoning went, so who cares if we insult them? During the height of the AIDS crisis, when approval of new treatments was delayed despite the fact that hundreds of people were dying, Health Minister Peter Dueck defended his government's dismal efforts to contain the disease by distinguishing the majority of people living with AIDS – gay or bisexual men and intravenous drug users – from those he described

as "innocent, [who] did not go out and wilfully or very carelessly through their lifestyle, contract that disease."[25]

The premier was outspoken in his categorical opposition to abortion, and he proposed defunding all abortions that were not medically necessary. However, his declarations on this front helped to rouse opponents within the caucus, who were emboldened by a growing recognition that the party's identification with religious conservatism was becoming an electoral liability. In 1990, the party's Christian clause was deleted in the face of objection from its supporters, who complained of a "secular humanist" conspiracy and insisted that this was "the final surrender to the secular and liberal forces within the party."[26] The internal revolt, however, intensified, and when conflict of interest charges arose from the sale of his biblically themed Fantasy Gardens theme park, Vander Zalm was forced to resign in the spring of 1991.

Social Credit's Collapse and the Rise of the BC Liberals

The contest to replace Vander Zalm pitted a more centrist candidate (Grace McCarthy) against one clearly identified with the party's right (Rita Johnston). And even if the field of candidates was far narrower than it had been in 1986, once again it was the right wing that prevailed with Johnston's selection. The 1991 election was disastrous for the party and produced a resounding New Democratic Party victory, with that party winning 41 percent of the vote to Social Credit's 24 percent. This election also saw the rebirth of the BC Liberals, who took 33 percent of the vote and 17 seats – their first in the legislature since 1979.

Social Credit all but collapsed as a party in the wake of this defeat. Grace McCarthy replaced Johnston as party leader but then lost a 1994 by-election to Gordon Campbell, the new leader of the Liberal Party. Four of the seven surviving Social Credit MLAs then joined the BC Reform Party. From the province's 1996 election on to the formal dissolution of Social Credit in 2013, it held no legislative seats. However, there was continuing uncertainty about where the rightist remains of Social Credit would go. Although organizationally independent, the federal Reform Party's 1993 breakthrough raised hopes for the provincial party's prospects, then boosted by the Social Credit defections. Jack Weisgerber, one of the four Social Credit MLAs to join Reform, became party leader, and Bill Vander Zalm provided public support. At the same time the Family Coalition Party was also attempting to win over moral traditionalists, contributing to a sense of fractiousness among moral conservatives.

The NDP that won office in 1991 had moved solidly toward social progressivism. Like the CCF before 1961, the NDP relied on the support of a strong labour movement that was more militant than most of its provincial counterparts. However, its time in government from 1972 until 1975 also demonstrated a willingness to govern pragmatically, in the tradition of other western New Democratic governments. At the same time, the party became significantly more secular, with the activists having any religious affiliation declining from 45 to 16 percent.[27]

In 1991, Premier Mike Harcourt appointed a cabinet that was significantly younger than those of previous Social Credit governments, and this change was reflected in the policy priorities of the government, including those related to identity politics and environmentalism. The 1980s had seen the political mobilization of the province's large gay and lesbian community, especially in Vancouver, and in the years to follow, advocacy on this front was intensified by growing support among the province's unions.[28] This strengthened considerably the hand of activists within the provincial NDP, who then helped educate the party's electoral candidates across the province and apply pressure on the government front benches. Within the first year of its mandate, Harcourt's government introduced legislation prohibiting discrimination on the grounds of sexual orientation and family status. Further measures would follow on relationship recognition and adoption by gays and lesbians, making BC the first province or territory in Canada to enact statutory change on such issues. Surprisingly, given the political climate in Ottawa and elsewhere in Canada, there was almost no opposition to these initiatives within the BC Legislative Assembly. Reform Party members did register some objections to the new adoption provisions in 1995, evoking prejudicial fears about the impact of gay and lesbian relationships on children, but this barely slowed enactment.[29]

The Liberals seemed ready to acquiesce to the changes, although not yet ready to stake out a clear policy position on such issues. In the first few years of the Harcourt administration, they were led by Gordon Wilson, who had previously protested Bill Bennett's rightist agenda and whose centre-left stances fit the moderate profile of the party's core activists. Further growth, however, confronted the Liberals with a dilemma. As Lynda Erickson points out, their electoral gains in 1991 were directly related to Social Credit losses, reflecting a distinct rightward shift in their voting base. Not surprisingly, Wilson experienced considerable internal caucus dissent in the two years following as well as sustained discontent from fiscally conservative business interests in Vancouver, who were now hoping for a more clearly right-wing alternative to the NDP government. Personal issues intensified the pressure on Wilson, who resigned as leader in 1993.

Gordon Campbell was the candidate most favoured by former Socred members and by fiscal conservatives. He had been mayor of Vancouver and had secured his local standing with the support of the Non-Partisan Association, the city's right-wing municipal-level "party." Campbell won the 1993 leadership race, which concluded just over a month before a federal election in which the Reform Party won 36 percent of British Columbians' votes. One consequence of this was that Campbell moved his party more clearly to the fiscal right. Positioning the Liberals on social issues was more difficult. In 1995, Campbell declared his opposition to NDP government legislation to extend same-sex adoption rights. On the other hand, he knew that he could not afford to alienate centrist voters, and there were Liberal insiders who paranoically read NDP measures on LGBT issues as partly designed to sow division among Liberal ranks.[30] Campbell, therefore, pursued a strategy of avoidance and silence, declining to speak on gay issues in the Legislative Assembly and frequently absenting himself from votes on gay-positive measures.

In the 1996 election, the Liberals cemented their place as the primary alternative to the NDP, receiving 33 percent of the vote and nearly doubling the party's seat total to 33. They did so on the basis of polarizing rhetoric and fiscal conservatism. But the right was still not completely united, and the BC Reform Party won 2 seats and 9 percent of the vote, enough to keep the NDP in power.[31] In the next few years, however, fractiousness among moral conservatives provided an opportunity for the Liberals to further broaden their support on the right. In 1997, Jack Weisgerber was replaced as Reform leader by Wilf Hanni, a strong social conservative who was soon exploring a merger with the fringe anti-abortion Family Coalition Party (FCP). His divisive leadership led the party's other sitting MLA, Richard Neufield, to defect to the Liberals, while Weisgerber himself became an independent. Hanni resigned as leader in 1999 and was replaced by none other than Bill Vander Zalm, who was then defeated in a by-election that year. He subsequently orchestrated a merger of rightist forces in the form of the BC Unity Party, aimed at bringing together the remnants of Reform, the FCP, Social Credit, the BC Conservatives, and the British Columbia Party, but it won only 3 percent of the vote in the 2001 election.

In the meantime, outside the legislative arena the province's religious conservatives were mobilizing in unprecedented numbers. The issue of LGBT visibility in provincial schools had exploded into public view when the Surrey School Board banned three lesbian/gay positive books from its elementary schools at a time when the BC Teachers' Federation was supporting calls for greater attention to the inclusion of sexual minorities across the province's educational system. In 1997, the newly re-elected NDP government, now with Glen Clark as leader, introduced legislation extending recognition of same-sex relationships, augmenting the pioneering legacy it had established in its first term in office. Evangelical ire had already been provoked on the schooling issue, and now it was mobilized in response to the Family Relations Amendment Act. The opposition was joined by BC's Catholic bishops and scattered representation from other religious communities. The Liberals were divided, as they had been when adoption was debated in 1995. When the vote came, twenty-two Liberals supported the government bill and nine opposed it. Tellingly, when the Human Rights Commission recommended the addition of gender identity to the province's anti-discrimination provisions, the Liberals immediately declared their opposition.

The Liberals won the 2001 election by riding a wave of anger directed at the governing NDP, securing a remarkable 58 percent of the popular vote and all but 2 seats in the legislature. Their success was based on drawing in the broad spectrum of voters on the right. As Dennis Pilon puts it, over the previous five years, "the BC Liberals worked hard to woo the remaining hold-outs on the right by adjusting their policy mix: greater resistance to Aboriginal land claims, support for privatization, and talk of democratic reform that appealed to populists."[32] The party was now remaining silent on issues that mattered to moral conservatives, a pattern that would reflect Gordon Campbell's style of leadership throughout the 2000s. The Liberals' positioning of themselves as the logical successor to Social Credit was reinforced by an endorsement from former premier Bill Bennett in the run-up to the 2001 election. Addressing reporters, Bennett spoke about the new Liberal coalition as "the British Columbia party that I always thought the Socreds were under me."[33] As one senior Liberal put it:

> Well, it's the old Socred party ... it is! The only way that you keep the NDP out in British Columbia is to have a coalition of the Tories and the Liberals. It's the only way you do it. I'm a federal Tory. And it's very hard for me to attach myself to the name "Liberal," but that is the one that is being used.[34]

This new version of the anti-NDP coalition, however, was not exactly the same as the old. As Mark Crawford argues, it relied more heavily on seats in the Vancouver area, and its core supporters included social policy centrists, and even some progressives, who assertively opposed the moral traditionalism of the religious right.[35] This combination severely complicated the challenge of retaining social conservative support by making it even harder for the party leadership to signal its sympathies to that segment of the electorate.

Liberals in Office under Gordon Campbell

The Liberals stayed away almost entirely from taking positions on the kinds of social issues that religious conservatives cared about. The highly contentious issue of same-sex marriage was prominent in national politics, but Campbell stayed out of that debate. On the other hand, the Liberals governed strongly to the right during their first term, cutting government expenditures sufficiently to force the closing of schools and hospitals, and provoking enough public outcry to strengthen the NDP's standing in the polls. For this reason, the Liberals pivoted to the centre in time for the 2005 election, as Dennis Pilon puts it, "rebranding themselves in their second term, de-emphasizing neoliberalism and embracing the post-material issues they had once decried."[36] They won a second majority government in that election, though with thirty-one fewer seats.

The party's move to the centre included a subtle change in approach to issues like LGBT rights. *Vancouver Sun* columnist Doug Ward describes BC Liberals as "trying to walk a tightrope ... quietly capitaliz[ing] on their connection to Christian and Sikh communities at the same time they protect themselves from being burned by voters' fears about the power of religious organizations."[37] Premier Campbell supported the change to Canada's marriage laws ultimately passed by Ottawa in 2005, though of course this was safely distant from provincial jurisdiction and followed a series of definitive court rulings, including those originating in British Columbia.

In May 2009, Campbell's Liberals were re-elected for a third consecutive majority government, with 46 percent of the popular vote, once again with no serious challenge from their right. (The BC Conservatives, somewhat revived after years of not winning even 1 percent of the vote, still received only 2 percent.) Liberal success, however, was quickly overtaken by a wave of protest aimed at the party's July 2009 announcement of the introduction of a harmonized sales tax (HST). The new measure would combine separate federal and provincial sales taxes into a single tax, but in doing so would include certain services that had previously been exempt from the latter. Opponents soon began organizing a drive to launch a referendum on the issue and to recall several government MLAs, taking advantage of the province's populist institutional structure to do so. They were led by former premier Bill Vander Zalm – whose government had passed the referendum and recall legislation being employed – and, by September 2010, they had gathered enough signatures to force a vote on the tax the following year. By the second half of 2010, support for the Liberals had declined to 24 percent. Significant gains were registered by the NDP and the Green Party, but discontent on the Liberals' right flank was also evident in the growth of support (up to 8 percent) for the BC Conservatives. Campbell's own approval rating fell to a low of just 9 percent, enough to force his resignation in November 2010.

Christy Clark and Liberal Revival

Christy Clark won the Liberals' 2011 leadership race, though she was not an obvious front runner at the outset. She had been first elected in 1996, and from 2001 to 2004 served as deputy premier and minister for education, but then dropped out of legislative politics in 2005. Her leadership victory, however, may have had at least as much to do with the fact that she had been out of the government at the time when the HST fight was being waged. Indeed, as the host of a radio talk show, she was at times critical of her former colleagues. She also campaigned for the leadership in a way that suggested a very broad political tent. She was enough of a social liberal to have marched in Vancouver's Pride Parade, but she promoted a "Family First" agenda that might have been aimed at securing conservative credentials (albeit in general enough terms to cast a wider net).[38] These strategies helped her to win, though only with a narrow 52 percent of votes on the third ballot. The candidate most favoured by social conservatives, Kevin Falcon, got 48 percent.

The threat to Liberals on their right flank had been intensified by the campaign against the HST, which resulted in a referendum defeat that summer. Later that year, one poll showed 18 percent support for the BC Conservative Party, compared to 31 percent for the Liberals and 40 percent for the NDP. The Conservatives were now led by John Cummins, a social conservative who had served as a federal MP for the Reform Party, the Canadian Alliance, and the Conservative Party of Canada. A number of Liberal activists who had supported Kevin Falcon's leadership bid had now moved over to the BC Conservatives, and in March 2012, long-time Liberal MLA John Van Dongen left the

Liberal caucus to sit as a Conservative, giving the party its first seat in the legislature in over thirty years. By that time, the Liberals were just 3 percentage points ahead of the Conservatives in the polls, and they were far behind the NDP.

Leaning Right

Christy Clark had always recognized the need to shore up the party's appeal to social conservatives, and now had more reason than ever. One of her first actions after becoming premier was to hire Dimitri Pantazo-poulos, a former Stephen Harper staffer and Conservative pollster, to be her principal secretary. She then stopped going to Vancouver's Gay Pride Parade, and no other Liberal MLAs went on her behalf. In the face of growing Conservative Party popularity, Clark's appeals to the right became even more visible. Preston Manning, former leader of the federal Reform Party, was invited to address an October 2011 meeting of the Liberal caucus, and in his remarks he specifically noted the danger of vote splitting. In January 2012, high-profile social conservative Ken Bossenkool was appointed chief of staff in the Premier's Office, and, at his suggestion, Stephen Harper's one-time press secretary Sara MacIntyre was hired to better focus the premier's messaging. In March, Clark appeared in Ottawa at the Manning Networking Conference, where Manning named her as an "Iron Snowbird" – a term he had previously reserved for Deborah Grey, the first Reform Party MP.[39] Clark responded by speaking about family values in addition to economic growth and pipelines, prompting columnist Gary Mason to suggest that the premier was undergoing a radical ideological makeover a year into the job:

> From routinely taking potshots at Prime Minister Stephen Harper and his party while a Liberal-friendly radio host, Ms. Clark has turned to the Conservative Leader and his acolytes in a painfully obvious attempt to reverse her dreary political fortunes ... Today, instead of deriding the views of Christian fundamentalists and hard-line conservatives such as Preston Manning, Ms. Clark seeks their blessings.[40]

By January 2013, public support for the Conservatives had slipped to 10 percent, but this was far from enough to allay Liberal fears. The premier had already advocated measures designed to flag her party's right-wing and populist credentials, but she also wanted to talk directly to faith communities. In February, she spoke to Vancouver-based evangelical organization City in Focus, discussing her Anglican faith and expressing her support for faith-based public service providers. She also implied that people of faith were more caring than others:

> I really do think the tragedy of our society is actually not that there are so many atheists – because atheists often express themselves as generously as non-atheists – it's the fact people don't go to a place of worship every week and get reminded anymore of how important it is that we care.[41]

In the meantime, the Liberals had drafted a "Multicultural Strategic Outreach Plan" largely inspired by the federal Conservatives' plan to lure ethno-cultural minority votes away from the federal Liberal Party.[42] In BC politics, the South Asian community is an essential part of the Liberals' electorate, and the party wanted to build on this. According to one close observer:

> It's a big factor in internal party politics because the BC Liberal membership is over 30 percent Sikh. Their influence is organized through family and temples ... all the temples play an important role in politics. More so in terms of getting nominations, and getting people to show up for those things.

Chinese evangelicals also constitute a set of communities whose loyalty party strategists wanted to gain or secure. Religious conservatives and family traditionalists are not necessarily a majority in either of BC's largest ethno-cultural minority groups, but some are an important enough segment within them to constitute a source of traditionalist pressure within the fold of Liberal voters and activists.

The 2013 Election

In the 2013 provincial election, the Liberal platform was almost singularly focused on the economy and on eliminating public-sector debt.

Formally, the campaign did not veer in the slightest into social conservative territory, and local candidates avoided the kind of embarrassing statements on morality policy that had so harmed the federal Conservatives in the early 2000s and Alberta's Wildrose Party in the early 2010s. However, appeals to conservative faith communities were part of the Liberals' strategy throughout. The Social Credit legacy was amplified by the high-profile endorsement of Brad Bennett, the son of Socred premier Bill Bennett and the grandson of W.A.C. Bennett. The Liberals' interest in courting religious conservatives was made obvious by the campaign profile given to Stockwell Day. The party's strategy of reaching out to its social conservative right without making policy commitments was aided by the BC Conservatives running a disorderly and gaff-prone campaign and by the very real prospect of an NDP victory. The NDP also had an interest in staying away from social policy questions because of their preoccupation with economic and environmental issues, not least to ward off a challenge from the provincial Greens. There was also no prospect of pointing to a hidden Liberal agenda of supporting the religious right since the government had so regularly avoided making the sort of concessions to social conservatism that had regularly featured in federal Conservative governance.

To the surprise of most informed observers, the Liberals won a majority in that election, with 44 percent of the popular vote. This was made possible, in part, by the relatively weak showing of the BC Conservatives, who won 5 percent, and whose votes resulted in the Liberals losing two seats at most. Popular support for the New Democrats dropped two points to 39 percent in an election in which they were expected to gain, a result that many insiders and outside observers blamed on a weak campaign by leader Adrian Dix. The broad coalition assembled by the Liberals, largely from Social Credit fragments, seemed to have remained intact, and it succeeded once again as a vehicle for a wide range of NDP opponents. The Liberals accomplished this by almost completely avoiding policies designed narrowly to appeal to moral traditionalists but, at the same time, using well-established social conservatives to endorse the party and to reinforce the belief among the province's many evangelical Christians that it was their only logical option.

Table 7.1   Vote choice within religious groups in British Columbia, 2013

	Liberals (%)	NDP (%)	Green (%)	Conservative (%)	Total (n)
Denomination					
Roman Catholic	64	15	13	8	53 (100%)
Mainline Protestant	41	38	13	8	141 (100%)
Evangelical	54	30	2	14	39 (100%)
Other	24	50	24	2	140 (100%)
Unaffiliated/atheist	32	54	12	2	294 (100%)
Total	36	45	14	5	668 (100%)
Importance of religion					
Very important	43	31	17	8	108 (100%)
Somewhat important	38	37	16	8	138 (100%)
Somewhat unimportant	34	50	12	3	149 (100%)
Very unimportant	34	51	13	2	273 (100%)
Total	36	45	14	5	667 (100%)

Source: Jared Wesley et al., Canadian Provincial Election Project, http://cpep.ualberta.ca/.

While the Provincial Election Study underestimated the level of Liberal support, there were few surprises in the voting patterns of religious groups, as we see in Table 7.1. Voters who see religion as important in their lives are significantly more likely to vote Liberal than NDP. This shows up not just in response to a question specifically about this but also in the disproportionate number of evangelicals voting Liberal. Their gravitation to the Liberals is nothing compared to their historical levels of support for Social Credit, which at some points reached over 80 percent.[43] This tempering of evangelical support comes partly from their wariness of any "Liberal" brand, having supported federal Reform and Conservative parties for years. There were also some evangelical voters drawn provincially to the BC Conservatives. Still, almost 10 percent of provincial Liberal supporters in 2013 were evangelical, and almost 20 percent declared religion very important in their lives. In a close election these sources of support matter, and on each of these dimensions, the proportions within the NDP were about half. (The greater draw of the

Liberals among Catholics is rooted partly in the long-standing British Protestant character of the BC labour movement but also in the long history of Catholic association with the federal Liberal Party.)

The Politics of Education in British Columbia

The BC electorate has sorted itself to an important degree along faith lines, providing parties on the right with a disproportionate block of religiously and socially conservative voters. Yet, is there any evidence of this having made a difference in public policy? We have already seen that schooling policy was an important flashpoint for evangelicals in the 1990s, and we know that education is a crucial area of concern for religious conservatives across the country. So it is here that we look for evidence of policy impact. It is here, too, that we explore public policy treatment of home schooling and independent schools as well as the recognition of sexual diversity in the public educational system. What we find is that social conservatives have certainly lost battles in this policy area, but they have also helped secure some gains that are important to them.

Home Schooling

There is little regulation of home schooling in British Columbia, even less than in Alberta (see Chapter 6). Students must be registered at a public, francophone, or independent school each year, and the education program offered at home is formally supervised by a certified teacher; however, neither the school nor the provincial education ministry requires the delivery of an approved curriculum. There is no direct financial support offered to families or guardians, but a small amount is provided to the registering school to cover administrative costs. "Distributed learning" (distance learning) is also widely offered at little or no cost to families but, of course, with no requirement that parents follow what is formally available as a curriculum. The Fraser Institute reports that home schooling enrolment grew almost 90 percent from 14,000 in 2006–07 to 27,000 in 2011–12.[44] A significant proportion of home-schooling families are evangelical, and various Christian home educator associations operating in the province provide families with resources, field trip opportunities, and support networks. There have been no moves to increase funding or other means of homeschooling support, but nor has there been any push to increase oversight.

Government Supports for Private Schools

"Independent schools" have also increased dramatically in popularity, from 4 percent of the overall student population in 1977 to 13 percent in 2014–15.[45] In BC, they include not only schools for Catholics, religious minorities, and elite private schools but also a significant number of those established by evangelical Protestants. These schools fall into four categories. Group 1 schools (about three-quarters of the total) follow a curriculum consistent with that used in the public system taught by certified teachers, and they receive 50 percent of BC's per student operating grant. Group 2 schools (about 20 percent of the total) are those with relatively high operating costs, mostly "elite" schools, and they receive 35 percent. Other private schools (enrolling 2 percent of students combined) are not required to employ certified teachers, and they are ineligible for provincial grants.

The provision of government funding for BC's private schools was inaugurated by Bill Bennett's Social Credit government in 1977.[46] This move encountered criticism for catering to the wealthy, whose children went to expensive schools, but it was a policy that played well among the party's religious supporters. As Lois Sweet argues, the NDP was split because some of its MLAs wanted funding for Catholic schools, and others felt that "equality of opportunity should be extended to religious minorities."[47] The NDP managed this divide by simply not voting for the government's bill at second reading, and the legislation was adopted with no opposing votes.

In 1996, an NDP policy convention voted to cut funding to independent schools, but the NDP government avoided the question. It finally did cut funding, at the end of its second mandate, but by only two dollars per student. After winning office in 2001, the Liberals increased funding somewhat, and, on their watch, evangelical Christians have occupied important roles as inspectors of independent schools. In the lead-up to the 2013 election, the BC Liberals reaffirmed their commitment to independent schools, boasting that they had increased funding by 86 percent and, thereby, had contributed to a 22 percent growth in student enrolment.[48] They also talked of "choice" being "a cornerstone of the BC Liberal government's educational policy agenda." Then opposition leader Adrian Dix indicated that an NDP government would not change the funding program for independent schools – a position the party continued to hold through 2016.

The Recognition of Sexual Diversity in BC Schools

Policy conflicts over making schools more welcoming of sexual minorities offer another lens, and a more directly confrontational one, through which we can gauge the influence of religious conservatives on BC political parties. Pressure to make schools more inclusive had been applied to provincial educational authorities since the early 1990s, almost always countered by opponents who have mobilized on a scale as imposing as that found anywhere in Canada. As a result, a series of provincial governments, left and right, have either avoided taking action altogether or have moved with great caution.

It was the Glen Clark NDP government in the late 1990s that first encountered massive opposition to the recognition of sexual diversity in schools. A few years before this, with Mike Harcourt as premier, statutory recognition of same-sex couples had been approved with relatively little organized opposition either inside or outside the legislature. A 1995 bill recognizing lesbian/gay adoption rights drew more opposition among religious conservatives but not sustained confrontation.

Schooling was becoming a more complicated matter – one that mobilized much more significant religious right opposition. In 1996, representatives of the British Columbia Gay and Lesbian Educators (GALE-BC) met the education minister to press for provincial action to challenge homophobic school climates at a time when departmental officials seemed willing to create more inclusive policies.[49] Paul Ramsey, the education minister, was at the time open to taking action, and, in 1997 when Surrey school trustees opposed the use of books depicting same-sex parents in elementary classrooms, he publicly condemned the action. That same year, GALE-BC activists secured support from the BC Teachers' Federation for a resolution calling for action to confront homophobia and heterosexism in schools.

A tidal wave of backlash was then mobilized by religious conservatives, who also mounted a campaign to recall Ramsey. While the campaign failed to gather enough signatures, it was effective enough to
slow the NDP policy drive to a stop. In 1998, the Ministry of Education
suspended its plans to establish a provincewide anti-homophobia program, and the following year, a new Safe Schools initiative was launched
without resource materials specific to LGBT issues.

As a result of this inaction, the Liberal government that took office
in 2001 inherited no LGBT-related policies on schooling that their morally conservative supporters wanted to change. On the other hand, the
social reformers within the party's very broad tent were open to calls
for more provincial action, which had been amplified by the intense
media coverage in 2000 of a gay teen suicide in Mission, BC. Around
this time, the province's two biggest urban school boards, Vancouver
and Victoria, both adopted inclusive policies addressing harassment
and bullying, increasing the pressure on the government to take action
that would apply across the province.[50]

During its first mandate, the Liberal government established the
Safe School Task Force, chaired by an openly gay Liberal MLA Lorne
Mayencourt. But despite hearing an enormous amount of evidence
about bullying in BC schools aimed at sexual minorities, the task force
report contained no recommendations regarding homophobic bullying, and the Ministry of Education guidelines on safe schools issued in
2003 had nothing specific to say about sexual diversity. One year later,
Mayencourt introduced a private member's bill on safe schools, including specific mention of LGBT students, but it died before getting approval – this in a legislature overwhelmingly dominated by government
members and with an opposition more than prepared to back the bill.

The only visible Liberal government action was in the face of activist
litigation. A 1999 human rights complaint over the absence of LGBT
representation in the BC curriculum led to a 2006 settlement in which
the Ministry of Education committed to a review of the inclusiveness
of the provincial curriculum and to the introduction of a new course
on social justice that would attend to sexual diversity. But the course,
to be inaugurated in 2008, was an elective, and local boards were not

compelled to offer it. This clearly meant that religious schools receiving major government subsidies, and required in principle to follow the provincial curriculum, would not have to adopt the course. And even if the settlement broadly committed the education ministry to create a more inclusive curriculum as various subject areas came up for routine updating, the government was silent on whether religious schools in that category would be obliged to comply. Even this very modest resolution aroused substantial discontent among religious conservatives, who had already opposed local school board moves towards recognizing sexual diversity. Evangelicals in Alberta cited this concession to LGBT activists in applying pressure on that province's government to shore up parents' right to exclude their children from teaching on sexuality.[51] This could hardly have encouraged the BC Liberals to interpret their human rights settlement more expansively.

In late 2011, Christy Clark began yet another consultation on anti-bullying legislation for BC schools, and, in 2012, the BCTF pressed the education ministry further on the importance of specifically addressing LGBT issues. But resistance was apparent from the beginning, with opponents favouring broadly generic policy rather than anything addressing the particulars of sexual and gender non-conformity. Doug Lauson, president of the Federation of Independent School Association of BC, argued that, while his organization "would be 100-per-cent behind a policy or legislation that was against all forms of bullying," he believed that "to emphasize one form of bullying would be problematic."[52] When the government's policy was released in mid-2012, the "Erase Bullying" strategy did not contain any specific measures designed to protect LGBT students. Three years later, following the passage of Alberta's gay-straight alliance bill in early 2015, Clark said no such legislation was needed in BC, claiming that she was looking for "balance" and asserting, without apparent irony, that "we lead the world in ... looking to create safe schools where there's a real climate of inclusion for all kids."[53] It can be no coincidence that the education minister during this period from 2013 to 2015 was Peter Fassbender, an evangelical former mayor of Langley. No new legislation had been proposed as of 2016.

Conclusion

Party politics in British Columbia were never shaped by the Catholic-Protestant differences that were so important in the history of major parties in eastern and central Canada. However, since the Second World War there has been a history of religious conservatives opting for whatever party was on the right, opposing the Co-operative Commonwealth Federation and then the New Democratic Party. In speaking of the role of faith in provincial party politics, then, we cannot talk of "realignment" since there was no enduring alignment on any other dimension apart from that which distinguishes social progressivism from its opposite. From its origins, the Social Credit Party had an important evangelical constituency, but it also drew such conservative Catholics as Bill Vander Zalm.

When the right-wing mantle shifted to the Liberals in the second half of the 1990s, Liberal history at the federal level would have made it a tough sell for evangelical Protestants. But, as the provincial Liberals moved to the neoliberal right, reflecting the Social Credit Party's shift under Bill Bennett and the rightward move of Alberta's PCs under Ralph Klein and Ontario's PCs under Mike Harris, many social traditionalists felt they had little choice. British Columbia may well have been distinctive in the number of its residents who were without a religious affiliation, but conservative faith constituencies were significant enough that, with a history of large-scale mobilization, they were important to Liberal electoral success. The Social Credit Party's disintegration after years of Bill Vander Zalm's leadership contained a lesson about the electoral risks of giving a high profile to moral traditionalism, but this did not mean that this viewpoint could be ignored.

This created some awkwardness within the party since the Liberals' electoral coalition stretched further into social reformism than did its Ontario and federal counterparts on the partisan right. However, the party's recent history of seeking endorsements from senior politicians with powerful credentials among religious conservatives, and the policy record of recent Liberal governments on issues related to schooling, demonstrate that the retention of moral conservative support is still considered important. It is no small matter that, in 2015, Premier Christy

Clark failed to march in Vancouver's Pride Parade and refused to sign the Pride organizers' pledge to support the inclusion of gender identity and gender expression in the province's Human Rights Code. The government did enact legislation to this effect one year later, by which time most other provinces had taken similar steps without controversy. The resistance on trans rights until 2016 reflects the presence of social conservatives in the party's electorate and the leadership's concern for their loyalty. Liberals' attention to shoring up their social conservative credibility also come from a continuing fear that those on the right flank of the party, evangelicals in particular, will defect to minor parties in enough numbers to bring the party to defeat at the polls.

The Liberals have pursued the federal Conservative strategy of reaching out to ethno-cultural minorities. It is not clear that they set out deliberately to use a "traditional" family pitch to attract social conservatives within those communities, but it is hard to avoid thinking that their reluctance to take policy steps specifically aimed at creating greater LGBT inclusiveness in schools would have been part of what they hoped would appeal to such communities. Their advocacy of school choice would also have been tempting to advertise within Christian and non-Christian segments of those communities. As is true for Ontario's PCs, the Liberals have stayed away from contentious issues related to the recognition of minority religious rights, not least because they see minorities as electorally important.

So of the three potential axes of religious contention, only one has shaped British Columbia's party system, and it has done so for decades. The grounds for governments on the right to make policy concessions to religious conservatives have narrowed considerably since the 1990s, and the explicit language of Christian faith used by Premier Bill Vander Zalm to oppose abortion and lesbian/gay rights is a phenomenon of the now receding past. But the Liberals' attention to shoring up their social conservative credentials tells us that religious faith continues to be influential even when the partisan right is represented by a very different label than we find elsewhere in Canada, and even in a province where so many citizens deny any religious attachment whatever.

PART 4
Canada's Most Distinctive Regions

Conflicted Secularism in Francophone Quebec Party Politics

8

One version of Quebec's distinctive story is that its French-speaking population moved rapidly from a political order thoroughly shaped by Roman Catholicism to a progressive society barely touched by religion. Churches emptied out to the extent that Quebec became the most secular region in North America. A powerful provincial state apparatus emerged, taking over functions once assumed by Catholic institutions. Emerging in the place of Catholic traditionalism was a broad societal consensus on expansive social policy and a commitment to a pluralist conception of Quebec society. From the late 1960s on, party divisions and electoral choices no longer had a significant religious component, in marked contrast to political patterns across most of North America and much of Europe.

An alternative view is that the shift towards secularism was slower and more equivocal than this, complicated, in part, by an attachment to the Catholic component of francophone Quebec identity among the lapsed as well as the faithful, and reinforced by non-Christian immigration. Until the new millennium, major parties were united in their caution in advancing state secularism, as they were in approaching such hot button issues as abortion and sexual diversity. Where political contention was most pronounced was in the recognition of minority religious practice, an area of public debate side-stepped by major parties across most of the rest of Canada. And finally, we find in Quebec, more than elsewhere in Canada, strong currents of what might be called assertive, or "strict," secularism, proposing clear rules that ensure not just the neutrality of the state with respect to religious practice but also the elimination of faith practices from the realm of the state. We find echoes of all such views elsewhere, but they are stronger in Quebec, in part for their association with the preservation of a distinct identity or as a reaction to the long period of Catholic social and political influence.

All debates over religion in Quebec have a distinctive colouration in the Canadian context because they are invariably refracted through the "national" question. For most of the nineteenth and twentieth centuries, the defence of French language and culture against assimilationist forces, and the assertion of francophone interests in the face of English-Quebec or English-speaking North American economic power, has been the single most influential shaper of party politics. Political conflict between Catholics and Protestants across Canada inevitably had (in a few cases still has) a language component, but nowhere is this more so than in Quebec. The unusual mixture of anti-clericalism and continued identification with Catholicism among francophones in Quebec is linked to the national question, as is the now-politicized debate between contrasting visions of secularism.

The pattern of partisan faith alignment and realignment is therefore quite different in Quebec than in any other region. Among francophones, Liberals were long the political home of reformist Catholics as well as anti-clericals, especially from the 1930s on. Traditionalist Catholics sided with parties on the right that defended the existing place of the church in francophone Quebec. During the late 1960s, the major parties came to a form of "soft," or "open," secular consensus, with little or no opposition to the state acquiring almost all of the service provision roles once occupied by the church. At the same time, no major party was ready to explicitly side with the religiously or morally traditionalist positions on contentious social policy issues. In the mid-2000s, a new faith alignment emerged that distinguished the two most established parties, the Parti Québécois shifting towards an assertively secularist position that, in effect, targeted religious minorities. It was supported by principled secularists, some influenced by what they perceived to be the French model of *laïcité*, but also by others who were discomfited by the growing visibility of religious minorities, especially Muslims. The Liberals retained an open secularist position, despite internal dissension, more in line with the pluralist and "interculturalist" rhetoric that had until then prevailed.

One of the Quebec paradoxes, then, is that, in this most secularized of Canadian regions, religiously based contention has been more intense than in any other region, not on denominational issues, and not on those issues that pit religious conservatives of all denominations against reformers, but on the one religious "axis" that has been most often avoided in provincial politics elsewhere.

After providing a portrait of religious practice in Quebec, this analysis explores the various currents of national identity, essential to understanding the play of faith in public debate and party politics. It then traces the shifting way in which the province's parties were "religiously" distinct from the nineteenth century to the early 1960s before going on to examine the Quiet Revolution's contribution to a faith realignment in partisan politics. After that, it takes up the impact of accelerated immigration and, particularly, the increased size of French-speaking religious minority communities. The final section examines survey evidence tracking the extent to which we can talk of faith-based party alignments in the electorate.

A Revolution in Quebec's Religious Make-Up

All but a few francophone Quebeckers are "nominally" Roman Catholic, and an extremely high proportion still identify themselves as such when asked for religious affiliation.[1] The persistence of this "affiliation" as part of québécois identity combines with dramatic shifts away from church attendance and from denominationally specific faith. The influence of Roman Catholicism on francophone Quebec society up to the 1960s is hard to exaggerate. Throughout the nineteenth century the church was inextricably tied to the defence of the French language, and, for most of the twentieth century, weekly attendance at mass was as high in Quebec as anywhere in the world. From the earliest years of white settlement,

Figure 8.1   **Weekly mass attendance by Quebec Catholics, 1945–2015**

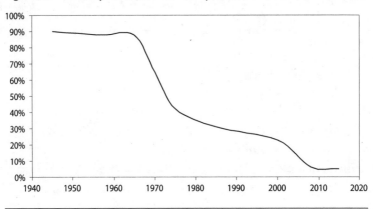

the church had built hospitals and charitable agencies, and from the 1920s on it supplemented these with Catholic youth movements, cooperatives, labour unions, and farmers' groups. And, of course, it exercised enormous control over the education of almost all French-speaking Quebeckers. As Hubert Guindon puts it, "the Church established an institutional system through which the French as a people could cope with the human life-cycle in their own way and in their own distinctive cultural style," maintaining a "protective mantle" over its insulated flock.[2]

Then, over the course of the half century after the Second World War, in the words of Kevin Christiano, "Quebec went from being one of the most socially traditional, politically conservative, and religiously devout regions of the developed world to one of the least."[3] He cites a 1945 Gallup poll showing that almost 90 percent of Quebec Catholics attended mass on a weekly basis.[4] It then dropped from the late 1960s on, eventually plummeting to less than 10 percent (see Figure 8.1).[5] Priestly ordinations declined in similarly dramatic fashion, from 127 in 1963 to seventeen in 1988.

During the time of the Quiet Revolution, francophone Quebeckers also turned away from traditional Roman Catholic Church teachings on reproduction, which until that point had encouraged large families and treated women as naturally focused on child-rearing. As Michael Gauvreau puts it:

What ultimately accelerated and widened the process of de-christian-ization was the large-scale defection from the Church's doctrines of contraception and prescribed family roles that occurred among adult Quebec Catholics between 1960 and 1968. By the end of the 1950s, the combination of increasingly higher rates of married women working outside the home and the rise of a discourse even within Catholic women's movements that acknowledged that an exclusive focus on women's familial obligations was stunting the female iden-tity, a critique that in some ways presaged that advanced in 1963 by Betty Friedan, established a very difficult terrain for Catholicism to navigate.[6]

Between 1959 and 1968, Quebec moved from having the highest birth rate of any province in Canada to having the lowest. In 1963, the average francophone woman had given birth to 3.5 children. Five years later, it was 2.3, and by 1986 it had declined to 1.4 – well below the population-replacement level.[7] Marriage rates declined rapidly, to the extent that, by 2000, 30 percent of co-habiting couples were un-married, compared to 12 percent for Canada as a whole. And according to Christiano, the abortion rate in Quebec also rose sharply to become one of the highest in the Western world.

Despite the appearances generated by such numbers, the Quiet Revo-lution was not at first a complete rejection of the church, in part because the church was actually not static during this upheaval. Strong "mod-ernizing" currents in Quebec society that emerged in the 1930s included important reformism within church circles, even more during the decade after the end of the Second World War. Dissidence was evident in the rise of intellectual challenges to the conservative Duplessis governments during the 1950s. Lay Catholics who had become socially engaged through Catholic Action or the Catholic workers movement were often at the forefront of these confrontations with tradition, joined by progres-sive clergy.[8] In the popular "marriage preparation" movement, many lay participants downplayed the exclusive emphasis on reproduction and encouraged women in the view that limiting the number of children, for example through the use of contraception, was an appropriate option.[9]

The energies and debates centred on Vatican II strengthened the hand of Quebec's Catholic reformers among the laity, the parish clergy, and the hierarchy. As a result, the changes that came with the Quiet Revolution did not encounter the kind of confrontational opposition that they would have in the past. In addition, the political advocates of a shift in power towards state institutions and away from the church included many practising Catholics, like Education Minister Paul Gérin-Lajoie, who believed in the importance of revisioning the relationships between church and state.

The forces of secularization in Quebec seemed not to be slowed by either reformers or traditionalists. In Michel Gauvreau's view, 1968 was a turning point: "When the Pope reiterated Catholic moral teaching and the church's opposition to what he termed 'artificial' types of birth control, it entailed an immediate and massive erosion of adherence among Catholicism's traditional constituency: married couples with families."[10] This contributed to a readiness to deny the legitimacy of clerical influence on politics and even to clear the public arena of expressions of religious faith.

Not all is what it appears, however. There are a few indicators of religiosity that show a less complete abandonment of religion than the analysis to this point suggests. Jeffrey Reitz, drawing on 2006 World Values Survey responses, reports that 71 percent of Quebeckers identified themselves as a "religious person," more than the 65 percent doing so in other parts of Canada.[11] On a 10-point scale, when asked how important God was in their life, 66 percent of Quebeckers gave scores from 7 to 10, less than 1 percent fewer than other Canadians and only slightly down from the 68 percent who provided such responses in 1990. None of this diminishes the significance of the great distance that opened up between most francophone Quebeckers and the Roman Catholic Church, though it does suggest that we use caution in our characterization of them as irreligious or antireligious.

Over recent decades, with the Catholic clergy playing a declining role in Quebec society, and even more so in politics, the anger that was once widespread slipped into what Christiano describes as "polite indifference." And yet there remained (and remains) an edgy vigilance about some forms of public religious practice that is less obvious in other parts of the country, reinforced by growing intellectual and cultural ties between Quebec and France. Sophie Therrien suggests that the response to religion is polarized in Quebec, with a strict form of secularism at one end.

> Le concept de laïcité s'avère souvent polémique. Il véhicule en effet un ensemble de représentations et une charge émotive suscietant des réactions polarisées. Son ancrage dans l'histoire de la France de même q'un certain anticléricalisme présent au sein des élites canadiennes françaises ont contribué à lui donner une allure rigide, voire antireligieuse.[12]

The varieties of secularism that grew out of the Quiet Revolution were accompanied by a growth in the number of immigrants to Quebec, including a significant number of adherents to non-Christian faiths. By the 2011 census, the proportion of foreign-born had risen to 13 percent, 80 percent with a mother tongue other than French or English, though over half with a reasonable knowledge of French.[13] The result is that, by this date, 5 percent of the total provincial population was non-Christian. The long-established Jewish population was just over 1 percent, almost all of whom used English as a home language. The more recently arrived Muslim communities were just over 3 percent of the population, a majority of them knowing at least as much French as English.[14] Language laws required immigrants to place their children in French-language schools, and, by the turn into the twenty-first century, in Montreal, about half of the student population in those schools was of immigrant origin. For the first time, the schools to which francophones sent their children included highly visible religious minority communities.[15]

Changes in Identity

Understanding contemporary contention over the public display of religious differences requires not just an examination of secularism and anti-clericalism but also of the interplay of distinct strands of national identity, typically arrayed along a spectrum that ranges from an ethnically based affection for a deeply rooted culture to a form of civic attachment to Quebec as self-consciously cosmopolitan. Jocelyn Maclure sees the Quebec "imagination" as saturated or besieged by these two contrasting portrayals.[16] Many observers characterize francophone Quebecers as moving from one towards the other, either slowly over the course of the last half of the twentieth century or rapidly in the midst of the Quiet Revolution, with allegiance to the Roman Catholic Church being central to earlier periods and dissipating in the later.[17] In the course of this transformation, nationalist sentiments spurned the purely ethnic and religious attachments that dominated the past in favour of support for an assertive state and for forms of identity open to pluralism. The once-contentious language laws of the 1970s in some ways reinforced this view by pressuring immigrants to send their children to French schools. What this has meant is that, for the first time, francophone québécois society, and not just territorial Quebec, was becoming ethnoculturally pluralized.

Maclure's own view of recent Quebec history is more complex, arguing that the space between the two identity "poles" (ethnic and pluralist) is open to continuing deliberation and conflict. On the one hand, he asserts that modern-day Quebec is relatively open, plural, and liberal and that "difference, whether it be sexual, cultural, linguistic, gender-based, or another kind, is starting to be seen as a wellspring from which identity can draw, instead of a problem it has to solve." Yes, adaptation to pluralism is slow and contentious, but no more so than in other liberal democratic systems. On the other hand, he acknowledges that there are many nationalists, including intellectuals and cultural producers, who believe "that there is a true and authentic way to be Québécois" and that identity is, therefore, based on assimilation to a fixed cultural mooring point.[18]

Among those who emphasize the building or maintenance of a common Quebec culture, Guillaume Lamy sets out two schools of thought.[19] One is what he sees as a progressive "civic republican" view, drawing inspiration from an idealized French model of *laïcité* in emphasizing a common civic culture built on rational Enlightenment ideals and calling for an end to all forms of official recognition of religion, including Roman Catholic. The other is "conservative republican," whose aim is to maintain a specifically québécois cultural community, one forged by a particular history that includes a Roman Catholic heritage, even if it sees value in the principle of separating church and state. Proponents of both schools of thought in effect argue that the integration required to forge community is one-way, with newcomers and minorities being expected to shed or marginalize their own communal attachments and particularities in the public square.

Ines Molinaro is one of those who argues that "the gradual broadening of the meaning of 'Québécois' to denote a civic identity has not overcome its elemental association with the French-Canadian nation in Quebec."[20] Daniel Salée, writing specifically about proponents of sovereignty, claims that "they remain imbued with a sense of *la nation québécoise* that is largely defined by the particular history of French-speaking Quebecers in Canada, and geared specifically toward the political emancipation and socioeconomic promotion of that group."[21] Rhetorical shifts towards "modernist, rationalist and universalist discourse" remain largely unconvincing to members of minority groups, not least because of nationalist tendencies to see francophones as "the true victims of Canadian history, whose claims for reparations supersedes the claims any other group might make on the Quebec polity."

Talk of "interculturalism" as Quebec's distinct approach to the integration of immigrants might appear to forge a middle ground between polarities. It suggests respect for both ethno-cultural diversity and for the existing language and culture of Quebec, balancing the right to distinctive identities and practices with the need to integrate not just in linguistic terms but also in one's commitment to norms of individual rights and equity that are said to be embedded in contemporary Quebec society. The explicit emphasis on "integration" in this pluralist model is deeply rooted in the understandable concerns of Quebec francophones regarding the cultural vulnerability of their society – and not just in an English-dominated North America. Such an approach is thought to lie between the *laïc* assimilationism of French Jacobinism and the multiculturalist approach assumed to prevail in the rest of Canada.[22] On the other hand, as Marie Mc Andrew points out, the understanding of québécois identity and common values has been subject to considerable disagreement.[23] She is also one of the few intellectuals in Quebec who challenges the stereotypes of what English Canadian multiculturalism represents.

One important factor in debates over identity is that faith matters for immigrants and religious minorities, in Quebec and across the rest of Canada, in a way that it often does not for majorities. As Pierre Anctil points out, social, economic, and political isolation elevates the significance of religious institutions and networks for many newcomers. The long-rooted Jewish community demonstrates that such linkages also maintain community solidarity in the face of a sometimes-unwelcoming society. To the extent that religious minorities encounter resistance or antipathy, their attachment to religious identity can be reinforced, among non-practitoners as well as among the faithful. This, in turn, can increase wariness among those in the majority culture who are hostile to the expression of faith in the public square.[24] Questions of religious faith, therefore, are inextricably linked to the contrasting approaches to identity at play in Quebec and to the place of immigrants in conceptions of "community."

Clericalism and Anti-Clericalism in Quebec's Earlier Party Systems

From the third decade of the nineteenth century until the early 1960s, Quebec's provincial parties were "bleu" or "rouge," and for almost all of this period there was a religious dimension to partisanship. Conservatives, and later the Union Nationale (UN), were more likely to side with the Catholic Church's interests and, as a result, to gain the support of the hierarchy. Liberals were more open to the exercise of state authority in the provision of services traditionally delivered by faith-based institutions and, in some cases, leaned towards anti-clericalism. Blue, after all, was the colour of heaven, and red the colour of hell.

This distinction was often blurred, up to and including the 1960s, largely because Liberals were reluctant to confront Catholic authority head on. Anti-clericals were never more than a minority among French-speaking legislators in the nineteenth century, and, in any event, defensive reaction to assimilationist pressures within and beyond Quebec often led them to acknowledge the church's culturally defensive role.[25] In the first half of the nineteenth century, secular nationalists joined other francophones in rallying round what Fernand Ouellette describes as "the curious process of identifying religion and nation" – for example, in creating a school system under church control.[26] By the time that the Liberals secured provincial office at the end of the nineteenth century, moderates on the clerical question were even more securely in control, though this did little to mollify the hierarchy.[27] Then, and for decades to follow, the church remained, in Vincent Lemieux's words, the "adversaire du Parti libéral."[28] This pattern endured through years of Liberal rule in the late 1920s and early 1930s.

The Union Nationale emerged as a reformist and nationalist successor to the provincial Conservatives, in part based on protests against the Liberals' promotion of industrialization, their acquiescence to English economic dominance, and their corruption.[29] As party leader and premier, Maurice Duplessis shifted the UN towards a conservative form of nationalism that attached itself to church interests and what were portrayed as rural values. In the postwar period, Catholic hierarchy support for the Duplessis bleus was reinforced when the premier added an anticommunist angle to the UN's defensive nationalist discourse and began targeting the province's Jehovah's Witnesses. If anything, traditionalist Catholic support for the UN hardened as dissenting voices in the 1950s began pushing against Catholic traditionalism.[30]

The death of Duplessis in 1959 was an important factor in his party's defeat one year later, but so was the steady growth through the 1950s of more reformist nationalism and growing unease among francophones about the role of the Roman Catholic Church – in Solange Lefebvre's words, "expremant à la fois son attachment et son ressentiment à l'égard de cette tradition religieuse qui l'a façonée."[31] Dissent was evident even within the hierarchy, for example, in a public rebuke of the government's repressive response to the 1949 asbestos strike from Montreal archbishop Joseph Charbonneau and the 1951 call for more reformist social policy from his successor Paul-Émile Léger. Working-class Catholics still remained largely loyal to the Union Nationale, but middle-class Catholics were increasingly turning to the Liberals.[32]

The State-Building Secularism of the Quiet Revolution

Quebec's Quiet Revolution of the 1960s represented a rupture that saw a major expansion of state authority and its sustained entry into and dominance of social service domains once under Roman Catholic Church control. The Liberal Party, however, was not uniformly devoted to dismantling church influence over Quebec society.[33] Once elected in 1960, the new Liberal government postponed the need for urgent action on education policy by appointing a Royal Commission on school financing (the Parent Commission). Throughout this period Premier Jean Lesage was intent on maintaining a cordial relationship with the Catholic hierarchy and, along with his education minister Paul Gérin-Lajoie, resisted calls for "neutral" schools from within his own party.[34] The government's Bill 60, introduced in 1964, created the Ministry of Education and centralized a great deal of authority in it. But it also retained denominationalism as the organizing principle behind public education and made additional concessions to the church, enough to provoke criticism from those who sought a more thoroughly secularized educational system.[35] Religious instruction remained for both Catholic and Protestant systems. Some have argued that such instruction "became more and more just another subject in the school curriculum and was often taught by persons with little or no theological training or religious convictions," yet Catholic school boards clung to that requirement.[36]

Early on in the decade, the Union Nationale staked out a position that echoed its earlier defence of social and religious traditionalism. Its 1962 program committed itself to "maintenir le caractère fondamental de la confessionalité dans toutes les écoles publiques de la province" and to respect the "droits prioritaires des parents en matières d'éducation."[37] By the time of the 1966 election, however, the party had more fundamentally renewed its appeal under Daniel Johnson's leadership, taking on a more assertive nationalism and supporting state intervention enough to greatly narrow the gap with the Liberals. After winning that election, the UN government made no attempt to roll back educational reforms. In addition, it created the entirely secular system of Colleges of General and Professional Education (CÉGEPs) in 1967 and the non-denominational Université du Québec system in 1968. The most significant "traditionalist" gesture of the UN government was to introduce legislation in 1968 that provided significant operational funding to private schools, the prime beneficiaries being the long-established Catholic *collèges classiques*. But this legislation was supported by the Liberals, and so, on this front too, there no longer seemed a clear-cut religious distinction between the parties.

Nationalist Rupture and Faith Realignment of the 1970s

The Liberal Party's internal divisions over the position of Quebec in the Canadian federation led to a schism in 1967–68, when René Lévesque formed the Mouvement Souveraineté-Association (merging with the Ralliement national to form the Parti Québécois a year later). The power of the national question was such that most Union Nationale supporters quickly split themselves between the Liberals and PQ, some also defecting (for a time) to the newly formed Ralliement créditiste – all this accelerated by the shock of the UN losing another leader with the death of Premier Daniel Johnson in 1968.[38] It lost all of its legislative seats in the 1973 election, with the Créditistes inheriting its nationalist conservatism for only a few years.

With only small exceptions, then, Quebec retained a two-party system, but with a significant turn in axis on the national question and the role of the state, with no major party left prepared to explicitly represent the views of Catholic traditionalists. On the other hand, both parties would retain a current of such believers, the PQ drawing the more *indépandistes* among them, and others going to a Liberal Party that was now more centrist than it had been in the 1960s. This meant that both parties had an interest in avoiding policy questions that could provoke religious contention, and in proceeding cautiously enough to allow for the gradual emergence of cross-party consensus.

The Tentative Secularism of the Parti Québécois

Under René Lévesque's skilful leadership, the Parti Québécois moved towards the social democratic left, but with no internal consensus on how to approach contentious moral issues and no apparent eagerness to confront religious authorities.[39] For example, the PQ government inherited a tangled legal web associated with the repeated prosecution of Henry Morgentaler for performing abortions in his Montreal clinic, in defiance of Criminal Code provisions requiring that the procedure be performed in a hospital and after the approval of a therapeutic abortion clinic. On taking office in 1976, the Lévesque government declared that it would no longer prosecute Morgentaler and would grant immunity to doctors who were qualified to do the procedure, but it actually moved only slowly in providing increased de facto access to abortion elsewhere. In fact, Lévesque for a time resisted further steps. Hospital abortions, for example, remained difficult to obtain in Quebec, particularly outside the English Montreal hospital system.[40] The PQ's 1977 congress had passed a resolution endorsing abortion on demand, and concerted pressure by feminists a year after that persuaded the government to acquiesce in the decision by five provincially organized local health clinics (*Centres locaux de services communautaires*) to perform abortions, though not until 1982.

The PQ seemed more assertive on the question of publicly recognizing lesbian and gay rights, but only very selectively. In late 1977, the province became the first to recognize sexual orientation by adding it to the Quebec Charter of Human Rights and Freedoms, far in advance of any other provincial or territorial jurisdiction. On the other hand, it did so quietly, by an amendment to its own bill in the final days of a December sitting of the National Assembly. In later years, when demands for the recognition of same-sex relationships grew in amplitude, PQ governments displayed just as much avoidance and delay as did governments in other provinces.[41]

During this time, the PQ did not have to confront particularly contentious debates over the recognition of religious minorities. In 1978, the government approved support for teaching "heritage languages" in schools, with some reservations but no major controversy.[42] However, there were indications of trouble yet to come. The party had rhetorically marginalized ethnicity-based conceptions of nationhood, which still represented an important current within the PQ, but there was a slowly expanding party activist core drawn to the assimilationist *laïcité* prevalent in France and promising full inclusion for those who fully adapted to French-Quebec language and culture.[43] And this was precisely during a time when Quebec's demography was shifting more noticeably than ever. Quebec was attracting more immigrants, and more and more of them were from outside Europe. The Quebec government was asserting its right to a role in selecting immigrants, prioritizing knowledge of French, and armed with language legislation that increased pressures on newcomers to integrate with the francophone community.[44]

The Liberal Party's Avoidance of Controversy

The Liberals may or may not have realized that they had a strategic dilemma. Though not the party for which most practising Catholics would have voted in the past, Liberals in this reconfigured party system were more likely to benefit from such voters having no obvious other party to choose. One 1981 survey indicates that, among francophones, the likelihood of voting Liberal was significantly higher among those who attended mass once or more a week.[45] At the same time, the party retained a significant number of secularists and anti-clericals, even if not drawn to *laïcité*. More significantly, the Liberals' anglophone and urban francophone voters were unlikely to favour even oblique appeals to social conservatism.

When the Liberals won the election of 1985, they inherited a still-contentious abortion file but reaffirmed support for the suspension of prosecutions inaugurated by the PQ government.[46] The 1988 Supreme Court of Canada decision to strike down the Criminal Code restrictions on access to abortion removed the issue of criminality from the provincial policy agenda, but there were continuing complaints of inadequate funding for abortion clinics. In response, the Liberals proved just as slow to act as had the PQ before them. In the years to follow, pro-choice advocates complained about regulatory complexities impeding access to abortion, but restrictions were eased only in 2009. Throughout this period, too, Liberal and PQ governments avoided taking measures to protect physical access to abortion services in the face of pro-life demonstrators, leaving the issue to the courts (which granted the first injunction in Gatineau in 2008).[47]

By the late 2000s, a cross-party consensus broadly supportive of reproductive choice appeared to have been solidified. This was demonstrated in a unanimous 2010 motion in the National Assembly that implicitly condemned the federal government's decision to ban funding for abortions under its new G8 Maternal Health Initiative (see Chapter 2). Liberal premier Charest, who had turned his party to the right on economic policy, was quoted as saying: "Abortion is an inalienable right and the consensus expressed in the National Assembly reflects the consensus on this issue in Quebec society ... the battle is over and there is no turning back."[48] By then, Quebec's population had moved towards the most pro-choice position of any region in Canada, one 2011 survey showing only 11 percent favouring a ban on abortion (compared to a Canadian average of 25 percent) and a 2012 poll showing 60 percent supporting the view that an abortion should be available when a woman decides (compared to 49 percent agreement countrywide).[49]

The Action démocratique du Québec (ADQ), a "third" party founded in 1994 and reconstituted as the Coalition Avenir Québec (CAQ) in 2011, seemed to be a revival of elements of the conservative coalition represented by the Union Nationale and the Créditistes in decades past, though there was no indication that it sought to roll back gains made by the women's movement and advocates of LGBT equity. We can therefore characterize the party system that emerged in the late 1970s and persisted into the new century as one with a soft secular consensus, without there being any party interested in aiming explicit appeals to the minority of Quebeckers who were still religiously faithful. On the other hand, there was also no party prepared to move too quickly on issues that might mobilize religious traditionalists.

Cross-Party Consensus on the Incomplete Secularization of the School System

No area of public policy better illustrates this pattern of cross-party caution than schooling. We have already raised questions about the standard characterization of Quebec's educational reforms in the 1960s, flagging accommodations made to denominational interests, particularly on the Catholic side. Even if the religious character of schools weakened substantially in the years following the Quiet Revolution, there was strong resistance to ending denominationally specific religious instruction.[50] In 1975, when the National Assembly was enacting the Quebec Charter of Human Rights and Freedoms, it included Section 41 to guarantee "the liberty of parents ... to ensure the religious and moral education of their children in conformity with their own convictions." In the late 1970s, according to Solange Lefebvre, there were "virulent" discussions on the confessional character of public schools arising from the young parents shaped by the Quiet Revolution who still wanted their children exposed to religious instruction and not simply "moral education."[51]

The increased enrolment of immigrant children in French-language (and Catholic) schools in the 1990s renewed debate over not only the appropriateness of religious instruction but also the denominational organization of schooling.[52] Finally, with cross-party support, a PQ government requested, and in 1997 obtained, federal parliamentary approval for a constitutional amendment that replaced that system with one based on language of instruction. This change took effect in 2000.

This did not remove conflict. During the transition, Education Minister Pauline Marois appointed the Proulx task force to examine the place of religion in schools, and the public consultations that ensued mobilized many voices on the francophone side who favoured the privileging of Catholicism. The committee's 1999 report acknowledged the strength of such sentiment in the many briefs submitted to it from the Catholic "side":

> All underline the primary importance of parental rights, Catholic educational philosophy that considers religion to be an essential component in the overall education of each child, Quebec's social identity as forged by Catholic tradition, and the presumed majority support among parents for Catholic tradition.[53]

The committee side-stepped these concerns by adopting what Stéphanie Tremblay refers to an as "open" version of *laïcité* that recognizes a variety of religious traditions. It recommended that all students be required to take courses in religion that were taught from a cultural perspective and not a denominational one, though schools could provide access to their facilities for religious groups after regular hours. It also recommended that Section 41 of the Quebec Charter be amended, recognizing it as a buttress to the existing pattern of religious instruction.

The PQ government's 2000 legislation on school reorganization was not prepared to go that far, retaining denominationally specific religious instruction alongside moral instruction. This tactic was clearly aimed at avoiding a confrontation with those in the population who were still attached to their Catholic faith as well as with those not yet ready to fully incorporate religious diversity into the curriculum.

Only in 2005, now with a Liberal government, was agreement reached on moving further – specifically, to create a compulsory ethics and religious culture program for all grades. Even then, implementation was to be delayed until 2008 and to entail an additional concession in the program's content, which was to be understood as including substantial coverage of Quebec's religious heritage, specifically acknowledging the historical role of Catholicism.[54] This was enough to rouse objections from secularists, who challenged the idea of a course that was devoted entirely to faith, marginalizing voices that comprehensively rejected religion.

Even this curricular compromise was not enough for religious traditionalists. One study shows that support for the common ethics and religious culture program was only 47 percent among parents in ethnically homogenous areas (francophone Catholic) and only 67 percent in pluralist settings.[55] Legal challenges to the legislation were subsequently launched, one from a Jesuit high school in Montreal that resulted in a Supreme Court ruling that the new course, while still compulsory, could be taught from a from a Catholic perspective.[56]

The Paradoxical Funding of Private Faith-Based Schools

Another aspect of the "incomplete" secularization of Quebec's educational system is the large number of faith-based private schools generously supported by state funding, a system sustained almost continuously, with the implicit agreement of major parties, from the late 1960s to the present day. The 1968 establishment of routinized support for private schools was motivated, to an important degree, by respect for the role that had been played historically by Quebec's *collèges classiques*, their important function in the transition to a reformed school system, their serious financial difficulties, and the inequities in earlier financial subsidies. When the Union Nationale government introduced the bill in 1968, the legislative debate had, in Lawrence Bezeau's words, "an air of nostalgia as members spoke of the education they had received in the province's private schools."[57] The resulting regime was, at the time, the country's most generous scheme for private schooling, though it was at first restricted to high schools. The system created two categories: those schools deemed by the ministry to be operating in the public interest (which were eligible for a subsidy amounting to 80 percent of the operating grants for public schools) and others (eligible for 60 percent).[58] Subsidies came with the requirement that schools use the official provincial curriculum, that they engage only certified teachers, and (in later years) that they respect the province's language legislation.

In the 1970s, there were objections to this system from the Parti Québécois' left flank, and these were strong enough to insert a provision pertaining to the subject in the party's electoral program. As Magnuson says, this became, for the first time, a hot campaign issue in 1976, and the PQ "boldly promised" to eliminate such funding altogether.[59] However, during that campaign, René Lévesque was quoted as saying that the time may not be right to take such a step.[60] In 1977, the government did declare a moratorium on the creation of new private schools, pending further study of the overall issues. But this aroused vocal resistance from the Liberal opposition, and a survey at the time suggests that almost 90 percent of Quebeckers supported parental choice in schooling, with little difference between supporters of the Liberals and supporters of the PQ. In 1981, the government did reduce grants to private schools somewhat more than it did the cuts imposed on the public sector, a move rationalized by the need for fiscal restraint, but the level of support for private schools was still the highest in Canada.[61] This was a factor in private school enrolment rising to 9 percent of the total student population in the mid-1980s and to 12 percent in the 2000s.

The cross-party aversion to questioning generous support for private schools remained in place in the decades to follow, including the 1994–2003 period, when the PQ was in power. Moreover, virtually no interveners in public discussion were prepared to acknowledge the importance of faith-based education in the private sector, except for the occasional concern expressed about religious minority schools. Controversy arose in 2005 when the Liberal government of Jean Charest proposed a boost to the funding provided for Jewish schools following an arson attack on a Jewish school library.[62] In 2014 a study was undertaken for the Mouvement laïque québécois showing that 80 of the 172 subsidized private schools were faith-based, that two-thirds of these were "assertively" religious, and that the majority of these were Christian, but the report received only a brief public airing.[63] In the election of that year, Québec Solidaire (a small party to the left of the PQ) questioned the continued public subsidies for private schools. It was the only party to do so, and this had little political traction.[64] In the fall, the newly elected Liberal government announced its intention to study a significant reduction in state support, this at a time when it was announcing major cuts to spending in other domains (principally health).[65] In the months to follow, however, the government displayed no haste in following through with its funding cuts, and the only sustained media coverage of faith-based schools was, once again, restricted to those associated with Jewish and Muslim communities.

What we learn from the history of schooling policy from the 1960s onward is that the secularist "revolution" in Quebec was more cautiously applied than is widely understood – and more contested. At first, the opposition was driven by a mixture of the continuing faith of a strong minority of Québécois, allied to a form of cultural nostalgia on the part of a majority. In more recent years, the minority still allegiant to and practising their faith has been smaller than ever, but it has been joined by a larger population with an attachment to Catholic heritage, intensified by the increased immigration of ethno-cultural-religious minorities.

Political Contention over Minority Religious Practice, 2000+

The half-way mark of the first decade in the new century marked an important shift in the axis of faith-based party alignment. From the late 1970s until the early 2000s, there seemed a broad cross-party agreement on "open," or "soft," secularism. From the Quiet Revolution onward, there were "civic republican" voices representing strict secularism, but they were never more than a minority voice, and did not generate much visible debate.[66] In the meantime, local institutions were developing patterns of accommodation with regard to the growing immigrant population. School authorities had developed an array of policies aimed not only at French language training but also at acknowledging ethno-cultural differences and providing room for teaching heritage languages in public schools.[67] This was always imperfect, as equity policies inevitably are, with continued exclusionary patterns evident in both the teaching materials used and the manner in which they were taught.[68] But there was an official commitment, backed by cross-party agreement, to a form of inclusiveness that recognized the public face of religious diversity. This would soon change.

The Sensationalization of "Reasonable Accommodation," 2005–07

The September 2001 attacks on iconic American institutions had repercussions for Muslims throughout the West, increasing the scrutiny they faced from governments and the broader public. Quebeckers would have had less reason to experience those attacks as a direct threat, but the comparative newness and size of Quebec's Muslim communities, their dramatically enhanced visibility in French-language institutions, and the religious homogeneity of the past provided ample feeding ground for prejudice about Islam.[69]

Muslim religiosity in Quebec had been the object of earlier controversy in 1995 and 1996, focused on school students wearing the hijab. This was an echo of controversies in France and other parts of Continental Europe, though in Quebec the right to wear such head coverings was defended by human rights groups, union leaders, and some feminist groups, with no political party seizing the issue.

A series of events in the first half of the next decade, however, heightened public reaction against making "accommodations" for religious minorities. In 2001, a Quebec court supported the Hassidic Jewish community's installation of a temporary "eruv" enclosure in Outremont, and three years later the Supreme Court of Canada supported the same community's right to construct temporary "succahs" on condominium balconies.[70] Much more serious public opposition to the institutional recognition of minority religion arose in 2002, when Sikh student Gurbaj Multani successfully challenged a 2002 school ban on his right to wear a ceremonial kirpan to school. In 2006, the Supreme Court of Canada sided with Multani – no surprise in the context of expanding jurisprudence on religious rights inside Quebec and across Canada.[71] That same year, an Ontario report recommending that a family arbitration regime that had already allowed for the use of religiously based law be extended to Muslim communities seeking the application of Sharia law received widespread media condemnation in Quebec. An Ontario court's decision later that year calling for the removal of a Christmas tree in a courthouse building also received overwhelmingly negative coverage in the Quebec media. What followed was a barrage of sensationalized media reports on what were framed as excessive concessions to minority religious claims, with much of the coverage resorting to a variety of rhetorical devices to characterize traditional Muslims and Orthodox Jews as threatening the province's victimized majority and the supposed neutrality of public spaces.[72]

The 2007 Quebec Election

Quebeckers went to the polls in March 2007, and for the first time in years a third party was in serious contention, this during a time when there were indications of an overall erosion of established party attachments.[73] Mario Dumont's campaign for the ADQ was populist, combining elements of neoliberalism with statements that played on francophone fears about threats to their identity. In the words of Pierre Anctil, he positioned himself as "an opponent of the so-called concessions made to the cultural and religious minorities, and as the defender of the historical identity of the francophone majority within Quebec."[74] Over the course of the two previous years, he had attacked the Liberal government for its response to questions of ethnic diversity, using the language of "special privileges" so often marshalled by the religious right in response to lesbian/gay rights claims. In early 2007, he publicly supported the mayor of the minority-free community of Hérouxville, who had secured approval of a community code of conduct that was unequivocally prejudicial against minorities, particularly Muslims. As Frédéric Boily points out, with assistance from the media, the ADQ helped to convince an important segment of the electorate that there was "un problème identitaire au Québec."[75]

Before the election, Liberal premier Jean Charest sought to punt the issue beyond the election date by appointing the Consultation Commission on Accommodation Practices Related to Cultural Differences. He was no doubt spooked by sensationalized media coverage, and he realized that his own party was not yet ready to develop a clear position. The Liberals won re-election, but with only a legislative minority, and with the ADQ increasing its vote share from 16 to 31 percent, surpassing the PQ to become the official opposition. The ADQ's inexperience and incompetence soon led to a dramatic decline in its popular support, but its 2007 surge had a lasting impact on the play of public contention over minority religious practices in the other two parties, especially the PQ.

The Bouchard-Taylor Commission Hearings and Report

The commission on "reasonable accommodation" was led by two of Quebec's most distinguished academics – the McGill philosopher Charles Taylor and the highly respected sociologist Gérard Bouchard (the younger brother of former PQ premier Lucien Bouchard). Their previous writings suggest a preference for the principles of open secularism that had once appeared to have wide popular and political support, but the consultation process they launched encountered a powerful wave of quite different sentiments. One study of the nine hundred briefs submitted to the commission shows that those upholding universalist or pluralist values paled in comparison to the number referring to families and communities shaped by common ethnicity, language, and history.[76] The importance attached to faith in many submissions was noteworthy, with a substantial portion either regretting the passing of faith as one of the foundations of québécois identity or arguing that it remained a central "communitarian glue" for that heritage. The commission's Montreal hearings were somewhat more balanced, with many presentations calling the high-stakes debate an artificial creation and advocating open secularism by highlighting modes of accommodation that had been around for some time at the local and/or institutional levels. But even in the metropolis there were many arguments based on a particular notion of identity that characterized immigration as a threat.

In May 2008, Bouchard and Taylor delivered a report that sought to defend a pluralist inclusiveness and to distance itself from the ethnically rooted anxiety that had surfaced so dramatically in many submissions. It acknowledged the very distinctive context that is represented by a Quebec housing a French-speaking majority in an English-dominated continent, but it promoted a version of interculturalism that unequivocally rejected what they saw as the restrictiveness of France's *laïcité*.[77] Bouchard and Taylor specifically rejected proposals for a blanket prohibition on public service employees wearing religious symbols, even if they did leave an opening for restrictions on a few public occupations (such as judges, prosecutors, and police officers) that "by their very nature embody the State and its essential neutrality." They recognized the heritage value of many Christian symbols across the province but argued that the crucifix over the speaker's chair in the National Assembly, and the recitation of Christian prayers at the opening of municipal council meetings, were no longer appropriate. They urged recourse to informal "citizen"-centred resolutions to requests for accommodation to religious practices rather than a more formal legal or codified approach.

The extent to which the ideas discussed and the recommendations made by Bouchard and Taylor had become politically explosive was in full view when former PQ premiers Jacques Parizeau and Bernard Landry immediately attacked the report, claiming – bizarrely – that it had little to say on promoting immigrant inclusion in French-speaking milieux and that the commissioners were blaming francophones for intolerance.[78] Pauline Marois, the PQ's leader at the time, expressed disappointment that the commission did not recommend a legislative codification of Quebec's common values, something she had proposed.

The Liberal government was reluctant to publicly embrace the Bouchard-Taylor recommendations, and Premier Charest immediately secured the unanimous consent of the National Assembly affirming the retention of the crucifix over the speaker's chair. In 2010, the government's Bill 94 additionally distanced itself from the report's tone and substance by proposing that the few women in Quebec who wore face coverings had to remove them if they worked anywhere in government service or were doing business with public officials. This was the first such legislation in North America, and there was no mistaking its targeting of Muslims. The bill elicited much response, some of it in the press, some of it in the form of submissions to the legislative committee examining the bill in detail. In early February, a "Manifest pour un Québec pluraliste" published in *Le Devoir* adopted the open secularist vision of the Bouchard-Taylor Report, as did the brief submitted by the

Ligue des droits et libertés, the Conseil des relations interculturelles, and the Commission des droits de la personne et de la jeuneesse. The Commission des droit, along with the Fédération des femmes du Québec, was especially concerned that regulating the dress of public service recipients would stigmatize Muslim women or "breathe new life into a xenophobic tendency."[79] On the other side were many presentations, among them by the Mouvement laïque québécois and a large group of signatories of the Déclaration des Intellectuels pour la laïcité, that talked of the long struggle for secularism seeking "emancipation from the yoke of religion" and a "bulwark against the rise of fundamentalism."[80] Submissions such as these typically urged much more expansive legislation, prohibiting those employed in the public sector (perhaps also school students) from wearing any "ostentatious" religious signs.

Any hope that the Bouchard-Taylor Report had created the basis for cross-party agreement on a version of open secularism, retaining a regime of state neutrality but one based on religious freedom, had now dissolved. The huge disparity of views now being aired was replayed inside the legislature and, to some extent, within the Liberal Party. Unsurprisingly, the bill languished in committee and then died (for a time) when the legislature was dissolved in advance of the 2012 election.

The Parti Québécois in Government and the Charter of Quebec Values

By 2010, the PQ opposition had moved to a much more assertive position on such issues, attacking the Liberals for not going further and calling for broad limits on accommodation to be incorporated into Quebec's Charter of Human Rights and Freedoms. At about the same time, it also criticized the government for a modification in the school calendar that it claimed had been requested by members of the Jewish community. This was the first time in modern Quebec history that a party in serious contention for power politicized contentious issues of minority religious recognition. This seemed a very different party from the one that, in 1993, had approved resolutions recognizing that Quebec culture was not monolithic and, in fact, was enhanced by citizens of diverse ethnocultural backgrounds.[81]

The PQ government's narrow defeat in the 1995 sovereignty referendum may have shifted the balance between assimilationists and pluralists who had long co-habited within the party. When Premier Jacques Parizeau declared that the defeat was a result of "money and the ethnic vote," he also used "we" to denote the francophones who had voted for independence. "Nous voulons un pays et nous l'aurons!"[82] Parizeau had long been associated with support for immigration and a pluralist vision of Quebec, and the bulk of the party leadership remained committed to a comparatively inclusive vision.[83] And yes, there was also widespread revulsion among many rank-and-file péquistes supporters at these remarks. However, the premier's comment in the heat of the moment was greeted by much applause.

The 1995 resignation of Parizeau and the selection of Lucien Bouchard as party leader seemed to reinforce the PQ's commitment to ethno-cultural inclusiveness, and the new premier wasted little time in declaring his pluralist credentials in highly publicized remarks aimed at Quebec anglophones in 1996. He affirmed that "the Quebec nationalism that we are building no longer defines itself as that of French-Canadians, but as that of all Quebecers: it no longer seeks homogeneity but it embraces diversity and pluralism."[84] The PQ's 2005 leadership victory on the part of André Boisclair, openly gay and previously responsible for immigration, also seemed to embody an outward-looking cosmopolitanism and a commitment to broaden the PQ's appeal without compromising its commitment to sovereignty. But it was he who led the party to defeat in the 2007 election, one in which the ADQ scored important electoral gains, opening the way for a challenge to his leadership and a shift in the party's approach to questions of immigration and assimilation.

Pauline Marois took the PQ leadership in 2007 and led the party into the 2012 election, in which she promised a "Charter of Quebec Values" with secularism at its centre. During the campaign, the mayor of Saguenay, already notable for defying the Quebec Human Rights Commission in opening council meetings by conducting prayers, attacked PQ candidate Djemila Benhabib for having supported the removal of the crucifix from Quebec's National Assembly: "They quietly start by removing the prayer in city hall, then they'll remove our religious objects, then they'll take away the crosses in cities and after that they'll go into the schools."[85] This provoked Marois into demanding an apology, though the mayor of Trois Rivières argued that Jean Tremblay was reflecting what many Québécois were thinking.

The PQ won in 2012 with 32 percent of the vote and a legislative minority. The Liberals held on to 31 percent; the Coalition Avenir Québec (successor to the ADQ) ate away at the other parties' right flank at a resurgent 27 percent; and Québec Solidaire bled support from the PQ's left to reach 6 percent. The election may have suggested that the new government be cautious in politicizing the issue of minority religious recognition, but the strength of the CAQ vote provided an incentive to carry on along the path already chosen by the PQ leadership. In fact, paradoxically, CAQ leader François Legault was less extreme on issues of minority religious recognition than the ADQ had been under Mario Dumont, and he was more focused on economic issues, leaving the PQ leadership as the most assertive champion of assertive secularism.[86] That spring, renewed media preparedness to sensationalize cases involving the recognition of minority religious practices further emboldened the government.

In September 2013, leading PQ minister Bernard Drainville presented the government's preliminary thinking on the "religious neutrality" of the state and a framework for religious accommodation.[87] The government proposed a revival of the ban on face coverings contained in the Liberals' Bill 94 and an additional ban on wearing conspicuous religious symbols among all public-sector employees, including teachers, child care workers, university employees, and health-sector workers. This was not yet a legislative bill, so there appeared to be a degree of openness to change as a function of public reaction.

Large demonstrations were soon organized in support of and against the proposed Charter of Quebec Values. Liberal leader Philippe Couillard immediately declared his firm opposition, saying that the charter would become law "over my dead body."[88] All of the major candidates for mayor of Montreal, along with all other sitting mayors on the Island of Montreal, expressed their opposition to the charter. Almost immediately, they were joined by prominent sovereigntists, including Lucien Bouchard, Jacques Parizeau, and Louise Harel (a respected former cabinet minister once responsible for outreach to immigrant and minority communities). Québec Solidaire was, one way or another, declaring its support for open secularism. The Fédération des femmes du Québec expressed its opposition in the name of defending women's rights, even if other well-known feminists supported the government. As Chantal Hébert argued at the time, the government proposal "clearly offends the core values of a significant and articulate segment of the party's base" and "has scores of long-time sovereigntist activists wringing their hands in despair over potentially irreparable damage to their cause."[89] Later, she lamented that the charter was distancing the PQ more than ever from the model of civic nationalism championed by René Lévesque.[90]

Both Drainville and Marois were unmoved by opposition, defending their proposals in the strongest terms. At one point Marois even referred to France as "le plus beau" example of minority integration, an astonishing claim for anyone who has visited the Paris banlieux, witnessed the policing response to ethno-religious diversity, or tracked the widespread local resistance to mosque construction.[91] Writing later, Lysiane Gagnon characterized the PQ strategy as "tak[ing] a wedge issue that will remobilize your base of core supporters, play on the widespread negative feelings toward visible immigrants (Muslims especially) while pretending to serve the noble goals of secularism and gender equity, ride on the instinctive reactions of the 'real people' against the 'disconnected elites' and there you are."[92]

The government introduced a bill in early November that went even further than the proposals sketched out in September, though putting off a final decision on the National Assembly's crucifix. This could not help but reinforce views that this legislation was not born of a principled commitment to civic republicanism, provoking many critics to assert "la présence de ce crucifix dans la plus importante enceinte de l'État Québécois est une atteinte flagrant à la laïcité, un flagrant symbole de la non-laïcité."[93] And, of course, neither the charter nor its government supporters breathed a word of ending state tax supports for religious buildings and subsidies for faith-based schools.

Bill 60 also extended its ambit to private contractors and publicly subsidized companies, and restricted the possibility of institutions opting out or delaying implementation. The PQ leadership was emboldened, in part, by dissension among Liberals, leading Philippe Couillard at first to consider a ban on religious dress for government officials in positions of authority (judges, police officers, corrections officers), thus reflecting an opening provided by the Bouchard-Taylor recommendations. He then further "clarified" in January, favouring a restriction on public-sector employees wearing face-covering garments and also retaining the National Assembly's crucifix.[94]

The convictions of government ministers were also strengthened by polls that showed that PQ support had increased enough – 18 percent ahead of the Liberals among francophones – to offer the prospect of a majority government. Unable to resist the temptations this provided, Premier Marois called an election for April 7, 2016, and party strategists seemed intent on keeping what appeared to be the winning issue of the Charter of Quebec Values in high relief. Montreal-based social scientist Denise Helly was in no doubt that the PQ's electoral calculations contributed to its launching "une campagne de stigmatisation de minorités religieuses," which then gave room for the expression of public intolerance and dramatically increased the number of physical and verbal attacks against Muslims.[95] In the view of another seasoned francophone academic:

> You can't imagine the atmosphere created by the PQ. It's not the same as in the rest of Canada; it's different than Europe – not as bad – but still. During the debate about the charter, it was awful: vulgar, violent, racist. It was amazing because we are not so used to this stuff in Canada, even in Quebec. We were hearing Islamophobia all round.[96]

It is possible that the prejudicial backdrop to at least some of the support for the charter alienated some voters. During the campaign, when long-time feminist and prominent media personality Janette Bertrand defended the charter by deploying stereotypes about Muslim men, "even staunch charter supporters cringed."[97] More significant, though, was the sovereignty issue, which was thrust onto centre stage by star candidate and future PQ leader Pierre Karl Péladeau and, in the process, alienated many voters by presenting the prospect of a third referendum. An election that had at first seemed like a sure victory for the PQ slipped away in the final weeks of the campaign. Instead, it was the Liberals who won a majority with 42 percent of the vote, as compared to 25 percent for the PQ, 23 percent for the CAQ, and 8 percent for Québec Solidaire.

The Persistence of Contention Following the 2014 Election

Newly elected premier Couillard promised to introduce a charter, but without apparent conviction. During the first year of his mandate, the one issue upon which he was prepared to declare himself concerned his support for banning the niqab among those delivering or receiving government services. He was induced to do so by virulent public reaction against a federal court ruling that supported a woman's right to wear the niqab at a citizenship ceremony.

In the fall of 2014 and the winter of 2015, prominent contenders for the PQ leadership took advantage of jihadist attacks on military officers in Canada and the French satirical magazine *Charlie Hebdo* to attack the Liberal premier's inaction on the broader front that they had opened up by introducing the idea of a secularism charter. Pierre Karl Péladeau, then the leading PQ leadership candidate, suggested that immigration was imperilling the sovereigntist project.[98] Following in the footsteps of Conservative prime minister Stephen Harper, the PQ's leading figures were rallying support around combatting Islamic terrorism and were feeding popular stereotypes that explicitly linked Islam to fundamentalism.

The Coalition Avenir Québec was now doing much the same. In early 2015, a decision by the Shawinigan city council to refuse planning permission for the construction of a mosque prompted François Legault to call for an amendment to Quebec's Charter of Rights and Freedoms to allow for routinized inquiries into whether applicants for new religious institutions have denigrated Quebec values – a suggestion transparently targeting Muslims. All this was fuelled by more media stories about Muslim and Jewish private schools not following the provincial curriculum.[99]

In the spring of that year, the provincial government reacted to stories about Muslim youth radicalization in Quebec by introducing two pieces of legislation on the same day. One was related to law enforcement and police surveillance; the second was a revival of the previous Liberal government's Bill 94, which restricted full-face coverings in cases in which a prohibition was warranted "in the context of security or identification reasons or because of the level of communication required."[100] Even if the face-covering bill was not explicitly tied to anti-radicalism measures, its being announced at the same time inextricably linked the two. It left out the more odious provisions of the PQ Charter of Quebec Values introduced almost two years before, but it was similar in its targeting of Muslim women. The head of the Muslim Council of Montreal characterized the double bill as marked by discrimination and prejudice, claiming that there had been none of the consultation that had been promised and adding: "every one of these debates makes life miserable for Muslims in Quebec."[101]

The niqab issue was revived during the 2015 federal election. The Conservative government, as we saw in Chapter 1, had banned the wearing of face coverings at citizenship ceremonies, but was found to have acted unconstitutionally. Harper re-raised the issue while electioneering in Quebec and was supported by Bloc leader Gilles Duceppe, who hoped to undercut the NDP's support in the province. Both leaders then also talked about banning face coverings for federal public servants. The Bloc focused on the issue, releasing ads featuring the niqab as an ominous threat, and talking of using the constitution's notwithstanding clause to protect against legal challenges. The ban for citizenship ceremonies played well across most of Canada, but especially in Quebec, and was seen as rescuing the Bloc from political oblivion. While earning fewer votes, the party took 10 seats, more than twice its 2011 result. The Conservatives also more than doubled their seat count from 5 to 12. In contrast, NDP leader Tom Mulcair's staunch opposition to any niqab ban was seen as contributing to the sharp drop in NDP support in Quebec.

In early 2016, the CAQ led an attack on a government announcement of moderately increased immigration levels, coupled with tying newcomer selection more closely to labour market needs. The PQ joined the complaint against what it claimed were high immigration numbers, and both parties applauded a government retreat shortly after introducing the policy. In May of that year, the Montreal suburb of Outremont, home to a significant Hasidic community, extended a ban on the establishment of new places of worship that now effectively covered the whole municipality. In the wake of the killing of forty-nine people at a gay nightclub in Orlando in June 2016, one of Quebec's most respected academics reinforced the characterization of Muslims and Islam as homogeneously resistant to LGBT inclusiveness, in contrast to a québécois political culture that had apparently adopted equality on the basis of sexuality and gender as a core value.[102] All this, for Gérard Bouchard, constituted an "obstacle à la pleine intégration des musulmans dans la société québécoise" – language disturbingly close to that evoking a clash of civilizations.

In the fall of 2016, former PQ cabinet minister Jean-François Lisée won the leadership of his party, after a campaign in which he played to anti-Muslim sentiment. In the wake of the PQ's electoral defeat in 2014, he voiced second thoughts about the outgoing government's secularism charter. Following his selection as leader, however, he mused about measures going beyond that of the charter. These measures included a ban on wearing burkas in public, bizarrely suggesting that they could be used to hide AK-47s. His statements were aimed at an important and enduring constituency within the PQ, but he also made clear his interest in luring CAQ voters.[103]

The CAQ leadership continued to play a similar card, repeating calls for testing new immigrants on "Quebec values," and floating the idea of a ban on teachers wearing headscarves. This continued even after the killing of six Muslims in a Quebec City mosque early in 2017. During revived debate on the Liberals' Bill 62, banning face coverings in the delivery and receipt of government services (itself almost certainly in violation of Quebec human rights law), both opposition leaders attacked the government for not going further in imposing restrictions that transparently targeted Muslims. Political commentator Yves Boisvert wondered if the mosque tragedy would induce a sustained commitment to embrace Quebec's Muslim community and retreat from inflammatory rhetoric, but he soon saw little sign of that in the National Assembly.[104]

Québécois Attitudes towards Minorities and Consequences for Voting Patterns

The question here is whether there is a belief pattern among Quebeckers that facilitates the kind of changes we have witnessed in party politics. After all, unease about at least some forms of minority religious recognition have been widespread across Canada, especially in relation to Islam. In Quebec, however, attitudes towards minorities have been shaped by the understandably complex interplay of different Québécois identity "strands," combined with a current of anti-clericalism that increasingly draws from the example of French *laïcité*. Public beliefs are also influenced by elements of discomfort with the religious "other," a reality well known in the rest of Canada but more widespread and intensely felt in Quebec. All these co-exist alongside the everyday recognition of ethno-cultural pluralism in many contemporary French-speaking institutions, in Montreal especially.

Survey Findings on Attitudes towards Minorities

Jeffrey Reitz has mined several large surveys from the early and mid-2000s to address the differences between Quebec and the rest of Canada (as well as France) with regard to attitudes towards minorities.[105] What he shows is that, within Canada, there are roughly similar attitudes towards immigration in general: slightly stronger support in Quebec than elsewhere for maintaining or increasing immigration levels (73 percent versus 64 percent), about the same agreement to the statement that immigrants improve society by bringing in new ideas and cultures (64 percent vs. 70 percent), but somewhat lower approval of the claim that immigrants are generally good for the country's economy (52 percent vs. 63 percent). These findings are confirmed by a 2015 Environics survey, which shows that Quebeckers were less likely to feel that there was too much immigration in Canada and that immigrants take jobs away from other Canadians than were inhabitants of any other region.[106]

However, attitudes towards Muslims, and to some extent Jews, are noticeably more negative in Quebec than elsewhere. Between 1990 and

Table 8.1   Attitudes in Quebec and Canada towards immigrants and minorities, 2007 (%)

	Quebec	Ontario	BC	Canada
Immigrants should adapt fully to culture in Canada.	77	50	41	53
Menu requirements of religious and cultural groups should never be accommodated.	25	11	12	14
Public places like schools, hospitals, and government buildings should have no religious or cultural accommodation.	64	27	26	37
The workplace should have no religious or cultural accommodation.	65	39	32	45

Source: "Canadians Overwhelmingly Support Limits to Reasonable Accommodation," Institute for Research on Public Policy, *Policy Options*, September 25, 2007.

2000, the percentage of Quebeckers indicating that they did not want Jews as neighbours increased slightly from 8 to 9 percent, while simultaneously declining in the rest of Canada from 5 to 2 percent. Antipathy towards Muslims as neighbours increased dramatically from 11 percent in 1990 to 22 percent in 2006, despite elsewhere falling from 10 to 8 percent.[107] Table 8.1 displays additional survey data from 2007 revealing similar shifts and contrasts. This particular survey was undertaken, of course, in the midst of media-fed controversy over reasonable accommodation, though attitudes had already been changing.

A Léger Marketing poll in 2009 shows that 40 percent of francophones saw non-Christian immigrants as threatening to Quebec society, up from 32 percent in 2007.[108] Only 40 percent viewed Muslims favourably, a drop of 17 percent from two years earlier, and just 32 percent approved the wearing of hijabs in school. A survey undertaken in 2014 for the Association of Canadian Studies suggests a further decline in positive attitudes towards Muslims to around 30 percent and an increase in disquiet about non-Christian immigrations.[109] A 2016 Forum

Research poll shows that 48 percent of Quebeckers had "unfavorable feelings" toward Muslims, more than double the percentage among Canadians in other regions.[110] A parallel survey of Muslims also indicates that Quebec Muslims were more likely than were those in other parts of the country to have experienced poor treatment because of their religion. At the same time, there has been an increase in the proportion of Quebeckers who recognize that Muslims are the target of frequent discrimination – 68 percent according to the 2015 Environics survey.[111] A 2016 Environics survey of Muslims also shows that those in Quebec are more likely than their co-religionists in other regions to believe that public attitudes towards Islam have improved, and they are relatively positive about how future generations will be treated.

Questions about the PQ secularism charter during the 2013–14 period showed much volatility. In the late summer and fall of 2013, when the government was first airing its proposals, francophone support ranged from around 50 percent up to 71 percent.[112] One poll showing 59 percent overall francophone approval of the charter also indicated 65 percent supporting the preservation of Quebec's Catholic heritage and 52 percent agreeing that Quebec's heritage was threatened by the influx of immigrants.[113] One early 2014 survey, conducted by Luc Turgeon and his colleagues, found that 47 percent of Quebeckers supported the charter.[114] Those on side with the government were evenly divided between those who also agreed that the crucifix over the speaker's chair in the National Assembly should be removed, a position that had the virtue of secular consistency, and those who did not. The 28 percent who supported the charter and the crucifix (32 percent among francophones) also held markedly more negative attitudes towards minority groups than did those holding other positions – almost half with extremely negative views. Sixty-five percent of these – dubbed Catholic secularists by the authors – believed that immigrants were having a negative impact on the culture of Quebec, compared to 39 percent of those we might describe as consistent secularists, and 26 percent among those who opposed the charter. Within the PQ, 54 percent of its supporters favoured the consistent secularist position and 46 percent the "Catholic secularist" position, which was in turn more likely to coincide with fear and prejudice.

Support for the charter, and unease about the extent of immigrant integration, is of course buttressed by anxieties about the retention of a distinct Quebec culture. Even if most of the recent waves of newcomers speak French, there may well be widespread belief that they will not be drawn to, or participate in, québécois cultural phenomena, so powerfully evident in film, theatre, music, and television. Some part of this anxiety is understandable, but it cannot but be shaped by prejudicial views that Muslims are unusually resistant to integration.[115] Versions of this overall anxiety are also built on the assumption that a society increasingly dependent on immigration can retain cultural patterns completely undisturbed by the backgrounds and interests of immigrants rather than seeing the process as a reciprocal exchange or as seeing Quebec culture as being in constant creative flux as it responds to newcomers.

Electoral Alignment and Realignment

To this point we have laid out a form of partisan realignment on faith-related public policies and set this within a context of changing public attitudes. The question posed here asks to what extent there has been a shift in the complexion of each party's electorate. We have already suggested that, in the aftermath of Quebec's Quiet Revolution, and particularly with the disappearance of the Union Nationale, there was no obvious party to champion religious and moral traditionalists, even if more of them ended up drawn to the Liberals than to the PQ.[116]

Systematic studies of the impact of religiosity on party voting are relatively scarce in Quebec, but an analysis of the 2007 and 2008 elections by Éric Bélanger and Richard Nadeau shows that most Liberal supporters had attended one or more religious services in the previous year (60 percent in 2007, 51 percent in 2008), compared to PQ supporters (37 and 39 percent, respectively).[117] The average Liberal supporter in 2007 scored .57 on a moral conservatism scale (ranging from 0 to 1.0), with the ADQ next at .52 and the PQ at .42, the distinctions declining modestly in 2008.[118] By 2012, intriguingly, religiosity appeared to have almost no impact on voting preference, as confirmed by Nadeau and Bélanger and by the findings of a provincial election study undertaken by Jared Wesley's team, displayed in Table 8.2.[119] Those

Table 8.2   Vote choice within religious groups in Quebec, 2012–14

Importance of religion	Year	PLQ (%)	PQ (%)	CAQ (%)	QS (%)	Total* (n)
Very important	2012	33	35	26	5	110 (100%)
	2014	62	18	16	4	203 (100%)
Somewhat important	2012	37	33	25	4	225 (100%)
	2014	55	20	21	4	463 (100%)
Somewhat unimportant	2012	23	41	26	8	284 (100%)
	2014	42	25	25	6	431 (100%)
Very unimportant	2012	17	39	22	17	278 (100%)
	2014	34	27	22	14	352 (100%)
Total	2012	26	38	25	9	897 (100%)
	2014	47	23	22	7	1,449

* Excludes votes for Option Nationale, for which under 3 percent expressed support in 2012 and 1 percent in 2014.

declaring religion very important in their lives were distributed across the three leading parties in close to the same proportion as those parties' overall support levels in 2012, though Liberals fared somewhat better among the religious and worse among those for whom religion was unimportant. (The preference for Liberals among the very religious was much stronger in 2014.)

Nadeau and Bélanger also find that the moral conservatism of each party's electorate varied little except for a slight tilt of moral conservatives towards the CAQ. David McGrane uses provincial election studies to compile indices of voter perspectives on such core values as "postmaterialism," based on attitudes towards race, gender, environmentalism, and "traditional values."[120] On a scale from 1 to 4, 2.5 is the mean and the lower end indicates progressive views. This is a quite broad cluster of attitudes, far beyond the notion of moral traditionalism, but it still suggests a Quebec population less progressive than is widely perceived, with most party differences relatively muted. Only supporters of Québec Solidaire provide average responses placing them on the progressive side of the mid-point, at 2.26. PQ supporters average 2.59, Liberals 2.73, and CAQ supporters 2.82.[121]

This leaves the question of whether PQ and ADQ/CAQ campaigning on minority religious practices, beginning in 2007 and continuing to the present, has produced a new faith alignment. The first step in responding is to examine the voting patterns of minorities themselves. The antipathy towards or anxiety about the sovereigntist project among minority voters, even if more fluent in French than in English, still induces most ethno-racial minorities and immigrants to support the Liberals.[122] In moving beyond those communities to the general public, we face a curious silence in academic analysis of the 2007, 2008, and 2012 elections regarding where supporters of the three parties stand in relation to immigration and minority religious practice. However, we do know from scattered public opinion polling that francophone supporters of the Liberal Party were significantly less likely than were their PQ counterparts to support bans on wearing faith-related symbols while at work in the public sector. A January 2014 Léger Marketing survey shows that support for restrictions on religious wear was 60 percent across Quebec but an extraordinary 91 percent among PQ supporters.[123] Support among Liberals may have been as high as 40 percent, but the gap between parties is still very significant and much more striking than the differences between supporters of the major parties on economic and social issues.

Overview and Conclusion

Faith-based contention in Quebec is now dominated by debate over whether limits should be imposed on the public practice of religious faith. Some of the rhetorical language associated with proposals to limit such displays reflects a rejection of a form of Roman Catholic hegemony that once so profoundly shaped Quebec society. In fact, there are many francophones motivated by this sentiment who adopt a consistent and principled view that all non-secular policies, including private school funding, should be eliminated. The civic republicanism that Lamy so artfully describes includes a "polyphony" of voices, but many are inspired by a categorical rejection of religion as limiting free thought, oppressive of those who do not share the faith, and, in most cases, denigrating to women.[124]

Another principled approach is born of a philosophical liberalism that champions religious liberty; it calls for official state secularism in the interests of ensuring the recognition of religious diversity as well as the rights of those who have no religious affiliation.[125] This was the position articulated in the manifesto issued by sixty prominent scholars in late 2013 in the heat of public contention over the Charter of Quebec Values.

Among most of those who articulate this view, there is a preparedness to accept that some historical legacies warrant retention. Gérard Bouchard recognizes that there are countless institutions and practices based on Catholic heritage that should be retained as an important part of Quebec's "symbolic foundation."[126] He cites the examples of the Christian bias in legal holidays, streets named after saints, the provision of public support for the preservation of historically important Catholic buildings, and the cross at the centre of Quebec's flag. These, he argues, are largely "de-activated" in their religious significance, as distinct from practices that more assertively declare a religious affiliation, such as the National Assembly's crucifix or opening Christian prayers in local councils. He acknowledges that there are important differences of view regarding what would count as contradicting the spirit of state neutrality and separation of church and state.

There are many debates in the rest of Canada about such issues, and disagreements about the extent to which governments and courts should recognize the rights of religious minorities, but party leaders at the federal level and in other provinces have largely avoided politicizing these issues. The major exception has been the federal Conservative Party, which during its time in government adopted several measures that played on anti-Muslim prejudice, including those linking Islam to terrorism and to "barbaric cultural practices." This pattern was also much in evidence during the party's 2016–17 leadership contest. What seems different in Quebec is the strength of support for strict secularism, however inconsistently applied, and the degree to which divisions over minority religious recognition have permeated the party system.

For the most of the second half of the twentieth century, Quebec's parties followed a relatively accommodative pattern in relation to issues that might have provoked political contention, though in distinctive ways and in a highly distinctive context. They responded to the enormous changes of the Quiet Revolution, and the social movement contestation that remained such an important part of Quebec's politics, with a gradualist approach that displayed caution until a cross-party consensus could be reached. This was also the approach taken towards policy making concerning the recognition of minority religions.

However, since the mid-2000s, the tempered and consensual response to difficult questions posed over the public recognition of minority faith requirements has been abandoned, at least for a time. The minor ADQ party led by Mario Dumont was the first to politicize the issue, though the Parti Québécois was not far behind. There was significant dissent within the PQ's Montreal base, though not enough to deter it from introducing the aggressively secularist Charter of Quebec Values in 2013, and fear-mongering over accommodating religious minorities. The Liberal Party's leadership has struggled to maintain unified support for open secularism within its ranks, but it has obviously faced internal dissent. Québec Solidaire also adheres broadly to the principles of open secularism, going further than the Liberals in challenging the ways in which the Quebec state supports faith-based institutions (e.g., in private schooling).

The politicization of minority religious rights has played on currents of identity politics that include a traditionalist and inward-looking resistance to pluralism, widely thought to have been replaced by cosmopolitan and civic nationalism invigorated by the Quiet Revolution. While not making Quebec's conflict over religious accommodation equivalent to the more insidiously prejudicial debate in France and other parts of Europe, the politicization of this issue does appear to have shifted some elements of public opinion in disturbing directions.

An important part of the popular support for the attacks on minority religious recognition reflects a secularist double standard, opposing ostentatious public displays of religiosity for minorities while remaining oblivious to the ways in which Catholicism is buttressed and/or supported by such displays in the name of tradition. Strict secularists in Quebec who draw inspiration from French *laïcité* routinely ignore the inconsistencies in French state policy and side-step the extent to which the meanings associated with that term have been twisted since the 1980s in ways that have fed off, and reinforced, right-wing xenophobia.

In fact, support for what many think of as *laïcité* arises in significant measure from a specific anxiety about, or antipathy towards, Muslims. In Quebec, as in much of Europe, the backdrop to public and partisan debates over religious restrictions was primarily taken up with the image of the Muslim woman, wearing either a simple headscarf or more concealing coverings that shielded all or most of her face. In a post-9/11 environment in which Muslim communities have been under so much public scrutiny, the Quebec public and the popular media are not immune to sentiments that can be found in all Western countries. Some of the intellectuals whom Guillaume Lamy cites as representative of a principled commitment to civic republicanism, supported by a current of Quebec feminism, believe that Muslim head coverings in and of themselves are suggestive of fundamentalist Islam and that it is the duty of the state to ensure that women are liberated from the pressure to conform – a position with disturbingly authoritarian instincts.[127] It is important to emphasize that attitudes towards Muslims in Quebec remain largely positive, but there is a growing minority that possesses quite negative views, coupled with sweepingly generalized views of Muslims and Islam. It is not helpful that the comparative strength of this sentiment is given little public airing.

At the core of the debate over alternative visions of secularism are questions about identity, which have long been at the centre of political discourse in a region with a French-speaking majority justifiably concerned about maintaining its linguistic and cultural distinctiveness. At the same time, a majority of Quebeckers support immigration at much the same level as we find in the rest of Canada. However, support for comparatively large-scale immigration into francophone society, widely recognized as necessary for longer term economic growth, will not sit easily beside a defensive approach to québécois distinctiveness that sees integration as a one-way street. The vast majority of those who live in Quebec accept that newcomers have an obligation to recognize the primacy of the French language, but successful integration over the long term also means acknowledging that québécois identity will evolve in the decades to come as a response to ethno-cultural and, yes, religious diversity.

The 2017 attack on a Quebec City mosque generated incisive and heartfelt reflections on just how receptive Quebec society has been to the Muslim population within it. Some attention was focused on the otherwise little-noticed presence of an extreme right fringe in Quebec. But there was also much commentary on the contribution to anti-Muslim prejudice by media-stoked "controversy" over minority religious practices, and by the rancorous partisan debate over restricting such practices in the name of high principle.[128] Soon after the mosque killings, however, legislative deliberation over restricting what was widely understood as specifically Muslim face coverings suggested that there was still a willingness to continue deploying such issues for partisan gain. Whether those favoring a more inclusive and pluralist vision of Quebec would prevail over the longer term is hard to judge. In the medium term, faith continues to have a role in party politics that few architects of the Quiet Revolution would have imagined.

Evangelical Christianity and Northern Territorial Politics

9

Across Yukon, the Northwest Territories (NWT), and Nunavut, socially conservative faith has a significant presence. Its political influence, however, is tempered by preoccupations with economic and social development in the territories and by the process of settling Indigenous land claims and self-government agreements.[1] Indeed, the North's distinctiveness lies to a large extent in its geographic remoteness and in its proportionally large Indigenous communities – one-quarter in Yukon, half in the NWT, and 85 percent in Nunavut – though religious affiliation is almost entirely Christian.[2] Elements of traditional Indigenous spirituality are evident in the faith practices of many, but declarations of exclusive attachment to such spirituality are found in only about 1 percent of the territorial population.

Overall, faith communities are least significant in the contemporary politics of Yukon, somewhat more prominent in the NWT, and more so in Nunavut, where levels of religious affiliation are particularly high. It is, in fact, only in Nunavut that we can detect any policy influence on the part of faith communities, but even there it is limited by the overwhelming priority accorded to issues related to socio-economic development.

In this chapter we argue that a mix of demographic and institutional factors has prevented explicitly religious constituencies from emerging as a political force in Yukon, whose population is the most secular in Canada. In the NWT, the absence of political parties has prevented a sustained articulation of faith-based policy positions. Even in Nunavut, where social conservatism is often expressed through the language of traditional Inuit practice and culture, and regularly characterized as under threat from the social norms of southern Canada, moral traditionalism has been only rarely voiced in politics.

Demographic and Institutional Constraints

In each of the three territories, the ability of religious conservatives to gain access to the political system has been constrained by a particular set of demographic and institutional circumstances. Yukon politics share remarkable similarities with those in British Columbia, not only in its comparative secularism but also in its ideologically polarized party systems. In the case of Yukon, this distinctive political environment has led to the emergence of one of Canada's most socially progressive jurisdictions – one in which the voices of religious conservatives are relatively marginal in political discourse. Especially in a party system whose primary cleavages run so strongly along economic lines, faith communities have had little room to influence the direction of territorial public policy.

The larger and more visible faith communities in the NWT have had difficulty finding a consistent advocacy voice in the Legislative Assembly. This is partly a result of the distinctive "consensus" form of parliamentary government found here and in Nunavut.[3] In the absence of political parties, some interests become subsumed within the internal compromises of the consensus system and the pragmatism that characterizes it. Without parties acting as "aggregators" of different ideas, and particularly in the absence of a party on the right open to social conservative pressure, even significant currents of popular opinion may not be heard.

Political discourse in the NWT is very much structured by other political cleavages, for example, those among the various Indigenous groups across the territory (including newly emerging sub-territorial governments resulting from treaty settlements); between Indigenous peoples as a whole and non-Indigenous settlers; and between Yellowknife and the territory's outlying communities. Here and in other territories, economic issues predominate, and the importance of the public sector in providing for material needs limits the room for an ideologically based right-wing alternative voice in NWT politics. The potential for a strong socially conservative voice is also limited by the historical rooted-ness of the territory's Roman Catholic clergy in economically progressive social justice theology.[4]

Of the three northern territories, Nunavut is perhaps the most surprising for the absence of a sustained morally traditionalist agenda among its political representatives. After all, conservative and evangelical Christianity is particularly strong here. But, rather than generating sustained advocacy for a policy agenda, this has reinforced a culture of silence and avoidance among the political class, especially around issues of sexual diversity. The absence of political parties, as in the NWT, prevents moral traditionalists from being organized into an effective voting block capable of applying pressure on the government.

This analysis of the northern territories begins with an examination of the distribution of faith communities across the region and the historical legacies that still shape their religious contours. We then turn to political development, focusing on the evolution of party politics in Yukon and consensus government in the NWT and Nunavut. We end the chapter by presenting case studies illustrating the comparative absence of traditionalist moral policy agendas in territorial politics.

Faith in Northern Canada

Christianity was introduced to Indigenous peoples first by enterprising missionaries and, later, in a more systematic fashion as part of the colonial policies of the federal government. The denominational differences across the territories, especially in the NWT and Nunavut, reflect the competing missions of Anglican, Roman Catholic, and Moravian churches in converting and ministering to Indigenous peoples. Evangelical Christianity was introduced much later, most widely in Nunavut and largely in the post-Second World War period.[5] Indigenous peoples had their own complex cosmologies and spiritual practices based in shamanism and animism, some of which have survived as independent spiritual currents or have been grafted onto Christian traditions.

Prior to European contact, the settlement patterns of Indigenous peoples were shaped entirely by environmental conditions.[6] While the areas generally north of the treeline and into the Eastern Arctic were occupied by Inuit peoples, the areas south of the treeline were occupied by First Nations peoples. Métis arrived later, particularly following the North-West Rebellion of 1885. Indigenous peoples have been encountering Europeans for over a thousand years – Vikings, Basques, and (later) Russians and other Europeans who were drawn by fishing and trapping, religious missions, and the search for trade networks. These encounters were often short lived and sporadic, but they paved the way for non-Indigenous peoples to permanently enter the North, largely for economic reasons, beginning in the eighteenth century. Canadian colonization was led by such institutions as the Hudson's Bay Company and the North-West Mounted Police (later the Royal Canadian Mounted Police). These had profound influences on trading and law, but it was missions established by churches to proselytize and to educate that most fundamentally altered the structure of families and communities and their relationship to the land.[7]

Contemporary denominational patterns reflect this early colonial period, with the predominant faith of each community reflecting either its particular Christian mission or, in cases of divided communities, the missionary competition between churches. The earliest missions were established among the Inuit (starting in Labrador) in the 1770s by the Moravian Brethren. From the 1870s on, starting in Baffin Island, the Anglican Church Mission Society spread its influence. Early in the twentieth century, Roman Catholic missionaries from the Oblates of Mary Immaculate established themselves in the Kivalliq region on the western shores of Hudson Bay.[8] Evangelical Christianity was introduced to the Eastern Arctic starting in the 1950s, with Pentecostalism (the dominant evangelical current) firmly established in the 1970s.[9] Many, although not all, residential schools in northern Canada were operated by Anglican and Roman Catholic churches, another key mechanism for the entrenchment of denominational patterns across the territories.

In Nunavut, as we see in Table 9.1, 50 percent of the population is Anglican, 24 percent Roman Catholic, and just over 5 percent evangelical. The moral traditionalism that is most commonly associated with

Table 9.1   Faith in northern Canada, 2011 (%)

Religion	Yukon	NWT	Nunavut
Indigenous spirituality	1	1	0.4
Protestant	28	28	62
Anglican	(8)	(10)	(50)
Evangelical	(4)	(4)	(5)
Roman Catholic	18	39	24
Other faiths	3	2	1
No religious affiliation	50	31	13
Total	100	100	100

Note: Evangelical numbers are derived from adding Pentecostals and Baptists.
Source: Statistics Canada, National Household Survey, 2011, www12/statscan.gov.ca/nhs-enm/2011/.

Pentecostals is bolstered by the conservatism of most of the territory's Anglican churches. In some respects, this is a legacy of the early preoccupations of Christian missionaries with supplanting earlier local practices with "Christian sexual morality."[10] New sexual taboos were introduced, though some also dovetailed with precolonial Inuit societal patterns, producing in the contemporary period a silence around issues of sexual diversity. In Nunavut, for example, it is commonly argued that homosexuality and/or bisexuality "did not exist in traditional Inuit culture," and that interpretation is certainly reinforced by church teachings.[11]

The spread of Christianity in the NWT followed the same pattern as in Nunavut, with non-Indigenous settlers bringing their own religious practices to such predominantly settler communities as Yellowknife, Hay River, and Fort Smith. Overall, evangelicals constitute less than 4 percent of the population, close to the Canadian average, and those with no religious affiliation constitute 30 percent of the population – above the Canadian average. The large Roman Catholic presence in the territory includes a strong current of liberation theology. It also includes a commitment, especially among the Oblates, to Indigenous struggles for self-determination. Father René Fumoleau's study on Treaties 8 and 11 was a foundational text of Dene political activism in the NWT, and he remains an important settler ally of Dene to this day.[12] Into the 1980s and 1990s, the Roman Catholic Church in Yellowknife partnered with environmental, labour, and women's groups to form a social justice coalition called Alternatives North.[13] The result has been a church presence in the NWT that, along with the United Church in Yellowknife, has had a noticeably more progressive hue than prevails among Anglican and evangelical churches in Nunavut. This has not necessarily translated into a reformist approach to sexuality and gender, but it does mean that the priorities for political intervention among these churches have lain elsewhere.

Yukon is a religious outlier, both in the North and in Canada as a whole. Those with no religious affiliation represent fully half the population. Non-Indigenous migrants to Yukon have long been attracted to its frontier lifestyle, breeding a sense of individualism and independence, along with a rejection of the traditional strictures of southern social life.[14] Yukon First Nations experience was similar to Indigenous peoples in its neighbouring territories, having been shaped by the same kinds of missionary outreach from Roman Catholic and Anglican churches, accompanied by the spread of church-controlled residential schools.[15] Now, Protestants represent 28 percent of the population, while 18 percent are Roman Catholic. About 4 percent are evangelical, with only a small number of these coming from the territory's Indigenous communities.

The Territorial Political Context

The development of consensus government and the implementation of Indigenous self-government have created unique political environments across Canada's North.[16] What are now Yukon, the NWT, and Nunavut were once part of Rupert's Land and the North-Western Territory, transferred from the Hudson's Bay Company to the Dominion of Canada in 1870. The Arctic Islands – which are today divided among Ontario, Quebec, and Nunavut – were transferred in 1888. These territories were governed at arm's-length by the uninterested and distant federal government that was content to leave the region open to traders, missionaries, prospectors, and homesteaders. As settler populations grew sufficiently large on the Prairies to organize and demand political representation, portions of the NWT were partitioned into smaller juris-dictions.[17] The first of Canada's three territories was Yukon, created in response to the influx of prospectors during the height of the Klondike Gold Rush in 1898.[18] The 1905 extension of Alberta and Saskatchewan borders to the 60th parallel resulted in the establishment of the modern NWT above that line. It was then divided in 1999 by the creation of Nunavut, part of a political settlement between Inuit and the Crown.

Yukon

In the decade following the gold rush, Yukon's population collapsed from an estimated 50,000 to 8,500 in 1911. Over that period, migrants to the territory agitated for political rights and were granted an elected but non-partisan council in 1909. The decline in population over the early twentieth century led the federal government, for a time, to strip away power from the territory; but, in the postwar period, a growing economy, the construction of the Alaska Highway, and the expansion of the welfare state led to rapid population growth and settler demands for responsible government.[19] In the late 1970s, political parties were introduced to the newly christened Yukon Legislative Assembly. In 1990, the first major Indigenous land settlement was agreed to by the federal and territorial governments, and, in the twenty-five years to follow, eleven of fourteen Yukon First Nations have settled self-government agreements, covering such areas as citizenship, social services, and educa-tion. On the other hand, in 2016, only three of the Legislative Assembly's nineteen members were Indigenous, even though Indigenous peoples make up one-quarter of the territory's population.

The territorial Progressive Conservative Party won the first party-centred election in 1978, reflecting territorial loyalty to the federal party and to Erik Nielsen, Yukon's champion in Ottawa. While Nielsen had espoused morally traditional positions throughout his thirty years as Yukon's MP, faith communities did not play a significant role in either his support base or that of the party's. Throughout the second half of the twentieth century, Yukon politics were dominated by debates over Indigenous land claims, the devolution of control over natural re-sources, and increased overall political autonomy. In 1991, and in the lead-up to the disastrous electoral defeat of Brian Mulroney in 1993,

Yukon PCs were reconstituted as the Yukon Party. This new conservative party, featuring the same party activists and voices, continued to promote the fiscal conservative values and individualism of its predecessor but avoided getting entangled with social conservatism. The territory's Liberal and New Democratic parties have held socially progressive positions, ranging from support for same-sex marriage to the protection of gender identity and expression in the territory's human rights code.

The Northwest Territories

The NWT had a caretaker commissioner appointed by the federal government from 1905 to 1921, when oil was discovered at Norman Wells. Fearing another population wave similar to Yukon's gold rush, the federal government revived the wholly appointed territorial council of the old North-West Territories. Even as elected members were added in the 1950s, the territorial capital remained in Ottawa until the designation of Yellowknife in 1967. The components of cabinet government were devolved so slowly that responsible government came only in 1986. Throughout this period, Indigenous peoples organized politically and pressed their land claims, framing the discussion of many political, economic, and social issues in the Legislative Assembly and beyond. Indigenous politicians often frame their interventions on social issues, for example, in terms of their impact on Indigenous self-government and what they see as traditional culture. Religious morality is only rarely invoked, and then only by a minority of non-Indigenous MLAs, particularly from outside Yellowknife.

The NWT legislature's consensus government system means that the premier and cabinet members are selected by MLAs from their own ranks after an election run without parties. This developed in the NWT for a series of historically specific reasons, among them the Legislative Assembly's long history as an appointed body. In the formative period of the 1960s and 1970s, the continuing federal leverage over territorial matters also militated against internal divisions. This pattern, as Ailsa Henderson writes, was not a product of Indigenous traditions but, rather, a matter-of-fact reflection of what were perceived to be political realities:

That consensus politics *currently* reflects the wishes of a northern Aboriginal population is not in question, but it was not designed to be a permanent feature of northern political life, it had nothing to do with efforts to acknowledge Aboriginal preferences, and its current existence owes as much to the tenor and pace of political change in the NWT as it does to the original intentions of administrators.[20]

This form of government has allowed for the development of distinct cleavages in the Legislative Assembly along identity and geographic lines, and divisions along such lines do structure political alliances or enmities among MLAs. But, in a system such as this, the sustained articulation of other interests is more difficult. As a result, morally traditional positions are presented only sporadically in the Legislative Assembly, and without enough force to challenge the social pragmatism that has characterized governments in the NWT.

Nunavut

Inuit in the NWT, northern Quebec, and Labrador formed the Inuit Tapirisat of Canada in 1971, which began the process of land claim negotiations with the federal government. A 1982 plebiscite on dividing the NWT into two territories passed, with 52 percent voting in favour of the creation of Nunavut. In 1990, an agreement in principle was signed between the federal government and the Inuit of the Eastern Arctic, leading to the finalization of the Nunavut Land Claims Agreement in 1993, in which the federal government agreed to create a new territory. Nunavut was officially established in 1999, with a governmental system similar in principle to that of the NWT, including a legislature operating under the consensus principle. The close relationship between the creation of Nunavut and the claims process has encouraged the close connection between Inuit identity and the territory as a whole.

There are important and politically relevant divisions in Legislative Assembly politics between the three regions of the territory (Baffin, Kivalliq, and Kitikmeot), but large-scale policy debates are for the most part absent in Nunavut. MLAs typically focus on the local issues of their constituencies – which is not surprising, given the absence of parties and the attention paid to natural resources and economic development through the land claim process.

There are, however, some discernible divisions along faith lines. As Henderson argues, "While initially division would have been between Christians and those practicing more traditional forms of Inuit spirituality, and later might have been characterized itself by rivalry between Christian denominations, it might now distinguish between evangelical and non-evangelical Christians (or between evangelical Christians and everyone else)."[21] The question for us to address here is whether this has had any significant influence on territorial policy making regarding the sorts of issues that have roused evangelicals in the south.

Sexual Diversity, Schooling, and Faith Communities in Northern Canada

If we use debates over the political recognition of sexual diversity as a gauge, we see dramatic contrasts across the three northern territories, broadly reflecting the differences in faith we outline above. But even in Nunavut, where religiously infused moral conservatism is most widespread, we see that its influence is constrained by consensus politics and economic preoccupations.

Yukon

Yukon has a strikingly progressive policy record on several social policy fronts, including those related to sexuality, though conservative resistance from outside the political system has been evident in recent years. In 1987, sexual orientation was included in the territory's Human Rights Code, and in 1990 Yukon became the first among provincial and territorial governments to extend full benefits to same-sex couples through its public-sector collective agreements, having done so partially in 1988. In 1998 and 1999, an NDP government changed the legislative definition of spouse to include same-sex couples, following pioneering steps in that direction taken by an NDP government in BC a few years earlier. One factor that facilitated this extraordinary record has been the preparedness of the conservative Yukon Party either to acquiesce in these measures or to support them.[22] In response to a successful court challenge on same-sex marriage in 2004, for example, Premier Dennis Fentie remarked: "It shows this country is very open to all views and I think that's a good thing and the Yukon is no different."[23]

Yukon has also been a leader in the recognition of sexual diversity within its public schooling system, and this, too, has elicited no party-based opposition. In 2012, the Ministry of Education approved a policy on sexual orientation and gender identity that recognized the presence of LGBTQ students and community members in Yukon schools, one of the first provincial-level jurisdictions in the country to develop policies specific to sexual minorities. The new policy also prohibited "homophobic and gender-based comments, discrimination, and bullying [that] are demeaning to all students, parents or guardians and employees regardless of their actual or perceived sexual orientation."[24] A year later, students and staff at F.H. Collins Secondary School in Whitehorse founded the first gay-straight alliance north of the 60th parallel, which then went on to win the Canadian Safe School Network/TD Award of Excellence Against LGBTQ Youth Bullying. None of these developments elicited legislative or extra-parliamentary protest.

The inclusion of sexual diversity within Catholic schools has been more controversial, even though they have been funded, managed, and operated by the Yukon government since 1962. In response to a 2012 Yukon policy on sexual orientation and gender identity, Catholic bishop Gary Gordon released a resource guide for schools and pastoral staff, *Living with Hope, Ministering by Love, Teaching in Truth*, that describes homosexuality as an "intrinsic moral evil" and "objective disorder."[25] Students at Vanier Catholic Secondary School, led by Grade 11 student Liam Finnegan, protested the guide in February 2013, garnering national media attention. The Yukon Party government moved immediately to have the guide removed from school websites, with Education Minister Scott Kent stating that what he was looking for was "a policy that conforms with the departmental policy on same-sex and gender equity, and that needs to be developed obviously in collaboration with the entire school community."[26] In an open letter to Bishop Gordon, Kent wrote: "Those parts of the Episcopal Corporation's policy that are inconsistent with and do not meet the requirements of existing laws and policies cannot have application in any publicly supported schools in the Yukon. This also includes religious instructional material in the Catholic separate schools."[27] Kent then ordered the development of a new policy that complied with the territory's human rights legislation and the Charter of Rights and Freedoms.

In response to the controversy, the Catholic board passed a new policy in December 2013, *One Heart: Ministering by Love*, which did affirm that "respect is due everyone regardless of race, gender, age, stage of development, disability, sexual orientation, class or religion," but then it opposed the creation of explicit LGBT anti-bullying clubs in its schools, favouring the creation of catch-all "One Heart" clubs.[28] The next spring, however, students at Vanier Catholic School formed a GSA, and a year later graduating Vanier students wore rainbow-coloured socks at their convocation ceremony to show support for LGBT students at the school. Promises of an updated Catholic-specific policy to address the concerns of parents, staff, and clergy, as well as to protect LGBT students, have yet to be realized.

Trans rights have seen less policy initiative by the territorial government. In April 2015, a petition was brought before the Legislative Assembly calling for the express inclusion of transgender rights in the territory's Human Rights Code. The Yukon Party government at first responded by stating that transgender rights were already protected in the legislation under the category of sex. The Legislative Assembly then unanimously supported an NDP motion asking the government to introduce "amendments to explicitly include gender identity and gender expression to the Yukon Human Rights Act *the next time the act is reviewed*," but it was clear that the government was not prepared to act before the 2016 election.[29]

In late 2016, the Yukon Liberal Party won a majority government, replacing the Yukon Party after fourteen years in power. Although the Liberals favoured including gender identity and expression in the human rights code prior to the election, when pressed on the subject in November 2016 by trans activists, the party refused to comment on whether it would amend the legislation.[30]

Northwest Territories

Sexual and gender diversity has been legislatively recognized in the NWT, though in the face of greater opposition from within the Legislative Assembly than in Yukon. Sexual orientation was added to the territory's Human Rights Code only in 2002. However, the Code itself was only developed at that time, and its inclusion of gender identity made NWT the first senior level of government to do so explicitly. The debate over the act as a whole, including these provisions, was, in the words of McGill and Kirkup, "short, collegial, and ultimately uncontroversial."[31]

In 1992, NWT civil service workplace benefits were extended to include same-sex couples, and, in 2002, in response to the Supreme Court of Canada's ruling in *M. v. H.* (1999), a wide range of statutes were amended to recognize same-sex families. There was little option but to proceed in this way, yet the government showed no sign of regret at presenting such legislation. The willingness to act on such fronts has also been shaped by a "rights culture" stemming from the struggle for Indigenous political and land rights, which was central to territorial politics from the 1970s. In supporting the 2002 legislation on family recognition, Premier Stephen Kakfwi also cited the importance of rights for his people and the inappropriateness of denying rights to others:

> One of the great pains or vacuums that some of us have grown up with is the denial of rights. Aboriginal people grew up with that. Until we experience it and live with it, it is difficult sometimes to understand how those who are oppressed and denied rights feel. There is no dignity in it. There is no respect and your self-worth is something you have to struggle to maintain.[32]

There has been opposition, however, usually framed by the language of traditional Indigenous culture and sovereignty, which often masks the role that conservative Christianity has played in shaping it. Jane Groenewegen, MLA for Hay River South, expressed her sentiments not only by invoking symbols of Indigenous spirituality but also by using arguments found among moral conservatives elsewhere in the country:

In this Territory, we stand to pray in this Legislature. We pray in our committee meetings. We pray to the Creator. I believe that the relationship that holds life between a man and a woman, that creates life, is a mystery. It is a beautiful thing. I think that as legislators, to enact laws that would contradict that shows disrespect to the Creator. Life continues on the basis of the way things were created. I believe it is a beautiful thing. I cannot personally be involved in an action I perceive to make a mockery of that or to show disrespect for that.[33]

David Krutko, a Gwich'in MLA representing the Mackenzie Delta, linked Indigenous and religious values, stating: "I, for one, believe that religious values, family values and aboriginal values are not being taken into account." He also couched the recognition of same-sex couples as a threat to the sovereignty of Indigenous nations. In his words, the recognition of sexual diversity limits the capacity of First Nations governments and organizations to "establish programs and services and determine exactly who their membership is and collectively how they will be able to allocate programs and services."[34] Future premier Floyd Roland talked of the threat LGBT communities posed to traditional values and also summoned widely used stereotypes about the risks of HIV transmission and the danger that recognition of LGBT rights posed to teaching about "family values" in schools.[35] Allowing same-sex couples to adopt would be detrimental to children, he argued, because they would eventually become sick and would no longer be able to provide the care necessary for healthy child development.

At the time that same-sex marriage was legislatively accepted by Parliament in 2005, there was little concerted opposition in the NWT, though some Indigenous governments have postponed accepting jurisdiction over marriage in their self-government agreements. For example, the Sahtu Deline have agreed to revisit the issue "following the tenth anniversary of the [agreement] and at a time agreed to by the parties."[36] Opposition has slowed policy development in education so that the NWT does not yet have a territory-wide policy on sexual diversity in schools. Still, the lack of a party system, and the pragmatism that generally characterizes political debate in the territory, means that moral traditionalism does not have a sustained influence on policy making. When the Yellowknife school board decided to create gender-neutral washrooms as a vehicle for recognizing LGBT student concerns, for example, there was no evidence of local protest.[37]

Nunavut

Faith has made its most visible appearance in Nunavut, where a growing evangelical presence supported by missions and resources from southern Canada has made its social and political presence felt. The Northern Canada Evangelical Mission, founded in 1946, has established strong programs in Nunavut and has found allies among MLAs such as Tagak Curley and James Arreak.[38] Evangelical voices have routinely been at the forefront of opposition to the political recognition of sexual diversity, though other church communities have also spoken out. In 2005, following the legalization of same-sex marriage by the federal government, the Anglican Diocese of the Arctic released a notice stating that "it will not employ the following: anyone having pre-marital sex, homosexuals, lesbians and bisexuals, those who willingly engage in sexual activities with a minor and with those whom they are counselling or supervising (excluding spouses) and those who fail to disclose a prior conviction of child sexual abuse," in addition to anyone who "supports and promotes such behaviour, lifestyle, or teaching."[39] Here in Nunavut, even more than in the NWT, opposition to LGBT rights has been framed in terms of Inuit traditional culture. Rebekah Williams said, in explaining opposition to same-sex marriage, that "Inuit had to survive all on their own and they tried to have morals. If the morals break down somewhere, the people might starve."[40]

The Nunavut government has, to be sure, enacted change that was required by the courts, framing such moves as meeting its constitutional obligations. For example, following the decision of two provincial appellate courts to legalize same-sex marriage in 2003, and the federal Liberal proposal to enact inclusive same-sex marriage legislation nationally, Nunavut premier Paul Okalik responded by saying: "If developments in the Parliament of Canada and the Supreme Court of Canada result in the definition of marriage being broadened, we will respect the law and comply with that."[41] In response to intense questioning from both government and regular MLAs, he acknowledged the forcefulness of moral traditionalism in the territory but shifted blame away from the territorial government:

> Because we know that there is a lot of opposition out there, we will not and do not have the authority and jurisdiction in this matter. If they say so in the Supreme Court of Canada, then we will follow in their footsteps according to that. We are not going to just go out of our way to do the opposite of what Nunavummiut want.[42]

The political awareness of the risks associated with proactive steps in such policy areas has been reinforced by successful local activism. Bibles are distributed in Arviat schools, and Ouija boards have been removed from Rankin Inlet's largest store following community opposition.[43] In 2014, angry protest greeted the raising of a Pride flag (for the first time) in front of Iqaluit City Hall. One city councillor complained in these terms: "People tell me it is not an Inuit custom to be gay."[44] Cathy Towtongie, president of the Inuit land claim beneficiary organization, commended the dissenting councillors for their position, stating that "Inuit culture have had no time to discuss same-sex ... In fact it was an agenda that was hijacked and there was the excuse of [homophobia] which Inuit should have time to digest."[45]

In the end, however, that rainbow flag was raised, and prominent Inuit leaders were prepared to defend the decision to do so. Former premier Paul Okalik stated in the Legislative Assembly: "As someone who has felt that type of discrimination, I have felt compelled [to say] that no one deserves that kind of treatment in our territory."[46] Young Inuit leaders and other political people influential in Nunavut seem more inclined to stake out more inclusive positions. Laakkuluk Williamson Bathory, an emerging Inuit leader and promoter of Inuit traditional culture, wrote Towtongie an open later after the flag dispute, stating:

> The prejudice you showed to fellow Inuit and to other human beings is not fit for your very important position in society ... As someone that grew up with you and someone who shares the work you do for

Inuit, I would like to ask you to publicly apologize for your statements and further to this, announce love and respect for all and everyone living in Nunavut – that is my understanding of Inuit values.[47]

Across the territory, the absence of a party system, and an overall preference for pragmatism, militates against religious conservatism being a sustained influence in politics. Canada-wide court rulings have narrowed the room for manoeuvre on issues that are most likely to mobilize traditionalist opinion, however framed. There are certainly legislators who are influenced by conservative Christianity, but there are no indications that they prioritize policy positions arising from that allegiance. As with other legislators, they can hardly escape the urgency of other policy areas more centrally related to Nunavut and Inuit development.

Conclusion

The politics of faith in northern Canada are in keeping with the diversity we have seen in the provinces, though we also find that the influence of moral traditionalism is refracted through the unique demographic and institutional features of each territory. In Yukon, high levels of secularization have left little room for faith communities to exert political pressure, and they have resulted in the territory being a policy leader on some issues related to sexual diversity. In the NWT, where levels of religiosity are higher, and conservative faith more widespread, pragmatic territorial governments have rebuffed opposition to change, especially around the recognition of same-sex relationships. In Nunavut, where faith plays an important role in Inuit communities, the territorial government has pursued progressive policies, though by and large only those required by its constitutional obligations. However, even in Nunavut, a Pride flag was raised in front of Iqaluit's city hall, reflecting what may be a shift in public sentiments, especially among the young. This is what we have seen in those parts of Canada below the 60th parallel that were traditionally the most resistant to change.

If this speaks to a form of convergence, we also see this in the growing visibility of religious minorities that adhere neither to Christianity nor to Indigenous spirituality. Yukon has the largest settler population in the region and also the largest communities of Buddhists, Hindus, and Sikhs. Though still only 2 percent of the population, they have become more visible in Whitehorse. In the NWT, where 1.5 percent of the population belong to minority religions, and in Nunavut, where the figure is less than 1 percent, there is a growing Muslim population, with Inuvik hosting the world's most northerly mosque, built in 2010. Whatever claims for recognition emerge from those communities are likely to be responded to with the pragmatism that we find in different forms across the territories, combined with the overarching dominance of economic considerations in all political deliberation. So on this front, too, conflict will likely be tempered and differences recognized.

In many ways, the region north of 60 is very different from the rest of Canada. It has much smaller populations and a much stronger Indigenous presence. Religion is an important part of Indigenous life and, in some areas, of settler life as well, but we find only limited indications of sustained political influence, and very little preparedness to mobilize in large numbers even around those issues that have mattered most to social and moral traditionalists. In the NWT and Nunavut, this is reinforced by institutionalized non-partisanship, but in Yukon too, there is evidence of a pragmatic willingness to avoid major confrontation.

Conclusion: Canadian Diversity in Comparative Context

Is there a distinctive Canadian pattern of religious influence on party politics? Could any answer or set of answers, distinctive or not, apply across a country as diversified as this one, with its variations in religious make-up and history of faith-based political contention across its many regions? We contend that there are indeed patterns that broadly apply across the country, and here in this conclusion we pull together strands of our case studies to highlight common patterns without underplaying the regionally distinct stories that are key to understanding the role of faith and faith communities in our politics. The Canadian political system has strong regional fault lines based on different settlement and demographic patterns, amplified by the jurisdictional strength of provincial and territorial governments, and by party systems that differ from one another in dramatic ways. Still, there are broad patterns that we can pull from the case studies presented in this volume.

The first pattern is the shift in lines of faith-based conflict. Denominationalism has declined as a factor across all the regions where it had historically shaped political contention. Up to the middle of the last century, and in some regions well beyond that, Protestant-Catholic animosity or estrangement were crucial sources of division between and within political parties at the federal level and across several provinces.

Then from the 1970s or 1980s onward, the religious axis that most commonly affected party alignments was the dividing line between moral traditionalists from across faith backgrounds and those seeking progressive responses to feminist, LGBT, and civil rights advocacy. Until then, there was an unspoken consensus among parties in favour of what were thought to be permanently entrenched family values. Slowly, the major parties in Ottawa and several provinces moved towards clearly distinguishing themselves over this line of electoral and policy demarcation.

The second pattern is the growing diversity of religious practice in Canada and its recognition by state institutions. In recent decades, the political and legal recognition of minority religious practices, and the very idea of large-scale immigration from countries with non-Christian majorities, might have produced a new party alignment. With important exceptions, however, the scale of routinized immigration to this country, and the widespread recognition of the long-term economic indispensability of such population inflows, has muted partisan differences. This does not suggest an absence of public contentiousness over government decisions, court rulings, and institutional adjustments that acknowledge growing religious diversity. It does suggest that major parties have by and large resisted politicizing them.

A third pattern is the widespread secularization across Canada. There is no question that the influence of religious communities on Canadian political parties, and of faith itself, has been reduced by the extraordinary decline in religiosity that has marked the last half century. In the 1950s, weekly attendance at services was 60 percent, high by any standard; it now stands at less than 15 percent. Only a little over one-quarter of the population now see religion as very important, and attachment to religious strictures seems much less than even that number would suggest.[1] Faith-infused moral traditionalism has declined, and debates over family roles, sexuality, and abortion, seem no longer to have the same capacity to generate sustained inter-party conflict.

Nevertheless, religious affiliation and personal faith are still very important to a diversified array of religious minorities who recurrently demonstrate an uncommon capacity to mobilize political resources. As such, the fourth pattern reflects the fact that Christian traditionalists, and moral conservatism in general, remain influential voices within most parties of the right. They continue to shape policy choices in schooling especially, whether by reinforcing support for private and faith-based schools or by slowing change in equity-related policies. The numerical decline in social conservative ranks may reduce the range of issues on which they have the potential for influence, but their minority status intensifies the concern among some that their voices will be politically ignored, leading to more fervent organizational development in recent years. Moral and religious conservatives also retain the capacity to mobilize social and cultural anxieties within the broader public, particularly around issues of schooling.

At times, these various patterns intersect. Parties on the right are much more likely to have legislators and strategists sympathetic to moral conservatism, and have sometimes curried the support of ethno-cultural minorities by signalling their support for what they describe as traditional family values. This has led to the development of sometimes surprising coalitions of religiously motivated actors who, under other circumstances, would find themselves on opposite sides of issues such as minority religious recognition. The growing size of Canada's non-Christian minority communities means that there are increased claims for recognition that in some cases rub against the attachment to Christian dominance that informs a portion of the political right. Such claims, of course, also create unease among those on the right or the left who believe that religion has no place in public policy debate.

What we see across the country are episodes that reflect disagreement on the public place of religious belief and practice. Most of these episodes have centred on the axis that separates moral traditionalists from progressive reformers, but we now see a few high-profile instances in which the rights of religious minorities are in question. We also see isolated cases in which secularist demands that there be no state support for faith-based institutions have opened the issue of Roman Catholic school funding – an issue fought decades ago on denominational grounds and broadly thought to be politically settled. The complex reality, then, is that a variety of issues related to faith have the potential to elicit political conflict, either dividing parties internally or distinguishing one from the others. Religious communities, Christian, Muslim, Jewish, Sikh, Buddhist, and Hindu, also exercise influence inside political parties at the provincial and federal levels, and, in a highly fluid electorate, political strategists and candidates pay attention to communities with already-established social networks.

In the pages to follow, we draw on analytical strands and examples in our provincial and federal case studies to weave together a larger picture of how faith-based partisan contention has changed over time, at the same time muddying any claim that religion is now inconsequential to an understanding of Canada's party systems. We finish by exploring the extent to which Canadian political patterns are distinctive in comparative terms.

Declining Denominational Conflict

Political differences and electoral preferences based on sectarian divisions between Protestants and Catholics have now all but disappeared from the Canadian partisan landscape, even if ancient community attachments are still reflected in candidate selection and party voting in parts of Atlantic Canada. Even there, the segmentation of social and educational worlds that once so shaped political allegiances has slowly dissolved, and parties have avoided any hint of favouring one religious community over another. In New Brunswick, language began replacing religion as the primary axis of political contention early in the twentieth century, and on that issue too party leaders have striven to cast appeals broadly rather than narrowly, particularly since the 1960s. It may be in Prince Edward Island where parties were most concerned about balancing their electoral tickets, but in most of the region religious affiliation now counts for much less in terms of which political candidates you support than it did even one generation ago.

The deconfessionalization of Quebec's school system at the turn of the millennium was only one of many steps taken towards reducing the role of religion in education, and in any event language had long before supplanted religious considerations in shaping the province's schools. Ontario has retained full state funding for Catholic schools, though increasing non-Catholic enrolment within the system has added to questioning about how religiously distinct they are. If in Ontario and other provinces there are continuing debates about the appropriateness of public funding for Catholic schools, they are driven less by Protestant resentment than by secularist calls for a single publicly funded system or religious minority claims that public funding should be extended to their schools. When Catholic bishops or lay leaders speak in defence of policy proposals that they claim infringe on the rights of Catholic institutions to operate according to faith-based principles, they usually do so in opposition to secularist or progressive pressures. When Ontario's Catholic school trustees resist provincial legislation requiring an explicit recognition of sexual diversity, they are not combatting Protestantism in the same way as did earlier generations. Anti-Catholic sentiment persists in parts of Canada, but it is a shadow of its predecessors, and there are no political parties prepared to take sides with such animus. This is a far cry from decades past when policy debates and elections would regularly be infused by denominational prejudice, and when party leaders in such provinces as Ontario, Newfoundland and Labrador, and New Brunswick could invoke foreboding stereotypes of Protestant or Catholic protagonists backed by civil society groups like the Orange Lodge.

With the decline of substantive issues that reflect Protestant-Catholic animosity has come an overall reduction in the party distinctiveness of votes among Catholics or mainline Protestants. At the federal level, the Catholic tilt towards the Liberal Party – even when controlling for the preference for Liberals among francophones – endured into the first decade of this century without any substantive issue preferences explaining the voting pattern. The apparent decline in political relevance of denominational identity among Catholics meant that their votes reflected more general population trends, though a few would also have been drawn by the Conservative Party's targeting of social conservatives. In Ontario, the classical denominational differences between Liberals and Progressive Conservatives were not at all apparent in the 2011 election, in part because of the PCs' direct appeal to social conservatives of all religious persuasions. West of Manitoba, denominational differences had little sustained influence on party preferences, and certainly none in the present period.

What does still matter across the country is evangelical affiliation, which correlates with electoral preference for parties on the right, especially in Ontario and western Canada. However, this is not the denominational distinction of old but, rather, a function of social conservatives moving towards parties that are more clearly identifying with the right and away from parties that that are more clearly breaking with traditionalist positions on issues related to gender, sexuality, and schooling.

Party Realignment on the Social Conservatism Axis

Social movement challenges to established family structure, gender norms, and sexual regulation ramped up during the 1960s and 1970s. Social democratic parties were the first to adopt progressive positions on such issues, though for some time they did not do so with either unanimity or fervour. This was especially evident in response to sexual diversity, and the recognition of same-sex relationships was sometimes a stumbling block. The BC New Democrats stood out in their relative unity on this front during the 1990s, while internal hesitation and division was dramatically evident within the Ontario NDP during the Rae government. The Parti Québécois claimed a reformist mantle but displayed great caution in granting lesbian and gay couples full recognition. Prior to then, even where social democratic parties were major contenders for power, their caution over this hot button issue, which still provoked social conservatives, reduced the potential for electoral realignment.

If social democrats were slow to stick their necks out on such issues, centrist or centre-left parties were even slower. At the federal level, in Ontario, Quebec, the Atlantic region, and other provinces, Liberal parties were occasionally willing to champion policies aimed at gender equity, but well into the new millennium abortion often divided them. As we see in our detailed exploration of reproductive politics at the federal level, the Liberal caucus retained a visible and outspoken pro-life minority well into the period of Conservative government. No Liberal party in the country with any realistic shot at government was firmly united around sexual minority rights until the late 1990s – and many not until the 2000s. In some parts of the country, Liberal Party leaders recognized that a sizable minority of their legislators and electors held relatively traditional beliefs on family-related issues.

For some time, the brokerage pragmatism of major parties on the right, both federally and in several provinces, contributed to the weakness of faith realignment and the persistence of traditional denominational divides. The federal Progressive Conservatives, and their provincial counterparts in Ontario, the Atlantic region, and Alberta, had little incentive to play the traditional family policy card since they had important legislators, and electoral currents, who were indifferent to such issues or in favour of moderate reform.

The table was set for realignment along the traditionalist/progressive axis in those cases where parties on the right had already firmly allied themselves with Christian conservatives, as was the case of Social Credit in BC and Alberta. The same was true in instances where parties on the centre-right turned sharply towards a free market ideology, as with the PCs in Alberta and Ontario, and then the federal Conservative Party.

Ralph Klein moved Alberta's Progressive Conservatives to the right largely on the strength of a neoliberal agenda, but no party leader was ready to affront the party's important socially conservative constituency, which it had inherited from the Social Credit. During much of his time in office, the partisan opposition was weak and focused primarily on the PCs' economic agenda. Eventually, when Alison Redford shifted the party to the political centre, the rapid growth of the Wildrose Party was driven, in part, by the changing allegiance of moral traditionalists. During Jim Prentice's brief leadership in 2014 and 2015, the PCs were obviously struggling to regain some portion of that constituency by messily compromising on LGBT rights, but by that time the electoral risks of playing on social conservative antipathy to such rights were obvious. However, the New Democratic Party victory in Alberta's 2015 election did not mean that either the political influence of social conservatives or the province's significant evangelical population had disappeared. The Wildrose opposition, still an important force in provincial affairs, continued to face the strategic dilemma, long a feature of PC internal politics, of keeping social conservatives loyal and active while also attracting more centrist voters. And as the PCs regained popularity in 2016, the prominence of its revived social conservative constituency was on vivid public display.

The Ontario story has some similarities with Alberta's. Mike Harris moved Ontario's Progressive Conservatives sharply to the right in the early 1990s. He focused on economic issues but was conscious of the electoral threat from small parties (real and potential) on his social conservative flank. Over the next decades, during which the PCs were mostly governed by leaders of a Harrisite hue, the party retained the votes of most evangelicals and made gains among traditionalist Catholics. As recently as the early 2010s, under Tim Hudak, the Ontario Progressive Conservative Party allied itself unequivocally with those who protested against the recognition of sexual diversity in schools. And, in 2015, the party chose as leader a federal social conservative, though one who then tried to distance himself from the policy concerns associated with that current within the provincial party.

During the time that Ontario's PCs have been firmly on the right, the NDP has been relatively united on social issues, overcoming its 1990s divisions over sexual diversity. In contrast, it took a long time for the Ontario Liberals to position themselves unequivocally on the progressive side of such issues. Their shift from a policy position at least as socially conservative as the PCs' during the postwar period only really began in the mid-1980s and proceeded in fits and starts. In the early 2010s, we saw in the controversy over sex education that the threat of religious right mobilization was enough to intimidate the Liberal premier and his election advisors – this at a time when few observers would have imagined that the religious right had much leverage left. The leadership of Kathleen Wynne reflected the ascendancy of the progressive side of the party, at the very least on social issues, and this was reinforced both by her openness about living in a lesbian relationship and her policy record in the education ministry. There was still going to be a noticeable constituency of moral traditionalists within the party's electorate, but there was no longer a serious question of this limiting the party's preparedness to highlight its contrast with the provincial PCs on any of the issues that had traditionally mobilized social conservatives.

The federal Conservative Party that resulted from the merger of the Canadian Alliance Party and the PCs was much more deliberate than its provincial counterparts in fashioning itself as the natural electoral home of social conservatives, even if it also focused its policy agenda on lowering taxes and reducing the role of the federal government. Indeed, this economic message often resonated well with conservative religious communities that prioritized individual responsibility. Under Prime Minister Stephen Harper's leadership, the party strategically targeted ethno-cultural communities and some religious minority communities (though not Muslims), hoping to pull them away from the Liberals, in part, with appeals to traditional family values. When combined with the Liberals' embrace of more progressive positions on sexual diversity, this contributed to the elimination of the overall Catholic preference for the Liberals, and it diminished Liberal support in some minority communities. The Conservatives' loss in the 2015 election may have jostled this strategy and raised deep questions about relying on the loyalty of core constituencies on the right, including social conservatives. But in the medium term, the party needs those votes and the activist energy that comes from such currents.

From the turn of the twenty-first century, the federal Liberals appeared ready to set themselves alongside the NDP in opposition to social and family traditionalism. However, it was not always clear if this strategy was driven by principled conviction or was simply a product of the party leadership recognizing the electoral advantage of campaigning against a Conservative moral agenda. A more thorough-going shift was evident when Justin Trudeau took over as party leader and declared his party's support for the pro-choice position on abortion. By that time, election studies showed that attitudes towards same-sex marriage and abortion closely aligned Liberals with supporters of the NDP and the Bloc Québécois, and sharply differentiated them all from Conservative voters.[2] In the 2015 federal election, Trudeau campaigned on positions that were clearly at odds with moral traditionalists, such as the legalization of assisted dying, sex work, recreational marijuana, and safe-injection sites.

In British Columbia, the story of party alignment on social conservatism is somewhat different from that in other provinces. Throughout the first few postwar decades, when Social Credit ruled in BC, there was no doubt about which party would draw most support from traditionalists. Under Bill Bennett, the party turned economically right, even before the Alberta and Ontario PCs, but the influence of the religious right within the party had already been established. It was this current that helped elect Bill Vander Zalm as leader and premier in 1986. A conservative Catholic, he was more explicitly committed to morally conservative social policy than any major government party leader in Canada. Social Credit's pole position on the right endured into the 1990s, at which point the Liberal Party emerged to take its place. Since that time, no BC Liberal leaders have had any obvious affinity with social conservatism, and religious traditionalists were more likely to have second thoughts about supporting a party with the Liberal label attached to it. Still, in a historically polarized system, no party on the right could ignore a faith-driven morally traditionalist constituency, however diminished in size. We therefore witness the intriguing spectacle of a BC Liberal premier talking openly about her faith, supported by evangelical luminary Stockwell Day, in a province with very high levels of secularism.

For its part, Quebec is distinctive for having long had no significant partisan voice in favour of social conservatism. Yes, there has been a third party challenge since the mid-2000s from the Action démocratique du Québec (and Coalition Avenir Québec), which embodies some elements of a traditionalist response to social change, but it is much more focused on immigration-related issues than on family, gender, and sexuality. The comparative absence of a party voice similar to those found on the partisan right in other parts of the country reflects, in part, the dramatically weakened influence of Quebec's Catholic hierarchy since the Quiet Revolution, the very small size of the province's evangelical community, and the tendency for nationalists to identify Quebec as defined by consensus on gender and sexual equality. At the same time, the relative lack of political contention on these issues also reflects a decades-long history of partisan caution on issues like abortion and LGBT family rights, with PQ and Liberal governments alike proceeding only after being sure of cross-party agreement.

In provinces like Newfoundland and Labrador, and to some extent New Brunswick, we also see policy delay on the most contentious issues related to gender and sexuality, but this occurs over a longer period and in a region where social and moral traditionalism has been more influential than in other provinces. Even when New Brunswick's Liberal government eventually shifted away from a cross-party consensus on relatively limited access to abortion, it did so with sufficient caution to reduce the likelihood of sustained opposition. Newfoundland and Labrador did not retain a restrictive policy on access to abortion for as long as New Brunswick and Prince Edward Island, but it delayed recognizing LGBT rights long enough to avoid significant opposition within or outside the legislature.

Electoral Alignment

What of the tendency for moral traditionalists to vote in ways that are clearly distinct from others? Table C.1 displays two indicators of the extent to which party electorates outside Quebec have been reshuffled to pull (and push) those who are relatively religious or specifically evangelical Protestants towards those parties most clearly identified with the right. One measure is the percentage of evangelicals who prefer such parties, which we set against the parties' level of support in the overall population. The survey numbers are small here since declared evangelicals constitute only 4 to 6 percent of respondents in some provinces (Ontario, Newfoundland and Labrador, BC) and rise to a still modest 9 to 12 percent in others (Alberta, New Brunswick, Manitoba,

Table C.1   Evangelical and "very religious" voting for parties on the right, 2011–15 (%)

Party	Year of election	Average voter	Evangelical voter	Those reporting religion very important
Cons Party of Canada	2015	30	52	38
BC Liberals	2013	36	54	43
Alberta Wildrose	2012	37	63	51
Saskatchewan Party	2011	67	84	70
Manitoba PCs	2011	46	81	59
Ontario PCs	2014	36	65	50
NB PCs	2014	41	75	56
NL PCs	2011	52	59	61

Source: Patrick Fournier et al., 2015 Canadian Election Study; Jared Wesley et al., Canadian Provincial Election Project, 2011–14, http://cpep.ualberta.ca/.

and Saskatchewan). Interpretation, therefore, has to be cautious, but we can see the general results that we would have anticipated. Elsewhere, we see evidence of evangelicals disproportionately supporting the federal Conservatives, the provincial PCs in Ontario and Manitoba, the Saskatchewan Party, Alberta's Wildrose Party, and the BC Liberals.

We might have imagined these numbers to be higher still. Sam Reimer and Lydia Bean both point to elements of political moderation among Canadian evangelicals, who are less likely than their American counterparts to see identification with a particular party as part of their core identity.[3] Yes, they tend towards traditionalist stances on a range of morality issues, but their policy priorities extend far beyond that.

The Narrowing but Persistent Policy Influence of Social Conservatives

The foothold that social conservatives have retained in those parties that most unequivocally allied themselves with religious and moral traditionalism has declined in recent years – quite a lot. What has happened at the federal level illustrates a pattern that is also evident in provinces such as Alberta and Ontario. As leader of the federal Conservatives, Stephen Harper had warned social conservatives within his own party about asking for too much, or moving too dramatically. Once in office, he made a token gesture in the direction of undoing same-sex marriage, and then, after predictably failing, made it clear that lesbian and gay marriage was a settled issue, not to be revived. He also became increasingly impatient with backbench MPs who sought to enact incrementalist steps to raise the issue of abortion. It did not escape notice, either in federal Conservative ranks or in their provincial counterparts, that, by the 2010s, well over 60 percent of Canadians supported same-sex marriage, and steadily growing majorities broadly supported a woman's right to have access to abortion services.[4] However, as we saw in Chapter 1, there are still sharp distinctions between the attitudes of Conservative Party supporters and those of other parties, especially on the moral acceptability of abortion and gay and lesbian relations.[5]

In Alberta, public opinion on issues related to sexuality no longer distinguishes its residents very much, if at all, from the Canadian average, and that has undoubtedly reduced the political leverage of social conservatives in the province. The upstart Wildrose Party, which had drawn religious conservatives away from the Progressive Conservatives, generated its own firestorm over anti-gay sentiments, eventually driving its leader Danielle Smith to abandon the party entirely. Brian Jean, her successor, himself rooted in social conservatism, has since politically disavowed a moral agenda. Meanwhile, PC leader Jim Prentice displayed a spectacular about-face on the question of recognizing sexual diversity in schools, abandoning a clumsy compromise on gay-straight alliances designed to retain or lure moral traditionalists and eventually securing the passage of more inclusive policy. Nonetheless, it is still premature to dismiss social conservative influence on the partisan right, as the race to succeed Prentice as party leader witnesses the resurfacing of the influential moral traditionalist constituency within that party.

Ontario's PCs dallied with religious and moral conservatives under the leadership of Tim Hudak, but this appears to have helped him lose two elections that the party seemed poised to win. A 2015 leadership race was then won by Patrick Brown, a candidate with a solid federal record of supporting morally conservative positions. Like his Alberta Wildrose counterpart, after winning the leadership campaign, he then repeatedly denied that he was a social conservative and stayed as far away as he could manage from the continuing controversy over sex education. But his party continues to draw a strong majority of evangelicals and other moral traditionalists, and they show no signs of being content with political marginalization.

In parts of the Atlantic region, moral traditionalism was buttressed by a shared reluctance among Liberal and PC leaders to embrace socially progressive policies. This gave way to very slow and belated policy shifts on LGBT rights, driven in part by court decisions. In New Brunswick and PEI, restrictive regimes narrowing women's access to abortion remained in place until the mid-2010s, but even there admittedly cautious steps have been taken towards reform. In the meantime, public opinion on these issues, which once reflected the overall traditionalism of those in the region, has shifted markedly towards the Canadian average and, on some issues, towards the progressive end of the regional spectrum.

In parts of the North, and most especially Yukon, social conservatism never had much of a foothold, and now it has less than ever. In other parts, most notably Nunavut, evangelicism and other forms of morally traditional Christianity are widespread, though a preoccupation with social justice issues and patterns of pragmatic consensualism have tended to reduce the play of such beliefs in territorial politics.

Overall, this study has provided us with many indicators that religious conservatism, while diminished, has *not* declined to the point of inconsequentiality in Canadian party politics. First, we have seen religious conservatives influencing the selection of party leaders. Even if they may fail to secure their first choice, they have wielded muscle in the selection of leaders such as the Ontario PCs' Patrick Brown. BC's Liberal premier Christy Clark was not a favourite of that party's religious right, but she has felt compelled to talk about her personal faith in a public way. Major front bench figures in the federal Conservative Party are adherents to the kind of traditional faith currents that helped fuel the Reform Party, and that wing of the party will remain consequential whoever is chosen successor to Stephen Harper.

Across much of the country, voters for whom religion is important, and especially evangelicals, still gravitate to parties on the right. This is more obviously the case for conservative white Christians since there is only mixed evidence of rightist parties peeling off large numbers of moral or family traditionalists within minority communities (both Christian and non-Christian). The Jewish community swung towards the federal Conservatives for a time at least, but very little of that shift came from the preferences of the relatively small portion of that community that is socially conservative. There are stronger currents of family traditionalism in other minority communities, but there is no indication of a wholesale shift in party allegiance towards parties on the right, and there is even less indication that what changes have occurred are motivated by such sentiments.

The ethno-cultural diversification of protest against LGBT-inclusive school policies in Ontario and, to some extent, BC is a relatively recent phenomenon, born of the increase in size of minority communities and their growing political confidence. This contributes to the potential of religious conservative influence on party politics in those regions where minority populations are largest, though fear of backlash in Quebec would significantly reduce the likelihood of traditionalist mobilizing there. In Ontario and BC especially, though, this diversity either strengthens the voice of social conservatism or at least slows its decline. As one writer put it when reflecting on those protesting against an updated sex education, "The result is something new in Ontario: a multicultural army of social conservatives who are angry, energized and eager to test their political power."[6]

The fact that voters and activists representing the "traditional" core of the religious right ally themselves disproportionately with parties on the right continues to give them a greater degree of heft within those parties than their share of the total population would suggest. And in a set of party systems in which turnout is relatively low, electoral loyalty much diminished, with parties winning seat-based pluralities instead of majorities, it would be a very brave party leader on the right who ignored this current altogether.

Across the country we can still find evidence of policy making being affected by moral traditionalists, most significantly in schooling. Provincial ministries of education have generally been slow to develop policies specifically addressing harassment based on sexual orientation and gender identity. Ontario's revised curriculum on sexual health education was delayed for years by fears of moral traditionalist backlash, and it is not altogether clear that the Liberal government would have persevered in the face of massive protest in 2015 had it not been for the embarrassment of caving in a few years earlier.

Most provinces provide significant public monies for private schools, and by and large they justify this in terms of choice. But across the country, most of the beneficiaries are faith-based schools, and the vast majority of these are Christian. Alberta also has an educational regime that allows for explicitly faith-based schools to be fully a part of public school boards, with what appears to be only modest curricular oversight. Controls on what is taught may well be tighter in other provinces, but the relatively generous taxpayer support for faith-based schools represents an important gain for religious conservatives in a policy sector more important to them than any other.

Party Response to Religious Diversification

The religious diversification that has come with shifts in immigration away from Europe in favour of regions with non-Christian majorities means that major parties across the country can no longer ignore religious minority voters. The 2011 census showed that 8 percent of Canadians were affiliated to non-Christian faiths, a proportion that is projected to grow to about 15 percent by 2031.[7] This trend affects the Atlantic region less than any other, but in Halifax there is now a noticeably growing population of religious minorities. In major urban regions elsewhere, significant Muslim, Hindu, Sikh, and Buddhist communities are now being added to the already-established Jewish minorities.

Outside Quebec, parties on the right were not in the past as successful as their centre or left-leaning competitors in securing votes in such minority groups, but they now routinely treat ethno-cultural and religious minority communities as important constituencies. This interest flows from the widening belief that minority voters include many natural supporters of the right, and moderates the temptation to play on the nativist xenophobia that is ubiquitous on Europe's far right and disturbingly strong even among some more centrist parties.

We have seen episodes of contention over the recognition of minority religious practices, sometimes paired with regret over the elimination of specifically Christian references in public institutions. In the early postwar years, anti-Semitism was widespread enough, and Christian hegemony assumed, that questions of minority practice were rarely raised in legislative or partisan arenas. Minority claims became more prominent with the 1982 enactment of the Charter of Rights and Freedoms, and the growing number of adherents to minority faiths. The first major public controversy arose in 1988 over the wearing of turbans by Sikh RCMP officers, but there have been others. Most such cases were resolved by specific institutional decisions or by the courts, and major party leaders were by and large willing to avoid engagement. The Reform Party seized the turban issue in the late 1980s and early 1990s, but eventually pulled back on policy stances associated with anti-immigrant sentiment. In 2003, the question of Ontario extending faith-based arbitration options to Muslims provoked a major wave of opposition, but the Liberal government's 2005 decision to roll back all such arbitration had no significant objectors in the party system, and the issue died almost as quickly as it had arisen. In other parts of the country, individual politicians have given voice to sentiments echoing unease with high levels of immigration or with accommodation to minority religious practices. But these have been relatively isolated examples, with major parties across the country supportive of comparatively high levels of immigration and willing to generally avoid issues related to minority religious recognition.

The most sustained exception to this pattern has been in Quebec since the mid-2000s, when the minor ADQ party joined with the tabloid press in stoking fears about recognizing or "accommodating" minority religious practice. The PQ then shifted towards a policy agenda that, in effect, targeted the province's sizable Muslim population, though it tried to dress up its proposals in the progressive garb of incorporating minorities into an equity-driven majority culture. The party lost the 2014 election, in which it most aggressively deployed this strategy, but its new leadership has shown no interest in backing down from that agenda, even in the wake of the 2017 mosque killings.

In the 2015 election, a similar pattern emerged at the federal level for the first time in modern Canadian history. The incumbent Conservative government had already taken small symbolic steps that played to anti-Muslim sentiment, including a requirement (later struck down by the courts) that required the removal of face coverings for the official swearing of Canadian citizenship oaths. The idea of such a ban was hugely popular in Quebec, but it also had strong majority backing across the rest of the country. Despite this support, the Conservatives lost the election, and many observers believed that the fear-mongering tone of their campaign was a contributing factor, whatever the popularity of particular platform commitments. Whether this defeat convinces federal Conservatives to stay away from exclusionary identity politics, however, remains an open question.

Outside Quebec, there is certainly no evidence of any other provincial parties systematically engaging in contention over minority religious practices. The question of state funding for faith-based schools, which certainly could be used as a vehicle for stoking anti-minority anxiety, has not been given prominence in the platforms of any major party across the country, whether in those provinces that offer no such funding or in those that offer generous support. In most of the country, even Quebec, the everyday institutional recognition given to minority faith practices passes with little comment.

An Overview of Regional Distinctiveness

There is a long history of arguments that regionalism is a defining element of Canadian social and political life. Confederation itself began on shaky foundations, geographic location has generated varied economic prospects, immigration histories have spawned distinct cultures and memories, and growth in provincial jurisdiction has entrenched political diversity.[8] We began the present analysis by pointing to growing differences in party systems between provinces and territories, and increased separation between federal and provincial parties. All this reinforces the belief that "region" counts heavily in public policy making, popular opinion, and the character of party oppositions.

In recent years, Jared Wesley has led a team of colleagues in administering and interpreting provincial election studies. In doing so, they have drawn a nuanced portrait that highlights both commonalities and differences. Wesley's own overview points to sometimes striking cross-regional similarities in attitudes towards issues such as taxation, the environment, health care, and morality, as well as towards overall left-right placement.[9] There are important regional differences, however, and he points to the increasing disentanglement of provinces party systems from one another as well as major variations across regions in the shape of political oppositions.

How does the play of religion in party politics fit into this discussion? We have already seen that Quebec stands out for the willingness of parties to politicize the recognition of minority faiths, a conclusion that echoes Wesley's analysis of variations on other fronts. Its residents are significantly less likely to attend religious services than are any other residents in Canada, even while francophones continue to identify themselves with Catholicism and support the retention of public displays reflecting their Catholic heritage. This is the province in which anti-clericalism is strongest, and, along with this comes significant public support for strict forms of secularism. Quebec has the weakest religious right and, therefore, the smallest sustained opposition to policies aimed at easing women's access to abortion or at securing sexual minority rights. While this has not translated into particularly avant-garde policy making on this front, when policy reforms have come, they have done so with cross-party support. These distinctive features have contributed to the prominence given to minority religious recognition in Quebec and to the willingness of the lead sovereigntist party to play on prejudicial sentiment, particularly towards Muslims.

There are important differences across other regional boundaries in Canada, even if not on quite this scale. British Columbia has a large population of non-believers but also sizable evangelical community relatively concentrated in one or two geographic areas. Alberta has an even larger population of religious conservatives, evangelicals prominent among them – and the same applies broadly to Saskatchewan and Manitoba. We have seen in our case studies that there have been important variations across other regions with regard to popular opinion and public policy in issue areas that have been the focus of faith-based mobilization.

At the same time, there are also notable signs of convergence. This derives, in part, from a significant decline in social conservatism in Alberta and the Atlantic region over recent years and, in part, from a recognition among parties that developing high-profile policy commitments reflective of the preferences of moral traditionalists loses more votes than it gains. Courts have played a role, of course, by limiting room for policy discretion on the rights of sexual minorities and women's access to abortion. On questions of minority religious recognition, courts have likewise played a role in narrowing the room for manoeuvre, but, as we have seen, most party leaders across Canada have also seen the potential for vote gains among religious and ethno-cultural minorities.

Canada in Comparative Context

The question of whether cross-country similarities overshadow regional distinctions depends in part on the size of our comparative frame. If we broaden our view to other Western industrialized democracies, some internal diversity diminishes in significance, potentially even in relation to Quebec. The basic contours of the Westminster parliamentary system apply across the country, and in their Canadian variants this comes with strong leader-dominated party discipline (outside of Nunavut and the Northwest Territories). The overall shape of the welfare state varies only modestly across Canada. All jurisdictions in Canada come under the purview of the Charter of Rights and Freedoms, which plays a particularly important role in the policy areas we have been considering.

Let us go beyond the institutional context, though, and explore levels of religiosity and public attitudes towards the issues around which faith groups have most often mobilized.

Religiosity

In exploring cross-national differences in religiosity, it is the Canadian-American contrast that leaps most strongly to the foreground. As Table C.2 shows, Canadians are significantly less likely to attend religious services than are Americans, even accounting for overstatements in survey respondents on questions such as this. They are also less likely

Table C.2   Religiosity in selected countries, 1981–2012 (%)

	Religion very important		*Attends weekly+*		*Never attends*
	2002	*2015*	*1981*	*2005–09*	*2005–09*
Canada	30	27	31	25	35
US	59	53	43	36	26
Britain	33	21	14	17	47
France	11	14	11	7	60
Italy	27	26	32	32	12
Poland	36	28	–	58	5
Australia	–	18	17	14	49

Sources: Pew Global Attitudes Project, "Among Wealthy Nations, US Stands Alone in Its Embrace of Religion," December 19, 2002, http://www.pewglobal.org/files/pdf/167.pdf; Pew Global Attitudes Project, "Americans Are in the Middle of the Pack Globally When It Comes to Importance of Religion," December 23, 2015, http://www.pewresearch.org/fact-tank/2015/12/23/americans-are-in-the-middle-of-the-pack-globally-when-it-comes-to-importance-of-religion/; World Values Survey, http://www.worldvaluessurvey.org/wvs.jsp.

to say that religion is very important in their lives. On such questions, of course, it is the United States that is the outlier among rich industrialized countries.[10] When looking at the reported importance of religion in respondents' lives, Canadians fit within the relatively secular set of responses found in Europe and Australia. Canadians are somewhat more likely to attend religious services than are Europeans as a whole, especially those living in western Europe. Setting such differences alongside the regional variations across Canada (see the Introduction), we find no region in this country that comes close to the religiosity of Americans. The data do indicate that Quebeckers are closer to the French and to northern Europeans in their abandonment of church attendance than to Canadians in other regions, but such variation is still broadly within the context of a relatively secularized society, closer to the European average than to that of the United States.

Canada is unusual in its religious diversity. The sizable Roman Catholic population in British North America prior to Confederation required some degree of protection of religious minority rights, if only for strategic reasons. The fact that no single denomination was numerically dominant on the Protestant side also prevented any sustained efforts to privilege one sect over others. Massive waves of immigration throughout the nineteenth and twentieth centuries contributed to further religious diversification, particularly when public policy changes resulted in dramatic increases in migrants from outside Europe and North America. Canada not only has a high proportion of immigrants in its population but also extraordinary diversity in countries of origin and ethno-religious background. A sizable set of Muslim communities, themselves highly varied in geographic roots, exists alongside significant and visible population of Jews, Hindus, Sikhs, Buddhists, and other faiths.

Public Beliefs on Abortion and Sexual Diversity

If we switch to a comparison of attitudes on abortion and sexuality, Canada is lodged even more firmly in the European camp. As we see in Table C.3, the proportion of Canadians who see abortion as "unacceptable" is half of that in the US, but it does not stand out particularly in other industrialized countries.[11] A similar pattern appears on attitudes

Table C.3   Conservative attitudes on abortion and
homosexuality, 2013

| | % saying morally unacceptable | |
	Abortion	Homosexuality
Canada	26	15
US	49	37
Britain	25	17
France	14	14
Italy	41	19
Poland	47	44
Australia	26	18

Source: Pew Global Attitudes Survey, "Global Views on Morality,"
April 15, 2014, www.pewglobal.org/category/datasets/2013.

to homosexuality, once again positioning this country close to the norm in western Europe. And here, too, the variations across regions within this country are relatively modest, especially when juxtaposed to US responses.

Religious Traditionalism and Party Politics

Where does Canada fit when it comes to the impact of faith on party systems? There are similarities, but also major contrasts, with the US case. For forty years, the American party system has born the unmistakable imprint of religious contestation, more so than the Canadian. Prior to that, the main US political parties were not as denominationally distinct as the Canadian Liberal and Progressive Conservative parties at the federal level, but Protestants did lean to the Republicans and Catholics favoured Democrats. In addition, denominational prejudice was widespread enough to generate concern over whether John F. Kennedy's Catholicism was a political liability in the 1960 presidential race. From the late 1980s on, however, the "axis" of contention shifted away from denominational considerations to one in which moral traditionalism was the centrepiece.[12] Even more than they already did, beginning in the 1970s the Republicans drew increasing support from religious conservatives across denominational lines, and, since that time, the party has explicitly associated itself with causes championed by the religious right. In return, evangelicals in particular have tended to see Republican support as an essential element of their religious identity.[13] This reflects, in part, the much more significant presence of evangelicals and other religious conservatives in the US than in Canada, and their effective mobilization of resources within the Republic Party.[14]

Religious conservatives in Canada represent a much smaller proportion of the population than do religious conservatives in the US, identify more equivocally with parties on the right, and work inside a disciplined party system that reduces their leverage. As a result, major parties across Canada, and their electorates, have been less polarized than the two main American parties and their supporters when it comes to the hot button issues of abortion and the political recognition of sexual diversity, even with the faith realignment of Canadian party systems that we have seen in recent decades. Though Canadian evangelicals are frequently in the front ranks of social conservative advocacy, there are elements of political "civility" among them and an accommodation to differences of view that are more difficult to find among their American counterparts.[15] If the metaphor of culture war has had resonance in American party politics over the last decades, it has only faint resonance, if any at all, north of the border.

Similarities to the Canadian pattern can be found in Britain, where the Conservative Party moved further right under Margaret Thatcher and more than ever became the main recipient of support from religious traditionalists across denominations. That party was traditionally thought the natural home of adherents of the Church of England, and Labour attracted disproportionate numbers of Protestant nonconformists and Catholics.[16] This distinction survives to some extent, but there have been subtle shifts produced by the Conservative Party's rightward turn, even if it was preoccupied by reducing taxation and the influence of labour unions. Like their contemporary Canadian counterparts, British Conservatives were much more selective than their Republican soulmates in advancing a morally traditionalist agenda – avoiding abortion almost entirely.[17] In recent years, the Conservative Party's leadership has moved towards embracing legal equality for sexual minorities, but in election campaigns they do attempt to signal their understanding of conservative Christians.[18]

Continental Europe has quite different stories. In the Protestant-dominated Scandinavian countries, the decline in religiosity has been more pronounced than in Canada, and recent decades have seen little sustained partisan conflict over morality issues. Where Catholicism was in the majority, Christian Democratic parties or their equivalents long relied on a solid core of support from those still adherent to the faith. Some such parties took their distance from the Roman Catholic hierarchy from early on in the post-Second World-War period, but the pressures of secularization have led to a further de-Christianization of their appeals.[19] In countries like Spain, France, and Belgium, all with very large nominally Catholic majorities, rates of attendance at religious services are significantly lower than they are in Canada. For a time, countries with a high proportion of Roman Catholics and strong Christian Democratic parties were slow to liberalize abortion regula-tion, and to recognize same-sex relationships, but in more recent years even centre right governments have lowered the access bars to abortion and opened the doors to the recognition of same-sex relationships. As Isabelle Engeli and her associates point out, "morality issues are becoming increasingly unpleasant because they tend to threaten the broad appeal of these parties by pushing them to reaffirm a set of pot-entially divisive Christian moral values."[20] Spain's Popular Party strongly opposed same-sex marriage and change in abortion regulation in 2005, though once elected to government it seemed to pay heed to changes in public opinion and took no significant steps to reverse those poli-cies.[21] Shifts in opinion are as dramatic in most of Europe as they have been in Canada, and this has been an important contributor to policy change. As Kelly Kollman argues, the legal recognition of same-sex re-lationships has become something of a norm in Europe and other Western regions, shaping policy in all but the most religious of coun-tries.[22] Changes in policy and opinion on abortion have not been as dramatic, and there are several countries in which access to abortion is still restricted, but the steady shift towards increasing access has crossed almost all of the Western democratic world.[23]

Most of Europe's extreme right-wing parties lack a strong religious foundation and show little interest in upholding traditional values. France's Front National and its equivalents across the continent have paid little attention to morality politics, focusing instead on portraying immigrants as a threat to jobs as well as to established social and cultural norms. In some cases, most notably the Netherlands, anti-immigrant mobilizing has framed Muslim communities as a religiously based threat to the progressivism of social policy.[24] Other parties on the right that focus on tax reduction and deregulation also have had little appetite for opposing moral change and often include libertarians advocating a reduction in state intervention on what they construe as family matters.

Throughout the "postindustrial" world, we find a gradual faith "dealignment" and a reduction in partisan conflict on the issues that have historically mobilized religious communities, with the exceptions being the United States and a few countries in southern and eastern Europe where religious faith still holds sway. As Norris and Inglehart point out, religiosity is still associated with traditionalist views, and it remains the most powerful "social background" predictor of voting for rightist parties.[25] But in the most advanced countries, this is a declining phenomenon, with a notable reduction in the strength of that relationship across almost all of Europe between the 1980s and the 2000s.

Religious Minorities and Party Politics

What has been more prominent across much of Europe, and now the United States, is the politicization of immigration in general, and Muslim community presence in particular. Anti-immigrant sentiment is a crucial driver of support for parties on the radical right from one end of Europe to the other, and the Muslim community is typically the explicit or implied target of attack.[26] Parties such as the Swedish Democrats, the National Front in France, Italy's Northern League, the Party for Freedom in the Netherlands, and the Alternative for Germany have all risen to prominence, and they are rising further on the crest of the refugee wave provoked by the civil war in Syria.

Muslims constitute the largest religious minority across most of western Europe, averaging 6 percent across the whole continent and between 5 and 8 percent in Austria, Belgium, France, Germany, the Netherlands, Sweden, Switzerland, and the UK (Muslims represent about 3 percent of the Canadian population and 1 percent of the US).[27] Several European countries have imposed restrictions on religiously associated clothing, almost always targeting head and face coverings associated with Islam.[28] In some cases, such measures have acquired wide cross-party support, most notably in France.

In the US, the 2016 campaign rhetoric of Republican candidate Donald Trump included language on immigrants, and Muslims in particular, that is much in tune with Europe's radical right. Anti-immigrant sentiment in that country is typically associated with immigration from the south and, especially, with the status of undocumented immigrants from Mexico. This has no obvious religious complexion, but Trump's attacks on Muslims most certainly do, linking Islam with terrorism and with cultural values that are seen as fundamentally inimical to "American" values. This drastic infusion of partisanship into such questions represents an important break from past practice, even if it has some roots in the Republican right's approach to immigration reform. At this point, even with Trump's electoral victory, it is impossible to know if this will remain a feature of the US party system.

Nothing in Canadian party politics displays anything close to these patterns. Religious garb and Muslim integration have been politicized in Quebec and federally, but politicians advocating a charter of Quebec values took pains to distance themselves from anti-immigrant politics in France. Marine Le Pen expressed admiration for that charter during a visit to Quebec in early 2016, but she was almost universally shunned by politicians across the spectrum. Elsewhere in Canada, there is at least as much resistance to the kind of politics waged against Muslims and immigrants that has become evident in recent decades in Europe and, even more recently, in the United States. There is no room for complacency here, but to this point there is an argument to be made about Canadian distinctiveness.

Wrapping Up

The most prominent source of faith-driven contention in Canadian party politics in recent decades has been centred on "family values." This has contributed to a long-term realignment of party politics at the federal level, and across several provinces, that has seen parties on the right become the focus of electoral support and policy aspiration for religious conservatives. At the same time, parties on the left or in the centre have gradually stiffened their backs in favouring progressive social policies at odds with the preferences of moral traditionalists. In much of the country, rightist parties prioritized economic issues, deregulation, and lower taxation as they embraced neoliberalism at various times from the 1980s to the early 2000s. However, their leaders knew that their electoral coalitions included social conservatives. This current is becoming less prominent than it was, but it remains a constituency that party leaders on the right have needed to court in closely fought contests.

In public policy areas where religious conservatives have most visibly and forcibly mobilized, they have made few gains. They have sometimes slowed change – for example, by reinforcing school officials' anxiety about LGBT inclusiveness or slowing improvements in access to abortion in Atlantic Canada. But beyond such issues, social conservatives have supported a range of policy options on school funding and childcare "choice" that are congruent with their values but that also appeal to free market or libertarian impulses. There is no scientific mechanism for isolating the influence of moral traditionalists on these policy fronts, but we have no doubt that their voices have added significant pressure on those files.

In no part of the country has the political advocacy of social conservatives translated into the kind of culture war that has beset American party politics since the early 1980s. It was not just that Canadian court rulings narrowed the field of dispute over the most explosive of the issues at the centre of American conflict but that the religious vanguard of moral conservatism was demographically and organizationally weaker in Canada and less absolutist in its political agenda.[29] There are also indications that many people of faith who have adopted what we see as traditionalist or conservative positions on sexual diversity and gender are also concerned that insufficient policy attention is being paid to the provision of social services to the disadvantaged, to environmental degradation, and to other forms of social injustice.[30] Such concerns are especially evident among the young, who have also been changing their attitudes towards issues like same-sex marriage as they have come to know people whose sexual and gender identities lie outside heterosexual norms. This has not swept aside concern for upholding what they see as traditional family values, but it does mean that they are developing more pragmatism in their approach to politics. For traditionalist constituencies of all sorts, support for parties on the right is not unshakable.

The most recent federal and Quebec elections showed us that partisan contention can arise on issues related to religious minorities. This may suggest a wider unease about the integration of immigrants, exacerbated by unfamiliarity with and prejudice directed at religious practices outside the Christian (or Judeo-Christian) tradition. It may also speak to support for preserving Christian traditions even among a portion of the increasing population of non-believers. But, even at its worst, the attempts by governing parties to play on anxieties about ethno-religious minority integration, particularly with regard to Muslims, has been a far cry from what has occurred in major parts of Europe and the United States. We should never assume that we are immune to such tendencies, but it cannot be lost on political leaders and their strategic advisors that parties leading with campaigns that targeted religious minorities lost their bids for re-election.

Canada has an unusual history of religious diversification, now being amplified by large waves of non-Christian migration. This has resulted in nearly continual debates over the extent to which religious practices and institutions should be given legal and political recognition – debates that predate the Canadian federation itself. It has also led to distinctive patterns for the accommodation of differences, evident in public policy and constitutional law. Partisanship has at times played on religious divides, though more intensely in the past than in the last several decades. Along none of the axes of faith-based contention that we explore in this volume is there partisan warring of the sort that we have seen in the United States or in the European debates over immigration and integration.

So yes, faith is less influential in the lives of Canadians now than it was in the past, and the intensity of partisan conflict based on religious differences is a shadow of what it once was. However, for a sizable minority of Canadians, including Protestants, Catholics, and members of minority communities retaining attachment to faith-based identities, religion counts heavily enough to influence partisan preferences or to shape the policy choices of party leaders. Most faith-based advocacy has been mobilized by religious conservatives or by religious minorities advocating for the public recognition of their faith. Much of what they traditionally fought for is now widely recognized, even by many social conservatives, as politically settled, but there are specific issues that still arouse the passions of a range of faith-based constituencies, including sex work, physician-assisted suicide, and the conscience rights of health professionals. There are also broader concerns over the scope of, or limitations to, religious rights; over the recognition of faith practice in the public square; and, yes, over how schools educate our young. These concerns will continue to provoke contention that will mobilize faith groups across the country.

Notes

Introduction

1 Kurt Bowen, *Christians in a Secular World: The Canadian Experience* (Montreal and Kingston: McGill-Queen's University Press, 2004), 13, 28.

2 Mark Noll, *What Happened to Christian Canada?* (Vancouver: Regent College, 2007), 15–16. He points out that, in 1950, rates of church attendance were one-third to one-half higher than in the US, with rates in Quebec among the highest in the world.

3 Richard Johnston, "Religion and Identity: The Denominational Basis of Canadian Elections," paper presented at the annual meeting of the Canadian Political Science Association, Waterloo, May 2011, 3.

4 The 2015 data are from the Angus Reid Institute, "Prayer: Alive and Well in Canada," May 8, 2015, http://angusreid.org/prayer-in-canada/. For earlier data, see Bowen, *Christians in a Secular World*, 13, 28, 32; Reginald Bibby, *Fragmented Gods: The Poverty and Potential of Religion in Canada* (Toronto: Stoddart, 1990), 17; Colin Lindsay, "Canadians Attend Religious Services Less than They Did 20 Years Ago," Statistics Canada, November 21, 2008, www.statcan.gc.ca/pub/89-630-x/2008001/article/10650-eng.htm; and "Canada's Changing Religious Landscape," Pew Forum on Religion and Public Life, June 27, 2013, www.pewforum.org/Geography/Canadas-Changing-Religious-Landscape.aspx. The 1945 Gallup Survey showed 67 percent of Canadians attending religious services within the last week; Bibby reports 31 percent in 1975, 24 percent in 1990, and 21 percent in 2000. Statistics Canada's General Social Surveys indicated that weekly attendance was 27 percent in 1985, 24 percent in 1990, 23 percent in 1995, 20 percent in 1997, and 19 percent

in 2000. Reginald Bibby writes extensively on religious belief and practice in Canada, including in his *Beyond the Gods and Back* (Lethbridge, AB: Project Canada, 2011).

5 Warren Clark and Grant Schellenberg, "Who's Religious?" *Canadian Social Trends* 81 (Summer 2006), http://www.statcan.gc.ca/pub/11-008-x/2006001/9181-eng.htm. The index combined four measures: affiliation with a religion, service attendance, personal religious practices, and affirmative responses on the importance of religion. The "high" proportion was 26 percent for people born in Canada and 41 percent among immigrants.

6 Charles Taylor, *A Secular Age* (Cambridge: Harvard University Press, 2007), chap. 1. See also José Casanova, *Public Religions in the Modern World* (Chicago: University of Chicago Press, 1999), chap. 1; Bowen, *Christians in a Secular World*, chap. 1; and Ahmet Kuru, *Secularism and State Politics toward Religion: The United States, France, and Turkey* (Cambridge: Cambridge University Press, 2009).

7 Janet Epp Buckingham is one of those arguing that we have travelled very far down the road to the privatization of religion. See her *Fighting over God: A Legal and Political History of Religious Freedom in Canada* (Montreal and Kingston: McGill-Queen's University Press, 2014).

8 According to a 2007 Pew survey, 71 percent of Canadians responded affirmatively to the statement "religion is a matter of personal faith and should be kept separate from government policy" (Pew Research Center, *Pew Global Attitudes Survey 2007*, http://www.pewglobal.org/category/datasets/2007/).

9 Bowen, *Christians in a Secular World*, 20. On the individualization of faith, see also Danièle Hervieu-Léger, "Individualism Religious and Modern," in *Re-Thinking Church, State, and Modernity*, ed. David Lyon and Marguerite Van Die, 52–65 (Toronto: University of Toronto Press, 2000).

10 For data on the question "women wanting an abortion," sources are, for 1970: Gallup – "Now thinking about the law on abortion, at the present time abortion is legal only to save a mother's life or her mental or physical health. Do you think this law should remain as is or should it be revised to permit an abortion for all who wish to have one? Yes, revise; No, do not revise." For 1985–2010: Environics – "Every woman who wants to have an abortion should be able to have one. Agree; Disagree." For data on the question of whether abortion should be legal, sources are, for 1975–92: Gallup – "Abortion should be legal under any circumstances, permitted in some circumstances, illegal under all circumstances." For 2012: Ipsos Reid – "Abortion should be permitted whenever a woman decides she wants one, should be permitted in certain circumstances, should not be permitted under any circumstances." (See Monica Boyd and Deirdre Gillieson, "Canadian Attitudes on Abortion: Results of the Gallup Polls," *Canadian Studies in Population* 2 (1975): 53–64; Environics Institute, Focus Canada 2010, 39.)

11 A 2012 Ipsos Reid survey with more choices indicates that 49 percent agreed that abortion should be permitted whenever a woman decides she wants one, up from

36 percent in 1988; and an additional 45 percent agreed that it should be permitted in "certain circumstances" (compared to 39 percent in 1988), with only 6 percent saying it should not be permitted in any circumstances. Ipsos Reid, Canadian Online Omni, June 18–25, 2012.

12   The 2002 poll is Josephine Mazzuca, "American and Canadian Attitudes on Abortion," *Gallup*, http://www.gallup.com/poll/6856/american-canadian-views -abortion.aspx. The 2005 poll is Lydia Saad, "Can a 'Reagan Revolution' Happen in Canada?," *Gallup*, http://www.gallup.com/poll/20986/can-reagan-revolution -happen-canada.aspx. The 2007 poll is Angus Reid, "Canadians Open-Minded on Relationships and Sexual Behaviour, but Not Drugs," December 20, 2007. The 2014 poll is from Pew Global Attitudes project (www.pewglobal.org). In the latter case, the survey offered as an option the response that this was not a moral issue, and fully 37 percent of Canadian respondents chose that.

13   The 2000 Canadian Election Study shows that 63 percent of Catholics agreed on easy abortion access, compared to only 27 percent of evangelicals, with the Canadian average being 66 percent. The 2011 survey asks about banning abortion, with 83 percent of Canadians disagreeing, 77 percent of Catholics, and only 43 percent of evangelicals. See André Blais, Elisabeth Gidengil, Richard Nadeau, and Neil Nevitte, 2000 Canadian Election Study (dataset), http://www.queensu.ca/cora/ces.html.

14   See Amy Langstaff, "A Twenty-Year Survey of Canadian Attitudes towards Homosexuality and Gay Rights," in *Faith, Politics, and Sexual Diversity*, ed. David Rayside and Clyde Wilcox, 49–66 (Vancouver: UBC Press, 2011); and Marc Zwelling, "Canada's Pulse: How the Gays Won" (Toronto: Vector Research and Development, 2004). For an analysis of early polling on homosexuality, see David Rayside and Scott Bowler, "Public Opinion and Gay Rights," *Canadian Review of Sociology and Anthropology* 25 (November 1988): 649–60. On questions related to moral disapproval, sources are for 1975–95: Reginald W. Bibby, The Bibby Report: Social Trends Canadian Style" (Toronto: Stoddard, 1995), http://www.reginaldbibby. com/images/The_Bibby_Report_MASTER.pdf. For 1975–2001: Gallup –"What about sexual relations between two adults of the same sex – do you think it is always wrong, almost always wrong, wrong only sometimes, or not wrong at all." For 2005–10: World Values Survey – "Homosexuality 'never' or 'always' justified." For 2014: Pew Global Attitudes – "Homosexuality as morally acceptable (30%); morally unacceptable (15%); not a moral issue (50%)."

15   Langstaff, "Twenty-Year Survey," 53. See also Mark Kennedy, *Poll Shows Wide Support for Abortion Rights, Gay Marriage*, http://o.canada.com/news/poll-shows-wide -support-for-abortion-rights-gay-marriage. Until 1987, only 10 percent of Canadians "approved" of homosexuality, and just 48 percent did so in 2004. Positive sentiment came only after that, with 70 percent agreeing in 2007 that homosexuality should be accepted by society.

16   Ipsos Reid, Canadian Online Omni, June 18–25, 2012.

17 Patrick Fournier, Fred Cutler, Stuart Soroka, and Dietlind Stolle, 2011 Canadian Election Study (dataset), 2011, http://www.queensu.ca/cora/ces.html. Note that the number of evangelical and Muslim respondents is quite small, reducing the reliability of these findings, though they accord with data from many other surveys.

18 Jonathan Malloy suggests 10 percent in "Canadian Evangelicals and Same-Sex Marriage," in Rayside and Wilcox, *Faith, Politics, and Sexual Diversity*, 145. Reginald Bibby suggests 8 percent, in "Restless Gods and Restless Youth," paper presented at the Annual Meeting of the Canadian Sociological Association, May 2009. See also Rick Hiemstra, "Counting Canadian Evangelicals," *Centre for Research on Canadian Evangelicism*, Church and Faith Trends, October 2007, http://www.evangelicalfellowship.ca/page.aspx?pid=5074.

19 When we present data throughout this study, we use the term "evangelical protestants," or "evangelicals," to refer to those who attend denominations that are full members of the Evangelical Fellowship of Canada. A full list is available at http://www.evangelicalfellowship.ca/denominations and includes Baptists, Mennonites, and Christian Reformed congregations in addition to those more traditionally thought of as evangelical, such as Pentecostals. We acknowledge that the denominations that make up the EFC hold a wide spectrum of views, with some, such as the various branches of the Mennonite faith, aligning more with mainline churches on matters of social justice and international solidarity. Beyond the confines of reporting on data, we also refer to evangelicals somewhat more broadly, recognizing that there are members of mainline Protestant denominations who see themselves as evangelical even if they would not be captured by a purely "denominational" definition. In data reporting, we treat the "mainline" protestant denominations as the Anglican, United, Presbyterian, and Lutheran churches, which do not belong to the EFC.

20 The 2015 Canadian Election Study did not include questions on abortion or traditional values, hence the use of 2011 data.

21 David McGrane, "Centrism, Ideological Polarization, and the Canadian Provincial Voter," in *Provinces: Canadian Provincial Politics*, 3rd ed., ed. Christopher Dunn, 184–216 (Toronto: University of Toronto Press, 2016).

22 The literature on religion and partisan alignments, mostly focused on denominational differences, includes: John Meisel, "Religious Affiliation and Electoral Behaviour: A Case Study," *Canadian Journal of Economics and Political Science* 22, 4 (1956): 481–96; William P. Irvine, "Explaining the Religious Basis of the Canadian Partisan Identity," *Canadian Journal of Political Science* 7, 3 (1974): 560–63; Richard Johnston, "The Reproduction of the Religious Cleavage in Canadian Elections," *Canadian Journal of Political Science* 18, 1 (1985): 99–113; James L. Guth and Cleveland R. Fraser, "Religion and Partisanship in Canada," *Journal for the Scientific Study of Religion* 40, 1 (2001): 51–64; Paul Bélanger and Munroe Eagles, "The Geography

of Class and Religion in Canadian Elections Revisited," *Canadian Journal of Political Science* 39, 3 (2006): 591–609.

23   There is little analytical literature on faith-based social movements in Canada, but that which exists includes Reginald Stackhouse Jr., "Bearing Witness: Christian Groups Engage Canadian Politics Since the 1960s," in *Rethinking Church, State, and Modernity*, ed. David Lyon and Marguerite Van Die, 113–28 (Toronto: University of Toronto Press, 2000). From an evangelical perspective, see Michael Wagner, *Standing on Guard for Thee*, 2nd ed. (St. Catharines, ON: Freedom Press, 2012); and from the point of view of an LGBT advocate, see Tom Warner, *Losing Control: Canada's Social Conservatives in the Age of Rights* (Toronto: Between the Lines, 2010). Marci McDonald argues the case that the federal Conservatives are substantially shaped by the evangelical predilections of their leaders in her *The Armageddon Factor: The Rise of Christian Nationalism in Canada* (Toronto: Random House of Canada, 2006).

24   Statistics Canada, 2011 National Household Survey: Data Tables, Religion (108), http://www12.statcan.gc.ca/nhs-enm/2011/.

25   It was formed in 2000 as the Canadian Council on American-Islamic Relations, basically a branch of an already established US group. In 2013, it adopted its new name.

26   Statistics Canada, 2011, National Household Survey.

27   Brian Clarke, "English-Speaking Canada from 1854," in *A Concise History of Christianity in Canada*, ed. Terrence Murphy (Toronto: Oxford University Press, 1996), 297.

28   See, for example, Ronald Manzer, *Educational Regimes and Anglo-American Democracy* (Toronto: University of Toronto Press, 2003).

29   Robert D. Putnam and David E. Campbell, *American Grace: How Religion Divides and Unites Us* (New York: Simon and Schuster, 2010), 2.

30   Janet R. Jakobsen, "Beyond Tolerance," in *Religion and Sexuality: Diversity and the Limits of Tolerance*, ed. Pamela Dickey Young, Heather Shipley, and Tracy J. Trothen (Vancouver: UBC Press, 2015), 22.

31   Putnam and Campbell point to pragmatism among conservative Christians, and to attitude shifts among the young, in *American Grace*, chap. 4 The co-existence of pragmatism and orthodoxy among Canadian and American evangelicals is also an important theme for Lydia Bean in *The Politics of Evangelical Identity* (Princeton, NJ: Princeton University Press, 2014), chap 1.

32   Janine Brodie and Jane Jenson, "Piercing the Smokescreen: Stability and Change in Brokerage Politics," and Steve Patten, "The Evolution of the Canadian Party System," in *Canadian Parties in Transition*, ed. Alain-G. Gagnon and A. Brian Tanguay, 33–53, 55–79, respectively (Toronto: University of Toronto Press, 2011); and various contributions in James Farney and David Rayside, eds., *Conservatism in Canada* (Toronto: University of Toronto Press, 2013).

33 Sam Reimer, "Are American and Canadian Evangelicals Really That Different?," *Faith Today*, May-June 2016; Bean, *Politics of Evangelical Identity*, 10–15. Through the 2000s and the 2010s, upwards of three-quarters of white US evangelicals voted Republican – over 80 percent in 2016. In Canada, during the late 2000s and early 2010s, about 70 percent of Canadian evangelicals voted for the federal Conservatives, but that declined to just over 50 percent in 2015.

34 *Canada (Attorney General) v. Bedford*, 2013 SCC 72, [2013] 3 S.C.R. 1101.

35 An Environics Survey conducted in 1990 shows that 70 percent of Canadians opposed this accommodation and 59 percent strongly opposed; see *Research Digest*, "Do Canadians Really Have a Problem with the Niqab?," Environics Institute, http://www.environicsinstitute.org/research-digest/research-commentary/do -canadians-really-have-a-problem-with-the-niqab.

36 See Environics Institute, *Survey of Muslims in Canada 2016* (Toronto: Environics Institute and Tessellate Institute, April 2016), http://www.environicsinstitute.org/ institute-projects/completed-projects/survey-muslims-canada-2016.

37 In 2016, 58 percent disagreed that there was too much immigration, a pattern with considerable uniformity across all regions. Environics Institute, Focus Canada Spring 2016: "Attitudes about Immigration and Citizenship," 3, http://www. environicsinstitute.org/institute-projects/current-projects/focus-canada-2016 -immigration-and-citizenship.

38 Jack Jedwab, "Identity, Intergroup Relations and Concerns over Racism," unpublished paper, April 2014. The proportion "worried" about immigration was 51 percent among francophones, 42 percent among anglophones, and 33 percent among speakers of other languages. Concern about non-Christian immigrants was expressed by 53 percent of francophones, 38 percent of anglophones, and 29 percent of those speaking other languages,

39 A 2016 Environics survey found that 33 percent of Canadians had a generally negative view of Islam, down from 38 percent in 2006, with 42 percent a positive view, down 7 percent. See Environics Institute, *Survey of Muslims in Canada 2016*.

40 Environics Institute, "Focus Canada 2010," 33, http://www.environicsinstitute.org/ uploads/institute-projects/pdf-focuscanada2010.pdf .

41 Between 1989 and 2001, attendance rates among the Canadian-born declined from 35 percent to 28 percent, but among the foreign-born it increased from 42 to 45 percent. See Warren Clark, "Pockets of Belief: Religious Attendance Patterns in Canada," *Canadian Social Trends* 5 (Spring 2003), http://www.statcan.gc.ca/ sites/default/files/6493-eng.pdf.

42 Bibby, *Beyond the Gods and Back*, 6.

43 The Bloc Québécois also used the niqab issue aggressively, though in the end it succeeded more in reducing Quebeckers' support for the NDP than in regaining electoral strength.

44 Environics Institute, Focus Canada 2010, 29. In 2015, 57 percent disagreed that there was too much immigration, a pattern with considerable uniformity across all regions. See Environics Institute, Focus Canada Spring 2015: "Canadian Public Opinion about Immigration and Multiculturalism," 3, http://www.environics institute.org/institute-projects/completed-projects/focus-canada-2015-immigration -and-multiculturalism.

45 For a discussion of the broader philosophical issues involved in schools debates, see Manzer, *Educational Regimes;* and Alison Bradley, "Religious Rights and Quebec's Ethics and Religious Culture Course," *Canadian Journal of Political Science* 44, 3 (2011): 613–33.

46 This is centred at the University of Alberta, under the direction of Jared Wesley. See Jared Wesley, ed., *Big Worlds: Politics and Elections in the Canadian Provinces and Territories* (Toronto: University of Toronto Press, 2015).

Chapter 1: Conservative Faith and Federal Parties

1 On the dramatic changes through this period, and the question of party realignment in general, see R. Kenneth Carty, William Cross, and Lisa Young, *Rebuilding Canadian Party Politics* (Vancouver: UBC Press, 2000); Lawrence LeDuc, "Realignment and Dealignment in Canadian Federal Politics," Janine Brodie and Jane Jenson, "Piercing the Smokescreen: Stability and Change in Brokerage Politics," in *Canadian Parties in Transition*, 3rd ed., ed. Alain-G. Gagnon and A. Brian Tanguay, 163–77, 33–53, respectively (Peterborough: Broadview Press, 2007); and Steve Patten, "The Evolution of the Canadian Party System," in *Canadian Parties in Transition*, 4th ed. ed. Gagnon and Tanguay, 3–27 (Toronto: University of Toronto Press, 2017).

2 John Meisel, "Religious Affiliation and Electoral Behaviour: A Case Study," *Canadian Journal of Economics and Political Science* 22, 4 (1956): 481–96.

3 William Irvine, "Explaining the Religious Basis of the Canadian Partisan Identity: Success on the Third Try," *Canadian Journal of Political Science* 7, 3 (1974): 560. See also Laura Stephenson, "The Catholic-Liberal Connection: A Test of Strength," in *Voting Behaviour in Canada*, ed. Cameron D. Anderson and Laura B. Stephenson, 86–104 (Vancouver: UBC Press, 2010); and Elisabeth Gidengil, Neil Nevitte, André Blais, Joanna Everitt, and Patrick Fournier, *Dominance and Decline: Making Sense of Recent Canadian Elections* (Toronto: University of Toronto Press, 2012), 19–21.

4 Richard Johnston, "The Reproduction of the Religious Cleavage in Canadian Elections," *Canadian Journal of Political Science* 18 (1985): 99–113; Richard Johnston, "Religion and Identity: The Denominational Basis of Canadian Elections," paper presented at the Annual Meeting of the Canadian Political Science Association, Waterloo, May 2011; James L. Guth and Cleveland R. Fraser, "Religion and Partisanship in Canada," *Journal for the Scientific Study of Religion* 40, 1 (2001): 51–64; Paul Bélanger and Munroe Eagles, "The Geography of Class and Religion in Canadian Elections Revisited," *Canadian Journal of Political Science* 39, 3 (2006): 591–609.

5 In 2015, Catholics outside of Quebec were more likely than were mainline Protestants to vote Liberal (+7 percent), less likely to vote Tory (–8 percent), and slightly more likely to vote NDP (+2 percent). Evangelicals are far more likely than either to vote Tory: +12 percent compared to mainline Protestants, and +18 percent compared to Catholics (Canadian Election Study).

6 This is noted by Guth and Fraser, "Religion and Partisanship in Canada," 52; and Bélanger and Eagles, "Geography of Class and Religion," 602.

7 An Angus Reid exit poll in 2015 indicates that 52 percent of evangelicals supported the Conservatives, 20 percent the Liberals, and 10 percent the NDP. See Sam Reimer, "Are American and Canadian Evangelicals Really That Different?" *Faith Today*, May-June 2016, 28–32. The 2015 Canadian Election Study similarly finds that 52 percent of evangelicals outside of Quebec supported the Conservatives, 25 percent the Liberals, and 17 percent the NDP.

8 It is difficult to track religiosity over a long period since the questions used to tap it have varied and the language used is often general enough to defy confident analysis.

9 In 1968, Canadian Election Study respondents were asked how often they attended religious services, with a not-very-demanding threshold of once a month or more. By this standard, Liberal support among attenders outside Quebec was 7 percent more than among non-attenders. The PCs had the same level of support among attenders and non-attenders overall, and the NDP had 7 percent less. The 1984 survey asked if respondents considered themselves religious. Liberals were most successful among those responding "very religious" (30 percent), a little less so among "fairly religious" (28 percent), and least among the "not very religious" (19 percent). Only 7 percent of very religious respondents supported the NDP, compared to 22 percent among the not religious. These results held both inside and outside Quebec. In 1988, a slightly different question was asked – "how important is religion in your life?" – and here, too, Liberals had a higher proportion of supporters who considered it important than any other party.

10 Gidengil and her associates, for example, find that, in the new Conservative Party's first two elections, personal religiosity tilted voters moderately towards it, but not in 2008. Gidengil et al., *Dominance and Decline*, 47. See also Joe Friesen, "Why Did Catholics Stop Voting Liberal?" *Globe and Mail*, February 24, 2014.

11 Ipsos Reid, "2011 Canadian Federal Election Exit Poll," May 2, 2011; and Sarah Wilkins-Laflamme, "The Changing Religious Cleavage in Canadians' Voting Behaviour," *Canadian Journal of Political Science* 49, 3 (2016): 499–518.

12 Gidengil et al. point out that, in 2008, 40 percent of religious Catholics supported the Conservatives, compared to 47 percent of the less religious. See Gidengil et al., *Dominance and Decline*, 25–26.

13 This is a point made by Ron Rayside, who indicates that respect for the community contributions of such agencies likely persists even in secular regions of Quebec.

14 See Stephenson, "Catholic-Liberal Connection," 95–98.

15 Tom Flanagan, interview with authors, May 17, 2011.

16 Elisabeth Gidengil, André Blais, Joanna Everitt, Patrick Fournier, and Neil Nevitte, "Back to the Future? Making Sense of the 2004 Canadian Election outside Quebec," *Canadian Journal of Political Science* 39, 1 (2006): 1–25. The estimated probability of voting for the Conservatives was enhanced substantially among Protestant literalists particularly, controlling for other factors.

17 The 2011 Canadian Election Study shows that, overall, 55 percent of voters outside Quebec supported the Conservatives, but, among literalists, the proportions were 84 percent for evangelicals, 77 percent for mainline Protestants, and 64 percent for Catholics.

18 The 1968 Canadian Election Study found that the criminalization of homosexuality was strongly opposed by just 36 percent among Liberals and 33 percent among Progressive Conservatives (and not much different at this early stage for NDPers – 37 percent).

19 Christopher Cochrane, *Left and Right: The Small World of Political Ideas* (Montreal and Kingston: McGill-Queen's University Press, 2015).

20 Gidengil et al., *Dominance and Decline*, 46. An index of moral traditionalism was constructed from responses to questions about women staying home with their children, how much should be done for women, sympathy with feminism, same-sex marriage, and feelings about gays and lesbians (189–90).

21 This is a point on which others agree, most notably Barry J. Kay, Steven D. Brown, and Andrew M. Perrella, "The Religion Enigma: Theoretical Riddle or Classificational Artifact," paper prepared for the annual meeting of the American Political Science Association, Toronto, September 2009, cited in Jonathan Malloy, "Between America and Europe: Religion, Politics and Evangelicals in Canada," *Politics, Religion and Ideology* 12, 3 (2011): 326–27.

22 No question related to abortion was included in the 2015 Canadian Election Study.

23 Abacus Data, "Canadians' Moral Compass Set Differently from That of Our Neighbours to the South," July 9, 2016, http://abacusdata.ca/canadians-moral-compass-set-differently-from-that-of-our-neighbours-to-the-south/.

24 Antoine Bilodeau and Mebs Kanji, "The New Immigrant Voter, 1965–2004," in *Voting Behaviour in Canada*, ed. Cameron D. Anderson and Laura B. Stephenson, 65–85 (Vancouver: UBC Press, 2010).

25 Gidengil et al., "Back to the Future?," 6–7.

26 Gidengil et al., *Dominance and Decline*, 24–25.

27 Darrell Bricker and John Ibbitson, *The Big Shift* (Toronto: HarperCollins, 2014), 25, 32–35. Among immigrants in the country fewer than ten years, 28 percent voted Conservative; more than ten years, 45 percent. Bricker and Ibbitson also suggest that the attraction to Conservatives was stronger among Asian voters than among minority voters from other parts of the world.

28 Reported in Selina Chignall, "Immigrants Are Not a Monolithic Voting Block," *iPolitics*, September 22, 2015, http://ipolitics.ca/2015/09/22/immigrants-are-not-a -monolithic-voting-block/.

29 Michael Adams and Robin Brown, "Are Immigrants Natural Conservatives? Think Again," *Globe and Mail*, December 27, 2013.

30 Jeffrey Simpson reports on an Ipsos Reid poll showing that, in the 2011 election, 52 percent voted Conservative, compared to 24 percent who voted Liberals, and 16 percent who voted NDP (Jeffrey Simpson, "How the Political Shift among Jewish Voters Plays in Canada," *Globe and Mail*, September 28, 2011). See also Craig Offman, "Jewish Community Finds a Friend in Harper," *Globe and Mail*, November 30, 2013.

31 An additional 26 percent of Conservatives "somewhat" agree. Environics Institute, Focus Canada 2012, Detailed Data Tables, 156, http://www.environics institute.org/uploads/institute-projects/focus%20canada%202012%20-%20 banner%20tables%20-%20february%201-2013.pdf.

32 This point is made by Lydia Bean in *The Politics of Evangelical Identity* (Princeton: Princeton University Press, 2014), 38–39.

33 See David Rayside, *On the Fringe: Gays and Lesbians in Politics* (Ithaca, NY: Cornell University Press, 1998), 109–11.

34 Michael Wagner, *Standing on Guard for Thee*, 2nd ed. (St. Catharines, ON: Freedom Press, 2012), 83–89.

35 See Rayside, *On the Fringe*, chap. 4; Wagner, *Standing on Guard for Thee*, 135–43.

36 Jonathan Malloy cites Michael Lisztig and Matthew Wilson ["A New Right? Moral Issues and Partisan Change in Canada," *Social Science Quarterly* 86, 1 (2005): 111] in suggesting that moral conservatism was an important force in evangelicals switching from the PCs to Reform, cited in Malloy, "Between America and Europe," 326.

37 For an analysis of the ways in which non-Conservative parties pushed religious conservatives away, see Don Hutchinson and Rick Hiemstra, "Canadian Evangelical Voting Trends by Region, 1996–2008," Centre for Research on Canadian Evangelicism, *Church and Faith Trends* 2, 3 (2009), http://files.efc-canada.net/min/rc/cft/ V02I03/Evangelical_Voting_Trends_1996-2008.pdf. On the 2000 election more generally, see Edward Greenspon, "Covering Campaign 2000," and Michael Marzolini, "The Politics of Values: Designing the 2000 Liberal Campaign," in *The Canadian General Election of 2000*, ed. Jon H. Pammett and Christopher Dornan, 165–90 and 263–76, respectively (Toronto: Dundurn, 2001).

38 Among the most helpful of several major analyses of Harper are Tom Flanagan, *Harper's Team: Behind the Scenes in the Conservative Rise to Power* (Montreal and Kingston: McGill-Queen's University Press, 2007); and Paul Wells, *The Longer I'm Prime Minister: Stephen Harper and Canada, 2006–* (Toronto: Vintage Canada, 2014). Marci McDonald emphasizes Harper's attachment to evangelicism in *The Armageddon Factor: The Rise of Christian Nationalism in Canada* (Toronto: Vintage Canada, 2011).

39 Quoted in Lawrence Martin, *Harperland: The Politics of Control* (Toronto: Viking Canada, 2010), 244.

40 Quoted in Wells, *Longer I'm Prime Minister*, 55. For his extended commentary on the Civitas speech, see 55–61. See also Bean, *Politics of Evangelical Identity*, 41–42.

41 Wells, *Longer I'm Prime Minister*, 11.

42 Tom Flanagan, interview with authors, May 17, 2011.

43 Wells cites the example of veteran Reform/Conservative MP Randy White urging that the Charter of Rights and Freedoms be ignored. See Wells, *Longer I'm Prime Minister*, 34.

44 See David Rayside, "The Conservative Party of Canada and Its Religious Constituencies," in *Faith, Politics, and Sexual Diversity in Canada and the United States*, ed. David Rayside and Clyde Wilcox, 282–85 (Vancouver: UBC Press, 2011). See also Faron Ellis and Peter Woolstencroft, "Stephen Harper and the Conservatives Campaign on Their Record," in *The Canadian Federal Election of 2008*, ed. Jon H. Pammett and Christopher Dornan (Toronto: Dundurn Press, 2009), 34. It was only in 2016, after Harper had resigned as leader, that a Conservative Party convention removed its official opposition to same-sex marriage, though there was no modification of, or any thaw in, opposition to abortion and to physician-assisted suicide.

45 Wells, *Longer I'm Prime Minister*, 297, 387. See also John Ibbitson, "Harper Unbound," *Globe and Mail*, April 28, 2012.

46 The estimate of caucus numbers is reported by Douglas Todd, "Playing 'God Car': Canadians More Skeptical than Americans," *Vancouver Sun*, October 4, 2008.

47 Paul Wells, *Right Side Up: The Fall of Paul Martin and the Rise of Stephen Harper's New Conservatism* (Toronto: McClelland and Stewart, 2006), 314.

48 Chantal Hébert, "Social Conservatives Have Gained Little Ground in Stephen Harper's Government," *Toronto Star*, November 9, 2012.

49 Bricker and Ibbitson, *Big Shift*, 125. See also 102–3.

50 Bean, *Politics of Evangelical Identity*, 12, 226.

51 Malloy, "Between America and Europe," 330–31.

52 Martin, *Harperland*, 246.

53 Jason Fekete, "Tories Repeal Sections of Human Rights Act Banning Hate Speech over Telephone or Internet," *National Post*, June 7, 2012.

54 Josh Wingrove, "Amendment to Protect Gender Identity in Criminal Code Fails," *Globe and Mail*, June 10, 2014.

55 Marci McDonald, "True Blue," *Walrus*, May 2014, 35.

56 See Karen Bird and Andrea Rowe, "Women, Feminism, and the Harper Conservatives," in *Conservatism in Canada*, ed. James Farney and David Rayside (Toronto: University of Toronto Press, 2013), 171; Wells, *Longer I'm Prime Minister*, 23.

57 Tom Flanagan, interview with authors, May 17, 2011.

58 John Whyte, "Russell Brown Doesn't Belong on the Supreme Court," *Toronto Star*, August 19, 2015.

59 Robin Sears, "Harper's Dog-Whistle Politics," *Toronto Star*, October 5, 2015.

60 Martin, *Harperland*, 247. In 2012 the CBC reported $20 million grants to thirteen colleges since 2009.

61 On feminist influence, see Linda Briskin and Lynda Yanz, eds., *Union Sisters: Women in the Labour Movement* (Toronto: Women's Press, 1983). On unions responding to sexual diversity, see Gerald Hunt, ed., *Laboring for Rights* (Philadelphia: Temple University Press, 1999); and Gerald Hunt and David Rayside, ed., *Equity, Diversity, and Canadian Labour* (Toronto: University of Toronto Press, 2007).

62 Paul Sniderman, Joseph F. Fletcher, Peter H. Russell, and Philip E. Tetlock, *Clash of Rights: Liberty, Equality, and Legitimacy in Pluralist Democracies* (New Haven: Yale University Press, 1996), 105–7. On public opinion, see David Rayside and Scott Bowler, "Public Opinion and Gay Rights," *Canadian Review of Sociology and Anthropology* 25, 4 (1988): 649–60.

63 Rayside, *On the Fringe*, 130.

64 See Amy Langstaff, "A Twenty-Year Survey of Canadian Attitudes towards Homosexuality and Gay Rights," in Rayside and Wilcox, *Faith, Politics, and Sexual Diversity*, 49–66.

65 The Abortion Rights Coalition of Canada claimed that 22 out of 103 Liberal MPs were pro-life, compared to 78 of 124 Conservatives, and no New Democrats (Abortion Rights Coalition of Canada, *Position Paper #50 Abortion and the Conservative Party*, August 2007, http://www.arcc-cdac.ca/postionpapers/50-Abortion-Conservative-Party.PDF). Classifying MPs as opposed to the choice position was determined either by their voting record, by whether they had attended or spoken at a pro-life rally, or by whether they had publicly stated a policy position that was pro-life or supportive of abortion only in limited circumstances.

66 John-Henry Westen, "Liberal Party of Canada Demands Abortion Push in Maternal Health Initiative," *LifeSiteNews*, 2010, http://www.lifesitenews.com/news/archive/ldn/2010/feb/10020207.

67 "Liberals Defeat Own Family Planning Motion," *CBC News*, March 24, 2010, http://www.cbc.ca/news/politics/liberals-defeat-own-family-planning-motion-1.867247.

68 Susan Delacourt, "No Choice but Pro-Choices, Trudeau Tells Candidates," *Toronto Star*, May 8, 2014.

69 Interview, June 8, 2015.

70 Gary Mason, "Political Discourse Has Become Un-Canadian," *Globe and Mail*, October 17, 2015.

71 Nancy McDonald, "Going Its Own Way," *Maclean's Magazine*, October 26, 2015; and Tim Harper, "Tory Sees Muslim 'Agenda,'" *Toronto Star*, August 23, 2015.

72 Ryan Maloney, "Joe Daniel, Tory Candidate, Alleges Muslim Refugee 'Agenda,'" *Huffington Post*, September 23, 2015.

73 Donovan Vincent, "Niqab Issue Bolsters Tory Support: Pollster," *Toronto Star*, October 1, 2015. Polls showed that, overall, Canadian support for a ban on wearing niqabs while taking a citizenship oath varied between about 65 percent and 80 percent.

74 As we see in Chapter 8, this borrowed legislative ideas from the rancorous politicized debate among Quebec's provincial parties. See Tonda MacCharles, "Harper Ramps Up Rhetoric against Niqab," *Toronto Star*, October 7, 2015.

75 Joseph Heath, "Conservative Party Moves beyond the Pale," *In Due Course: A Canadian Public Affairs Blog*, October 5, 2015, http://induecourse.ca/conservative -party-moves-beyond-the-pale/.

76 Tim Harper, "Trudeau Challenges Harper's Politics of Fear," *Toronto Star*, October 5, 2015.

77 In the midst of the 2016 debate over physician-assisted suicide, Chantal Hébert observed that she had never seen a governing party caucus with so little dissent on a "conscience" vote and so little influenced by the religious right. See Chantal Hébert, "Unlikely Liberal Unity on C-14 Will Last," *Toronto Star*, May 7, 2016.

78 Jaime Watt, "Why the Liberals Struck a Cord," *Globe and Mail*, October 23, 2015.

79 A very large set of polls showed that 34 percent of immigrant citizens supported the Conservatives, compared to 27 percent of the native-born. See Sakshana Bascaramurty, "Rhetoric on Muslims Finds Little Backlash," *Globe and Mail*, October 14, 2015.

80 Lorna Dueck, "Why Did the Conservatives Lose so Badly?," *Context with Lorna Dueck blog*, October 20, 2015, http://www.contextwithlornadueck.com/blog/why-did -the-conservatives-lose-so-badly.

81 Reimer, "American and Canadian Evangelicals"; and Bean, *Politics of Evangelical Identity*.

82 Tom Flanagan, interview with authors, May 17, 2011.

83 Bob Hepburn, "Beware: Kellie Leitch Is on a Winning Role," *Toronto Star*, September 29, 2016. See also Laura Stone, "Leitch Defends Immigrant Screening Plan as Way to Promote Tolerance," *Globe and Mail*, September 7, 2016.

84 Forum Research, "Muslims the Target of Most Racial Bias," December 8, 2016, http://poll.forumresearch.com/post/2646/muslims-the-target-of-most-racial-bias/. The same poll showed that an even higher proportion of Bloc Québécois supporters – 44 percent – held unfavorable views.

Chapter 2: Abortion Politics and Federal Parties

1 "Harper Says He Won't Reopen Abortion Debate," *CBC News*, April 21, 2011, http:// www.cbc.ca/news/politics/harper-says-he-won-t-reopen-abortion-debate-1. 1010714.

2 Raymond Tatalovich, *The Politics of Abortion in the United States and Canada: A Comparative Study* (New York: Routledge, 1997), 84–89.

3 L. Marvin Overby, Raymond Tatalovich, and Donley T Studlar, "Party and Free Votes in Canada Abortion in the House of Commons," *Party Politics* 4, 3 (1998): 381–92.

4 Tim Bloedow, "Parliamentary Pro-Life Caucus Re-Established," *The Interim*, September 12, 1998, http://www.theinterim.com/politics/parliamentary-pro-life -caucus-re-established/; Lloyd Mackey, "Groups Explore Faith-Based Issues in

Minority Parliament: Two Parliamentary Cross-Party Groups Could Take on New Importance in 38th Minority Parliament," *Hill Times*, October 18, 2004.

5 R. Kenneth Carty, William Cross, and Lisa Young, *Rebuilding Canadian Party Politics* (Vancouver: UBC Press, 2000), 94.

6 David Rayside, "The Conservative Party of Canada and Its Religious Constituencies," in *Faith, Politics, and Sexual Diversity in Canada and the United States*, ed. David Rayside and Clyde Wilcox, 279–99 (Vancouver: UBC Press, 2011).

7 Munroe Eagles, "Constituency and Personal Determinants of MPs' Positions on Social Conservative Issues in the 37th and 38th Canadian Parliaments," in *Parties, Elections, and the Future of Canadian Politics*, ed. Amanda Bittner and Royce Koop, 67–93 (Vancouver: UBC Press, 2013).

8 James Farney, *Social Conservatives and Party Politics in Canada and the United States* (Toronto: University of Toronto Press, 2012); Melissa Haussman and L. Pauline Rankin, "Framing the Harper Government: Gender-Neutral Electoral Appeals while Being Gender-Negative in Caucus," in *How Ottawa Spends 2009-2010*, ed. Allan Maslove, 241–62 (Montreal and Kingston: McGill-Queen's University Press, 2009).

9 CBC Radio, "Abortion and the Conservative Caucus," *The Current*, February 15, 2012, http://www.cbc.ca/thecurrent/episode/2012/02/15/abortion-and-conservative -caucus/.

10 Leah A.D. McKeen, "Canadian Christian Nationalism? The Religiosity and Politics of the Christian Heritage Party of Canada" (PhD diss., Wilfrid Laurier University, 2015), 9.

11 Confidential interview, May 2012.

12 Campbell Clark, "Harper Must Make Abortion Part of Health Pledge, Ignatieff Says," *Globe and Mail*, February 2, 2010.

13 John-Henry Westen, "Liberal Party of Canada Demands Abortion Push in Maternal Health Initiative." *LifeSiteNews*, February 2, 2010, https://www.lifesitenews. com/news/liberal-party-of-canada-demands-abortion-push-in-maternal-health -initiative.

14 Campbell Clark, "Birth Control Won't Be in G8 Plan to Protect Mothers, Tories Say," *Globe and Mail*, March 17, 2010.

15 Tonda MacCharles, "Liberals Lose Vote on 'Abortion,'" *Toronto Star*, March 24, 2010.

16 Confidential interview, May 2012.

17 Ibid.

18 Aaron Wherry, "Brad Trost Goes Rogue," *MacLean's: Beyond the Commons*, September 28, 2011.

19 Keith Martin eventually crossed the floor to the Liberals in 2004 but was a Reform MP in 1997 when he introduced a bill that would have made it a criminal offence for women to harm a fetus by consuming drugs or alcohol.

20 Haussman and Rankin, "Framing the Harper Government," 242.

21 Farney, *Social Conservatives and Party Politics*, 126.
22 Parliament of Canada, *Bill C-484: An Act to Amend the Criminal Code (Injuring or Causing the Death of an Unborn Child While Committing an Offence)* (Ottawa: House of Commons, 2007), 3, http://www.parl.gc.ca/legisinfo/BillDetails.aspx?Language =E&Mode=1&billId=3097460.
23 Marci McDonald, *The Armageddon Factor: The Rise of Christian Nationalism in Canada* (Toronto: Random House, 2010), 170.
24 Campbell, "Harper Ups Ante on Election Ultimatum," *Globe and Mail*, August 26, 2008.
25 Confidential interview, May 2012.
26 Paul Wells, *The Longer I'm Prime Minister: Stephen Harper and Canada, 2006* (Toronto: Random House, 2013), 386–87.
27 Confidential interview with parliamentarian, May 2012.
28 Mark Warawa, "MP Mark Warawa Introduces Motion to Condemn Discrimination against Females via Sex-Selective Pregnancy Termination," *Mark Warawa, MP for Langley-Aldergrove*, September 27, 2012, http://www.markwarawa.com/stop -gendercide/news-releases/mp-mark-warawa-introduces-motion-to-condemn -discrimination-against-females-via-sex-selective-pregnancy-termination.
29 Glen McGregor, "Anti-Abortion Group Looking to Run Candidates as Conservatives in Ottawa Ridings," *Canada.com*, December 5, 2013.
30 Parliament of Canada, *Order Paper and Notice Paper No. 33* (Ottawa: House of Commons, December 9, 2013), http://www.parl.gc.ca/HousePublications/ Publication.aspx?Language=E&Mode=1&Parl=41&Ses=2&DocId=6375360& File=7.
31 Ibid.
32 Ibid.
33 C-484 contained exemptions lacking in C-291; C-510 did not actually recognize the fetus in law but, rather, dealt with coercion of the mother; M-312 would not have changed any laws directly but, instead, would have established a committee to investigate them.
34 Michel Viatteau, "Sex-Selective Abortion Could Be Prevented by Keeping Fetuses' Sexes Secret: Canadian Medical Association Journal," *National Post*, January 16, 2012.
35 Paul Saurette and Kelly Gordon, "Arguing Abortion: The New Anti-Abortion Discourse in Canada," *Canadian Journal of Political Science* 46, 1 (2013): 157–85.
36 As we pointed out in the Introduction, Mennonite denominations are members of the Evangelical Fellowship of Canada, but many of their congregations tend towards more moderate positions and also ally themselves with the Canadian Council of Churches in addition to the EFC.
37 Confidential interview, May 2012.
38 Ibid.
39 Ibid.

40 Alice Musabende, "Long-Time Social Conservative MPs Bid a Bittersweet Farewell to Ottawa," *iPolitics*, June 23, 2015, http://ipolitics.ca/2015/06/23/long-time-social -conservative-mps-bid-a-bittersweet-farewell-to-ottawa/.

41 The Christian Heritage Party had mobilized its membership in defence of the pro-life private member's initiatives brought forward by Conservative backbenchers during the Harper years. See McKeen, *Canadian Christian Nationalism?*, 163–66.

42 This assessment comes from a well-connected observer, interview, June 8, 2015.

43 Trinh Theresa Do, "Harper Won't Fund Abortion Globally because It's 'Extremely Divisive,'" *CBC News*, May 29, 2014, http://www.cbc.ca/news/politics/harper -won-t-fund-abortion-globally-because-it-s-extremely-divisive-1.2658828.

44 Mark Kennedy, "Stephen Harper Takes Jab at Trudeau's Abortion Policy, Says Tories Won't 'Impose Views on People.'" *National Post*, June 20, 2014.

45 This a point that Lydia Bean makes in her ethnographic exploration of four evangelical communities on either side of the Canadian-American border. See Lydia Bean, *The Politics of Evangelical Identity* (Princeton: Princeton University Press, 2014), 207.

46 Kelly Grant, "Health Canada Decision on Abortion Pill Set for Mid-January," *Globe and Mail*, December 23, 2014.

47 Harold Albrecht, *Government of Canada, House of Commons Debates* 147, 86 (May 14, 2014): 5372.

48 Laura Payton, "Abortion Drug Decision Pushed Back by Health Canada," *CBC News*, January 13, 2015, http://www.cbc.ca/news/politics/abortion-drug-decision -pushed-back-by-health-canada-1.2899723.

49 Grant, "Health Canada Decision."

50 "Why the Abortion-Pill Delays, Health Canada?," *Globe and Mail*, January 15, 2015.

51 David Anderson, "MP David Anderson Questions Health Canada's Approval of Unsafe Drug RU-486," *David Anderson, MP for Cypress Hills-Grasslands*, July 30, 2015, http://www.davidanderson.ca/mp-david-anderson-questions-health -canadas-approval-of-unsafe-drug-ru-486/.

52 Mike Schouten, "Canada Approves Dangerous RU 486 Abortion Pill That Kills Women and Unborn Babies," *LifeNews.com*, July 30, 2015, http://www.lifenews. com/2015/07/30/canada-approves-dangerous-ru-486-abortion-pill-that-kills -women-and-unborn-babies/.

53 "Rona Ambrose Denies Role in RU-486 Abortion Pill Approval," *CBC News*, July 30, 2015, http://www.cbc.ca/news/canada/edmonton/rona-ambrose-denies-role -in-ru-486-abortion-pill-approval-1.3174361.

54 *Campaign Life Coalition*, "Federal Elections: October 19, 2015 is Decision Day for Canada," http://www.campaignlifecoalition.com/index.php?p=Federal.

55 Teresa Wright, "Trudeau's Abortion Stand Divides PEI MPs," *Guardian* (Charlottetown), May 16, 2014.

56 Don Butler, "Catholic MPs Stand Ground on Abortion Despite Threat," *Ottawa Citizen*, March 14, 2008, A1.

57 Teresa Wright, "PEI Women Have Their Abortion Rights Respected: Justin Trudeau," *Guardian* (Charlottetown), April 18, 2015.

58 The Liberal platform, quoted in Amanda Connolly, "Liberals Would Fund Abortion Services under Maternal Health Initiative," *iPolitics*, October 16, 2015, http://ipolitics. ca/2015/10/16/liberals-would-fund-abortion-services-under-maternal-health -initiative/.

59 David Akin, "Trudeau OKs Canadian Dollars for Foreign Abortion Services," *Toronto Sun*, May 10, 2016.

60 Jeffrey Simpson, "The Nepean Contest Wasn't about Substance," *Globe and Mail*, July 2, 2015.

61 Kathleen Charlebois, "Twenty-Nine-Year-Old Arnold Viersen Leads the Conservative Party in Peace River-Westlock," *Whitecourt Star*, September 3, 2015.

62 Lorna Dueck, "Why Did the Conservatives Lose So Badly?," *Context with Lorna Dueck blog*, October 20, 2015, http://www.contextwithlornadueck.com/blog/ why-did-the-conservatives-lose-so-badly.

Chapter 3: Religion in Atlantic Provincial Politics

1 Ronald Manzer, *Educational Regimes and Anglo-American Democracy* (Toronto: University of Toronto Press, 2003), 40. See also 41–45.

2 Rand Dyck, *Provincial Politics in Canada*, 3rd ed. (Scarborough: Prentice Hall Canada, 1996), 130.

3 See Frederick W. Rowe, *The Development of Education in Newfoundland* (Toronto: Ryerson Press, 1964); Gertrude E. Gunn, *The Political History of Newfoundland, 1832–1864* (Toronto: University of Toronto Press, 1966); and Sean T. Cadigan, *Newfoundland and Labrador: A History* (Toronto: University of Toronto Press, 2009).

4 Gunn, *Political History of Newfoundland*, 182.

5 Cecil J. Houston and William J. Smyth, *The Sash Canada Wore: A Historical Geography of the Orange Order in Canada* (Toronto: University of Toronto Press, 1980), 78. See also Mark Graesser, "Religion and Voting in Newfoundland: Party Alignment and Realignment, 1889–1949," paper presented at the Annual Meeting of the Canadian Political Science Association, Ottawa, 1993, 6.

6 Manzer, *Educational Regimes*, 42; Rowe, *Development of Education in Newfoundland*.

7 Gunn, *Political History of Newfoundland*, 185; Gordon O. Rothney, "The Denominational Basis of Representation in the Newfoundland Assembly, 1919–1962," *Canadian Journal of Economics and Political Science* 28, 4 (1962): 557–70.

8 Houston and Smyth, *Sash Canada Wore*, 79; and Cadigan, *Newfoundland and Labrador*, 145, 217.

9 Susan McCorquodale, "Newfoundland: Plus ça change, plus c'est la même chose," in *Canadian Provincial Politics*, 2nd ed., ed. Martin Robin, 138–69 (Scarborough: Prentice-Hall of Canada, 1978).

10 Mark Graesser, "The 1989 Newfoundland Provincial Election," unpublished manuscript, May 1991, 10–11. Graesser also points out that the Liberal Party had been

the party of choice for Catholics until an early-twentieth-century realignment that was cemented by the early 1930s and then further reinforced by Smallwood.

11 See Mark Graesser, "Education Reform in Newfoundland, 1990–1995," paper presented at the Annual Meeting of the Canadian Political Science Association, St. John's, Newfoundland, 1997; and Philip Warren, "The Politics of Educational Change: Reforming Denominational Education," in *Education Reform: From Rhetoric to Reality*, ed. Gerald Galway and David Dibbon (London, ON: Althouse Press, 2012), 56–57.

12 Gerald Galway and David Dibbon, "A Perfect Storm: Conceptualizing Educational (Denominational) Reform in Newfoundland and Labrador," in Galway and Dibbon, *Education Reform*, 18, 22–25.

13 Phillip McCann, "From Christian Humanism to Neoliberalism: A Decade of Transition, 1985–1995," in Galway and Dibbon, *Education Reform*, 88–89.

14 Ibid., 91.

15 Galway and Dibbon, "Perfect Storm," 30.

16 Warren, "Politics of Educational Change," 49–50.

17 Other surveys during this period show an increase in the number of Newfoundlanders favouring a single non-denominational school system, from 50 percent in 1976 to two-thirds in 1991. See Graesser, "Education Reform in Newfoundland," 8–10.

18 Warren, "Politics of Educational Change," 46–47.

19 Graesser, "Education Reform in Newfoundland," 23.

20 One survey shows that only 48 percent of Catholics voted "yes," and that, if forced to choose between the present system and a totally non-denominational one, 62 percent of all Catholic respondents would opt for the former. See Graesser, "Education Reform in Newfoundland," 26, 28.

21 The injunction was supported in the 1997 ruling, *Hogan v. Newfoundland (School Boards for Ten Districts)*, throwing the school system into even more turmoil.

22 In the view of Alex Marland, the end of denominational education was the last nail in that particular coffin. Personal correspondence with authors, March 17, 2014.

23 See Mark Graesser, "Religion and Voting in Newfoundland: Party Alignment and Realignment, 1889-1949," paper presented at the Annual Meeting of the Canadian Political Science Association, Ottawa, 1993.

24 McCorquodale, "Newfoundland," 159.

25 Ibid.," 157; Graesser, "Religion and Voting in Newfoundland."

26 McCorquodale, "Newfoundland," 159.

27 Graesser, "1989 Newfoundland Provincial Election."

28 Graesser, personal correspondence with authors, May 22, 2014.

29 See Brenda O'Neill, "Variation in Women's Status across the Provinces, 1999–2014," in *Provinces: Canadian Provincial Politics*, 3rd ed., ed. Christopher Dunn (Toronto: University of Toronto Press, 2016), 127.

30 "Frank Coleman Abortion Controversy: Who Has Said What," *CBC News*, April 22, 2014, http://www.cbc.ca/news/canada/newfoundland-labrador/frank-coleman -abortion-controversy-who-has-said-what-1.2617571.

31 See Joanna Everitt, "Mobilization on the Periphery: LGBT Activism and Success in Atlantic Canada," in *Queer Mobilizations: Social Activism and Canadian Public Policy*, ed. Manon Tremblay (Vancouver: UBC Press, 2015). See also Tom Warner, *Never Going Back: A History of Queer Activism in Canada* (Toronto: University of Toronto Press, 2002), 206–7.

32 P.J. Fitzpatrick, "New Brunswick: The Politics of Pragmatism," in Robin, *Canadian Provincial Politics*, 120–37.

33 Edmund A. Aunger, *In Search of Political Stability: A Comparative Study of New Brunswick and Northern Ireland* (Montreal and Kingston: McGill-Queen's University Press, 1981), 138–39.

34 Ibid., 74, quoting M. Hatfield, "H.H. Pitts and Race and Religion in New Brunswick Politics," *Acadiensis* 4 (1975): 60.

35 Dyck, *Provincial Politics in Canada*, 173; and Aunger, *In Search of Political Stability*, 69.

36 Hugh Mellon, "New Brunswick: The Challenge of New Brunswick Politics," in *The Provincial State in Canada*, ed. Keith Brownsey and Michael Howlett (Peterborough: Broadview Press, 2001), 76.

37 This was what Nelson Wiseman characterizes as a Maritime version of the western-based Reform movement, and he emphasizes the point by reminding us that, in the federal elections of 1993 and 1997, Reform candidates did well (with 15 percent of the overall vote and over 20 percent in some ridings). See Nelson Wiseman, *In Search of Canadian Political Culture* (Vancouver: UBC Press, 2007), chap. 6; Agar Adamson and Ian Stewart, "Changing Party Politics in Atlantic Canada," in *Party Politics in Canada*, 8th ed., ed. Hugh G. Thorburn and Alan Whitehorn (Toronto: Prentice-Hall, 2001), 306.

38 William Cross, "Leadership Selection in New Brunswick: Balancing Language Representation and Populist Impulses," in *Political Parties, Representation, and Electoral Democracy in Canada*, ed. William Cross (Toronto: Oxford University Press, 2002), 49.

39 Jacques Poitras, *The Right Fight: Bernard Lord and the Conservative Dilemma* (Fredericton: Goose Lane, 2004), chap. 20.

40 Cross, "Leadership Selection." See also Mario Levesque, "New Brunswick," in *Big Worlds: Politics and Elections in the Canadian Provinces and Territories*, ed. Jared J. Wesley (Toronto: University of Toronto Press, 2015), 63–64.

41 Poitras, *Right Fight*, 335. As he points out, this was to some extent being replaced by a new divide between urban areas, more likely to experience a degree of economic growth and prosperity, and rural areas, the new solitudes of provincial politics.

42 Joanna Everitt, personal correspondence to authors, March 14, 2014.

43 This is a point made by Levesque, "New Brunswick," 60.

44 Katrina Ackerman, "'Not in the Atlantic Provinces': The Abortion Debate in New Brunswick, 1980–1987," *Acadiensis* 41, 1 (2012): 75–101.

45 Michael O. Nowlan, *A Century of Service: The Knights of Columbus in New Brunswick* (Moncton: Faye Editions, 2004).

46 Ackerman, "'Not in the Atlantic Provinces,'" 77; Rachael Johnstone, "The Politics of Abortion in Canada after Morgentaler: Women's Rights as Citizenship Rights" (PhD diss., Queen's University, 2012), 83–97.

47 Federal government pressure eased when the federal Conservatives won office in Ottawa, with Health Minister Tony Clement indicating less interest than his predecessor in the issue. See Abortion Rights Coalition of Canada, Position Paper #3 Clinic Funding – Overview of Provincial Situation, August 2007, http://www.arcc-cdac.ca/postionpapers/03-Clinic-Funding-Overview.PDF.

48 Johnstone, *Politics of Abortion*, 88.

49 Ibid., 143–44.

50 "NDP Accuses Liberals of Misleading Public on Abortion Stance," *CBC News*, April 11, 2014, http://www.cbc.ca/news/canada/new-brunswick/ndp-accuses-liberals-of-misleading-public-on-abortion-stance-1.2606505.

51 Shawn Berry, "Capital City March for Life Rally at Legislature Attracts MLAs," *Daily Gleaner*, March 16, 2014.

52 Jane Taber, "Incoming NB Premier Moves to Remove Barriers to Abortion," *Globe and Mail*, September 25, 2014.

53 Kelly Grant, "Province Fell Just Shy of Fulfilling Commitment to Expand Abortion Access, Documents Reveal," *Globe and Mail*, May 22, 2015.

54 Kelly Grant, "Funds Raised for Clinic Offering Abortions," and "Single New Site to Perform Abortions," in *Globe and Mail*, January 17, 2015 and February 25, 2015, respectively.

55 These are Canadian Election Study data, reported in O'Neill, "Variation in Women's Status," 127.

56 Thirty-one percent said that abortion should be available only in limited circumstances, and 13 percent were completely opposed ("Abortions May Not Be Offered at All Hospitals, Gallant Says," *CBC News*, January 8, 2015, http://www.cbc.ca/news/canada/new-brunswick/abortions-may-not-be-offered-at-all-hospitals-gallant-says-1.2894056).

57 Roman Catholic responses were 39 percent strongly agree, 30 percent agree, 16 percent disagree, 16 percent strongly disagree. Mainline Protestant numbers were 40 percent, 24 percent, 16 percent, and 20 percent, respectively. Evangelicals were not quite as different as we might imagine, with 9 percent strongly agreeing, a remarkable 47 percent more or less agreeing, 39 percent strongly disagreeing, and 5 percent more or less disagreeing.

58 Warner, *Never Going Back*, 203–4.

59 Everitt, "Mobilization on the Periphery," 134.

60 "Government Formally Backs School Gay-Straight Alliances," *CBC News*, July 22, 2014, http://www.cbc.ca/news/canada/new-brunswick/government-formally-backs-school-gay-straight-alliances-1.2714771.

61 These numbers represent the proportion of each set of partisans scoring 8, 9, or 10 on a composite 10-point scale in which these scores represent the most "progressive" responses.

62 Reginald Bibby, *Fragmented Gods* (Toronto: Irwin, 1987), 90.

63 Kurt Bowen, *Christians in a Secular World: The Canadian Experience* (Montreal and Kingston: McGill-Queen's University Press, 2004), 55. In 2011, Bibby pointed to levels of weekly attendance at religious services that were higher (at 39 percent) than in any other region (Saskatchewan-Manitoba at 36 percent, Ontario at 28 percent, Alberta at 28 percent, British Columbia at 17 percent, and Quebec at 15 percent). He also points to relatively high levels of identification with a religion – 92 percent, second only to Quebec at 94 percent, ahead of Alberta, the Prairies, Ontario, and British Columbia, ranging between the mid-80s and 54 percent. See Reginald W. Bibby, *Beyond the Gods and Back* (Lethbridge: Project Canada Books, 2011), 53.

64 David Eagler, "Changing Patterns of Attendance at Religious Services in Canada, 1986–2008," *Journal for the Scientific Study of Religion* 50, 1 (2011): 187–200. The drop in attendance likelihood among Catholics in Quebec fell over the same period from 0.18 to 0.04 percent.

65 Josephine Mazzuca, "American and Canadian Views on Abortion," *Gallup*, September 24, 2002, www.gallup.com/poll/6856/american-canadian-views-abortion.aspx.

66 Angus Reid Strategies, "Canadians More Open-Minded on Relationships and Sexual Behaviour: But Not on Drugs," December 20, 2007; Ipsos Reid, Canadian Online Omni Survey, June 18–25, 2012.

67 David Rayside, *Queer Inclusions, Continental Divisions: Public Recognition of Sexual Diversity in Canada and the United States* (Toronto: University of Toronto Press, 2008), 52.

Chapter 4: Ontario's PCs and Denominational Politics

1 The 2011 National Household Survey shows that 27 percent of Ontario's Catholics were immigrants. The 2006 census shows that francophones constituted only 14 percent of the province's Catholics.

2 Franklin A. Walker, *Catholic Education and Politics in Ontario: A Documentary Study* (Toronto: Thomas Nelson and Sons, 1964); R.D. Gidney, *From Hope to Harris: The Reshaping of Ontario's Schools* (Toronto: University of Toronto Press, 1999), chap. 1.

3 W.G. Fleming, *Education: Ontario's Preoccupation* (Toronto: University of Toronto Press, 1972,) 253.

4 This direction was evident in such encyclicals as *Quanta Cura*, the *Syllabus Errorum*, and *Rerum Novarum*.

5 Joseph Schull, *Ontario since 1867* (Toronto: McClelland and Stewart, 1978), 40–41.

6 Walker, *Catholic Education*, 127.

7 Schull, *Ontario since 1867*, 78–79; Walker, *Catholic Education*, 110–11.

8 Schull, *Ontario since 1867*, 79. See also Cecil J. Houston, *The Sash Canada Wore: A Historical Geography of the Orange Order in Canada* (Toronto: University of Toronto Press, 1980).

9 Walker, *Catholic Education*, 126. Irish-Canadian clergy, for example, were frequently at odds with francophone clerics from the nineteenth century on.

10 Walker, *Catholic Education*, 234.

11 Peter Meehan, "The East Hastings By-Election of 1936 and the Ontario School Tax Question," *Historical Studies* 68 (2002): 105.

12 Walter G. Pitman, "The Limits to Diversity: The Separate School Issue in the Politics of Ontario," in *Government and Politics of Ontario*, ed. Donald C. MacDonald (Toronto: Macmillan, 1975), 18.

13 Schull, *Ontario since 1867*, 302.

14 Robert M. Stamp, *The Schools of Ontario, 1876–1976* (Toronto: University of Toronto Press, 1982), 177.

15 Robert Vipond, *Making a Global City: How One Toronto School Embraced Diversity* (Toronto: University of Toronto Press, 2017), chap. 3.

16 Stamp, *Schools of Ontario*, 178.

17 Vipond, *Making a Global City*, chap. 3. As Vipond indicates, too, the curricular guides issued by the Ministry of Education made clear the moral superiority of Christianity over Judaism and pointed unequivocally to Jewish responsibility for the killing of Jesus.

18 Donald MacDonald's memoir talks extensively about his and the CCF's position on Catholic school funding but not at all about religious instruction, though it is true he became party leader only in 1953. See Donald MacDonald, *The Happy Warrior: Political Memoirs* (Toronto: Dundurn Press, 1988).

19 This was the Hope Commission, on which see MacDonald, *Happy Warrior*, 220. On Liberal and Conservative centrism, see Robert J. Williams, "Ontario Party Politics in the 1990s: Comfort Meets Conviction," in *The Government and Politics of Ontario*, 5th ed., ed. Graham White (Toronto: University of Toronto Press, 1997), 227–29.

20 Fleming, *Education*, 257; Pitman, "Limits to Diversity," 19–20.

21 The first quote comes from Pitman, "Limits to Diversity," 20; the second from MacDonald, *Happy Warrior*, 221.

22 Fleming, *Education*, 260–61.

23 Pitman, "Limits to Diversity," 17; Stamp, "Schools of Ontario," 215–16.

24 In mid-1971, they presented the government with a petition carrying 120,000 names. See Claire Hoy, *Bill Davis* (Toronto: Methuen, 1985), 270.

25 Stamp, *Schools of Ontario*, 213–14.

26 Hoy, *Bill Davis*, 270–71.

27 Only after the NDP position was declared did the Liberals emerge with a pro-extension stance, fearful of losing the Catholic support on which it so depended. See MacDonald, *Happy Warrior*, 227.

28 Gidney, *From Hope to Harris*, 124–25; Rosemary Speirs, *Out of the Blue: The Fall of the Tory Dynasty in Ontario* (Toronto: Macmillan, 1986), 24.

29 Hoy, *Bill Davis*, 265. At least one legislative insider at the time attaches no credence to this story (confidential interview, November 9, 2013).

30 Gidney, *From Hope to Harris*, 124–25.

31 Confidential interview, November 18, 2013.

32 Gidney, *From Hope to Harris*, 127.

33 He compared the move to Hitler's decrees changing education in prewar Germany.

34 Gidney, *From Hope to Harris*, 131.

35 Graham White contributed this observation, in personal correspondence, August 2015. Polling for the party had in fact showed that opposition to full funding was very strong among Protestants, with Catholics evenly divided (Speirs, *Out of the Blue*, 127, 168).

36 Gidney, *From Hope to Harris*, 135. On this controversy, and for a broader discussion of the religious dimensions of Ontario schooling history, see James Farney, "Contextualizing and Explaining Stability of an Educational Regime: The Case of Religious Schools in Ontario," paper presented at the annual meeting of the American Political Science Association, Philadelphia, August 2014.

37 Speirs, *Out of the Blue*, 225.

38 Fleming, *Education*, 270–71.

39 Ronald A. Manzer, *Educational Regimes and Anglo-American Democracy* (Toronto: University of Toronto Press, 2003), 212; Gidney, *From Hope to Harris*, 134–35.

40 Farney, "Contextualizing and Explaining," 12–13.

41 Ibid., 12.

42 Stamp, *Schools of Ontario*, 223.

43 See Ministry of Education and Training Ontario, *Education about Religion in Ontario Public Elementary Schools* (Toronto: Ministry of Education and Training, 1994). See also Vipond, *Making a Global City*, chap. 3.

44 At the federal level, in *R. v. Big M Drug Mart*, 1985, and in Ontario, in *R. v. Edwards Books and Art*, 1986. See Bruce Ryder, "The Canadian Conception of Equal Religious Citizenship," in *Law and Religious Pluralism in Canada*, ed. Richard Moon, 87–109 (Vancouver: UBC Press, 2008).

45 Fleming, *Education*, 270.

46 During the PC leadership campaign to replace William Davis, candidate Dennis Timbrell indicated during one debate that he was pro-life, but he then backed away from the issue in the face of protests. See Speirs, *Out of the Blue*, 45.

47 In 1981, an NDP MPP introduced an amendment to add sexual orientation to the code, but the NDP leader at the time indicated that gay rights were not a priority,

and only a handful of Liberals were prepared to support it. See Chris Bearchall, "Ontario Finally Says No," *The Body Politic* 80 (January/February 1982): 8–9. See also Tom Warner, *Never Going Back: A History of Queer Activism in Canada* (Toronto: University of Toronto Press, 2002).

Chapter 5: Sexual Diversity and Faith Communities in Ontario

1 The 2006 census shows that 46 percent of the Toronto "census metropolitan area" population was born outside Canada and that numbers for several of the regions around it were just over or just under 50 percent.

2 Kurt Bowen, *Christians in a Secular World: The Canadian Experience* (Montreal and Kingston: McGill-Queen's University Press, 2004), 54–55; Ipsos Reid, Canadian Online Omni poll, August 29–September 6, 2011.

3 Ipsos Reid Canadian Online Omni poll, June 18–25, 2012, http://www.ipsos-na.com/news-polls/pressrelease.aspx?id=5690.

4 This echoes the findings of William P. Cross, Jonathan Malloy, Tamara A. Small, and Laura Stevenson, *Fighting for Votes: Parties, the Media, and Voters in an Ontario Election* (Vancouver: UBC Press, 2015), 172–79.

5 David McGrane, "Centrism, Ideological Polarization, and the Canadian Provincial Voter," in *Provinces: Canadian Provincial Politics*, ed. Christopher Dunn (Toronto: University of Toronto Press, 2015), 192. On 4-point scales, where 4 is the conservative position, the average PC supporter is 2.95 on the post-materialism index, compared to 2.28 for Liberals and 2.27 for New Democrats. On the market liberalism index, PCs are 2.80, compared to 2.04 for Liberals and 1.85 for New Democrats.

6 Cross et al., *Fighting for Votes*, 173. On their 0-to-1 scale, the average PC supporter is .68 and the average for both NDPers and Liberals is .45.

7 This is an argument made by Graham White, personal correspondence, August 2015.

8 Tom Warner, *Losing Control: Canada's Social Conservatives in the Age of Rights* (Toronto: Between the Lines, 2010), 111–16.

9 Rosemary Speirs, *Out of the Blue: The Fall of the Tory Dynasty in Ontario* (Toronto: Macmillan, 1986), 78.

10 Rachael Johnstone, "The Politics of Abortion in Canada after Morgentaler: Women's Rights as Citizenship Rights" (PhD diss., Queen's University, 2012), 98.

11 According to Michael Wagner, Cardinal Carter, Roman Catholic archbishop, worked out an agreement with Attorney General Scott in 1985 aimed at limiting the number of protestors at Morgentaler's clinic. See his Michael Wagner, *Standing on Guard for Thee*, 2nd ed. (St. Catharines: Freedom Press, 2012), 76–77.

12 See David Rayside, "Gay Rights and Family Values," *Studies in Political Economy* 26 (Summer 1988): 109–47; and Tom Warner, *Never Going Back: A History of Queer Activism in Canada* (Toronto: University of Toronto Press, 2002), chap. 9.

13 The Premier's Office received ninety-six hundred letters and over one thousand phone calls, over three-quarters of which were opposed to the amendment.

14 This account relies heavily on Rayside's earlier account of this episode in, "The Fight for Relationship Recognition in Ontario," chap. 5 in *On the Fringe: Gays and Lesbians in Politics* (Ithaca, NY: Cornell University Press, 1998).

15 Craig McInnes, "Vote on Same-Sex Issue Test of NDP Solidarity," *Globe and Mail*, May 12, 1994.

16 On the Harris impact, see Randall White, *Ontario since 1985* (Toronto: Eastend Books, 1998), chap. 5; and Peter Woolstencroft, "Reclaiming the Pink Palace: The Progressive Conservative Party Comes in from the Cold," in *Government and Politics of Ontario*, 5th ed., ed. Graham White, 365–400 (Toronto: University of Toronto Press, 1997).

17 John Ibbitson, *Promised Land: Inside the Mike Harris Revolution* (Scarborough: Prentice-Hall Canada, 1997), 189.

18 Woolstencroft, "Reclaiming the Pink Palace," 379; and Rand Dyck, *Provincial Politics in Canada*, 3rd ed. (Toronto: Prentice-Hall, 1996), 355.

19 The CHP never did get many votes in federal elections and was soon supplanted by the Reform Party. See Chris Mackenzie, *Pro-Family Politics and Fringe Parties in Canada* (Vancouver: UBC Press, 2005); Wagner, *Standing on Guard for Thee*, 146–50.

20 See Geoffrey Hale, "Changing Patterns of Party Support in Ontario," in *Revolution at Queen's Park: Essays on Governing Ontario*, ed. Sid Noel (Toronto: James Lorimer, 1997), 111.

21 Warner, *Losing Control*, 162.

22 Johnstone, "Politics of Abortion in Canada after Morgentaler," 98–100.

23 Cross et al., *Fighting for Votes*, chap. 2.

24 Duncan MacLellan, "Faith-Based Schools and the Politics of Education: A Case Study of Ontario, Canada," *Politics and Religion* 6, 1 (2012): 37–60; "Ontario Budget Trims Taxes; Introduces Private School Tax Credit," *CBC News*, June 17, 2002, http://www.cbc.ca/news/business/ontario-budget-trims-taxes-introduces-private-school-tax-credit-1.281508.

25 See Anver Emon, "Islamic Law and the Canadian Mosaic: Politics, Jurisprudence, and Multicultural Accommodation," *Canadian Bar Review* 87 (2009): 391–425; and Anna C. Korteweg, "The Sharia Debate in Ontario," *ISIM Review* 18 (2006): 50–51.

26 See Cross et al., *Fighting for Votes*, 46.

27 See Warner, *Never Going Back*; Tim McCaskell, *Race to Equity: Disrupting Educational Inequality* (Toronto: Between the Lines, 2005).

28 Government of Ontario, *Shaping a Culture of Respect in Our Schools: Promoting Safe and Healthy Relationships*, December 11, 2008, 13, https://www.edu.gov.on.ca/eng/teachers/RespectCulture.pdf.

29 An implementation memorandum (no. 144), *Bullying Prevention and Intervention*, required boards to develop and implement policies in this area by February 2010.

30 Cameron McKenzie, "Is Queer Sex Education in Ontario Finally Out of the Closet?" *Aporia* 7, 3 (2015): 6–18.

31 McKenzie, "Queer Sex Education in Ontario," 14; Ontario Physical Health and Education Association, "Sexual Health Education in Schools across Canada," Toronto, 2013, https://www.ophea.net/sites/default/files/pdfs/advocacy/ADV_SexEdReportFINAL_31MY13.pdf.

32 Patrick B. Craine, "Mandatory Curriculum for Ontario Schools Promotes Homosexuality, Masturbation," *Lifesite News*, March 2, 2010, https://www.lifesitenews.com/news/mandatory-curriculum-for-ontario-schools-promotes-homosexuality-masturbatio.

33 Carmelina Prete, "Sexual Diversity Policy on Agenda," *Hamilton Spectator*, April 15, 2010.

34 Lydia Bean, in her exploration of evangelical beliefs in two Canadian religious communities, points out the extent to which McVety was viewed as out of touch with contemporary evangelical priorities, particularly among the young and in ethno-cultural minorities. See Lydia Bean, *The Politics of Evangelical Identity* (Princeton: Princeton University Press, 2014), 20–23.

35 Kate Hammer and Karen Howlett, "The End of Innuendo: Ont. Schools Making Sex Education More Explicit," *Globe and Mail*, April 21, 2010; and Kristin Roshowy and Robert Benzie, "Opponents to Protest New Sex-Ed Curriculum," *Toronto Star*, April 21, 2010.

36 Annie Kidder, the head of People for Education, reported to the group's membership that, when she got calls about the story, "reporters were very specific in their requests – they only wanted to talk to parents who were upset. They absolutely did not want to talk to me or any other non-outraged parents." Posted on April 23, 2010 (available at http://schools-at-the-centre.ning.com/forum/topics/sex-education-in-schools). See also Kathryn Blaze Carlson, "Flash Points in the Sex-Ed Curricula across Canada," *National Post*, October 8, 2011.

37 Robert Benzie, "Ontario and Sex-Ed: We're Starting Over," *Toronto Star*, April 27, 2010.

38 Ibid.

39 "Hudak Says McGuinty Keeps Parents in Dark on Sex Ed," *iPolitics*, September 23, 2011, http://ipolitics.ca/2011/09/23/hudak-says-mcguinty-keeps-parents-in-dark-on-sex-ed/.

40 Richard Brennan, "Cross-Dressing for 6-Year-Olds? Hudak Sticks up for Anti-Liberal Flyer," *Toronto Star*, October 3, 2011.

41 Cross et al., *Fighting for Votes*, 57.

42 Karen Howlett, "Anti-Bullying Legislation: Parents Urge Quick Passage to Avoid More Tragedy," *Globe and Mail*, December 8, 2011; and Tim McCaskell, "The Politics of *Common Cause*: Using 'Values Framing' to Understand the Battle Over Bullying in Our Schools," *Our Schools/Our Selves* 21, 4 (2012): 45–78.

43 Boards had to "promote the awareness and understanding of, and respect for, people of all sexual orientations and gender identities, including organizations with the name gay-straight alliance or another name." Section 9(d).

44 McCaskell, "Politics of *Common Cause*," 72.

45 The Liberal bill had some elements of that disciplinary and punishment approach. See McCaskell, "Politics of *Common Cause*," 67–69.

46 "Get It Right with Anti-Bullying Legislation," *Catholic Register*, May 8, 2012.

47 Andrea Houston, "Ontario Tightens Bill 13 So School Boards Can't Reject GSAs," *Xtra!*, May 31, 2012; and "Mission Accomplished," *Xtra!*, June 14, 2012.

48 Kristin Rushowy and Rob Ferguson, "'We Support Catholic Education,'" *Toronto Star*, June 5, 2012.

49 "Bill 13 Passed into Law," *Catholic Register*, June 8, 2012; and Robert Benzie, "Majority of Ontarians Favour Gay-Straight Alliances and Oppose Catholic School Funding, Poll Finds," *Toronto Star*, May 16, 2012.

50 Andrea Houston, "Breaking Rank on GSAs," *Xtra!*, May 17, 2012.

51 Laura Armstrong, "Premier Seeks Review of New Prostitution Law," *Toronto Star*, December 8, 2014. The Conservative legislation was in response to a Supreme Court ruling that struck down crucial elements of the existing regulatory regime.

52 Remarks delivered at a symposium in honour of Graham White, May 30, 2014.

53 Vidya Kauri and Adrian Morrow, "Toronto Prof Facing Child Pornography Charges Was Target of Probes in Ontario, New Zealand," *Globe and Mail*, July 8, 2013. Right-wing commentators such as Christina Blizzard and Ezra Levant immediately identified Levin as having been deputy minister during the development of the HPE curriculum, the latter describing it as "hyper-sexualized" and wondering if "changing the Ontario curriculum to bring sex lessons to children of tender years was coloured by Levin's alleged proclivities." See Christina Blizzard, "Disturbing Questions about Sex Education Policy," *QMI Agency*, July 10, 2013; Ezra Levant, "Innocence Violated," *QMI Agency*, July 13, 2013.

54 Keith Leslie, "Ontario Liberals to Introduce Updated Version of Sex Education Curriculum Pulled in 2010 over Religious Objections," *National Post*, October 30, 2014.

55 Adrian Morrow, "Back to Class: What to Expect from Ontario's New Sex-Ed Curriculum," *Globe and Mail*, February 24, 2015; and Jillian Kestler-D'Amours, "How Ontario's New Sex Education Program Compares to Other Provinces," *Toronto Star*, February 26, 2015.

56 Brian Lilly, "Ontario Sex Ed: They're Teaching My Kids to Do What?" *The Rebel*, February 19, 2015.

57 See, for example, Michael Coren, "Why Critics of Ontario's New Sex Ed Curriculum Are Wrong," *National Post*, February 26, 2015; and Margaret Wente, "Sex Education, Then and Now," *Globe and Mail*, February 24, 2015.

58 "Toronto Protest: My Child My Choice!!! Stop Age Inappropriate Sex Ed in Ontario!!!," *Campaign Life Coalition*, April 14, 2015, http://www.campaignlife coalition.com/index.php?p=Events,View&id=20.

59 Nicholas Hune-Brown, "The Sex Ed Revolution: A Portrait of the Powerful Political Bloc That's Waging War on Queen's Park," *Toronto Life*, September 2015.

60 Kevin Van Paassen, "Christian Fundamentalists Would Limit the Public Schools' Ability to Teach Curriculum," *Globe and Mail*, September 14, 2014.

61 Ashley Goodfellow, "Parents Angered by Sex Ed Changes," *Mississauga News*, February 9, 2015.

62 "A Letter to Parents and Friends," *Parents Alliance of Ontario*, March 6, 2015, http://www.parentsalliance.ca/node/49. See also Selena Ross and Sahar Fatima, "Coalition of the Pure," *Globe and Mail*, May 9, 2015.

63 "Parent Meeting with Premier Wynne," and "After Meeting – Parent Meeting with Premier Wynne," press releases, April 29, 2015.

64 Chris Selley, "Muslim Community Taking the Lead in Latest Round of Ontario Sex-Education Protests," *National Post*, May 5, 2015; and Louise Brown, "35,000 Kids Stay Home in Sex-Ed Boycott," *Toronto Star*, May 5, 2015.

65 For thoughtful analyses of the ethno-cultural diversity of protesters, see Joseph Heath, "Sex Education and the Dilemmas of Immigrant Integration," *In Due Course: A Canadian Public Affairs Blog*, September 3, 2015, http://induecourse.ca/sex-education-and-the-dilemmas-of-immigrant-integration/.

66 The modified version in Thorncliffe removed specific mention of genitalia and offered "private parts" instead. See Kristin Rushowy, "Sanitized Sex-Ed Offered at Toronto School," *Toronto Star*, May 13, 2016; and Selena Ross, "Some Students Falling through the Cracks after Sex-Ed Shuffle," *Globe and Mail*, May 25, 2016.

67 These groups made clear that they didn't necessarily endorse the curriculum but felt that parents needed information (Kristin Rushowy, "Peel's Sex-Ed Debunking Gets Help," *Toronto Star*, November 4, 2015).

68 Jane Taber, "Ontario Buys Ad Campaign to Promote Sex-Ed as Protests Loom," *Globe and Mail*, September 1, 2015.

69 Allison Jones and Keith Leslie, "New Sex-Ed Curriculum Leads to Showdown between Premier, PC Critic," *Global News*, February 24, 2015, http://globalnews.ca/news/1847436/new-sex-ed-curriculum-leads-to-showdown-between-premier-pc-critic/.

70 Robert Benzie, Rob Ferguson, and Richard Brennan, "Patrick Brown Wins Ontario PC Leadership," *Toronto Star*, May 9, 2015; "Campaign Life Coalition Congratulates Patrick Brown on PC Leadership Victory," press release from Campaign Life Coalition, May 9, 2015, https://www.campaignlifecoalition.com/index.php?p=Press_Room&id=154.

71 Lawrence Martin, "The Sagging Liberals Need a Shakeup," *Globe and Mail*, April 21, 2015.

72 Jane Taber, "Duelling Elliott, Brown Campaigns Made Efforts to Maintain Party Solidarity," *Globe and Mail*, May 12, 2015.

73 Rob Ferguson, "Ontario Becomes First Province to Ban 'Conversion Therapy' for LGBTQ Children," *Toronto Star*, June 4, 2015.

74 Rob Ferguson and Robert Benzie, "PC Leader Set to Go Toe-to-toe with Wynne," *Toronto Star*, September 14, 2015.

75 Patrick Brown, "My Sex-Ed Letter Was a Mistake," Toronto Star, August 29, 2016; Adrian Morrow, "PC Leader Won't 'Scrap' Ontario Sex-Ed Curriculum," *Globe and Mail*, August 30, 2016.

76 Adrian Morrow, "Brown Privately Said He Opposed Same-Sex Marriage: Christian Leaders," *Globe and Mail*, September 22, 2016.

77 Mike Crawley, "Patrick Brown Aiming to Shed 'Social Conservative' Tag," *CBC News*, December 12, 2016, http://www.cbc.ca/news/canada/toronto/ontario-pc-leader -patrick-brown-1.3888170.

78 Ainslie Cruickshank, "So-Cons Warn Split with Religious Right Could Cost Ontario PCs Next Election," *ipolitics*, Oct 25, 2016.

79 In May 2016, for example, a slim majority of Halton Catholic trustees voted against an anti-bullying policy because of its specific references to sexual orientation and gender identity.

80 Marci McDonald, *The Armageddon Factor: The Rise of Christian Nationalism in Canada* (Toronto: Random House Canada, 2011), 87. Focus on the Family, of course, established a Canadian branch.

81 According to the 2011 Canadian Election Study, only 23 percent of Canadian Catholics responded "yes" to a question concerning whether abortion should be banned (compared to 17 percent of all Canadians). Outside Quebec, where pro-choice sentiment is especially strong, 34 percent of Catholics supported a ban, significantly more than the average (20 percent), though still a minority. The same survey found that 66 percent of Canadian Catholics supported same-sex marriage, the same proportion as in the total population. The World Values Surveys conducted between 2005 and 2009 found that 29 percent of Canadian Catholics attended mass at least weekly.

82 On the attitudes of Muslims towards sexual diversity, see Momin Rahman and Amir Hussain, "Muslims and Sexual Diversity in North America," in *Faith, Politics, and Sexual Diversity in Canada and the United States*, ed. David Rayside and Clyde Wilcox, 255–74 (Vancouver: UBC Press, 2011); and David Rayside, "Muslim American Communities' Response to Queer Visibility," *Contemporary Islam* 5, 2 (2011): 109–34. The accumulation of polling evidence in both Canada and the United States indicates that Muslims are comparatively centrist or progressive on such issues as state intervention and taxation, and that they are not distinctive in their attitudes towards abortion; however, they are broadly similar to evangelical Protestants in their disapproval of homosexuality.

83 Debbie Epstein and Richard Johnson, eds., *Schooling Sexualities* (Buckingham, UK: Open University Press, 1998), 174. See also C.J. Pascoe, *Dude, You're a Fag: Masculinity and Sexuality in High School* (Berkeley: University of California Press, 2007); M. Kehler, "Hallway Fears and High School Friendships: The Complications of Young Men (Re)negotiating Heterosexualized Identities," *Discourse: Studies in the Cultural Politics of Education* 28, 2 (2007): 259–77.

84 Margaret Schneider and Anne Dimito, "Educators' Beliefs about Raising Lesbian, Gay, Bisexual, and Transgender Issues in Schools: The Experience of Ontario, Canada," *Journal of LGBT Youth* 5, 4 (2008): 49–71; Gabrielle Richard, "L'Éducation 'aux orientations sexuelles': Représentations de l'homosexualité dans les curricula formel et informel de l'école secondaire québécoise" (MA thesis, Université du Québec à Montréal, 2010).

85 Louise Brown, "Critical Mass," *Toronto Star*, August 30, 2014.

Chapter 6: Declining Influence of Conservative Faith in Alberta

1 The comment was by Allan Hunsperger, in a 2011 blog, the full text of which appears in Thomas Flanagan, *Winning Power: Canadian Campaigning in the Twenty-First Century* (Montreal and Kingston: McGill-Queen's University Press, 2014), 180–81.

2 Nelson Wiseman, "The Pattern of Prairie Politics," in *Party Politics in Canada*, 8th ed., ed. Hugh Thorburn and Alan Whitehorn (Toronto: Prentice-Hall, 2001), 353, 355. See also his *In Search of Canadian Political Culture* (Vancouver: UBC Press, 2007), and "Provincial Conservatism," in *Conservatism in Canada*, ed. James Farney and David Rayside (Toronto: University of Toronto Press, 2013), 222.

3 Clark Banack, "Religion and Political Thought in Alberta" (PhD diss., University of British Columbia, 2012); and Clark Banack, "Conservative Christianity, Anti-Statism, and Alberta's Public Sphere: The Curious Case of Bill 44," in *Religion in the Public Sphere: Canadian Case Studies*, ed. Solange Lefebvre and Lori G. Beaman, 257–74 (Toronto: University of Toronto Press, 2014).

4 Rand Dyck, *Provincial Politics in Canada*, 3rd ed. (Toronto: Prentice-Hall, 1996), 517–18; and David Laycock, *The New Right and Democracy in Canada: Understanding Reform and the Canadian Alliance* (Toronto: Oxford University Press, 2002).

5 Jared Wesley, *Code Politics: Campaigns and Cultures on the Canadian Prairies* (Vancouver: UBC Press, 2011), especially chap. 3.

6 Linda Trimble, "The Politics of Gender," in *Government and Politics in Alberta*, ed. Allan Tupper and Roger Gibbins, 219–45 (Edmonton: University of Alberta Press, 1992).

7 David J. Elkins and Richard Simeon, eds., *Small Worlds: Provinces and Parties in Canadian Political Life* (Toronto: Methuen, 1980).

8 Ailsa Henderson, "Regional Political Cultures in Canada," *Canadian Journal of Political Science* 37, 3 (2004): 595–615.

9 Allan Tupper and Roger Gibbins, "Alberta Politics: Change and Continuity," in *Government and Politics in Alberta*, ed. Tupper and Gibbins, xv-xxvii (Edmonton: University of Alberta Press, 1992). This view is also evident in Howard Palmer and Tamara Palmer, *Alberta: A New History* (Edmonton: Hurtig, 1990).

10 Mark Lisac, *Alberta Politics Uncovered: Taking Back Our Province* (Edmonton: NeWest Press, 2004), 3.

11 Ibid., 87, 79.

12 Confidential interview, May 30, 2011.

13 Peter Smith, "Alberta: A Province Just Like Any Other?" in *The Provincial State: Politics in Canada's Provinces and Territories*, ed. Keith Brownsey and Michael Howlett (Mississauga, ON: Copp Clark Pitman, 1992), 251–52.

14 Smith, "Alberta," This is also evident in the campaign priorities tracked by Jared Wesley in *Code Politics*.

15 Smith, "Alberta," 258; Wesley, *Code Politics*, 95–99.

16 Dyck, *Provincial Politics in Canada*, 554–56. See also several of the contributions to Gordon Laxer and Trevor Harrison, eds., *The Trojan Horse: Alberta and the Future of Canada* (Montreal: Black Rose, 1995).

17 This view was articulated by several close observers of Klein during the heated debate over the addition of sexual orientation to Alberta's Individual Rights Protection Act in 1998 (confidential interviews) and by Neil Thomlinson (personal correspondence). This is also Don Martin's view in *King Ralph: The Political Life and Success of Ralph Klein* (Toronto: Key Porter, 2002).

18 Sheldon Alberts, "Don't Interfere with Morality, Klein Tells UA," *National Post*, February 20, 1999.

19 Smith, "Alberta." See also David Stewart and Anthony Sayers, "'Christian Conservatives' in the Conservative Heartland: A Preliminary Analysis," paper presented to the Annual Meeting of the Prairie Political Science Association, Winnipeg, October 2010.

20 Trevor Harrison, "The Reform-Ation of Provincial Politics," in Laxer and Harrison, *Trojan Horse*, 48. See also Palmer and Palmer, *Alberta*, 361–62.

21 David Taras and Allan Tupper, "Alberta's Challenge to the Canadian Political Agenda," in *Canada: The State of the Federation*, ed. Douglas Brown and Janet Hiebert (Kingston: Institute of Intergovernmental Relations, 1994), 71.

22 Marta Gold, "Abortion Hot Topic for Tories," *Edmonton Journal*, April 1, 1995.

23 This section is based substantially on confidential interviews conducted by Rayside from 1998 to 2001.

24 Survey by University of Alberta Population Research Lab, reported in "Gays Fighting an Uphill Battle in Alberta," *Edmonton Journal*, January 21, 1991. In his analysis of regional differences in Canadian attitudes, Michael Ornstein shows that, in 1981, 55 percent of Albertans supported the protection of "homosexuals" from employment discrimination, somewhat lower than Ontario (60 percent) and British Columbia (63 percent), but not radically so ("Regionalism in Canadian Political Ideology," in *Regionalism in Canada*, ed. Robert Brym, 64–67 (Toronto: Irwin Publishing, 1986).

25 Mark Lisac, "Cultures Clashed When Tory Caucus Faced Gay Rights," *Edmonton Journal*, April 10, 1998.

26 Interview, April 28, 1999.

27 *Globe and Mail,* "Foes of Gay Ruling Bombard Klein," April 8, 1998.
28 "Alberta Justice Issues Research, Final Report" (December 1998), cited in Ashley Geddes, "Cabinet Tackles Gay Rights," *Edmonton Journal,* March 3, 1999.
29 Interview, April 28, 1999.
30 Larry Johnsrude, "Private Bill Would Block Recognition of Gay Marriage," *Edmonton Journal,* February 24, 2000.
31 "Alberta May Invoke Notwithstanding Clause over Same-Sex Marriage," *CBC News,* July 27, 2005, http://www.cbc.ca/news/canada/alberta-may-invoke-notwithstanding -clause-over-same-sex-marriage-1.528949.
32 This is a point also made by Clark Banack in "Understanding the Influence of Faith-Based Organizations on Education Policy in Alberta," *Canadian Journal of Political Science* 48, 4 (2015): 933–59.
33 This is a point that Rayside's work suggests and that is made forcefully by Clark Banack in "Conservative Christianity" and in "The Activity and Influence of Faith-Based Organizations with Respect to Education Policy in Alberta," paper presented to the American Political Science Association, Washington, DC, August 2014.
34 Alison Taylor, *The Politics of Educational Reform in Alberta* (Toronto: University of Toronto Press, 2001). See also Michael Wagner, "Charter Schools in Alberta: Change or Continuity in Progressive Conservative Education Policy?" *Alberta Journal of Educational Research* 45, 1 (1999): 52–66.
35 Wagner, "Charter Schools in Alberta."
36 Ibid.
37 Alison Taylor, "'Fellow Travellers' and 'True Believers': A Case Study of Religion and Politics in Alberta Schools," *Journal of Education Policy* 16, 1 (2001): 23.
38 Taylor, *Politics of Educational Reform in Alberta,* especially chap. 1.
39 Taylor, "'Fellow Travellers,'" 19.
40 Taylor, *Politics of Educational Reform in Alberta,* 14 (see also chap. 10).
41 Alison Taylor and Jesse Mackay, "Three Decades of Choice in Edmonton Schools," *Journal of Education Policy* 23, 5 (2008): 549–66. For all its faith-based schools, the board would be responsible for the assignment of teachers and administrators, but such appointments would not be made without the approval of the not-for-profit society that created the school in the first place.
42 In one of these cases, the Mennonite Education Society of Calgary asked that its Menno Simon Christian School be allowed to join the Palliser board. The society owns the building but receives full financial support for its academic and extra-curricular activities.
43 See Banack, "Conservative Christianity," 257–74; and Pamela Dickey Young, "'Severely Normal' Sexuality and Religion in Alberta's Bill 44," in *Religion and Sexuality: Diversity and the Limits of Tolerance,* ed. Pamela Dickey Young, Heather Shipley, and Tracy J. Trothen (Vancouver: UBC Press, 2015), 48.
44 Dickey Young, "Severely Normal," 50, 56.

45 Stewart and Sayers, "'Christian Conservatives' in the Conservative Heartland.

46 Confidential interview, May 30, 2011. Jim Farney makes a similar point in *Social Conservatives and Party Politics in Canada and the United States* (Toronto: University of Toronto Press, 2012), 115.

47 Confidential interview, May 30, 2011.

48 Ibid.

49 Trimble, "Politics of Gender," 219–45.

50 She saw herself very much in the mould of Peter Lougheed and Joe Clark. See Jason Markusoff, "Our Surprising Premier," *Alberta Views* 16, 1(2013): 34–39.

51 Markusoff, "Our Surprising Premier," 35.

52 "Alberta's Premier-Elect Signals a Province in Transition," *Toronto Star*, October 3, 2011.

53 This compared to 48 percent of the PC voters, 22 percent of Liberals, and 29 percent of NDPers. See Stewart and Sayers, "'Christian Conservatives' in the Conservative Heartland."

54 Confidential interview, June 1, 2011.

55 Personal interview, June 13, 2012.

56 David Climenhaga, "Has Wildrose Alliance Support Peaked? If So, It's All Downhill from Here!" *Rabble.ca Blog*, July 3, 2011, http://rabble.ca/blogs/bloggers/djclimenhaga/2011/07/has-wildrose-alliance-support-peaked-if-so-its-all-downhill-here.

57 Jason Fekete, "Wildrose Unveils Its Vision," *Calgary Herald*, November 10, 2009.

58 Interview, May 17, 2011.

59 Confidential interview, June 1, 2011.

60 Confidential interview, May 29, 2011.

61 Josh Wingrove and Dawn Walton, "In Alberta, an Election, and a Horse Race," *Globe and Mail*, March 27, 2012.

62 Quoted in Josh Wingrove and Dawn Walton, "Opposition Piles on in Bid to Slow Wildrose," *Globe and Mail*, April 7, 2012. As Tom Flanagan points out, "It took Smith a couple of days to arrive at the simple position that she wouldn't legislate on conscience rights." See Flanagan, *Winning Power*, 178.

63 Thaddeus Baklinski, "Alberta Pro-Life Rolls Out Defund Abortion Campaign," *LifeSiteNews*, March 1, 2012, https://www.lifesitenews.com/news/alberta-pro-life-rolls-out-defund-abortion-campaign.

64 Flanagan, *Winning Power*, 178.

65 The full text appears in Flanagan, *Winning Power*, 180–81.

66 James Wood, "Wildrose Candidate Tells Gays in Lady Gaga-Inspired Blog Post: 'You Will Suffer the Rest of Eternity in the Lake of Fire, Hell,'" *National Post*, April 15, 2012.

67 Josh Wingrove, "Alberta Race Hinges on a Changing Alberta," *Globe and Mail*, April 17, 2012; and Jeffrey Simpson, "Nothing's Rosy for Climate if Wildrose Wins," *Globe and Mail*, April 20, 2012.

68 Jen Gerson, "'Caucasian Advantage' Quip Casts Shadow over Wildrose Campaign Despite Poll Lead," *National Post*, April 17, 2012.

69 Danielle Smith, http://www.wildrose.ca/blog/danielle-speaks-about-mondays -election/ (n.b., page no longer exists).

70 Yannick Dufresne and Gregory Eady, "Social Conservatism in Alberta," presentation made to "Alberta Election 2012: Continuity or Seismic Shift?," panel discussion, Department of Political Science, University of Toronto, May 14, 2012.

71 David McGrane, "Centrism, Ideological Polarization, and the Canadian Provincial Voter," in *Provinces; Canadian Provincial Politics*, 3rd ed., ed. Christopher Dunn (Toronto: University of Toronto Press, 2015), 198.

72 "Wildrose May Reconsider Some Policies, Smith Says," *CBC News*, April 24, 2012, http://www.cbc.ca/news/canada/manitoba/wildrose-may-reconsider-some -policies-smith-says-1.1178620.

73 Personal interview, June 13, 2012.

74 Confidential interview, June 12, 2012.

75 Karen Dleiss, "Danielle Smith Attends Edmonton Pride Event, Won't Apologize for Former Candidate's Fiery Comment," *Edmonton Journal*, June 13, 2012.

76 Keith Gerein, "Smith Pledges Wildrose Will Be More Careful in Selecting Candidates," *Edmonton Journal*, November 25, 2012.

77 Confidential interview, May 2012.

78 Quoted in Jason Markusoff, "Our Surprising Premier," 35.

79 Gary Mason, "Defections the Latest Thorny Issue for Fading Wildrose," *Globe and Mail*, November 26, 2014.

80 Paula Simons, "The Lake of Fire Is Just Too Crowded to Burn the Wildrose This Time Around," *Edmonton Journal*, April 16, 2015.

81 "Debate over Gay-Straight Clubs 'Hateful,' Nenshi Says," *Toronto Star*, December 13, 2014.

82 Rick Bell, "Wildrose Leadership Contender Brian Jean on 'Nutbars' and 'Crazies,'" *Calgary Sun*, March 4, 2015.

83 Simons, "Lake of Fire Is Just too Crowded."

84 Gary Mason, "Brian Jean Enters Critical Stretch," *Globe and Mail*, April 23, 2015.

85 Andrea Huncar, "Two Private Schools Won't Comply with Alberta LGBTQ Policy, Says Pastor," *CBC News*, August 30, 2016.

86 Justin Giovannetti, "Tory MLA Defects to NDP, Cites Sexism and Personal Attacks," and Gary Mason, "Not So Progressive: U.S.-Style Politics Seep into Alberta," *Globe and Mail*, November 18, 2016.

87 Lisac, *Alberta Politics Uncovered*, 87.

88 Kurt Bowen, *Christians in a Secular World: The Canadian Experience* (Montreal and Kingston: McGill-Queen's University Press, 2004), 54–55.

89 Brenda O'Neill, "Women's Status across the Canadian Provinces, 1999-2002," in *Provinces: Canadian Provincial Politics*, 2nd ed., ed. Christopher Dunn (Peterborough: Broadview, 2006), 481; Warren Clark, "Pockets of Belief: Religious Attendance

Patterns in Canada," *Canadian Social Trends* 5 (Spring 2003), http://www.statcan. gc.ca/sites/default/files/6493-eng.pdf. See also Howard Palmer, with Tamara Palmer, *Alberta: A New History* (Edmonton: Hurtig, 1990), 337.

90 David Stewart and Anthony Sayers, "Albertans' Conservative Beliefs," in *Conservatism in Canada*, ed. James Farney and David Rayside, 252–55 (Toronto: University of Toronto Press, 2013).

91 McGrane, "Centrism," 191.

92 Brenda O'Neill, "Variation in Women's Status across the Provinces, 1999–2014," in Dunn, *Provinces*, 127. This is also reflected in Reginald Bibby's survey of Canadian teens, indicating that 38 percent of those in Alberta agreed that abortion should be available for any reason – the same percent as for Canada as a whole. See Reginald Bibby, *The Emerging Millennials* (Lethbridge: Project Canada, 2009), 157.

93 Doreen Barrie, in *The Other Alberta: Decoding a Political Enigma* (Regina: Canadian Plains Research Centre, 2006), cites a number of surveys from the early 2000s indicating the same patterns (53–54).

Chapter 7: Schooling, Sexuality, and Religious Conservatism in BC Politics

1 *100 Huntley Street*, July 27, 2012. Clark stated: "So I think that's the hard part, because many times as with many decisions that we face, and we learn this in the Bible, it's much easier to make a short-term decision that will make everybody happy or that will make your life a little bit easier, than it is to make a long-term decision that's good for the future but may be tough in the short run."

2 Michael Bolen, "Christy Clark: Bible Helps Me Make Tough Decisions," *Huffington Post*, August 2, 2012, http://www.huffingtonpost.ca/2012/08/02/christy-clark -bible-100-huntley-street_n_1732502.html.

3 BC Humanists Association, "New Poll Shows British Columbia Largely Non-Religious, Supports Separation of Religion and Government," press release, April 29, 2013.

4 See Figure I.1, and in particular the 2011 Canadian Election Study results for a question on the importance of religion, which indicates that 37 percent of British Columbians responded that religion is very important to them, exactly the Canadian average, and the Ipsos 2011 poll, which indicates that weekly attendance is only slightly lower than the Canadian average.

5 The 2011 Canadian Election Study shows 5.1 percent, the Canadian provincial Election Study of 2013 shows 5.0 percent.

6 Statistics Canada, "British Columbia, Religion," National Household Survey, 2011.

7 In considering the role of Christianity among the province's Asian communities, Don Baker argues that "ethnic and cultural differences are reinforced by religious institutions," which can lead to greater resistance to social change in secular society. See his "Korean Religiosity in Comparative Perspective," in *Asian Religions in British Columbia*, ed. Larry DeVries, Don Baker, and Dan Overmyer, 163–83 (Vancouver: UBC Press, 2010).

8 Kurt Bowen, *Christians in a Secular World: The Canadian Experience* (Montreal and Kingston: McGill-Queen's University Press, 2004), 54–55. Across Canada, 21 percent of the religiously committed were conservative Protestant. Levels of religious commitment overall, in his analysis, were much the same as the Canadian average.

9 R.K. Carty, Lynda Erickson, and Donald E. Blake, "Leaders, Parties and Polarized Politics: British Columbia," in *Leaders and Parties in Canada*, ed. R.K. Carty, L. Erickson, and D.E. Blake (Toronto: Harcourt Brace Jovanovich, 1992), 101; and Mark Crawford, "Pluralism, Institutionalism, and the Theories of BC Politics," *BC Studies* 172 (2011): 13.

10 Donald Blake, *Two Political Worlds: Parties and Voting in British Columbia* (Vancouver: UBC Press, 1985), 13.

11 Donald Blake, R.K. Carty, and Lynda Erickson, *Grassroots Politicians: Party Activists in British Columbia* (Vancouver: UBC Press, 1991), 5.

12 Chris Mackenzie, *Pro-Family Politics and Fringe Parties in Canada* (Vancouver: UBC Press, 2005), 257.

13 Robert Burkinshaw, *Pilgrims in Lotus Land: Conservative Protestantism in British Columbia, 1917–1981* (Montreal and Kingston: McGill-Queen's University Press, 1995), 4.

14 Despite this finding, relative few evangelicals held prominent political positions in 1950s British Columbia, though when they did it was almost always through Social Credit. See Burkinshaw, *Pilgrims in Lotus Land,* 196; Mackenzie, *Pro-Family Politics,* 95.

15 Cited by Burkinshaw, *Pilgrims in Lotus Land,* 196.

16 Walter D. Young, "Political Parties," in *The Reins of Power: Governing British Columbia,* ed. John Terence Morley (Vancouver: Douglas and McIntyre, 1983), 97.

17 Daniel Gawthrop, *Highwire Act: Power, Pragmatism, and the Harcourt Legacy* (Vancouver: New Star, 1996), 16–17.

18 Blake, *Two Political Worlds,* 87. In comparing BC's party system to its federal counterpart, he argues that, "insofar as national conflicts revolve around cultural and language issues, as they surely have done in the 1970s, they engage regional, ethnic and religious loyalties which are largely irrelevant in provincial politics" (7).

19 Donald Blake, "The Politics of Polarization: Parties and Elections in British Columbia," in *Politics, Policy, and Government in British Columbia,* ed. R. Kenneth Carty (Vancouver: UBC Press, 1996), 74.

20 Vander Zalm had deep roots within BC's Catholic community. In 1984, for example, he was a key organizer of Pope John Paul II's visit to the province. See William Rayner, *British Columbia's Premiers in Profile* (Surrey: Heritage House, 2005), 215.

21 Mackenzie, *Pro-Family Politics,* 13.

22 Sarah Cox, "Turning to Christ Will Aid Poor, Vander Zalm Says." *Vancouver Sun,* April 18, 1988.

23 David Rayside and Evert Lindquist, "Canada: Community Activism, Federalism, and the New Politics of Disease," in *AIDS in the Industrialized Democracies,* ed. David

Kirp and Ronald Bayer, 67–75 (Montreal and Kingston: McGill-Queen's University Press, 1992).

24 Denny Boyd, "Sex Education, Not Foolish Piety, Might Halt AIDS," *Vancouver Sun*, January 29, 1987.

25 Gawthrop, *Highwire Act*, 60.

26 Mackenzie, *Pro-Family Politics*, 14–15.

27 Blake et al., *Grassroots Politicians*, 26. Liberal party activists with no religious affiliation grew from 21 percent in 1974 to 27 percent in 1987.

28 David Rayside, *Queer Inclusions, Continental Divisions: Public Recognition of Sexual Diversity in Canada and the United States* (Toronto: University of Toronto Press, 2008), 98.

29 David Rayside, "Social Democracy, Labour Unions, and Same-Sex Relationship Recognition in British Columbia," paper presented at the annual meeting of the American Political Science Association, Boston, September, 1998.

30 Confidential interview with Liberal strategist, June 3, 2011.

31 P. Smith, "Completing the 'Three-Peat': Recent Provincial Elections in British Columbia," *Canadian Political Science Review* 4, 2–3 (2010): 90–96.

32 Dennis Pilon, "British Columbia: Right-Wing Coalition Politics and Neoliberalism," in *Transforming Provincial Politics: The Political Economy of Canada's Provinces and Territories in the Neoliberal Era*, ed. Bryan M. Evans and Charles W. Smith (Toronto: University of Toronto, 2015), 299.

33 Doug Ward, "Bennett Endorses Campbell," *Vancouver Sun*, April 20, 2001.

34 Confidential interview with Liberal strategist, June 3, 2011.

35 Crawford, "Pluralism," 81.

36 Pilon, "British Columbia," 299.

37 Doug Todd, "The Politics of Spirituality," *Vancouver Sun*, May 13, 2005.

38 Christy Clark, *The Families First Agenda for Change*, 2011, http://www.deslibris.ca/ID/233017.

39 The term came from Manning's description of Grey as a combination Margaret Thatcher, Britain's "Iron Lady," and Anne Murray, who had the hit song "Snowbird." See Peter O'Neil, "Clark Tries to Win Over the Right: Enlists Manning," *National Post*, March 10, 2012.

40 G. Gary Mason, "Christy Clark Morphs from Premier Mom to Iron Lady," *Globe and Mail*, March 16, 2012.

41 Douglas Todd, "Christy Clark Stands up for Her Anglican Faith," *Vancouver Sun*, February 6, 2013.

42 Kim Haakstad, *Multicultural Strategic Outreach Plan*, 2012. The NDP obtained a copy of the Liberal's Multicultural Outreach Strategy and criticized the party for using apologies to minority communities as ways to get "quick wins" that could increase the odds of a Liberal victory at the next election. See Craig McInnes, "Ethnic Vote Report Finds Serious Misuse of BC Government Resources," *Vancouver Sun*, March 4, 2013.

43 Blake, *Two Political Worlds*, 87.

44 Deani Neven Van Pelt, "Home Schooling in Canada: The Current Picture – 2015 Edition," *Fraser Institute*, 23, https://www.fraserinstitute.org/sites/default/files/home-schooling-in-canada-2015-rev2.pdf.

45 British Columbia Ministry of Education, *Student Statistics – 2014/15*, http://www.bced.gov.bc.ca/reporting/province.php.

46 Mackenzie, *Pro-Family Politics*, 30.

47 Lois Sweet, *God in the Classroom: The Controversial Issue of Religion in Canada's Schools* (Toronto: McClelland and Stewart, 1997), 117.

48 BC Liberals, *Today's BC Liberals Party Response*, http://bccpac.bc.ca/sites/default/files/articles/bccpac.liberal.response.pdf.

49 See Rayside, *Queer Inclusions*, 225–27; David Rayside, "The Inadequate Recognition of Sexual Diversity by Canadian Schools: LGBT Advocacy and Its Impact," *Journal of Canadian Studies* 48, 1 (2014): 202–3; Elizabeth Meyer, "Teachers, Sexual Orientation and the Law in Canada: A Human Rights Perspective" *Clearing House* 83 (2010): 89–95.

50 In 2003, the Greater Victoria School Board adopted recommendations aimed at fostering respect and safety for minority students, including transgender students. In 2004, the Vancouver School Board introduced anti-LGBT bullying policies as well as curricular reform.

51 See Clark Banack, "Conservative Christianity, Anti-Statism and Alberta's Public Sphere: The Curious Case of Bill 44," in *Religion in the Public Sphere: Perspectives across the Canadian Provinces*, ed. Solange Lefebvre and Lori G. Beaman, 257–74 (Toronto: University of Toronto Press, 2014).

52 Janet Steffenhagen, "BC Plans Tougher Anti-Bullying Policies to Protect Students," *Vancouver Sun*, December 16, 2011.

53 Craig Takeuchi, "Alberta Passes Gay-Straight Alliance Bill But BC Won't Follow," *Georgia Straight*, March 16, 2015.

Chapter 8: Conflicted Secularism in Quebec Party Politics

1 The 2011 census reports that 75 percent of Quebeckers identify as Roman Catholic, 5 percent as Protestant, 3 percent as Christian Orthodox, and 5 percent as affiliated with non-Christian religions. Eighty-two percent of the population used French at home entirely or part of the time. See Statistics Canada, *2011 National Household Survey Data Tables*: Religion (108), Immigration Status and Period of Immigration (11).

2 Hubert Guindon, "The Crown, the Catholic Church, and the French-Canadian People: The Historical Roots of Quebec Nationalism," in Hubert Guindon, *Quebec Society: Tradition, Modernity, and Nationhood* (Toronto: University of Toronto Press, 1988), 108–9.

3 Kevin Christiano, "The Trajectory of Catholicism in Twentieth-Century Quebec," in *The Church Confronts Modernity: Catholicism since 1950 in the United States, Ireland,*

and Quebec, ed. Leslie Woodcock Tentler (Washington, DC: The Catholic University of America Press, 2007), 21. See also Maurice Pinard and Richard Hamilton, "Les Québécois votent non: Le sens et la portée du vote," in *Comportement électoral au Québec*, ed. Jean Crête (Chicoutimi: Gaëtan Morin, 1984), 381. Various surveys of the Institut canadien d'opinion publique are used to show that, among francophones, weekly attendance remained high (over 80 percent) through the late 1940s, the 1950s, and the early 1960s, declining to 61 percent in 1975 and 46 percent in 1978. Among Quebec Protestants, the decline set in earlier, from 60 percent in 1946, to 32 percent in 1965, and 27 percent in 1978.

4 Christiano, "Trajectory of Catholicism," 30.

5 The data for this figure are drawn from Mark A. Noll, *What Happened to Christian Canada?* (Vancouver: Regent College Publishing, 2007), 14; Christiano, "Trajectory of Catholicism," 26–32; E.-Martin Meunier, Jean-François Laniel, and Jean-Christophe Demers, "Permanence et recomposition de la 'religion culturelle': Aperçu socio-historique du catholicisme québécois (1970–2006)," in *Modernité et religion au Québec*, ed. Robert Mager and Serge Cantin (Québec: Les Presses de l'Université Laval, 2010), 86–87; Pinard and Hamilton, "Les Québécois votent non," 338–86; Angus Reid Institute, "Prayer: Alive and Well in Canada," May 8 2015, detailed data tables, http://angusreid.org/wp-content/uploads/2016/05/2016.05.04_Prayer_ReleaseTables.pdf.

6 Michael Gauvreau, "'They Are Not of Our Generation': Youth, Gender, Catholicism, and Quebec's Dechristianization, 1950–1970," in Tentler, *Church Confronts Modernity*, 82.

7 Christiano, "Trajectory of Catholicism," 34–35. It increased only fractionally to 1.5 in the early 2000s, after years of pro-natalist policies.

8 In Yvan Lamonde, *La Modernité au Québec*, 2 vols. (Montreal: Fides, 2011).

9 Gauvreau argues that, until the late 1960s, the messages conveyed in such family planning groups included suggestions that the use of contraception was not prohibited in Catholic doctrine. See Gauvreau, "They Are Not of Our Generation," 84, 64–77; and Michael Gauvreau, "From Rechristianization to Contestation: Catholic Values and Quebec Society, 1931–1970," in *Contemporary Quebec: Selected Readings and Commentaries*, ed. Michael D. Behiels and Matthew Hayday, 127–56 (Montreal and Kingston: McGill-Queen's University Press, 2011).

10 Gauvreau, "They Are Not of Our Generation," 85. As Michele Dillon argues, many Catholics already using birth control were now being told that they were in a state of sin and concluded that it was pointless attending mass. This produced a precipitous decline in mass attendance on the part of American Catholics, though not quite as much as in Quebec. See Michele Dillon, "Decline and Continuity: Catholicism since 1950 in the United States, Ireland, and Quebec," in Tentler, *Church Confronts Modernity*, 244.

11 Jeffrey G. Reitz, "National Models and Public Receptivity to Immigrants in Europe and North America: France, Canada, and Quebec in Comparative Perspective,"

paper presented at "Muslim Integration in Europe and North America: New Directions in Comparative Research," Fondation maison des sciences de l'homme, Paris, November 2015. See also Jeffrey G. Reitz, "Multiculturalism Policies and Popular Multiculturalism in the Development of Canadian Immigration," in *The Multiculturalism Question: Debating Identity in 21st Century Canada*, ed. Jack Jedwab, 107–26 (Montreal and Kingston: McGill-Queen's University Press, 2014).

12 "The idea of laïcité is often polemical. Indeed, it channels an ensemble of discontents and emotional loadings that provoke polarized reactions. Its anchoring in the history of France as well as a certain anticlericalism among French Canadian elites have given it a rigid, even anti-religious, attraction." Sophie Therrien, "La Diversité religieuse et les institutions publiques: Quelques orientations," in *La Religion dans la sphère publique*, ed. Solange Lefebvre (Montréal: Presses de l'Université de Montréal, 2005), 80–81.

13 Pierre Anctil, "Un Patrimoine en mouvance: L'apport décisif des communautés non chrétiennes," in *La Patrimoine religieux du Québec*, ed. Solange Lefebvre (Québec: Presses de l'Université Laval, 2009), 68–69.

14 Across the country, over 8 percent are attached to one or another non-Christian faith, Muslims being the largest at 3.2 percent. Among those who migrated to Quebec between 2006 and 2011, half were Christian; and Muslims were by far the largest non-Christian group – at 29 percent of the total. Across Canada, half of immigrants in those years were Christian, and Muslims constituted 17 percent.

15 Marie Mc Andrew, "Immigration, Pluralism, and Education," in *Quebec: State and Society*, 3rd ed., ed. Alain-G. Gagnon (Toronto: University of Toronto Press, 2004) 309, 315.

16 Jocelyn Maclure, *Quebec Identity: The Challenge of Pluralism* (Montreal and Kingston: McGill-Queen's University Press, 2003), Introduction. See also Raymond Breton, "From Ethnic to Civic Nationalism," *Ethnic and Racial Studies* 11, 1 (1988): 85–102.

17 Luc Turgeon, "Interpreting Quebec's Historical Trajectories: Between La Société Globale and the Regional Space," in Gagnon, *Québec*, 55.

18 Maclure, *Quebec Identity*, 13, 136–37, chap. 4.

19 Guillaume Lamy, *Laïcité et valeurs québécoises: Les sources d'une controverse* (Montréal: Québec Amérique, 2015), especially chaps. 3 and 4.

20 Ines Molinaro, "Context and Integration: The Allophone Communities in Quebec," in Behiels and Hayday, *Contemporary Quebec*, 461.

21 Daniel Salée, "Quebec Sovereignty and the Challenge of Linguistic and Ethnocultural Minorities: Identity, Difference, and the Politics of *Ressentiment*," in Behiels and Hayday, *Contemporary Quebec*, 474.

22 Gérard Bouchard, *Interculturalism: A View from Quebec*, trans. Howard Scott (Toronto: University of Toronto Press, 2015), 4, 59.

23 Mc Andrew, "Immigration, Pluralism, and Education," in Gagnon, *Québec*, 310–11. See also Bouchard, *Interculturalism*, though Bouchard's argument is that

multiculturalism has evolved since its origins in ways that reduce the apparent starkness between its early conception and interculturalism (chap. 3). Jeffrey Reitz argues that the complex policy mix related to immigration differs in few substantive terms between Quebec and the rest of the country.

24 Anctil, "Un Patrimoine en mouvance," 79. Alongside many commentators, Anctil side-steps the long history (up to the present) of Catholic and Protestant claims that faith could not be restricted to the private realm.

25 André Siegfried, *The Race Question in Canada* (Montreal and Kingston: McGill-Queen's University Press, 1966), 26. As Lamy points out, civic republicans point to the long roots of Quebec's anti-clericalism outside of legislative politics, including the period of the 1837 rebellion (*Laïcité et valeurs québécoises*, chap. 3). See also André Lamoureux, "Le Système partisan au Québec," in *La Politique québécoise et canadienne: Une approche pluraliste*, ed. Alain-G. Gagnon, 423–26 (Québec: Presses de l'Université du Québec, 2014).

26 Fernand Ouellet, "The Historical Background of Separatism in Quebec," in *French Canadian Nationalism: An Anthology*, ed. Ramsay Cook, 58–60 (Toronto: Macmillan of Canada, 1969); and Jean-Paul Bernard, *Les Rouges: Libéralisme, nationalisme et anti-cléricalisme au milieu du XIXe siècle* (Montréal: Presses de l'Université du Québec, 1971).

27 See Vincent Lemieux, *Le Parti Libéral du Québec* (Sainte-Foy: Les Presses de l'Université Laval, 1993), 14; H. Blair Neatby, *Laurier and a Liberal Quebec: A Study in Political Management* (Toronto: McClelland and Stewart, 1973); and Dale C. Thomson, *Jean Lesage and the Quiet Revolution* (Toronto: Macmillan of Canada, 1984), 29–91.

28 Lemieux, *Le Parti Libéral*, 27, 37–38.

29 Herbert Quinn, *The Union Nationale: A Study in Quebec Nationalism* (Toronto: University of Toronto Press, 1963), 72; and Kenneth McRoberts, *Quebec: Social Change and Political Crisis*, 3rd ed. (Toronto: McClelland and Stewart, 1993), 105–6. It was the UN government, in 1936, that placed a crucifix over the speaker's chair in the Quebec legislature.

30 Réjean Pelletier, "Évolution du système de partis au Québec," in *Les Partis politiques québécois dans la tourmente*, ed. Réjean Pelletier (Québec: Presses de l'Université Laval, 2012), 57; and Pierre Drouilly, "La Structure des appuis aux partis politique québécois, 1998–2008," in Pelletier, *Les Partis politiques*, 155–56.

31 Solange Lefebvre, *Cultures et spiritualités des jeunes* (Montréal: Bellarmin, 2008), 219.

32 See Maurice Pinard, "Classes sociales et comportement électoral," in *Quatres élections provinciales au Québec, 1956–1966*, ed. Vincent Lemieux (Québec: Les Presses de l'Université Laval, 1969), 158.

33 Jean Hamelin and André Garon, "La Vie politique au Québec de 1956 à 1966," in Lemieux, *Quatres élections provinciales au Québec*, 14.

34 Pelletier, *Partis politiques*, 101, 193–95; Jennifer Wallner, *Learning to School: Federalism and Public Schooling in Canada* (Toronto: University of Toronto Press, 2014), 131, 164.

35 Among these were voices associated with the influential journal *Parti Pris*. See Lamy, *Laïcité et valeurs québécoises*, 125–26, 199.

36 Thomson, *Jean Lesage and the Quiet Revolution*, 309. Francois Rocher also points out the persistent support for religious instruction in the Quiet Revolution period, in "Quebec's Secularism Regime under (High) Tension," in *Revealing Democracy: Secularism and Religion in Liberal Democratic States*, ed. Chantal Maillé, Greg M. Nielsen, and Daniel Salée (Bruxelles: P.I.E. Peter Lang, 2014), 131.

37 Quoted from the official 1962 program by Pelletier, *Partis politiques*, 285.

38 On the UN's difficulty in navigating the space between Liberals and the PQ, see Pelletier, "L'Évolution du système de partis au Quebec: Un bipartisme tenace," in Pelletier, *Partis politiques*, 30–31.

39 Hubert Guindon, "The Rise and Demise of the Parti Québécois," in Guindon, *Quebec Society*, 157.

40 In 1970, of the 181 legal therapeutic abortions performed in the province, only one was in a francophone hospital. Eighty percent of the total were performed by one hospital – the Montreal General. In 1976, the numbers had increased to over 7,200, but only 14 of 95 hospitals had functioning abortion committees, and 70 percent of abortions were performed at the Montreal General. See Canadians for Choice and Fédération du Québec pour la planning des naissances, *Focus on Abortion Services in Quebec* (Quebec: CFC and FQPN, 2010), 14–15.

41 When an Ontario NDP government bill recognizing such relationships ended up in legislative defeat, the PQ government of Jacques Parizeau visibly backed off commitments to proceed on the matter. It took its first significant step only in 1999, with a measure that was far from being a pioneer in the area.

42 Bouchard, *Interculturalism*, 33–34.

43 Dimitrios Karmis, "Pluralism and National Identity(ies) in Contemporary Quebec: Conceptual Clarifications, Typology, and Discourse Analysis," in Gagnon, *Québec*, 82–91.

44 Carolle Simard, "La Politique migratoire," in Gagnon, *La Politique québécoise et canadienne*, 659–62.

45 Among the 54 percent who reported rarely or never attending mass, 78 percent supported the PQ, and 22 percent other parties (overwhelmingly the Liberals). Among those attending once/week, 56 percent supported the PQ. See André Blais, "L'Appui au Parti Québécois: Évolution de la clientèle de 1970 à 1981," in Crête, *Comportement électoral au Québec*, 296–97.

46 CFC and FQPN, "Focus on Abortion Services in Quebec," 23.

47 Ibid., 36.

48   This was only a week after Quebec cardinal Marc Ouellet condemned abortion in very strong uncompromising language. See Ingrid Peritz and Rhéal Séguin, "Quebec MNAs Challenge Harper's Abortion Stance," *Globe and Mail*, May 19, 2010.

49   The first is based on the 2011 Canadian Election Study, reported in Brenda O'Neill, "Variation in Women's Status across the Provinces," in *Provinces: Canadian Provincial Politics*, 3rd ed., ed. Christopher Dunn (Toronto: University of Toronto Press, 2016), 127.

50   Stéphanie Tremblay, *Écoles et religions: Genèse du nouveau pari québécois (1996–2009)* (Montréal: Fides, 2010), 26.

51   Lefebvre, *Culture et spiritualités des jeunes*, 220.

52   Tremblay, *Écoles et religions*, 29–39.

53   Quoted in Spencer Boudreau, "From Confessional to Cultural: Religious Education in the Schools of Quebec," *Religion and Education* 38, 3 (2011): 217.

54   See Alison Braley, "Religious Rights and Quebec's Ethics and Religious Culture Course," *Canadian Journal of Political Science* 44, 3 (2011): 613–33; and Lamy, *Laïcité et valeurs québécois*, 30–32.

55   Tremblay, *Écoles et religions*, 47–48; Boudreau, "From Confessional to Cultural," 220. Howard Adelman points to polling that shows that only half of francophones supported the new course, compared to 78 percent of non-francophones. See Howard Adelman, "Conclusion: Religion, Culture, and the State," in *Religion, Culture, and the State: Reflections on the Bouchard-Taylor Report*, ed. Howard Adelman and Pierre Anctil (Toronto: University of Toronto Press, 2011), 101.

56   *S.L. v. Commission scolaire des Chênes* [2012] 1 SCR 235; *Loyola High School v. Québec (Attorney General)* 2015 SCC 12. See Benjamin L. Berger, "Religious Diversity, Education, and the 'Crisis' in State Neutrality," *Canadian Journal of Law and Society* 29, 1 (2013): 103–22.

57   Lawrence M. Bezeau, "The Public Finance of Private Education in the Province of Quebec," *Canadian Journal of Education* 4, 2 (1979): 25.

58   The ministry could declare a school to be "of public interest" if it "ensures services of quality and contributes to the advancement of education in Quebec, by reason of the characteristics of the education which it provides, the competence of its staff and the pedagogical methods which it employs." See Canadian Education Association, "Information Note: The Public Funding of Private Schools in Canada" (February 1992), in *State Support of Religious Education: Canada versus the United Nations*, ed. Anne Bayefsky and Arieh Waldman (Leiden: Nijhoff, 2007), 554.

59   Roger Magnuson, "A Profile of Private Schools in Quebec," *McGill Journal of Education* 28, 1 (1993): 8.

60   Bezeau, "Public Finance of Private Education," 38–39.

61   Estimates for the per-pupil funding for private schools vary, in part because the Ministry of Education has the capacity to alter the proportion of funding given to public schools from year to year. See Bayefsky and Waldman, *State Support of Religious Education*, Introduction.

62 Ronan Teyssier, "The Public Funding of Private Education: A Quantitative Study of 'Who Gets What, When and How' in Four Canadian Provinces," paper presented at the Annual Meeting of the Canadian Political Science Association, Ottawa, May 2009.

63 Reported in Francis Vailles, "Les Écoles privées ne sont pas toutes laïques," *La Presse*, September 23, 2014. The report's author, Michel Lincourt, refers to most faith based schools as "aggressivement religieuses." Of all subsidized private schools, 16 were Jewish, 4 Muslim, 3 Armenian, and 1 Greek. Now, as before, the education ministry kept track of ethnicity but not of religiosity.

64 Québec Solidaire, *Electoral Platform*, 2014 Elections, Section 1.6 (a).

65 Daphnée Dion-Viens, "Écoles privées: Des coupes massives déplaceraient 30% des élèves vers le public," *La Presse*, September 27, 2014.

66 Lamy, *Laïcité et valeurs québécoises*, 125–26, 280–81.

67 Marie Mc Andrew, "Immigration, Pluralism, and Education," 312–13; Micheline Milot, "The Secular State in Quebec: Configuration and Debates," *Canadian Diversity* 10, 1 (2013): 40.

68 Ratna Ghosh and Amina Triki-Yamani analyze school textbook treatment of Muslims, and, although they find marked improvements in the late 1990s and early 2000s, they still tend to discuss Muslims outside Quebec and Canada and, therefore, to portray them as making up only a very little part of the contemporary local environment. See their "Casting the 'Other': The Treatment of Muslims in Quebec and Indian Textbooks," *Canadian Diversity* 10, 1 (2013): 82.

69 Micheline Labelle, *Racisme et antiracisme au Québec: Discours et déclinaisons* (Québec: Presses de l'Université du Québec, 2010), 113.

70 *Syndicat Northcrest v. Amselem*, [2004], 2 SCR 551, 2004 SCC 47. These and other cases are reviewed by Lamy, *Laïcité et valeurs québécoises*, 23–25.

71 *Multani v. Commission scolaire Marguerite-Bourgeoys*, [2006] 1 SCR 256, 2006, SCC 6.

72 Jack Jedwab and Maryse Potvin, "Public Opinion and Media Treatment of the 'Reasonable Accommodation' Crisis in Quebec," *Canadian Diversity* 10, 1 (2013): 96–99. For an account of these incidents and the media coverage of them, see Gérard Bouchard and Charles Taylor, *Building the Future: A Time for Reconciliation*, abridged report (Quebec: Commission de consultation sur les pratiques d'accommodement reliées aux différences culturelles, 2008).

73 See Lamoureux, "Le Système partisan au Québec," 432.

74 Pierre Anctil, "Introduction," in Adelman and Anctil, *Religion, Culture, and the State*, 5–6. See also Howard Adelman, "Monoculturalism versus Interculturalism in a Multicultural World," in the same volume, 45.

75 Frédéric Boily, "L'Action démocratique du Québec: Si près, si loin du pouvoir," in Pelletier, *Les Partis politiques*, 317.

76 Bina Toledo Freiwald, "'Qui est nous?' Some Answers from the Bouchard-Taylor Archive," in Adelman and Anctil, *Religion, Culture, and the State*, 85.

77   See Bouchard and Taylor, *Building the Future*, 42. See Section 4.

78   Anctil, "Introduction" in Adelman and Anctil, *Religion, Culture, and the State*, 14; and Howard Adelman, "Monoculturalism versus Interculturalism in a Multicultural World," in Adelman and Anctil, *Religion, Culture, and the State*, 49.

79   Rocher, "Quebec's Secularism Regime," 139–41.

80   Ibid., 142–44.

81   Karmis, "Pluralism and National Identity(ies)," 89.

82   Quoted in Karmis, "Pluralism and National Identity(ies)," 89.

83   This is a point made by Luc Turgeon, private correspondence, July 2015.

84   Quoted in Karmis, "Pluralism and National Identity(ies)," 91.

85   Sue Montgomery and Kevin Dougherty, "Pauline Marois Struggling with 'Hijab' Backlash," *Montreal Gazette*, August 15, 2012; Antonio Maioni, "Saguenay Mayor Merely a Sideshow of Quebec Election," *Globe and Mail*, August 17, 2012.

86   This is a point made by Luc Turgeon, personal correspondence, July 2015.

87   Government of Quebec, "Charte de valeurs québécoises: Québec présente ses propositions en matière de neutralité religieuse de l'État et d'encadrement des accommodements religieux," communiqué de presse, September 10, 2013.

88   John Ibbitson and Bill Curry, "Liberal Leader Couillard Dares Marois to Call Election over Secular Charter," *Globe and Mail*, September 16, 2013.

89   "Marois Treads Perilous Road with So-Called Code of Values," *Toronto Star*, September 17, 2013.

90   Ibid.

91   See, for example, Lysiane Gagnon, "Even Further Than France?," *Globe and Mail*, September 18, 2013. See also Laurence Kirmayer and Jaswant Guzder, "The Charter of Quebec Values: A View from Cultural Psychiatry," *Canadian Diversity* 10, 3 (2013): 50.

92   Lysiane Gagnon, "Wedge Politics Are the PQ's Best Friend," *Globe and Mail*, January 22, 2014.

93   Yvan Lamonde and other signatories to the Charte de la laïcité, quoted in Lamy, *Laïcité et valeurs québécoises*, 207.

94   Rhéal Séguin, "On Heels of MNA Dismissal, Liberals Define Charter Position," *Globe and Mail*, January 22, 2014.

95   Denise Helly, "L'Islam, épouvantail électoraliste péquiste," *Canadian Diversity* 10, 3 (2013): 64.

96   Confidential interview, December 2016.

97   Sophie Cousineau, "Make No Mistake: This Was a Self-Inflicted Debate," *Globe and Mail*, April 8, 2014.

98   PQ MNA and leadership candidate Alexandre Cloutier took strong exception to the remarks, though earlier Cloutier had been criticized by secularism-charter-champion Bernard Drainville, another leadership candidate, for insufficient commitment to the affirmation of a distinctly laïc Quebec identity. See "Une Déclaration de Pierre Karl Péladeau sur l'immigration crée un malaise," *Radio-Canada*, March

18, 2015; "La Survie du PQ passera par l'affirmation identitaire selon Bernard Drainville," *Radio-Canada*, March 16, 2015.

99   One example is Rima Elkouri, "Ces Prisons appelées 'écoles," *La Presse*, May 26, 2014. On Legault, see Guy Veillette, "Non à la mosquée à Shawinigan," *La Presse*, February 11, 2015. Legault separately recommended that immigrants be admitted for a probationary period, awaiting their successful sitting of a test on Quebec values.

100   Bill 62: An Act to Foster Adherence to State Religious Neutrality and, in Particular, to Provide a Framework for Religious Accommodation Requests in Certain Bodies.

101   Quoted in Les Perreaux, "Secularism Debate Roils Quebec Again," *Globe and Mail*, June 11, 2015.

102   Gérard Bouchard, "Terrorisme islamiste et rapport aux musulmans québécois," *La Presse*, June 18, 2016.

103   Cited in Konrad Yakabuski, "Lisée Does the Full Trump to Sway PQ Faithful," *Globe and Mail*, October 3, 2016.

104   Yves Boisvert, "A Week of Kindness, Then Identity Politics as Usual," *Globe and Mail*, February 10, 2017.

105   Reitz, "National Models and Public Receptivity to Immigrants."

106   Environics Institute, "Canadian Public Opinion about Immigration and Multiculturalism," Focus Canada Spring 2015, http://www.environicsinstitute.org/uploads/institute-projects/environics%20institute%20-%20focus%20canada%20spring%202015%20survey%20on%20immigration-multiculturalism%20-%20final%20report%20-%20june%2030-2015.pdf. Fifty-seven percent of Canadians disagree with the statement "overall, there is too much immigration in Canada," and that level of disagreement has held steady since 2000, at which point it increased significantly from the typical disagreement proportion of 35 percent before that. On "taking away jobs," 30 percent of Canadians agreed, with only 18 percent of Quebeckers agreeing.

107   The proportion of respondents in Quebec reacting in 2006 to immigrants and foreign workers in general as neighbours was 8 percent; to people of a different race, 5 percent; and to people speaking another language, 3 percent.

108   Adelman, "Conclusion," 100–1.

109   This was a cross-Canada survey, and it reported differences between anglophones, francophones, and speakers of other languages, regardless of province. The vast majority of francophone respondents, of course, were from Quebec, and there are not strong differences between francophones inside and outside Quebec. This survey shows that 53 percent of francophones, compared to 38 percent of anglophones, agreed that society is threatened by the influx of non-Christian immigrants. In response to the statement that religious freedom should include wearing visible religious symbols in public institutions, 34 percent of francophones, 62 percent of anglophones, and 60 percent of other language speakers agreed. Among

francophones the percentages with positive views of immigrants was 67 percent, and of Muslims 29 percent (compared to 65 percent and 46 percent, respectively, among anglophones). See Jack Jedwab, "Identity, Intergroup Relations and Concerns over Racism," *Association of Canadian Studies*, April 2014.

110   Forum Research, "Muslims the Target of Most Racial Bias," December 8, 2016, http://poll.forumresearch.com/post/2646/muslims-the-target-of-most-racial-bias/. Unfavorable views were held by 22 percent of Ontarians, for example, 26 percent of Albertans, and 21 percent of British Columbians.

111   Environics Institute, "Canadian Public Opinion," 9. The average percent agreement across Canada was 51 percent.

112   "Quebec Values Charter Support Down, Poll Shows," *CBC News*, September 16, 2013, http://www.cbc.ca/news/canada/montreal/quebec-values-charter-support -down-poll-shows-1.1855972; Christopher Curtis, "Let Courts Weigh Charter of Quebec Values, Poll Shows," *Montreal Gazette*, September 21, 2013.

113   Jack Jedwab, "What's Behind the Secularism Charter?" *Canadian Diversity* 10, 2 (Summer 2013): 28. A CROP poll taken at about the same time shows 42 percent support for the idea of a Charter among Quebeckers overall. Overall support was also strongest in requiring the uncovering of the face (81 percent) but lowest for the proposed limitations on wearing religious symbols in the public service (42 percent). See Michel Cobeil, "Sondage CROP: L'interdit sur les signes religieux accentue la division," *Le Soleil*, September 18, 2013. See also Jack Jedwab and Maryse Potvin, "Public Opinion and Media Treatment of the 'Reasonable Accommodation' Crisis in Quebec," *Canadian Diversity* 10, 1 (2013): 96–99.

114   Luc Turgeon, Antoine Bilodeau, Stephen White, and Ailsa Henderson, "Hijab, Crucifix and the Public Sphere: Support for a Ban on Minority and Majority Religious Symbols in Quebec," paper presented at the annual meeting of the Canadian Political Science Association, Ottawa, June 2015.

115   Jean-Marc Léger is among many Quebec commentators who essentially sidestep the question that prejudice is an important driver of public reactions to religious accommodation, in part on the basis of responses to the strikingly unhelpful question asking if respondents considered themselves racist. See Jean-Marc Léger, Jacques Nantel, and Pierre Duhamel, *Le Code Québec: Les sept differences quo font de nous un people unique au monde* (Montréal: Éditions de l'homme, 2016).

116   Maurice Pinard was perhaps the first, and remains one of the only, social scientist to explore the composition of each party's electoral constituency and to include religion as a factor. See his "The Ongoing Political Realignments in Quebec," in *Quebec Society and Politics*, ed. Dale C. Thomson (Toronto: McClelland and Stewart, 1973), especially 130. See also Vincent Lemieux, *Le Parti libéral du Québec* (Sainte-Foy: Les Presses de l'Université Laval, 1993); Vincent Lemieux, "The Provincial Party System in Quebec," in Thomson, *Quebec Society and Politics*, 99–118; Kenneth McRoberts, *Quebec: Social Change and Political Crisis*, 3rd ed. (Toronto: McClelland and Stewart, 1999), 105–7; Blais, "L'Appui au Parti Québécois," 297.

117 Éric Bélanger et Richard Nadeau, *Le Comportement électoral des québécois* (Montréal: Les Presses de l'université de Montréal, 2009), 67, 109. See also their "L'Élécteur québécois et les partis," in Pelletier, *Les Partis politiques québécois*, 174–75. In 2007, 47 percent of ADQ supporters attended religious services. Note how low the "attendance" threshold is.

118 The scale was a composite of responses opposing same-sex marriage, agreeing that society would be improved if people practised their faith more regularly, and supporting "traditional family values."

119 Richard Nadeau and Éric Bélanger, "Un Modèle général d'explication du vote des québécois," in *Les Québécois aux urnes: Les partis, les médias et les citoyens en campagne*, ed. Éric Bélanger, Frédérick Bastien, and François Gélineau (Montréal: Les Presses de l'Université de Montréal, 2013), 200, 203–4.

120 David McGrane, "Centrism, Ideological Polarization, and the Canadian Provincial Voter," in *Provinces: Canadian Provincial Politics*, 3rd ed., ed. Christopher Dunn, 184–216 (Toronto: University of Toronto Press, 2016).

121 McGrane also finds a similar clustering of supporters for the three parties on an index measuring respondents' attitudes towards government spending and taxation, this time with "0" representing willingness to pay more taxes and countenance higher spending, compared to "1" favouring low taxation and spending. Here the average CAQ supporter is .47, Liberals; .45, Péquistes; .39. Québec Solidaire supporters are at .30. See McGrane, "Centrism," 197–98.

122 Antoine Bilodeau, "L'Avantage libéral: Le vote des minorités visible à l'élection québécoise de 2012," in Bélanger et al., *Les Québécois aux urnes*, 237–50.

123 Chris Selley, "How Quebec's Secularism Debate Could Fizzle," *National Post*, February 7, 2014.

124 Lamy, *Laïcité et valeurs québécois*, chap. 3.

125 See, for example, Guy Rocher, "Rapport Bouchard-Taylor: Une majorité trop minoritaire," *Le Devoir*, June 12, 2008.

126 Bouchard, *Interculturalism*, 118.

127 Ibid., 239–45.

128 For a thoughtful intervention after the mosque shooting, see Alain Dubuc, "Ce sera quoi, l'après," *La Presse*, February 2, 2017.

Chapter 9: Evangelical Christianity and Northern Territorial Politics

1 Nunavut has a population of 37,000, with Iqaluit as the largest town with 6,700 inhabitants. Yukon also has 37,000 people, with Whitehorse the largest community at 23,000. The NWT has 44,000 people, with Yellowknife having almost half that population at 19,000.

2 Among the southern provinces, Manitoba and Saskatchewan have the largest Aboriginal populations – 15 percent each – and Alberta is next with 6 percent.

3 Frances Abele, "Northern Development: Past, Present, and Future," in *Northern Exposure: Peoples, Powers, and Prospects in Canada's North*, ed. Frances Abele, Thomas

J. Courchene, F. Leslie Seidle, and France St-Hilaire, 19–68 (Montreal: Institute for Public Policy Research, 2009).

4 June Helm, *The People of Denendeh: Ethnohistory of the Indians of Canada's Northwest Territories* (Montreal and Kingston: McGill-Queen's University Press, 2000), 159; Bern Will Brown, *End-of-Earth People: The Arctic Sahtu Dene* (Toronto: Dundurn, 2014), 10.

5 Frédéric B. Laugrand and Jarich G. Oosten, *Inuit Shamanism and Christianity: Transitions and Transformations in the Twentieth Century* (Montreal and Kingston: McGill-Queen's University Press, 2010), 343.

6 Kerry Abel, *Drum Songs: Glimpses of Dene History* (Montreal and Kingston: McGill-Queen's University Press, 1993); Thomas R. Berger, *Northern Frontier, Northern Homeland: Report of the Mackenzie Valley Pipeline Inquiry, Vol. 1* (Ottawa: Minister of Supply and Services, 1977); Helm, *People of Denendeh.*

7 Morris Zaslow, *The Opening of the Canadian North, 1870–1914* (Toronto: McClelland and Stewart, 1971).

8 Ailsa Henderson, *Nunavut: Rethinking Political Culture* (Vancouver: UBC Press, 2007), 51.

9 Laugrand and Oosten, *Inuit Shamanism*, 37.

10 Ibid.

11 Henderson, *Nunavut*, 194.

12 René Fumoleau, *As Long as This Land Shall Last* (Toronto: McClelland and Stewart, 1973).

13 Jerald Sabin, "Alternatives North: A History," in *The Social Economy in the North*, ed. Frances Abele and Chris Southcott (under review).

14 Jim Lotz, *Northern Realities: The Future of Northern Development in Canada* (Toronto: New Press, 1970), 71.

15 Paul Nadasdy, *Hunters and Bureaucrats: Power, Knowledge, and Aboriginal-State Relations in Southwest Yukon* (Vancouver: UBC Press, 2003), 43.

16 Graham White, "Go North, Young Scholar, Go North," *Canadian Journal of Political Science* 44 (2011): 747–68.

17 Lewis Herbert Thomas, *The Struggle for Responsible Government in the North-West Territories, 1879–1897* (Toronto: University of Toronto Press, 1957, 1978).

18 C.E.S. Franks, "How the Sabbath Came to Yukon," *Canadian Public Administration* 10, 1 (1967): 123–35.

19 Jerald Sabin, "Contested Colonialism: Responsible Government and Political Development in Yukon," *Canadian Journal of Political Science* 47, 2 (2014): 375–96.

20 Henderson, *Nunavut*, 113.

21 Ibid., 133.

22 John Devries, PC member for Watson Lake, expressed his opposition to changing the definition of spouse in the following terms: "I would also like to go on record that I cannot support the definition of 'spouse,' due to the implications of it possibly

referring to a same-sex couple on moral grounds. If one of my children came home and indicated to me that they had homosexual tendencies, I could still love them and put my arm around them, but I certainly could not condone any actions that took place from that point on." See Yukon Legislative Assembly, *Hansard*, May 4, 1992.

23 "Yukon Gold: Justice Continues to Spread," *Equal Marriage for Same-Sex Couples*, July 15, 2004, http://www.samesexmarriage.ca/legal/yu150704.htm.

24 Yukon Government, Ministry of Education, "Policy Subject: Sexual Orientation and Gender Identity," May 5, 2012, http://www.education.gov.yk.ca/pdf/sogi_policy_updated_dec_14.pdf.

25 Diocese of Whitehorse, *Living with Hope, Ministering by Love, Teaching in Truth*, 2012, 3, https://www.lifesitenews.com/images/pdfs/Living_with_Hope-Ministering_by_Love-Teaching_in_Truth.pdf.

26 Jacqueline Ronson, "Catholic School's Same-Sex Policy Revoked," *Yukon News*, March 6, 2013.

27 Letter from Minister Scott Kent to Bishop Gary M. Gordon, March 19, 2013, http://www.yukon-news.com/media/documents/kent_letter.pdf.

28 Catholic Schools of Whitehorse, *One Heart: Ministering by Love*, 2013, http://www.whitehorsediocese.org/documents/One_Heart-Ministering_by_Love.pdf.

29 Emphasis added. Yukon Employee's Union, "Trans* Rights in Yukon; One Small Victory at a Time," May 28, 2015, http://theunionbillboard.com/2015/05/28/trans-rights-in-yukon-one-small-victory-at-a-time/.

30 Pierre Chauvin, "Concerns Arise over Liberal Plans for Trans Rights," *Yukon News*, Novermber 21, 2016.

31 Jena McGill and Kyle Kirkup, "Locating the Trans Legal Subject in Canadian Law: *XY v Ontario*," *Windsor Review of Legal and Social Issues* 33 (2013): 96–140.

32 Northwest Territories, Legislative Assembly, *Hansard*, June 17, 2002: 824.

33 Ibid., February 28, 2002: 265.

34 Ibid., 262–63.

35 Ibid., June 17, 2002: 882.

36 *Deline Final Self-Government Agreement*, article 20, sub-section 1.1.

37 Yellowknife's school board has explored creating all-gender washrooms in its schools, a measure that has so far not encountered concerted local opposition. See Meagan Leonard, "Gender-Neutral Bathrooms in Public Schools Considered," *Yellowknifer*, August 12, 2015.

38 *Northern Canada Evangelical Mission*, "About Us," http://www.ncem.ca/about-us.

39 Marites N. Sison, "Arctic Diocese Bans Gays from Employment," *Anglican Journal*, September 1, 2005.

40 Patricia D'Souza, "Nunavut Decides against Same-Sex Marriage Ceremonies," *Nunatsiaq News*, November 7, 2003.

41 Nunavut, Legislative Assembly, *Hansard*, October 30, 2003: 4297.

42   Ibid., 4219.

43   "Arviat DEA Okays Bible Giveaways in Nunavut Schools," *Nunatsiaq News*, November 16, 2011; Jane George, "Complaints Prompt Rankin Inlet's Northern to Stop Selling Ouija Boards," *Nunatsiaq News*, November 16, 2011.

44   Peter Varga, "Rainbow Flag at Iqaluit City Hall Not Favoured by All, Councilor Says," *Nunatsiaq News*, February 14, 2014.

45   Sarah Rogers, "NTI President Won't Apologize for Comments about Iqaluit's Rainbow Flag," *Nunatsiaq News*, March 6, 2014.

46   David Murphy, "Iqaluit MLA Okalik Defends Gay Community in the Nunavut Legislature," *Nunatsiaq News*, March 7, 2014.

47   Rogers, "NTI President Won't Apologize."

Conclusion

1   According to The Pew Research Centre's 2016 global survey, 28 percent of Canadians reported that religion was "very important" in their lives. See "The Gender Gap in Religion around the World," March 22, 2016, http://www.pewforum.org/files/2016/03/Religion-and-Gender-Full-Report.pdf.

2   Among supporters of the Liberals, the NDP, and the Bloc Québécois, support for same-sex marriage varied between 73 percent and 82 percent, in contrast to Conservatives at 43 percent. Those favouring easy access to abortion among the then opposition parties in 2006 ranged from 71 to 85 percent, contrasted with 56 percent among Conservatives.

3   Sam Reimer, *Evangelicals and the Continental Divide* (Montreal and Kingston: McGill-Queen's University Press, 2003); Sam Reimer, "Are American and Canadian Evangelicals Really That Different," *Faith Today* (May-June 2016); and Lydia Bean, *The Politics of Evangelical Identity* (Princeton: Princeton University Press, 2014), chap. 8.

4   A variety of data on this are presented in the Introduction of this volume. The 2015 Canadian Election Study shows that 71 percent of Canadians supported same-sex marriage. The 2011 Canadian Election Study finds that just 18 percent agreed that abortion should be banned, and a 2012 Ipsos Reid survey indicates that 50 percent supported an uncompromising pro-choice position that favoured access without restriction.

5   Abacus Data, "Canadians' Moral Compass Set Differently from That of Our Neighbours to the South," July 9, 2016, http://abacusdata.ca/canadians-moral-compass-set-differently-from-that-of-our-neighbours-to-the-south/.

6   Nicholas Hune-Brown, "The Sex Ed Revolution: A Portrait of the Powerful Political Bloc That's Waging War on Queen's Park," *Toronto Life*, September 3, 2015.

7   Statistics Canada, "Projections of the Diversity of the Canadian Population, 2006-2031," cat. no. 91–551-X, March 2010. Estimates for all non-Christian affiliates for that year range from 13.4 to 15.1 percent, with Muslims constituting about half of that total by 2031 (see p. 25).

8 Among the major contributions to the ongoing debate over the power of regionalism are: David J. Elkins and Richard Simeon, eds., *Small Worlds: Provinces and Parties in Canadian Political Life* (Toronto: Methuen, 1980); R. Kenneth Carty, Lynda Erickson, and Donald E. Blake, *Leaders and Parties in Canadian Politics: Experiences of the Provinces* (Toronto: Harcourt Brace Jovanovich, 1992); Nelson Wiseman, *In Search of Canadian Political Culture* (Vancouver: UBC Press, 2007); Christopher Dunn, "Comparative Provincial Politics: A Review," in *The Provincial State in Canada: Politics in the Provinces and Territories*, ed. Keith Brownsey and Michael Howlett, 441–78 (Peterborough: Broadview Press, 2001); and David Stewart and R. Kenneth Carty, "Many Political Worlds: Provincial Parties and Party Systems," in *Provinces: Canadian Provincial Politics*, 2nd ed., ed. Christopher Dunn, 97–113 (Peterborough: Broadview Press, 2006).

9 Jared J. Wesley, "Introduction: From Small to Big Worlds," and "Conclusion: Explaining the Worlds of Difference," in *Big Worlds: Politics and Elections in the Canadian Provinces and Territories*, ed. J. Wesley, xiii–xxxvi and 206–21 (Toronto: University of Toronto Press, 2016).

10 For a dramatic graphic illustration of the relationship between wealth (GNP/capita) and religiosity, see Pew Global Attitudes Project, *World Publics Welcome Global Trade – But Not Immigration*, October 4, 2007, 41, http://www.pewglobal.org/files/2007/10/Pew-Global-Attitudes-Report-October-4-2007-REVISED-UPDATED-5-27-14.pdf.

11 Gallup surveys in 2016 display similar patterns, with 69 percent of Canadians and 43 percent of Americans saying that abortion was "morally acceptable. Similar gaps are evident on other "moral" questions related to sex between unmarried men and women, gay and lesbian relationships, and doctor-assisted suicide. See Abacus, "Canadians' Moral Compass."

12 Robert D. Putnam and David E. Campbell, *American Grace: How Religion Divides and Unites Us* (New York: Simon and Schuster, 2010), chap. 1.

13 Bean makes this point in *Politics of Evangelical Identity*, Introduction and chap. 1.

14 See, for example, Clyde Wilcox and Carin Robinson, *Onward Christian Soldiers: The Religious Right in American Politics*, 4th ed. (Boulder, CO: Westview Press, 2011), chap. 3; Kenneth D. Wald and Allison Calhoun-Brown, *Religion and Politics in the United States*, 6th ed. (Lanham, Rowman and Littlefield, 2011), chap. 6.

15 This was evident in Bean's interviews with evangelicals on both sides of the border. See Bean, *Politics of Evangelical Identity*, especially chap. 8; and in various writings by Sam Reimer, including "Are American and Canadian Evangelicals Really That Different."

16 See Steve Bruce, *Politics and Religion in the United Kingdom* (London: Routledge, 2012), 26.

17 See Lars Thorup Larsen, Donley T. Studlar, and Christoffer Green-Pederson, "Morality Politics in the United Kingdom: Trapped between Left and Right," in *Morality Politics in Western Europe: Parties, Agendas, and Policy Choices*, ed. Isabelle

Engeli, Christoffer Green-Pedersen, and Lars Trump Larsen, 114–36 (Basingstoke: Palgrave Macmillan, 2012).

18 In the 2010 election, for example, the Conservatives (in some instances) used a form of "God talk" widely used in the US. On this, see Brian Robet Calfano, Paul A. Djupe, and Angelia R. Wilson, "God Save This 'Broken' Land: The Efficacy of Closed Circuit Voter Targeting in a UK Election," *Politics and Religion* 6, 1 (2013): 50–73. See also Ben Clements and Nick Spencer, *Voting and Values in Britain: Does Religion Count?* (London: Theos, 2014), 64.

19 See Pippa Norris and Ronald Inglehart, *Sacred and Secular: Religion and Politics Worldwide* (Cambridge: Cambridge University Press, 2004), 200; Martin Conway, "The Age of Christian Democracy," in *European Christian Democracy*, ed. Thomas Kselman and Joseph A. Buttigieg, 44–67 (Notre Dame: University of Notre Dame Press, 2003); and Kees van Kersbergen, "The Christian Democratic Phoenix and Modern Unsecular Politics," *Party Politics* 14, 3 (2008): 259–79.

20 Isabelle Engeli, Christoffer Green-Pedersen, and Lars Trump Larsen, "Theoretical Perspectives," in Engeli et al., *Morality Politics in Western Europe*, 15.

21 Laura Chaqués Bonafont and Anna M. Palau Roqué, "From Prohibition to Permissiveness: A Two-Wave Change on Morality Issues in Spain," in Engeli et al., *Morality Politics in Western Europe*, 62–87.

22 Kollman may somewhat overstate the extent to which such norms have developed at the transnational level, given the tortuously slow path followed by European Union institutions in accepting same-sex relationships. However, there can be little doubt that, by the 2010s, such norms were indeed powerful. See Kelly Kollman, *The Same-Sex Union Revolution in Western Democracies: International Norms and Domestic Policy Change* (Manchester: Manchester University Press, 2013), especially 92–95.

23 See, for example, Isabelle Engeli, "The Challenges of Abortion and Assisted Reproductive Policies in Europe," *Comparative European Politics*, 7, 1 (2009): 56–74.

24 P. Mepschen, J. Duyvendak, and E. Tonkens, "Sexual Politics, Orientalism, Multicultural Citizenship in the Netherlands," *Sociology* 44, 5 (2010): 962–79; and Gert Hekma and Jan Willem Duyvendak, "The Netherlands: Depoliticization of Homosexuality and Homosexualization of Politics," in *The Lesbian and Gay Movement and the State*, ed. Manon Tremblay, David Paternotte, and Carol Johnson, 103–18 (Farnham: Ashgate, 2011).

25 Norris and Inglehart, *Sacred and Secular*, 200–8.

26 See, for example, Roger Eatwell and Cas Mudde, *Western Democracies and the New Extreme Right Challenge* (London: Routledge, 2004); Raymond Taras, *Xenophobia and Islamophobia in Europe* (Edinburgh: Edinburgh University Press, 2012); and Aziz al-Azmeh and Effie Fokas, *Islam in Europe: Diversity, Identity, and Influence* (Cambridge: Cambridge University Press, 2007).

27 See estimates in Pew Research Centre, "Muslim Population by Country," January 27, 2011, http://www.pewforum.org/2011/01/27/table-muslim-population-by-country/, and "The Future of World Religions," April 2, 2015, http://www.pewforum.org/2015/04/02/religious-projections-2010-2050/.

28 In the now-large literature on this, see especially Joan Wallach Scott, *The Politics of the Veil* (Princeton: Princeton University Press, 2007).

29 Samuel Reimer, *Evangelicals and the Continental Divide: The Conservative Protestant Subculture in Canada and the United States* (Montreal and Kingston: McGill-Queen's University Press, 2003).

30 There is little systematic analysis of changes in attitudes among, for example, evangelicals, but, in the United States, Clyde Wilcox points to significant shifts among young evangelicals in particular, and most notably on sexual diversity. See Clyde Wilcox and Rentaro Iida, "Evangelicals, the Christian Right, and Gay and Lesbian Rights in the United States: Simple and Complex Stories," in *Faith, Politics and Sexual Diversity in Canada and the United States*, ed. David Rayside and Clyde Wilcox, 101–20 (Vancouver: UBC Press, 2011).

Index